Lecture Notes in
Computer Science

Lecture Notes in Computer Science

Vol. 324: M.P. Chytil, L. Janiga, V. Koubek (Eds.), Mathematical Foundations of Computer Science 1988. Proceedings. IX, 562 pages. 1988.

Vol. 325: G. Brassard, Modern Cryptology. VI, 107 pages. 1988.

Vol. 326: M. Gyssens, J. Paredaens, D. Van Gucht (Eds.), ICDT '88. 2nd International Conference on Database Theory. Proceedings, 1988. VI, 409 pages. 1988.

Vol. 327: G.A. Ford (Ed.), Software Engineering Education. Proceedings, 1988. V, 207 pages. 1988.

Vol. 328: R. Bloomfield, L. Marshall, R. Jones (Eds.), VDM '88. VDM – The Way Ahead. Proceedings, 1988. IX, 499 pages. 1988.

Vol. 329: E. Börger, H. Kleine Büning, M.M. Richter (Eds.), CSL '87. 1st Workshop on Computer Science Logic. Proceedings, 1987. VI, 346 pages. 1988.

Vol. 330: C.G. Günther (Ed.), Advances in Cryptology – EUROCRYPT '88. Proceedings, 1988. XI, 473 pages. 1988.

Vol. 331: M. Joseph (Ed.), Formal Techniques in Real-Time and Fault-Tolerant Systems. Proceedings, 1988. VI, 229 pages. 1988.

Vol. 332: D. Sannella, A. Tarlecki (Eds.), Recent Trends in Data Type Specification. V, 259 pages. 1988.

Vol. 333: H. Noltemeier (Ed.), Computational Geometry and its Applications. Proceedings, 1988. VI, 252 pages. 1988.

Vol. 334: K.R. Dittrich (Ed.), Advances in Object-Oriented Database Systems. Proceedings, 1988. VII, 373 pages. 1988.

Vol. 335: F.A. Vogt (Ed.), CONCURRENCY 88. Proceedings, 1988. VI, 401 pages. 1988.

Vol. 336: B.R. Donald, Error Detection and Recovery in Robotics. XXIV, 314 pages. 1989.

Vol. 337: O. Günther, Efficient Structures for Geometric Data Management. XI, 135 pages. 1988.

Vol. 338: K.V. Nori, S. Kumar (Eds.), Foundations of Software Technology and Theoretical Computer Science. Proceedings, 1988. IX, 520 pages. 1988.

Vol. 339: M. Rafanelli, J.C. Klensin, P. Svensson (Eds.), Statistical and Scientific Database Management, IV SSDBM. Proceedings, 1988. IX, 454 pages. 1989.

Vol. 340: G. Rozenberg (Ed.), Advances in Petri Nets 1988. VI, 439 pages. 1988.

Vol. 341: S. Bittanti (Ed.), Software Reliability Modelling and Identification. VII, 209 pages. 1988.

Vol. 342: G. Wolf, T. Legendi, U. Schendel (Eds.), Parcella '88. Proceedings, 1988. 380 pages. 1989.

Vol. 343: J. Grabowski, P. Lescanne, W. Wechler (Eds.), Algebraic and Logic Programming. Proceedings, 1988. 278 pages. 1988.

Vol. 344: J. van Leeuwen, Graph-Theoretic Concepts in Computer Science. Proceedings, 1988. VII, 459 pages. 1989.

Vol. 345: R.T. Nossum (Ed.), Advanced Topics in Artificial Intelligence. VII, 233 pages. 1988 (Subseries LNAI).

Vol. 346: M. Reinfrank, J. de Kleer, M.L. Ginsberg, E. Sandewall (Eds.), Non-Monotonic Reasoning. Proceedings, 1988. XIV, 237 pages. 1989 (Subseries LNAI).

Vol. 347: K. Morik (Ed.), Knowledge Representation and Organization in Machine Learning. XV, 319 pages. 1989 (Subseries LNAI).

Vol. 348: P. Deransart, B. Lorho, J. Małuszyński (Eds.), Programming Languages Implementation and Logic Programming. Proceedings, 1988. VI, 299 pages. 1989.

Vol. 349: B. Monien, R. Cori (Eds.), STACS 89. Proceedings, 1989. VIII, 544 pages. 1989.

Vol. 350: A. Törn, A. Žilinskas, Global Optimization. X, 255 pages. 1989.

Vol. 351: J. Díaz, F. Orejas (Eds.), TAPSOFT '89. Volume 1. Proceedings, 1989. X, 383 pages. 1989.

Vol. 352: J. Díaz, F. Orejas (Eds.), TAPSOFT '89. Volume 2. Proceedings, 1989. X, 389 pages. 1989.

Vol. 353: S. Hölldobler, Foundations of Equational Logic Programming. X, 250 pages. 1989. (Subseries LNAI).

Vol. 354: J.W. de Bakker, W.-P. de Roever, G. Rozenberg (Eds.), Linear Time, Branching Time and Partial Order in Logics and Models for Concurrency. VIII, 713 pages. 1989.

Vol. 355: N. Dershowitz (Ed.), Rewriting Techniques and Applications. Proceedings, 1989. VII, 579 pages. 1989.

Vol. 356: L. Huguet, A. Poli (Eds.), Applied Algebra, Algebraic Algorithms and Error-Correcting Codes. Proceedings, 1987. VI, 417 pages. 1989.

Vol. 357: T. Mora (Ed.), Applied Algebra, Algebraic Algorithms and Error-Correcting Codes. Proceedings, 1988. IX, 481 pages. 1989.

Vol. 358: P. Gianni (Ed.), Symbolic and Algebraic Computation. Proceedings, 1988. XI, 545 pages. 1989.

Vol. 359: D. Gawlick, M. Haynie, A. Reuter (Eds.), High Performance Transaction Systems. Proceedings, 1987. XII, 329 pages. 1989.

Vol. 360: H. Maurer (Ed.), Computer Assisted Learning – ICCAL '89. Proceedings, 1989. VII, 642 pages. 1989.

Vol. 361: S. Abiteboul, P.C. Fischer, H.-J. Schek (Eds.), Nested Relations and Complex Objects in Databases. VI, 323 pages. 1989.

Vol. 362: B. Lisper, Synthesizing Synchronous Systems by Static Scheduling in Space-Time. VI, 263 pages. 1989.

Vol. 363: A.R. Meyer, M.A. Taitslin (Eds.), Logic at Botik '89. Proceedings, 1989. X, 289 pages. 1989.

Vol. 364: J. Demetrovics, B. Thalheim (Eds.), MFDBS 89. Proceedings, 1989. VI, 428 pages. 1989.

Vol. 365: E. Odijk, M. Rem, J.-C. Syre (Eds.), PARLE '89. Parallel Architectures and Languages Europe. Volume I. Proceedings, 1989. XIII, 478 pages. 1989.

Vol. 366: E. Odijk, M. Rem, J.-C. Syre (Eds.), PARLE '89. Parallel Architectures and Languages Europe. Volume II. Proceedings, 1989. XIII, 442 pages. 1989.

Vol. 367: W. Litwin, H.-J. Schek (Eds.), Foundations of Data Organization and Algorithms. Proceedings, 1989. VIII, 531 pages. 1989.

Vol. 368: H. Boral, P. Faudemay (Eds.), IWDM '89, Database Machines. Proceedings, 1989. VI, 387 pages. 1989.

Vol. 369: D. Taubner, Finite Representations of CCS and TCSP Programs by Automata and Petri Nets. X. 168 pages. 1989.

Vol. 370: Ch. Meinel, Modified Branching Programs and Their Computational Power. VI, 132 pages. 1989.

Vol. 371: D. Hammer (Ed.), Compiler Compilers and High Speed Compilation. Proceedings, 1988. VI, 242 pages. 1989.

Vol. 372: G. Ausiello, M. Dezani-Ciancaglini, S. Ronchi Della Rocca (Eds.), Automata, Languages and Programming. Proceedings, 1989. XI, 788 pages. 1989.

Vol. 373: T. Theoharis, Algorithms for Parallel Polygon Rendering. VIII, 147 pages. 1989.

Vol. 374: K.A. Robbins, S. Robbins, The Cray X-MP/Model 24. VI, 165 pages. 1989.

Vol. 375: J.L.A. van de Snepscheut (Ed.), Mathematics of Program Construction. Proceedings, 1989. VI, 421 pages. 1989.

Vol. 376: N.E. Gibbs (Ed.), Software Engineering Education. Proceedings, 1989. VII, 312 pages. 1989.

Vol. 377: M. Gross, D. Perrin (Eds.), Electronic Dictionaries and Automata in Computational Linguistics. Proceedings, 1987. V, 110 pages. 1989.

Vol. 378: J.H. Davenport (Ed.), EUROCAL '87. Proceedings, 1987. VIII, 499 pages. 1989.

Lecture Notes in Computer Science

Edited by G. Goos and J. Hartmanis

436

B. Steinholtz   A. Sølvberg
L. Bergman (Eds.)

Advanced Information Systems Engineering

Second Nordic Conference CAiSE '90
Stockholm, Sweden, May 8–10, 1990
Proceedings

Springer-Verlag

Berlin Heidelberg New York London Paris Tokyo Hong Kong

Editors

Bo Steinholtz
Department of Computer and Systems Sciences
Stockholm University, Electrum 230
S-164 40 Kista, Sweden

Arne Sølvberg
Department of Electrical Engineering and Computer Science
The Norwegian Institute of Technology
N-7034 Trondheim, Norway

Lars Bergman
SISU-Swedish Institute for Systems Development
Box 1250, S-164 28 Kista, Sweden

CR Subject Classification (1987): D.2.1, D.2.3, H.2.1

ISBN 3-540-52625-0 Springer-Verlag Berlin Heidelberg New York
ISBN 0-387-52625-0 Springer-Verlag New York Berlin Heidelberg

Printing and binding: Druckhaus Beltz, Hemsbach/Bergstr.
2145/3140-543210 – Printed on acid-free paper

Preface

The CAiSE '90 conference is the second of a series of Conferences on Advanced information Systems Engineering. The location of each of the future annual conferences will be chosen to be in one of the four Nordic countries.

The first conference in the series was arranged in Stockholm in 1989. The initiative to arrange the conference was taken by Professor Janis Bubenko of Stockholm University and SISU, the Swedish Institute for Systems Development. Even if the first conference was given a fairly restricted publication outside of the Nordic countries, the number of submissions from other countries were high. This indicated a need for this type of conference in the international research community. So we decided to make the conference a truly international event.

The calls for papers have been widely distributed in Europe for the CAiSE '90 conference. The program committee was chosen among very well reputed European researchers in the field of information systems engineering, and from key professionals in Nordic industrial companies and consultancy companies. This gave very encouraging results. The quality of the submitted papers were as good as could reasonably be expected. We are very satisfied, indeed, with the quality that we have achieved for the conference. There is also a very good international spread of the authors, who come from ten different countries. This gives a very good basis for future arrangements.

The CAiSE conferences try to ride two horses simultaneously. On the one hand, they are scientific conferences, where papers are chosen in the usual way: each submitted paper is reviewed by three members of the program committee, and chosen according to the ratings given. These papers are published in the conference proceedings. On the other hand, they are also conferences of invited speakers, who treat subjects that are known to be of central importance to the advanced practitioner. These presentations will only partly be supported by papers, which are usually not written within the deadlines for the submitted papers. Most experiences show that it is difficult to have the invited contributions fully documented in time for printing of the proceedings. We have consequently decided to publish only abstracts of the invited papers in the proceedings.

The program committee has made great efforts to compose a program of submitted papers and invited presentations that is appealing both to the advanced practitioner and to the information systems engineering researcher. It is our hope that the two groups of people can find a fruitful intersection of interesting topics and presentations in the CAiSE '90 conference.

The CAiSE '90 conference program could not have been created without the efforts of the authors, and of the program committee members, who have donated their time to the conference. They deserve our deepest thanks.

The editors

Bo Steinholtz   Arne Sølvberg   Lars Bergman

CAiSE '90 Organization

General Chair
Janis Bubenko Jr, *SISU and Stockholm University, Sweden*

Program Chair
Arne Sølvberg, *Norwegian Institute of Technology, Norway*

Program Coordinator
Bo Steinholtz, *Stockholm University, Sweden*

Program Committee

Rudolf Andersen, *Norwegian Inst. of Technology, Norway*
Bertil Andersson, *Televerket, Sweden*
Frans van Assche, *James Martin Associates, Belgium*
David Bruce, *Sparekassernes Datacenter, Denmark*
Peter Dadam, *IBM Scientific Center, FRG*
Christer Dahlgren, *IT-plan, Sweden*
Anne-Cecilie Fagerlie, *Arthur Andersen & Co., Norway*
Jacques Hagelstein, *Philips Research Laboratory, Belgium*
Kees van Hee, *Technical Univ. Eindhoven, The Netherlands*
Keith Jeffery, *SERAC Rutherford Appleton Lab., England*
Gregor Jonsson, *IBM Nordic Laboratories, Sweden*
Pertti Järvinen, *University of Tampere, Finland*
Kari Känsälä, *Technical Research Centre of Finland, Finland*
Paul Lindgreen, *Copenhagen School of Economics, Denmark*
Peri Loucopoulos, *UMIST, England*
Henrik Maegaard, *Computer Resources Int., Denmark*
Robert Meersman, *Tilburg University, The Netherlands*
Helge Moen, *Kvärner Engineering, Norway*
Risto Nevalainen, *TIEKE, Finland*
Björn Nilsson, *SISU, Sweden*
Markku Nokso-Koivisto, *TT-Innovation, Finland*

Örjan Odelhög, *Cap Gemini Logic, Sweden*
Ari Okkonen, *Nokia Research Center, Finland*
Antoni Olive, *Univ. Politecn. de Catalunya, Spain*
Barbara Pernici, *Politecnico di Milano, Italy*
Reind van de Riet, *Free University, The Netherlands*
Colette Rolland, *Université de Paris, France*
Ola Sannes, *Statoil, Norway*
Günther Schlageter, *Fern Universität, FRG*
Gert Schmeltz Pedersen, *Computer Resources Int., Denmark*
Amilcar Sernadas, *INESC, Portugal*
Matti Sinto, *TEKES, Finland*
Henk Sol, *Technical University of Delft, The Netherlands*
Svein Stavelin, *EDB, Norway*
Peter Stocker, *University of East Anglia, England*
Costantino Thanos, *IEI/CNR, Italy*
Berit Thaysen, *Crone & Koch, Denmark*
Yannis Vassiliou, *FORTH, Greece*
Peter Vendelbo, *Mentor Informatik, Denmark*
Herbert Weber, *Universität Dortmund, FRG*
Staffan Westbeck, *Digital Equipment, Sweden*

Organizing Committee
Lars Bergman, *SISU, Chair*
Anna Resare, *SISU*
Helena Persson, *SISU*
Marianne Sindler, *SISU*

Chairman's message

It is a great pleasure for me to welcome the participants of CAiSE '90 to Stockholm and Electrum. We are proud to be your hosts for the second year. We also very much appreciate the international response to the conference, in terms of paper submissions as well as attendance.

CAiSE '90 has several objectives. The first one is technology and knowledge transfer between research and business and industry in the field of information systems engineering. This two-way transfer is achieved by presenting current high-quality research as well as experiences and ideas from advanced applications in business and industry. The second objective is to improve communication between the research and the business and industry communities. We hope the structure of the conference program will effectively contribute to this objective. The third objective is to stimulate increased communication and exchange in this field within the Nordic countries (while doing our best at being international).

The CAiSE '90 conference program looks very promising and encouraging in all these respects. In my opinion, it is one of the few conferences to strike a good balance between scientific contributions and contributions from business and industry. CAiSE is also the first truly international conference series on information systems engineering in the Nordic countries.

I would like to thank all the people, worldwide, who made this possible by contributing interesting and high quality papers. Credit must also be given to our colleagues on the program committee, who have devoted much of their time to reviewing. A special acknowledgement and thanks should be given to the program committee chairman Professor Arne Sølvberg, the program coordinator Dr. Bo Steinholtz, and the organizing committee chairman Mr. Lars Bergman. Together with staff from SISU they have skillfully managed the complex conference development process.

CAiSE is an annual Nordic conference event in the area of information systems engineering with sites alternating between the Nordic countries. Next year's event will take place in Trondheim, Norway. CAiSE '91 will be hosted by the Norwegian Institute of Technology. I am sure you will find Trondheim a beautiful city full of hospitality and excellent facilities for professional as well as leisure activities. I am looking forward to seeing you all in Trondheim in 1991.

Janis Bubenko jr
General Chairman

TABLE OF CONTENTS

Practice & Experience sessions feature invited speakers. Only
abstracts of these presentations are included in the proceedings.

Sessions 1, 2: CASE
(Practice & Experience)

Chair: Ola Sannes, *Statoil, Norway*

CASE in the '90s 1
Anthony I. Wasserman, *Interactive Development Environments, USA*
CASE in Action: IEF at Nykredit 2
Jørgen G. Nielsen, *Nykredit, Denmark*
FOUNDATION - CASE Tools for the Success of the French Stock Exchange 3
Filippo De Capua, *SICOVAM, France*
A Common Repository and Information Model –
A Base for Integration of Development Tools 4
Christoph Engemann, *IBM, Switzerland*

Session 3A: Experiences of CASE
(Technical Papers)

Chair: Keith Jeffery, *SERAC Rutherford Appleton Lab., England*

Experiences with the Use of CASE-tools in The Netherlands 5
G.M. Wijers, *Delft University of Technology, The Netherlands*
H.E. van Dort, *Cap Gemini Pandata, The Netherlands*
Making CASE Work 21
John Parkinson, *Ernst & Young, England*

Session 3B: CASE Past, Present and Future
(Technical Papers)

Chair: Rudolf Andersen, *Norwegian Institute of Technology, Norway*

CASE Tools and Software Factories 42
Erik G. Nilsson, *Center for Industrial Research, Norway*
Selecting System Development Tools: Some Experiences 61
Reima Suomi, *Turku School of Economics and Business Administration*
& Sampo Insurance Company, Finland

Session 4A: The Software Process
(Technical Papers)

Chair: Yannis Vassiliou, *Foundation of Research and Technology - Hellas, Greece*

Software Configuration Management for Medium-Size Systems 79
W. Reck, H. Härtig, *GMD, FRG*
Automated Support of the Modelling Process:
A View based on Experiments with Expert Information Engineers 88
G.M. Wijers, *Delft University of Technology & SERC, The Netherlands*
H. Heijes, *Delft University of Technology, The Netherlands*
Software Process Modelling in EPOS 109
Reidar Conradi, Anund Lie, Espen Osjord, Per H. Westby, *NTH, Norway*
Vincenzo Ambriola, *Univ. of Pisa and Udine, Italy*
Maria Letizia Jaccheri, *TecSiel, Italy*
Chunnian Liu, *Beijing Polytechnic University, P.R. China*

Session 4B: Conceptual Modelling
(Technical Papers)

Chair: Peter Stocker, *University of East Anglia, England*

A Communication Oriented Approach to Conceptual Modelling of Information
Systems 134
Jan L.G. Dietz, *University of Limburg, The Netherlands*
Correction of Conceptual Schemas 152
C. Souveyet, *Université Pierre et Marie Curie, France*
C. Rolland, *Université de la Sorbonne, France*
A Natural Language Interpreter for the Construction of Conceptual Schemas 175
Leone Dunn, Maria Orlowska, *University of Queensland, Australia*

Session 5A: Selecting CASE Tools
(Technical Papers)

Chair: Björn Nilsson, *SISU, Sweden*

How to Combine Tools and Methods in Practice – a Field Study 195
Kari Smolander, Veli-Pekka Tahvanainen, Kalle Lyytinen,
University of Jyväskylä, Finland
Application of Relational Normalforms in CASE-tools 215
Béla Halassy, *Computing Application and Service Co. (SZÁMALK), Hungary*

Session 5B: Requirements Specification
(Technical Papers)

Chair: Colette Rolland, *Université de la Sorbonne, France*

The Conceptual Task Model: a Specification Technique between Requirements
Engineering and Program Development 228
S. Brinkkemper, A.H.M ter Hofstede, *Software Engineering Research Centre &*
University of Nijmegen, The Netherlands
Rule-Based Requirements Specification and Validation 251
A. Tsalgatidou, *Greek P.T.T., Greece*
V. Karakostas, P. Loucopoulos, *UMIST, England*
Requirements Specification in TEMPORA 264
C. Theodoulidis, P. Loucopoulos, *UMIST, England*
B. Wangler, *SISU, Sweden*

Sessions 6, 7: ESPRIT
(Practice & Experience)

Chair: Janis Bubenko jr, *SISU and Stockholm University, Sweden*

ESPRIT Today – An Overview 283
Janis Folkmanis, *Commission of the European Communities, Belgium*
ESPRIT at the Age of Seven – Its Industrial Impact Seen from a Participant's Viewpoint 284
Günter R. Koch, *2i Industrial Informatics, FRG*
From Software Engineering to Business Engineering: ESPRIT Projects in Information Systems Engineering 285
Pericles Loucopoulos, *UMIST, England*

Sessions 8, 9: Quality Assurance
(Practice & Experience)

Chair: Bo Steinholtz, *Stockholm University, Sweden*

Quality Auditing: The Necessary Step towards the Required Quality Objectives 286
Donald Davies, *Compex, England*
Quality Engineering: Designing for Quality – the SW Engineering Challenge 287
Ulf Olsson, *Bofors Electronics, Sweden*
Quality Control: A Cornerstone to Quality – Measurement and Motivation are Key Issues 288
Rikard Almgren, *RSA Software Quality Systems, Sweden*
Quality Management: The Business Asset and Its Competitive Advantage 289
Alvaro de Portugal, *Deportic International Consultancy, The Netherlands*

Session 10A: Prototyping
(Mixed session)

Chair: Arne Sølvberg, *Norwegian Institute of Technology, Norway*

Software Prototyping: Implications for the People Involved in Systems Development 290
Pam Mayhew, *University of East Anglia, England*
Experiences from Prototyping (Abstract) 306
Peter F. Elzer (Invited speaker), *ABB Corporate Research, FRG*

Session 10B: Design Support
(Technical Papers)

Chair: Pericles Loucopoulos, *UMIST, England*

IRIS – A Mapping Assistant for Generating Designs from Requirements 307
Yannis Vassiliou, Manolis Marakakis, Panagiotis Katalagarianos, Michalis Mertikas,
Foundation of Research and Technology - Hellas, Greece
Lawrence Chung, John Mylopoulos, *University of Toronto, Canada*
RECAST: A Tool for Reusing Requirements 339
M.G. Fugini, *Università di Brescia & Politecnico di Milano, Italy*
B. Pernici, *Politecnico di Milano, Italy*
A Design Tool for Object Oriented Databases 365
Mokrane Bouzeghoub, Elisabeth Métais, *Université Pierre et Marie Curie, France*
Farid Hazi, Laurent Leborgne, *Infosys, France*

CASE in the '90 s

Anthony I. Wasserman
(Invited speaker)

Interactive Development Environments, Inc.
595 Market Street, San Francisco, CA 94105, USA

Abstract

Modern CASE tools have now been commercially available for about five years, and have shown to improve the quality of software projects and the productivity of software designers. Most of these tools address a specific task within the software development life cycle, without giving significant attention to how they fit into a suite of integrated tools in a comprehensive software development environment. As the next generation of CASE tools emerges over the next couple of years, integration of tools will be a central issue.

This talk addresses some of the characteristics of these forthcoming CASE environments, including *integrated life cycle support, emerging standards, tool integration, distributed CASE, software reengineering and object orientation and reusability*.

Examples are taken from various products, research projects, and standardization efforts to present the likely future direction in CASE environments. This presentation emphasizes the above technical issues, giving secondary attention to organizational and managerial issues associated with the introduction and successful use of CASE within organizations.

Anthony I. Wasserman is founder and President of Interactive Development Environments (IDE), developer of the Software through Pictures® integrated CASE environment, and is regarded as a pioneer of the CASE industry. Before starting IDE, Tony was a University of California professor. He was the founder and first elected Chairman of ACM's Special Interest Group on Software Engineering (SIGSOFT).

He has edited seven books and written many articles on software engineering and software development environments. He is co-editor of the best selling tutorials, Software Design Techniques, and editor of Software Development Environments, both published by IEEE Press. He is a co-developer of the Object-Oriented Structured Design notation. Wasserman received his Ph.D. degree in Computer Sciences from the University of Wisconsin – Madison. He is a member of ACM and the IEEE Computer Society. Wasserman is also a recipient of the IFIP Silver Core award.

CASE in Action: IEF at Nykredit

Jørgen G. Nielsen
(Invited speaker)

Nykredit,Tiendeladen 7
DK-9000 Aalborg, Denmark

Abstract

The need for application development productivity and application adaptability to business changes leads to the search for new tools and methods. The formation of a new organisation gave Nykredit the challenge and opportunity to introduce new methods and new tools. Nykredit selected the method IEM, Information Engineering Methodology, in 1987 and the supporting I-Case-tool IEF, Information Engineering Facility, on Christmas Eve the same year. The first application was developed during 1988 and put into production in February 1989. We have now started the re-engineering of the central part of our main applications using IEM and IEF. The challenges are two-fold:

* Educational: Setting up a decent educational programme re-indoctrinating the old staff of programmers.

* Technical: Make the product operational in our environment. Set up the right procedures for development, testing and installation. Co-existence with old applications and procedures.

We still believe that we made the right decision and are determined to continue the effort of converting old applications and people to the new religion: Information Engineering and I-Case-tools. To us, the use of tools and method has already demonstrated a much higher degree of productivity and responsiveness to changes.

Jörgen G. Nielsen is manager of the technical department in the EDP-company within the Nykredit Corporation, one of the largest financial institutions in Denmark. The department is technically responsible for all aspects of the Information Systems Engineering process, from strategy to selection of methods, tools and techniques, and for proper software implementation, maintenance and operations. Prior to his involvement with Nykredit, Jörgen G. Nielsen spent 20 years with IBM Denmark as a Systems Engineer, supporting large customers in the system software and application development area. He holds a M. Sc. degree in Mathematics and Computer Science from the University of Copenhagen.

FOUNDATION - CASE Tools for the Success of the French Stock Exchange

Filippo De Capua
(Invited speaker)

SICOVAM, 5 Rue du Centre
93 167 Noisy le Grand, France

Abstract

When the French Stock Exchange decided to renovate its procedures and systems, in order to compete with the biggest worldwide exchanges, a large project was set up. Numerous participants were involved in the project (banks, brokers, service providers, vendors, ...).

The presentation will show how the use of FOUNDATION helped deliver a quality system within deadlines and budget. It will present measurements of that quality. It will also explain how FOUNDATION helped SICOVAM maintain quality and control of its developments during its growth from a 2 Mips site to an 80 Mips site. The presentation will also summarize some of the issues implementing CASE in the development system's and production groups.

Filippo De Capua is DP Manager (Directeur Informatique) of SICOVAM (Société Interprofessionnelle de Compensation des Valeurs Mobilières). SICOVAM manages the central database of the French Stock Market. It is a company of 350 people. The Data Processing Department represents 100 people, plus an important number of subcontractors. Filippo De Capua joined SICOVAM in 1988 to manage the rapid growth of the DP Department (now 2 3090-200) and the implementation of the brand new back office system of the French Bourse (RELIT).

A Common Repository and Information Model - A Base for Integration of Development Tools

Christoph Engeman
(Invited speaker)

IBM Switzerland
8048 Zurich, Switzerland

Abstract

This presentation will address the potential benefits of AD/Cycle, announced in September 1989 by IBM, for its users.

AD/Cycle intends to 'industrialize' the application development and maintenance cycle over the lifetime of applications. AD/Cycle is the CAD/CAM of Information Systems for application development.

The presentation will present the AD/Cycle Concept and some highlights of the Repository Manager/MVS upon which AD/Cycle is based.

Chris Engeman joined IBM (Switzerland) 1971 as a System Engineer at the Bern Branch office, where he supported various customers for several years. After an assignment at the World Trade System Center in the Boeblingen Lab, where he had world-wide responsibility for supporting IBM's database products, he returned to the Field System Center in Zurich. There he gave second level support to the Swiss customers and IBMers in the Database/Data Communication area. With the announcement of DB2 his primary responsibility was the implementation and support of this software at the country level. Today, Chris Engeman is the person responsible in the IBM Field Support Center Zurich for AD/Cycle and Repository Manager/MVS. During the first three months of 1990 he was a resident of the Country Introduction Center La Hulpe (Belgium) to install RM/MVS. In this residency he worked with early code of RM/MVS to establish a base for enabling customer workshops.

Experiences with the use of CASE-tools in the Netherlands

G.M. Wijers

Delft University of Technology
Faculty of Technical Mathematics and Informatics
Department of Information Systems
P.O. Box 356, 2600 AJ Delft, The Netherlands

and

H.E. van Dort

Cap Gemini Pandata
P.O. Box 3164, 3502 GD Utrecht, The Netherlands

Abstract

In April of 1989 the working group "Experiences with the use of CASE-tools" of the Dutch User Group of Structured Development Methodologies conducted an inquiry into the use of CASE-tools among 834 Dutch organizations. This paper presents the most interesting results of this survey. The results are grouped into five major sections: the characteristics of CASE-tool users, the selection criteria for CASE-tools, the implementation in organizations, the actual usage of CASE-tools and future expectations for the use of CASE-tools.

1. Introduction

The Dutch User Group of Structured Development Methodologies (in Dutch: "NGGO") was established at the end of 1985 to be a forum for organizations that use structured methodologies, like those published by Yourdon (1989), Ward and Mellor (1986) and Hatley and Pirbhai (1987). Since the outset, many NGGO-members have been very interested in CASE-tools. The NGGO produced a report that contained an overview of the characteristics of the main CASE-tools on the Dutch market (NGGO, 1988).

As an usergroup the NGGO is particularly interested in the practical experiences of users with CASE-tools. For this reason they tried in 1986 to establish a working group to record the experiences of CASE-tool use. This attempt failed because it appeared that the use of these tools was very limited at the time.

In September 1988 a new working group was established. This time it resulted in a survey of 834 organizations that use CASE-tools. The findings of these were published in September 1989 (NGGO, 1989), both authors of this paper were members of the working group. The current paper discusses the purpose and structure of this survey together with the major results.

The results presented give a general picture of the use of tools in the Netherlands. The results of the three most popular tools will be presented separately where interesting. These three tools are: SDW, which stands for "System Development Workbench", a relative new CASE-tool of Dutch origin (Cap Gemini Pandata), Excelerator a world-wide well known workbench from "In Tech" (USA) and IEW, the "KnowledgeWare" (USA) workbench that supports the Information Engineering Methodology.

2.   Structure of the study

The purpose of the working group was to make an inventory of the experiences of Dutch CASE-tool users. In this paper "user" is defined as an organization in which CASE-tools are being used and "CASE-tool" as a software product which, at least during analysis and design, contributes to the construction of the required specifications. Examples of CASE-tools are apart from the three already mentioned: IEF, Promod, Prokit, Graphdoc, Teamwork, Blues, Design/1, PSL/PSA, ISEE, ProNiam, BOIE, Yourdon A/D Toolkit, Maestro, etc.

A questionnaire was considered to be the most appropriate way to reach as many users as possible. A mailing list was compiled, based on addresses obtained from CASE-tool vendors and addresses gathered by the NGGO of organizations interested in CASE-tools. The list finally comprised the addresses of 834 organizations. The results of the survey have been analyzed using SPSS/PC+ and Graph-in-a-Box.

The questionnaire was divided into several sections, each covering a different part of the life cycle of a CASE-tool. A multiple-choice question format was adopted. This resulted in a 12-page questionnaire divided into seven sections:

- Introduction

    Explanation of the purpose of the survey plus some instructions for the respondent.

- Background information

    Questions about the line of business, the size of the organization and about the number and kind of CASE-tools available in the organization (see section 3).

- The selection process

    Questions about reasons for purchase and the means of selection (see section 4).

- Implementation of the CASE-tool in the organization

    Questions about how the CASE-tools were introduced in the organization (see section 5).

- Use of the CASE-tool in the organization

    Questions about the impact on design-process and the opinion of users on the different aspects of the CASE-tool, such as: price, consistency checks, ease of use, documentation, etc.

- Expectations for the future

    Questions about the planned use of CASE-tools in the next two years.

- General remarks on the questionnaire

    An open question to get an impression whether the questionnaire was both complete and correct of the questionnaire.

3. Profile of the Dutch CASE-tool users

In this section we discuss the entire response and the size of the organizations using CASE-tools.

3.1. Response

Of the 834 questionnaires sent, 237 were returned and used in this analysis, which corresponds with a response-rate of 28.6 %. The response-rate for the individual CASE-tool is shown in figure 1. The results where checked to see whether they were influenced by the source of the address. It appeared that the division between brands did not differ significantly between addresses supplied by vendors and those compiled by the NGGO. This confirms that the inquiry gives a reliable indication of the experiences of organizations that use CASE-tools.

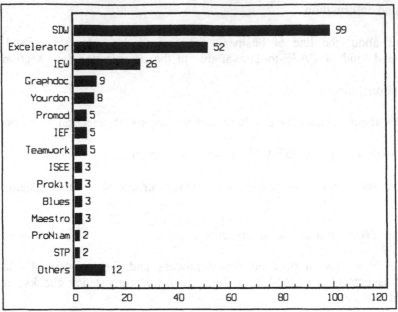

Figure 1 Response by brand in numbers

3.2. Size of organizations

From figure 2 it is clear that large organizations, in particular, use CASE-tools: 63.1 % of the organizations employing more than 500 peoples. If the figures for software houses/consultancy organizations are ignored this figure rises to 73.0 %.

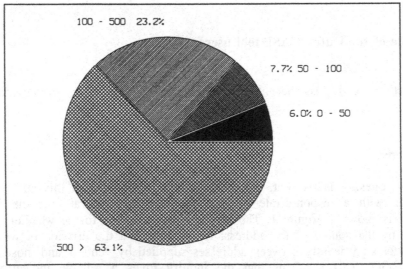

Figure 2 Number of people in the organization

4. Selection of CASE-tools

The working group was interested to discover: (1) the major reason for purchase, (2) the type of information used in decision-making, (3) the kind of test performed, and (4) the major selection criteria.

4.1. Major reason for purchase

In the literature, the word "CASE-tool" tends to be associated with productivity improvement. CASE-technology is said to be the certain way of decreasing the "application backlog" through improved productivity (McClure, 1989). Dutch users emphasize the importance of another tool characteristic: quality improvement is the most important reason for purchase.

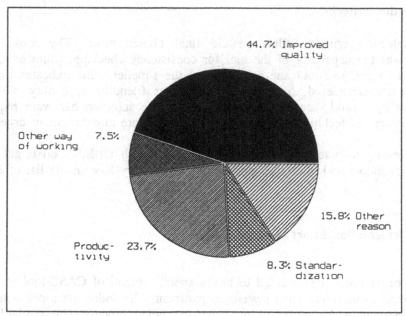

Figure 3 Major reason for purchase

4.2. Information sources

The most important information source in the selection process is a demonstration of the CASE-tool, preferably conducted on site by their own employees.

4.3. Number of CASE-tools compared

It was surprising that more than 23% of the respondents stated that only one tool was considered in the selection process. Less than 17% of the users had compared three other CASE-tools before buying.

4.4. Tests performed

In more than 75% of the situations the CASE-tool was tested at the own site before final purchase took place. In half of these this test took the form of a pilot-project, while also in a considerable number of situations the test was performed by a staff department responsible for methods and techniques. The test was usually short: nearly 80% of the tests were completed within three months.

4.5. Selection criteria

Which selection criteria influenced the final choice most? The most important criterion was the capability of the tool for consistency checking, followed by growth potential of the CASE-tool and continuity of the supplier. This indicates that CASE-tools are not considered to be perfect yet. User friendliness, quality of diagrams, integration by central data dictionary, support of the supplier, hardware requirements and correctness of techniques and methods supported are also important criteria.

It is interesting to note that interfacing capabilities with DBMS's on target machines or code-generators and multi-user possibilities come very low on the list of criteria.

5. Implementation in organizations

Once an organization has decided to buy a specific brand of CASE-tool, it has to be implemented in its information systems department. The following aspects are thought to be important in the course of this implementation process: (1) standardization of CASE-tools and techniques, (2) procedures to achieve a correct use of CASE-tools and (3) training of CASE-tool users.

5.1. Standardization

An indication of how definitively an organization has chosen to use a certain CASE-tool is the fact that it makes the tool an official company standard. Slightly more than half (51.9%) of the organizations had taken this step.

This figure is similar to the response to the question on how many CASE-tools the organization owns. Over 40% of the organizations have more than one brand of CASE-tool.

If the answer to the question on standardization is related to that on the length of experience with the CASE-tool, that the longer a tool is owned, the more frequently it becomes a standard. In 61.2% of the situations, organizations with more than one year of practical experience have made their CASE-tool standard.

It is always a point of discussion whether the technique or the tool is chosen first. In this survey we asked whether or not the tool supported the techniques that were standard at the moment the tool was purchased. In 64.2% of the organizations the CASE-tool supported the standard techniques. The other 35.8% of organizations apparently used other or no techniques prior to the purchase of the CASE-tool. It is to be expected that the implementation of a CASE-tool in such a situation, causes considerably more problems than implementation in an IS department that already has practical experience in the use of the techniques supported by the tool.

5.2. Procedures

The introduction of a CASE-tool in an organization in 43.8% of cases lead directly to the establishment of formal procedures to standardize the way the tool is used. Main points in these procedures are: drawing conventions, naming conventions and producing standard reports. A significant number (45%) of the organizations which did not establish procedures immediately, say that they plan to do so.

5.3. Training

Becoming acquainted with a new tool is usually achieved by self-study. In most cases the regular manual is used for this purpose, but sometimes a tutorial is used. Only a relatively small number of users attend training sessions.

In addition, it must be said that the response differs significantly between the various CASE-tools: for SDW-users self-study is more than four times as important as training by the supplier, for IEW-users both possibilities are equally important. Excelerator-users have a very high score for the use of the tutorial and in-house training.

These figures probably vary in different countries because of the influence of the marketing strategies of the dealers. On the other hand it is likely that there is a real relationship between the praise of SDW-users for the user-friendliness of the tool and the fact that they feel confident enough to learn to use the tool themselves.

Most users (36%) do not make an explicit planning for the time they need to master the tool. When they plan, they select a very optimistic period of one week. The differences between brands are considerable: the expectations of SDW- and Excelerator-users are in line with the overall answer, while most IEW users plan a month to get familiarized with the CASE-tool. These users also very often attend training courses.

6. Practical experiences with the use of CASE-tools

The major part of the questionnaire dealt with the practical experience in the day-to-day use of CASE-tools. The following questions were asked: how long has the CASE-tool been used, how does the organization use it, and how satisfied is the organization with various aspects of the tool?

6.1. Length of experience

The answers show that the use of CASE-tools is still relatively new in the Netherlands. More than 57 % of the organizations have used their current tool for less than one year. Not more than 11.4% has worked with the tool for more than two years. For this question there is an important difference between the various tools. The Excelerator-users have the longest experience, followed by the IEW-users. The shortest period of experience is found in the SDW-users; 50% of whom have used the tool for six months or less. These figures are in line with the time these different brands have been on the Dutch market.

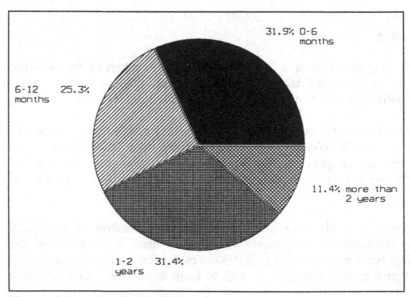

Figure 4 Length of experience

6.2. Consequences for the way of working in I.S. development

It is interesting to discover whether the introduction of CASE-tools in Information Systems Departments leads to a change in the way that software developers design and build systems.

The respondents were asked to indicate how their work had changed as a consequence of the use of CASE-tools. This introduces a difficulty in the interpretation of the results: it is of great importance to know the situation in the IS department before the tools where introduced. In general it can be said that the use of information system methodologies and structured techniques is quite common in the Netherlands. It is important to realize this while interpreting the following information.

6.2.1. Iteration

James Martin (1988) claimed that "the classical single-iteration 'waterfall' life-cycle does not work in many situations". In his view, development should be a multi-iteration or evolutionary process. The use of "design tools" will facilitate easy modification of the design. On the question whether tool use has resulted in more iteration in the design process: 56% of the respondents answer that this is the case. However almost 37% indicate that iteration does not change.

In a closely related question we asked whether prototyping was employed more often after the introduction of CASE-tools. This suggestion was clearly rejected: 80% of the respondents answer that tool use does not lead to prototyping.

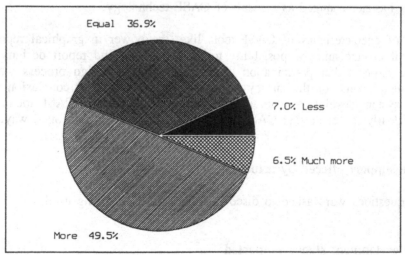

Figure 5 Iteration in development process

6.2.2. Duration of a project

As stated earlier, CASE-tools are often promoted as the ultimate solution for the "development backlog" or "software crisis". McClure (1989) reported "dramatic" increases in software productivity as a result of computer-aided software engineering.

In order to avoid confronting the issue of "productivity" directly, the questionnaire asked respondents to indicate what the duration of a project utilizing CASE-tools was as a percentage of that duration when CASE-tools were not used. 100% would mean "just as long as before", 50% would mean "half of the time". It appears that the most frequent answer to this question is 100% and the average answer is 95% ! No matter what definition one uses for "productivity", these figures do not support the idea that the available CASE-tools solve the software crisis.

6.2.3. Standardization

A great majority of respondents (88%) indicate that the use of CASE-tools leads to more standardization.

6.2.4. End user participation

In paragraph 6.2.1 we saw that the use of prototyping was not growing as a result of tool use. Does this mean that there is no change in the way the professional software developer communicates with the end-users of the system? A considerable number of respondents (40.7%) state that the participation of end-users has increased and that the users have become more active. However 58.4% answer that the role of the end-users has not changed as a result of CASE-technology.

Because of characteristics of CASE-tools like, the power in graphical representation, its ease of change and the possibility to present screen and report designs in a easy way, one expects that participation of end-users in the design process would really grow. The outcome of the survey however supports our final conclusion that today the way system developers work is not strongly influenced by CASE-tools. Or to put it more clearly: it seems that CASE-tools are used in an old-fashioned way.

6.3. The support offered by a tool

Several questions were asked to discover how tools were being used.

6.3.1. Development stages supported

As expected, tools are mainly used for analysis and design. IEW is used considerably more often during information planning than the overall average, but is not used during maintenance. SDW and Excelerator are quite often utilized during the latter phase. If the average period of experience is taken into account, it is likely that use during maintenance is mainly concerned with providing documentation for existing systems.

6.3.2. Techniques supported

In the questionnaire respondents were asked to indicate which techniques they used, with or without the support of the tool. The answers clearly show that dataflow and entity-relation diagrams are the most popular structured techniques among Dutch tool-users (more than 80% of the respondents used them). Matrices and decision tables are important techniques which are often not supported by tools. In the set of programming techniques, the Nassi-Shneiderman diagrams are considered to be the most popular (although often not supported by a tool). It is followed by Jackson diagrams, while the relatively modern "action diagrams" are hardly used among Dutch tool-users. Decomposition diagrams are also very popular with IEW-users (81% of them use this technique). Excelerator-users often use Structure Charts (60%).

6.3.3. Interfaces with other tools

Currently there is no tool which really supports the complete life-cycle of an information system. This means that automation of software development can only be achieved using several tools which use each others results.

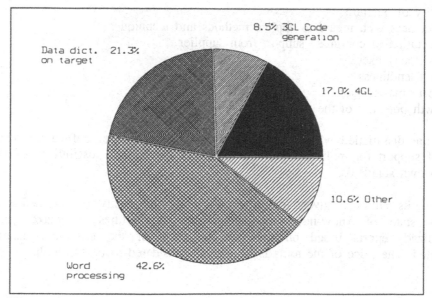

Figure 6 Interfaces

However this is hardly done in the Netherlands with the exception of wordprocessing interfaces. The majority of users do not have any interface with other tools. Apart from interfaces with word processing programs (merely a sign of weakness of the editors in the present CASE-tools): 20 respondents had realized an interface with the data-dictionary of a target-machine, 16 interfaced with a fourth generation language and 8 with a third generation language code-generator. Without doubt it can be said that, in the Netherlands, CASE-tools are currently used stand-alone.

6.4. Evaluation of CASE-tool characteristics

Respondents were asked to evaluate their tool by giving it a mark for several of its aspects. They were offered a range of 1 to 10 (the usual way of evaluating performance at school in the Netherlands): "1" meaning very poor, "10" meaning excellent.

Table 1 below shows the overall averages for all tools, together with individual scores for SDW, Excelerator and IEW. The average for all tools is weighted: for each brand an average was calculated, the averages were summed and divided by the number of brands. A brand was excluded from the calculation when its average showed a standard deviation that was too large. To give an example: the average of the aspect "price" is based on 11 brands, excluding the tools Promod, Software Through Pictures and Teamwork.

The most highly appreciated aspects of current tools are:

1. quality of diagrams
2. correctness with regard to applied methods and techniques
2. expectation of continued support from supplier
4. consistency checks
5. user friendliness
6. time to master tool
6. growth potential of the tool

Users are dissatisfied with the poor interfaces with all other software products, the lack of support for multi-user environments and the limited possibilities to adapt the tool to own standards.

Poor marks are also given for factors which could easily be avoided given the current state of know-how: text-editors and possibilities to make your own customized reports based on the data-dictionary of the tool, are insufficiently supported. The price of the tools is in general considered to be too high.

CRITERIA BY SUBJECT	AVE-RAGE	EXCEL 52	IEW 26	SDW 99
METHODS AND TECHNIQUES SUPPORTED				
Correctness methods and techniques	7.3	6.8	7.6	7.1
Consistency checks	7.2	6.1	7.9	7.0
Central data dictionary	6.7	6.0	7.0	6.8
Adaptability tool	5.0	5.1	3.9	5.4
SUPPLIER				
Received support	6.7	7.4	7.3	6.8
Continued support	7.3	7.8	8.1	7.9
Price	5.7	6.3	5.2	6.3
Growth potential tool	7.0	7.0	7.9	7.7
Number of new releases	6.0	5.9	5.8	5.4
EDITORS				
Time to master tool	7.0	6.5	6.6	7.8
User friendliness	7.1	7.6	7.1	8.0
User manual	6.3	7.1	6.8	6.1
Quality text-editor	5.6	4.6	4.9	5.6
OUTPUT QUALITY				
Quality of diagrams	7.4	7.2	7.5	7.6
Standard reports	6.1	7.0	6.0	6.2
Customized reports	5.1	6.2	3.8	5.0
TECHNICAL ASPECTS				
Hardware requirements	6.9	7.4	6.0	7.9
Reliability	6.9	7.5	6.8	7.0
Response-time	6.7	6.8	5.9	6.8
INTERFACES				
Interface to code-generator	5.0	4.1	5.0	4.2
Interface to DBMS	4.7	3.8	5.3	4.0
Interface to other software	4.0	4.7	5.0	3.8
MULTI-USER				
Multi-user possibilities	5.8	4.5	3.6	3.8
TOTAL RATING				
Overall qualification	6.8	6.6	7.1	7.1

Table 1 Marks of CASE-tool characteristics

When we compare the scores for Excelerator, IEW and SDW with the overall average scores, the following can be observed:

tool	better than average	less than average
Excelerator	received support user manual standard reports customized reports	consistency checks central data-dictionary price quality text-editor interface code-generator interface DBMS interface other software multi-user possibilities
IEW	consistency checks continued support growth potential of tool interface other software	adaptability tool quality text-editor customized reports hardware requirements response-time multi-user possibilities
SDW	growth potential tool time to master tool user friendliness hardware requirements	interface code-generator interface DBMS multi-user possibilities

Table 2 Comparison between Excelerator, IEW and SDW

The respondents were also asked to give an overall mark for the tool. It must be emphasized that this mark has to be interpreted as the overall general feeling about a tool expressed in one mark. The average over all tools was 6.8 meaning "reasonably good". For the most important tools these scores were slightly higher (7.1) for SDW and IEW, and slightly lower (6.6) for Excelerator.

7. Expectations for the future

Finally the respondents were asked their future plans for CASE-tools: 51% of them expected to increase use of their current tool; 17% plan to use more tools of different brands in the future; less than 10% plan to switch to another tool; 22% of respondents intend to stabilize at their current level of usage.

The open questions at the end of the questionnaire were provided in order to give an opportunity to comment freely on the future directions of tools (or on the questionnaire itself). The remarks made seem to be a reflection of the hot items in publications on software development: full life-cycle support, integration of tools, reverse engineering and better interfaces with the DBMS's on target machines. Another popular answer was the need for multi-user tools.

8. Conclusions

In general we can say that CASE-tool users are moderately positive about the CASE-tools which they use. The average overall qualification for CASE-tools is "reasonably good". The most highly appreciated aspects of current tools are quality of diagrams, correctness and consistency with regard to applied methods and techniques, user friendliness and future potentials. Users are dissatisfied with the poor interfaces with other software products, the lack of support for multi-user environments and the limited possibilities to adapt the tool to own standards.

The main reason for purchasing tools, is to achieve quality improvement. The most important criteria in selecting a tool are consistency checks, growth potential of the CASE-tool, reliability of the supplier and correctness with regard to applied methods and techniques. Other important criteria include ease of use, quality of the diagrams and integration into one central data-dictionary. Interfaces with 4th generation languages and code-generators were not considered to be as important as some suppliers would possibly like them to be. Another aspect that was surprisingly unimportant in the selection process was multi-user possibilities. The appreciation of these aspects in current CASE-tools is low, while in their future plans users mention a growing importance of these aspects. This seems to indicate that these criteria only become of more importance in the selection process when the primary criteria are handled in a satisfactory way.

Quality improvement of information systems can be reached best in the early phases of the development process. Tools that support these phases are more likely to contribute to quality. In our inquiry CASE-tool users mentioned quality improvement, standardization and consistency as very important issues. This agrees with the authors opinion that CASE-tools should in particular address the first phases of the development process.

From the length of experience and from the way tools are used, we have concluded that CASE-tool users in the Netherlands have just made a start with CASE-tools. However, if we look at the expectations for the future, we see ambitious plans such as: code-generation, multi-user environments, interfaces, reverse-engineering, entire life-cycle support, etc. We are not sure whether these ideas are based on the general presentations of CASE-tool suppliers, articles in the press or on realistic needs. When we see how CASE-tools are used today it is definitely necessary to pay more attention and put more effort to the adaptation of system development methodologies and project-management techniques to the use of (current) CASE-tools and vice versa. This is more important than quickly following all new CASE-technology enhancements.

Based on the results of this survey, we have come to the conclusion that CASE-tools are only slowly and very cautiously introduced into the organizations. The view on CASE-technology seems to be: make use of it, but do not completely depend on it.

Note

The NGGO working group that published the results of the survey in september 1989 consisted of 8 members employed by universities, consulting firms, government and industry. The chairman, and co-author of this paper was at the time employed by Cap Gemini Nederland BV. On January 1, 1990 this company merged with "Pandata", a Dutch softwarehouse and manufacturer of the CASE-tool SDW, into a new company called Cap Gemini Pandata.

References

Hatley, D.J. and I.A. Pirbhai, Strategies for real-time system specification, Dorset House, New York, N.Y., 1987
Martin, J., Documentation for the James Martin Seminar, 6th edition, 9th series, Savant Institute, Carnforth, Lancashire, 1988
McClure, C.L., CASE is software automation, Prentice Hall, Englewood Cliffs, N.J., 1989
NGGO, Computer ondersteuning van gestructureerde ontwikkelingsmethoden, een inventarisatie van tools, NGGO, Amsterdam, 1988
NGGO, Ervaringen met tools, NGGO, Amsterdam, 1989
Ward, P.T. and S.J. Mellor, Structured Development for real-time systems, vol.1. & vol.2. Prentice Hall, Englewood Cliffs, N.J., 1986
Yourdon, E., Modern Structured Analysis, Prentice Hall, Englewood Cliffs, N.J., 1989

Making CASE work

John Parkinson

Ernst & Young Management Consulting Services
Rolls House, 7 Rolls Buildings, Fetter Lane
London EC4A 1NH, UK

Abstract

Much of the attraction of Computer Aided Software Engineering (CASE) tools lies in the sophistication of the technology and the claims made for the tools to solve major problems of quality and productivity in system development. The number of tools available has grown from a handful in the early 1980s to over 1000 today. Yet despite the promises, users have been slow to adopt the tools and benefits have been equally slow to appear. So what has gone wrong? Do the tools actually work, or are users failing to appreciate how to get the best out of them? What can we learn from the experience of those who have successfully introduced CASE? This paper looks at how far these claims for CASE are justified, and examines what organisations have to do to get the best, or indeed anything out of their use of CASE tools.

Introduction

Tools that broadly match the definition of CASE have been available in the UK since c. 1984, and in the USA for about 18 months longer. Individual software productivity tools, particularly code generators and 4GLs have of course been available much longer than this, but were not offered on the same basis as current CASE tools. We will therefore take 1984 as the baseline for reviewing experiences so far with the use of CASE, giving us a 5 year period and at least two generations of tools to consider. The adoption process, from initial review to widespread, or at least relatively common use (or, in the case of failure, virtual abandonment) has typically taken between 18 and 24 months, and some organisations have repeated the process with several tools, or tried out more than one simultaneously.

Thus, those organisations that started with the first generation of tools in 1983 or 1984 and stuck with the same tool throughout, now have between two and three years of experience. However, there are relatively few examples of anyone using CASE extensively for this length of time. Most current tools did not become commercially available until 1986 or later, and users of these products have barely reached the stable use phase.

User Experiences

User experience of CASE tools has been extremely mixed, ranging from a high level of successful use through to a series of costly failures. Looked at as a whole, there are a number of common experiences that point at reasons why CASE has been slow to be adopted:

- **Confusion**. What is a CASE tool anyway? Once the CASE bandwagon got rolling in 1986, everything from a full function applications generation environment to a C compiler with window-based editor on a PC became a CASE tool. It's no wonder those IS departments who started looking at CASE were (and probably still are) confused

- **Over-sold capability**. Early tools were limited in the functions and features they offered and in the size and type of project they could support. The exact limits weren't known to either the vendors or the buyers, so users kept running into "edge case" problems with the products. They didn't know if the problem was with the tool or with their inexperience. Vendors didn't have sufficient experience with field support to easily identify the source of errors, and users often made slow progress, with frequent stops and starts, blind alleys and detours

- **Changes in working methods**. Adopting CASE tools changes more than just the look of the deliverables from a project. IS departments were slow to adopt the necessary new methods and management approaches, and did not therefore realise some of the expected benefits from the tools. Of course, the vendors did not emphasise this aspect of CASE, so users were as often as not expecting to be able to install the tools and keep everything else the same. It didn't work out like that, however, and may copies of tools ended up being used as documentation aids

- **Too little initial support.** Vendors as well as users were new to the CASE market, and did not have answers to all (in some cases any) of the necessary "how do I do this with your tools" questions. Once in the hands of "real" users, the tools got used for things that their developers had never intended. Often the tools actually couldn't help with some of the problems, but vendor support couldn't recognize that this was the position and blamed user incompetence. Tools were often put aside or abandoned altogether by their users in the interests of fixing a crisis

- **Learning curve effects** were underestimated. Many of the early CASE tools had very easy to learn graphics interfaces, and there was a common mis-conception that, having learnt to "use the controls", analysts and designers would be able to make productive use of the tools. In fact, the exact opposite was often true. Users could draw diagrams and collect information easily enough, but they had little idea what should go into the diagrams or what information should be collected. A lot of time was wasted learning effective ways to use the tools, and while this learning was going on, mistakes were made. Because no one was very experienced with CASE, not all these mistakes were recognised until they had had an impact on the project being used to evaluate the tools. In many such instances, the difficulties were remembered long after the easy to use interface had been forgotten

- **Poor match to audience**. Given the supposed importance of CASE, it's amazing how often the initial evaluation and selection process was carried out by relatively junior and inexperienced staff. Tools were often selected on features that were irrelevant to their proposed use. By the time decision makers and IS management got involved, the project was already underway with an appropriate tool. This was very frustrating for vendors who tried to sell the tools on the basis of what they believed the current benefits to be, yet found them being bought on the basis of future features. Quite a lot of the early tools were actually difficult to learn and use, because they were technicians tools, built by programmers and not suited for use by Business Analysts

- **The Critical Mass effect**. Everyone involved in the introduction of CASE should have been aware that there were certain to be critical mass effects with use of the tools. These effects actually manifested themselves in two ways.

- Until a tool covers a large proportion of all the activities required during a project, using it is actually counter-productive, even if it's very useful for the things that it does do. The coordination and communication overheads required to keep tool-based and non-tool-based activities in step outweigh the local advantages provided by using the tool

- Until a sufficient body of experience in the practical use of the tools develops, an IS department can't leverage new projects with the results of previous tool-based work, and much time is consumed in trying to fit existing designs into the new approach. This is where retrofit tools would be invaluable, if only they existed. A second flavour of this effect concerns the process of handing over the tool-based products of one team for use by another. Because the recipients have not seen the models developed, they tend to distrust them, or at best to feel that they did not understand them fully. This lack of confidence meant that they either proceed much more slowly than expected, or, worse, re-do all the modelling work

By and large, CASE vendors did not help the adoption process. Many did not build their CASE tools any better than their customers had traditionally built applications systems, and early tools were far from bug-free or reliable. Users of such unreliable tools quickly discovered that, for all its limitations, paper-based information is at least accessible. A corrupted design database on a CASE tool may not be. Added to this, early tools did not address some significant problems of practical use, particularly the issue of multiple users on a single project, and of shared access to a central repository of information. There were good technical reasons for this but many users were reluctant to get started on large projects with single user tools and the vendors waited too long to come up with a credible approach.

Nevertheless, there have been successes with CASE, some significant, many more modest but worthwhile. It should come as no surprise that the most successful cases tend to be in organisations that were already well organised and able to understand the requirements for a major change in the way they worked. CASE was not seen as an instant cure for all systems development problems, more as an essential component of an overall improved approach to the management of the development life cycle. Successful CASE users also tend to assemble a small portfolio of tools, recognizing that there is more than one problem to solve, and that no one tool addresses all requirements. They then persevered with their selection, discarding a tool only when it was clear that it did not work or could not meet users' requirements.

Does CASE really work ?

One of the most common questions asked about CASE is "does it really improve productivity and quality - and if so, by how much?". Vendors usually sidestep this question, with some justification, for two good reasons:

- There is little real performance data on the use of CASE, since few organisations have completed enough real projects, as opposed to trials and pilots, to establish controls for interpreting information on use

- Few CASE users (or any other type of IS department) have accurate or comprehensive performance data from their previous tools and methods, and most did not bother to establish baselines against which to measure the impact of introducing CASE

Despite the fact that everyone professes interest in productivity, there are really very few well established metrics, and those that do exist assume stable operating environments, not subject to multiple changes. This makes comparisons difficult, especially when measuring the combined effects of learning new tools and methods of working. For what it's worth, my own experience with several clients, tools and methods indicates that during planning and analysis, much better quality is achieved with about the same IS resources in slightly greater elapsed time. This is in part due to the increased involvement of users, and the extended time for achieving agreement and approval for requirements models. A further, albeit unquantified gain comes from the increased confidence that end users have when they are involved in and understand the results of the specification process.

A distinct and significant gain can be achieved during the Design and Construction phases, but this is primarily dependant on the nature of the implementation environment selected for the application. Where code or application generation tools have been used, the gain has been large. Where conventional hand coding is used, the gain is still apparent, because the coding and testing cycle is less affected by design changes, but is much less.

No one yet has much (any) hard data on the impact on reduced maintenance effort, although some (good) anecdotal information is appearing. The jury is still out on this one.

Getting Started with CASE

Buying and trying out a CASE tool can be either very cheap or very expensive. Single phase workbenches for analysis cost only a few hundred pounds, and can be learned in a day or so of "hands on" effort. If hardware and human resources are costed in, "trying out" CASE on this basis still costs only £20,000 to £25,000 - an insignificant amount for a major IS department and in most organisations less than half the annual cost of an analyst. At the other extreme, a full I-CASE toolkit may cost upwards of £250,000 to buy and another £250,000 to install and implement.

In each situation, however a plan for the introduction and effective use of CASE tools of any sort is really an essential. Without it, much time and expense can be wasted for little or no return. This section looks at some of the key issues in adopting CASE, in particular:

- Getting effective commitment from IS and user management

- Setting reasonable expectations for what CASE can do

- Making the cost/benefit case

- Starting in the right place in the development life cycle

- Starting with a pilot project vs the "Big Bang" approach

- Choosing a tool or tool kit

- Picking a good first project

In the next sections, we will also look at some of the major practical problems with current tools, and at some of the factors that have proved critical to the successful adoption of CASE tools in organisations that have made them work effectively.

Getting Effective Commitment

One of the real dangers with CASE is that it will be used by IS managers as "something to keep the technicians happy" and that there will be no real commitment to adopting it. Given that CASE is just one element of a change in the way the IS department works, it's not surprising that many middle level managers are reluctant to look at it seriously. In particular, changes that require much more direct user contact and accountability are often strongly resisted. In working with a number of organisations to introduce CASE, I have found that most analysts, designers and programmers take to CASE fairly readily. Senior managers are also reasonably easy to convince. It's the levels in between who offer the strongest resistance, and who are often the ones who actually control the selection process.

Without effective commitment, however, CASE will be just another "evaluation exercise" and even the best CASE tools can't demonstrate their true potential in isolation. So ensuring that there is commitment at senior levels in the IS Management to carry through the implementation is essential. Equally essential is the communication of this commitment to all levels of the IS Organisation. Users will also be involved in the introduction process, and the impact on them may be just as great. It's also necessary, therefore, to keep them and their management informed of what's going on, how it will affect them, and what benefits can be expected.

This makes the adoption process essentially a corporate decision, with implications that go well outside the IS department, and hence there has to be corporate commitment as well. In most organisations, that's a lot to ask for, as senior general management is not used to having to decide on these sorts of issues. Nevertheless, the adoption process will go much more smoothly if everyone involved knows that the Chairman or Chief Executive is behind the project and actively watching progress. It also raises the stakes for the IS department. With this level of visibility, they will be under a lot of pressure to make the introduction successful.

Setting Everyone's Expectations

CASE is far from being the answer to all IS development problems and it's important for those directly involved to understand this, and to make the point clear to everyone else. In particular, CASE does not:

- Remove the need for understanding and analysis of users' business problems

- Do all the work of information gathering, model building and evaluating options - it just makes some of the activities involved less tedious and time consuming

- Speed up the overall process of Analysis or Design. The requirement to use a structured method correctly and to introduce rigour into the modelling process actually slows things down - that's the price of improved quality

- Make life easier for users during the requirements definition process. Users may be required to become more involved, not less, and will be expected to take on a more responsible role in agreeing and quality assuring deliverables

Many extravagant claims are made for CASE tools and in every instance where they were believed they've re-bounded on the implementors and delayed or destroyed real but less extravagant benefits. Setting realistic expectations may make the selling process more difficult, but in the end it's always easier to do well against an expectation that was realistic in the first place.

Making The Cost/Benefit Case

There is a long standing joke among management consultants that something that you really want but can't cost justify ends up as an essential part of corporate strategy. CASE tools are no exception. Few organisations have so far taken on CASE as a necessary strategic tool for future IS developments, although the number is increasing as the tools improve. That means that most IS departments will have to provide a credible cost justification for the tools they want. The costs are relatively easy to identify (although they vary considerably from tool to tool) but are usually understated by ignoring or reducing the estimates for training and learning curve effects. Costs associated with the integration of new tools with the existing environment are also generally forgotten. If you add everything up, it turns out that the cost of the tools themselves is a fairly trivial element in the overall equation.

Benefits assessments are divided between:

- Quantifiable, which usually means estimates of:

    - Improved staff productivity from analysts, designers and programmers

    - The benefits in terms of reduced maintenance from better quality systems

    - Reduced machine resources from better designed and integrated applications using common data bases

    Of course, the reliability of some of these estimates may be in doubt, but so long as the underlying assumptions are stated and seen to be reasonable, estimates can usually be derived for these categories of "benefit"

- Unquantifiable which covers:

    - Other aspects of quality, such as usability, common standards and reduced requirements for user training and support

    - Increased user confidence in key operational systems through enhanced reliability

    - Improved contribution of information systems to the support of corporate objectives

    - Improved responsiveness of the IS department to changing business needs

    - The ability to attract and retain better quality IS staff through an improved image as a "leading edge" department and the resulting decrease in disruption caused by staff turnover

    Some of these "Unquantifiable" areas can actually have significant quantifiable savings attached to them, (user training and reduced staff turnover are two obvious examples) but few IS departments have any baseline information from which to generate a reliable estimate

As with all cost/benefit calculations, the value of the exercise depends on how well the current situation is quantified and whether the proposed savings can be realised in cash (or at least budgetary) terms. In IS departments, the position is usually fairly grim on both counts. Very few departments keep detailed productivity records. Quite a lot don't even keep accurate resource utilisation records structured by application development and maintenance and recorded on the basis of individual applications. So the baselines for estimating savings are weak at best.

The answer in most instances is to use the accounting equivalent of a "thought experiment" - see what the answer has to be to justify the cost, and then show that, within very conservative margins, this will be easily achievable if only x% of the claims for CASE are correct. Provided x is low enough, this usually passes scrutiny.

Starting in the right place

Most CASE implementations start with an Analysis project. There's nothing really wrong with this - requirements specification is one area where CASE is supposed to make a big impact - and it's an area that most IS departments feel that they already know. Unfortunately, it's often a bad place to start from the point of view of a successful implementation because:

- Structured methods, which CASE tools need to have in place to realise their full benefits, are often absent, or if present, are used badly or not at all. Analysts don't understand how to use the tools effectively because they don't really understand the techniques that the tools support

- Many of the architectural issues raised by using CASE can't be resolved if there is no Strategic Information Systems Plan in place

- Scoping an Analysis project is very difficult without corporate models for organisation, data and functions, so pilot projects have to be adjusted as they go along

- Good pilot projects are not always available, so inappropriate projects or "make work" exercises get used instead

- There is a significantly reduced opportunity for added value from the first project if the models built with the CASE tools are limited to one business area and are not readily usable in others

- Training often gets skimped in the rush to get started, resulting in confusion and uncertainty in the project team and low morale during the project

- There is a severe danger of "the blind leading the blind" on the project. Recently trained or even untrained CASE users have to become instant experts, and they make mistakes in their use and understanding of the tools. These mistakes can easily become working practice because there's no one to tell them how to do things correctly or effectively

All these potential problems make analysis projects a less than optimum place to start the CASE adoption process.

The best place to start is with a proper Information Strategy Planning exercise on a major organisational division, so that the key corporate models (organisation, data, function) are in place and agreed and the essential architectures (data, applications, technology) are identified, planned and understood. Subsequent analysis projects can then work from a common and consistent baseline, with assigned and agreed priorities and high added value from the planning models. The information strategy planning process is also less dependant on structured methods skills (although it still requires the basic skills of data and function modelling to be available to the team) and planning teams usually consist of more experienced staff. The duration of the planning phase also allows time for sensible methods and tools training for analysts and designers who will be involved in later projects.

There seems to be an strong case for starting with an ISP project, so why do so few organisations actually start somewhere else ? I think there are a few specific reasons why this happens:

- The choice of CASE tools that support planning is limited. If your favourite vendor's tool doesn't provide support (yet), you won't want to start with a project that will show it in a bad light. There's a much bigger range of choice in Analysis, so it's safer to start there and move on to Design

- Decisions about "trying out" CASE are made in the IS department at a level below that which could initiate or propose an ISP project. CASE is often brought in without senior management's knowledge or consent, "just to get some experience" and this isn't possible if the ISP route is chosen. Starting with a small low risk analysis project also avoids facing the issue of convincing senior managers that CASE is a good idea

- Not everyone feels confident that an ISP is necessary or desirable, or the organisation already has, or claims to have, one, and doesn't want to repeat the exercise

If a SISP already exists, a good approach is to use the CASE tools to document it thoroughly, and to construct the relevant corporate models. This helps validate the contents of the plan and gives any subsequent Analysis projects a head start with tool-based data and function models.

Nevertheless, 8 out of 10 users start their use of CASE with an Analysis project.

Pilot Projects vs Big Bang

Conventional wisdom in IS departments and elsewhere recommends that you start something new with a pilot project. The rationale is that pilot projects can fail without doing serious damage to the business, so the risk is contained. They also involve only a small proportion of the IS department's resources, so they're relatively cheap to run and not too difficult to manage. There's not much published data on the success rate of this approach in terms of achieving rapid implementation of new technology, even when the projects themselves are successes, but from my own experience and from anecdotal material, it's not high. There are some relevant reasons for this:

- Because pilot projects don't really matter, they seldom actually fail. If everyone knows that this is "just a pilot" they tend to relax and get on with things in a way that you don't see on "real" projects. If they do hit serious problems, that doesn't really matter either - its assumed that the problem will get fixed before the tools get used "for real"

- No one believes that pilots actually prove anything except that a basic level of functionality is present and works. Pilots are used as "exclusion" tests not "inclusion tests", yet no one considers the logic of trying out a tool that is in such poor shape that it's going to fail on this basis. From this point of view, pilots are just extended demonstrations without the salesman present

- Pilots are seldom chosen so that the experience gained on them can be transferred to larger or more complex projects, with different staff involved. They're just not typical enough to be useful indicators of how the tools will work for other people in other situations

- The process takes too long to produce any relevant results. In particular, any significant benefits are likely to be delayed well beyond the end of the pilot project until sufficient additional use has been made of the tools

That's not to suggest that pilot projects should be abandoned altogether - just that the project used needs to be chosen carefully, and that the attitude of the organisation towards the trial needs to be carefully managed.

The alternative to the pilot project approach is to recognize the strategic role that CASE will play in IS developments, and mandate its use on all projects, without going through the pilot stage. This "Big Bang" approach certainly demonstrates commitment but does require that the tools chosen be suitable for the work to be done and the environment in which they will be used. From that point of view, this is a much more risky approach. On the other hand, given a good choice of tool, the benefits will be available that much sooner.

There's no doubt that this approach can work, but it imposes a considerable strain on the management of the organisation attempting it.

Choosing a Tool Set

How to choose which tool or tools to use is a very common question. Like most selection processes, there's no simple answer to making the right choice, but there are some practical guidelines. At the very least, an organisation planning to adopt CASE tools needs to know why it wants them and what it expects to use them for. If you think that this is stating the obvious, you're absolutely right, but my experience is that it needs stating, over and over again. Here are a few of the key items that should be considered, not in any order of priority:

- **Match to methodology.** If you don't actively use a structured analysis and design methodology, you're not going to get much benefit out of CASE tools. If you already have, and actively use, a methodology, and you're happy that it will fit in with automated support, select from the tools that fit the approach used by the method. Methodology is a key determinant for the success of CASE tools, and, on a more trivial level, determines the type and format of diagrams that users feel comfortable with. Cosmetic issues may seem trivial in the selection process, but they turn out to play a significant role in the ease and success of the initial adoption

- **Match to technology architecture.** Pick tools that are consistent with your technology architecture and infrastructure. You are going to have to support the hardware and software platforms used by the tools, and if it's a new one for your support staff, there will be costs associated with this. Don't expect to have all the necessary hardware and software available already. Virtually all CASE tools require some additional investment in suitable platform resources

- **Match to development and implementation environments.** Pick tools that fit in with your development environment. For example:

  - If most of what you do is maintenance, retrofit tools and re-engineering generally will be important - planning tools won't be, although you'll probably need them eventually

  - If you are oriented towards using packages, you don't have much need for code generation tools, but you might still want end user or information centre oriented tools for package customisation

  - If you are involved in real time developments make sure that the functional modelling facilities of the tools will support this requirement

and so on.

Also pick tools that are a good match for your implementation environment. You don't want to spend a lot of time manually adapting automated designs to fit the target environment, although some manual tuning is almost always necessary. If you have more than one of these environments (as is increasingly the situation), expect to select a set of complimentary tools covering all the targets, although all the tools selected should be able to use a single repository

- **Match to organisational style and culture.** If you're a sophisticated IS department that already has a data administration or information resource management function, you'll be able to use more sophisticated tools than someone who has yet to install a DBMS. Pick tools that match the level of sophistication you can achieve, but remember that you will become more sophisticated much faster than the tools will, so don't go for something too basic that you will outgrow quickly. If your organisation is highly centralised with tight central control and strict design and documentation standards, pick a tool that can help to enforce these. If you're not so strictly controlled, or operate in a highly decentralised fashion, you'll need a tool that allows for more user flexibility, while still maintaining consistency between users' views

- **Match to implementation approach.** Select tools that fit in with they way you've planned to implement CASE. The tools will need to be strong in the areas that will be addressed first, because that's where the most mistakes will be made. Make sure that the selected tools cover all the areas you plan to address for the period of your implementation plan, not just the initial project

- **Match to budget.** If your budget is tight, select a tool that lets you start small and grow in easy increments, and that minimises all the hidden costs of adoption, like support, training and learning curve effects

- **Match to Vendors.** You're going to have to live with your tool choices for some time, so select vendors that you are comfortable working with and who can provide the type and amount of support that you're going to need. This includes satisfying yourself that the vendors will continue to be in business to provide the required support. If you're selecting more than one tool, make sure that the different vendors can and will work together to help to integrate your use of their products

The final choice is almost always a balancing act between conflicting objectives and compromises between what the buyer would like and what the tools can actually do. Using CASE changes many things related to the development life cycle and the choice of tools can make a big difference to the ease with which these changes are accomplished. So it's worth putting some effort into the selection process. Don't give the job to a couple of junior analysts to do in their spare time. Vendors are good at spotting who is serious about CASE tools and who is just "kicking tyres". Since they have a living to make, they tend to concentrate on those they believe to be the serious prospects. If you don't behave like one, you won't get treated like one.

Once you have identified a few tools in which you are really interested, arrange a product demonstration by the vendor, and go prepared to ask, and get answers to, the "make or break questions" that decide whether the tool is really a contender or not. Insist that the vendor makes technical expertise available to answer your questions, and does not just leave it to the salesman to "get back to you on that". If possible, prepare a short exercise that you want the tool to be put through, and let the vendor have a copy in advance, so that they know what to expect and can plan their time accordingly. Expect to spend at least a day on each product demonstration, but don't expect that this will prove all that much. The true test of a tool can only be on a project, and the purpose of a demonstration is to generate sufficient confidence to make setting up a trial project worthwhile.

Picking a Good First Project

If you are one of the 8 out of 10 installations for whom the preferred implementation route is a pilot project in Analysis, followed by Design, then there are some important issues to consider. Picking a good first project can make the difference between getting CASE going successfully and missing the opportunity. Some of the things to consider are:

- The project should be one that's going to be done anyway, not something invented for the purpose of the pilot. That means that it is a "real" project, the outcome of which matters to the IS department and to the business. Given that there is a risk in introducing CASE tools, it should not be a strategically vital development. It should, however be a non-trivial development that will be implemented on completion and for which the IS department has made delivery commitments

- The project should be one that's already been scoped and sized, so that some comparison can be made between what was expected without the use of CASE tools, and what actually happened

- The Project should be the right size, so that:

    - It's not too big, giving training and co-ordination problems to an inexperienced team, and not so small that the results will be dismissed as un-representative

    - It lasts long enough to get the team over the worst of the learning curve effects, but not so long that the benefits assessment and evaluation are delayed

    A good guide-line to use is a team of 3 - 5 people for 4 - 6 elapsed months, with an absolute upper limit of 9 months for the elapsed time. The team should include at least one user from the area under investigation. Larger projects can be considered, if adequate account is taken of the additional management input and co-ordination effort that will be required

- The project should be in an area that is already well understood by the business and the IS department, to minimise additional learning effects. Try to avoid areas that are changing for other reasons, or have serious organisational or managerial problems

- The area to be investigated should not be associated with the use of unfamiliar technology or software apart from the CASE tools. Once again, the idea is to minimise the number of variables that the project team has to cope with

- If possible, the project should provide opportunities to add value to the modelling work by re-using it in subsequent projects

Most medium and large scale installations will have a project that fits the majority of these criteria, although it may be a problem in smaller departments. Where no obvious candidate can be found, you should consider exactly why you are introducing CASE, and select a project that will best allow the performance of the products selected to be matched against these reasons.

And just to prove that all the above is really only a guide-line, I have also seen a successful installation (at a merchant bank) where they changed virtually everything in the IS department all at once (hardware vendor, operating system, DBMS, development language and departmental location), and still managed a successful implementation project in a critical business area.

Resources

What's needed for the first project is a team that will have a good chance of being successful, but not one that's so unlike normal project teams that everyone knows that the results aren't typical. It's also advantageous if the team members can be used to form the nucleus of future project teams and thus spread experience as rapidly as possible. In practice, it is very difficult to satisfy both of these criteria simultaneously. The main considerations are:

- The team members need to be enthusiastic about CASE, but not to the point of fanaticism. They must be prepared to be positive in the face of the difficulties that will inevitably arise, but also objective in their assessment of the contribution that the tools make to the success of the project. They should be people whose views and abilities are trusted and respected by their colleagues in the IS and user departments, so that they can act as ambassadors for the CASE approach once it has been proven

- Avoid using only "star" analysts or designers. The average CASE tool user will be someone with less than 2 years experience in their current job, and the tools must be useful to someone at this level. If they can only be used by real experts, they won't get used effectively by 80% or more of those who really need them

- At the same time, avoid using people who are very inexperienced and who will require constant supervision and help from other team members, who may themselves be uncertain as to what they should be doing. Also avoid those who are strongly against the CASE concept for whatever reason. They will spend their time on the project in trying to prove that CASE doesn't work, rather than finding out what it can actually do

- Get at least one user on the project team, and pick someone who is pro-technology. If the project creates a favourable impression with users and generates a lot of positive interest outside of the IS department, it will be difficult for IS staff not to accept CASE tools

- Pick a really good project manager. Project management skills are one of the main determinants of success for any development project, and ensuring that the project will be effectively managed is a key issue

Provided that the pilot CASE tools project has sufficient management commitment, the staff needed can usually be made available. Once the team has been selected, it's a good idea to train them in the use of the tools as a team, so that they get used to working together, and understand each other's strengths and weaknesses. This also makes life a lot easier for the project manager, who will know what to expect from each team member, and adjust the project roles and responsibilities accordingly.

It's also a good idea to budget for additional review and presentation time to allow non-team members to be briefed on progress during the course of the project. A monthly seminar, given by the project team to groups of colleagues, will stop the project being seen as "only for the privileged few". Using CASE tools should not be seen as difficult, and keeping everyone informed is one way to avoid this happening.

Timescales

All these considerations mean that the CASE tools implementation process can't easily be rushed through without risking longer term success. In the ideal approach, starting with an ISP project, the selection, preparation and first project will normally take between 9 and 15 months. A shorter elapsed time than this can be achieved if the choice of tools is relatively simple, but a minimum of 6 months is really the lower limit. Any longer and there is a danger that other factors, such as new tool developments or changing business requirements will invalidate the selected approach and tools.

Starting with an Analysis project gives a similar timescale. Three months to review and select the tools. A month for team training and project start-up and then four to six months for the project itself gives an elapsed time of 8 to 10 months. About a year seems to be typical. One of the major hold ups experienced by a lot of sites when starting up their first CASE project relates to ordering the correct hardware and software configuration for the selected tools. Why this should be I have no idea, it may be that the complexities of the PC world are simply unfamiliar to IS departments, or that the defences erected by many organisations to prevent end users buying PCs indiscriminately get in the way. Whatever the reasons, expect the process to be difficult, time consuming and error prone.

Getting Beyond Getting Started

All that the initial project really does is confirm that the CASE approach is potentially viable for an organisation, and that the tools selected work to an acceptable degree in the circumstances in which they were used. There is still the much larger problem of how a successful first project involving only half a dozen people can be transformed into widespread use of the tools in an IS department that may be hundreds strong. More than one organisation has put so much effort into its initial CASE projects that it had no energy or enthusiasm left to continue the implementation process once the first project proved successful. Yet CASE implementation is not complete until everyone who could be using a CASE tool is routinely doing so.

There are two main issues to consider once the first project has been completed successfully:

- How do we "finish" the application that has just been specified and/or designed?

- What should the second CASE-based project be?

If you wait until the first project is over before making these decisions, there will be an inevitable loss of momentum and enthusiasm and interest will be lost. You will also lose the opportunity of starting up subsequent projects before the end of the first. Because there are inevitably a lot of factors to be juggled, it's a sensible idea to start the process with a strategy for CASE tools implementation that covers more than just the initial project.

I hope that it is now clear why the right place to start the CASE implementation process is with an Information Strategy Planning project, even if it's only for the IS department itself. If you start with this, you and your organisation will already have done most of the work required to plan the development projects to be undertaken over a two to five year period, and you will understand the priorities, project dependencies and opportunities for added value from one development to another. Under these circumstances, it's easy to answer the "what should we do next" questions, and possible to plan ahead for the additional tools and facilities that will be required for later projects.

Despite all this logic, most installations still won't opt for this approach, but should still develop a strategy that will get them to the same end, albeit with more effort and risk. The strategy should cover:

- Extending the business models produced during the initial project, particularly the data model, to cover the whole business division or the complete organisation

- Identifying subsequent development projects and project phases, for which CASE will be used

- Planning the acquisition of any additional tools and training that will be required by these projects

- Continuing an education and training program for IS department and user management and staff

The plan should also address the overall migration issues concerned with converting existing systems into the CASE tools environment.

Most IS departments have the beginnings of an architecture for their use of technology. Without an SISP, however, there probably won't be equivalent architectures for data, organisation and applications. These architectures are essential for the planning and control of application development, whether or not you use CASE tools. An ISP project builds them explicitly. An Analysis project doesn't, but does create sufficient "seed corn" models, allowing a separate architecture development project to start once the business area models are available. The data and function models generated during Analysis become available fairly early on in the course of the project, especially at the level needed for architecture development work, so there is no need to wait for the end of the project before starting. In particular, the data model for a business area will usually contain most of the major organisation wide entities needed for the data architecture, and can form a starting point for a corporate data model. As the architectures for data, applications and technology develop, they need to be consolidated into a single corporate information model, under the aegis of the corporate data administration function. This is an iterative process, which should be started as early as possible during the development of each individual architecture, and which is greatly assisted by the use of CASE tools.

So, if the first CASE implementation project is not an ISP, the second should be an architecture development project, building on the business modelling work from the first and starting as soon as the models are stable. This will usually be about halfway through the planned elapsed time for the first project. Following the same approach as was used to prepare the initial project team, a selection and team training programme will be needed. Since CDA will take over responsibility for the architectures one they are developed, it's sensible to use some CDA staff on this project. The team should also contain some IS department analysts, who will be future "customers" of CDA and who will use the architecture on future projects. Their involvement prevents the worse aspects of "not invented here" being associated with the architectures and, particularly in the case of the data model, helps to stop the worst excesses of abstract data analysis from occurring.

It is actually possible to start the architecture project effectively at the same time as the first Analysis project and combine the modelling efforts. This approach provides the Analysis team with additional start-up resources and helps to get the models built quickly, but requires a larger initial training effort and introduces possible co-ordination problems.

Selecting subsequent projects is still going to be something of a problem. The architecture team will need longer to finish their development than the first project team will need to finish their requirements definition, so selection on the basis of the architectures will not be possible. The best approach is often to select a project that's a larger version of the first. There should be some value from the data models that will by now be available, but added value opportunities will probably be limited.

Education and Training

Good CASE tools look easy to use, in fact ease of use is one of their strong selling points. In terms of "operability" it's true that most people can learn the controls in a few hours and be comfortable and efficient with them in a few days. The leading tools are, however, extremely rich in functionality and highly integrated via their repositories. It takes much longer to learn how to use these facilities in an effective fashion. This learning process can't be effectively carried out without a significant amount of education and training:

- **Education**, because many analysts and designers are unfamiliar with the approaches required to make effective use of the tools, and need to be shown the assumptions that tool developers make about how their tools will be used

- **Training**, because there are new skills to be acquired, and these skills require both demonstration and practice

Much of the training needs to take place in order to ensure that analysts and designers understand structured techniques well enough to use the tools sensibly. This increases the training requirement substantially, but we have found it to be necessary in almost every organisation adopting CASE tools. Training in the basic techniques of data analysis is particularly necessary. In addition to basic skills acquisition, project teams may need to work together on exercises at the start of major projects. 3 - 5 day workshop classes based on prepared case studies can be used to re-enforce basic skills and establish understanding of the role the tools play in the project as a whole.

This is a lot of training for an IS department to commit to, and there will be a tendency to skip some of it, or to train just a few staff, and expect them to pass on their skills and knowledge to the rest of the department. This won't work. Training doesn't have to be done all at once, but it does all have to be done, and it's cheaper in the long run to buy high quality professional training than it is to rectify the problems caused by badly trained staff. CASE tools don't reduce the skill levels required for good analysis and design. All they do is make it easier for skilled staff to deploy their skills, and help to catch routine errors of detail. A badly analysed problem can be modelled perfectly on a CASE tool - but the solution designed from the model will not be the one required. So training may be expensive, but not training people is even more expensive, and can be disastrous.

What works and what doesn't

Like most new technologies, CASE promises many functions and facilities for users that are not fully developed or readily usable. This situation is not the fault of the tool developers alone, although they get blamed for any deficiencies or difficulties. Actually, tool developers have a major problem when trying to decide which functions and facilities to develop, and how to package them into sets that match the way users work. Only by trying out tool features on real projects is it possible to tell what will be required by users, and what approaches work well. When you add in the difficulties caused by variations in project management, user skills and all the other variables in real life development projects, it's not surprising that the developers don't get everything right first time.

It's important therefore to ensure that all those who are to be involved in CASE projects know what to expect, and are not led to believe that the tools will do things that they can't. This is important for both:

- **IS staff**, who may become frustrated if the tools don't meet their expectations and make their work slower or more difficult. If the IS staff don't believe in what they are trying to do, it's highly unlikely that the project will succeed

- **Users,** who will rapidly lose confidence in both the development process and the CASE technology. Since their co-operation is essential to a successful implementation, this loss of confidence must be avoided. Once it's happened it's much more difficult to re-establish.

Setting realistic expectations is therefore important, and needs to be done from the outset of a CASE implementation programme. Those involved need to understand that:

- CASE is expected to work effectively, but not necessarily all at once, or immediately

- Problems are to be expected, but resources and skills are available to deal with them

- There is management commitment to see the process through to a successful conclusion

Everyone involved must also understand that CASE tools are just that - tools - and their effect depends on how well they are used, not just on the fact that they are being used. The tools help developers to carry out some procedures more effectively, but they don't remove the need for those procedures.

Keeping it simple

The approach, therefore, should be to formulate a simple message about the use of CASE, and to set expectations relatively low, but to provide visible encouragement and support for initial projects. Do:

- Emphasise commitment to enhancing the development process and to furthering the development of the IS department's ability to respond to user needs

- Support the requirement to develop high standards of professional skill, and to enhance the effectiveness of those skills through the use of CASE

Don't:

- Stress the technology of CASE

- Make the tools seem easier to use than they really are

- Force the use of the technology in user contacts until the IS staff are comfortable with it

Since the initial CASE experience will surface problems and concerns, try to anticipate where they might occur, and be prepared to deal with them quickly and decisively.

Where and when do the benefits appear ?

Given the significant costs of introducing CASE tools, IS and business management are always keen to know when the benefits and payback will appear. Predicting and measuring benefits is difficult, in part because of the lack of information about current performance and quality in IS development. Nevertheless, the benefits question needs to be answered sooner or later, and there are a number of considerations that need to be taken into account when trying to predict where and when benefits will occur.

Learning to operate CASE tools is generally simple and quick. Learning to use them effectively is not. In addition, CASE tools focus on the need to carry out planning, analysis and design activities with much greater attention to detail, and with much more awareness of users requirements. Learning how to do this effectively is not easy for most IS departments, and while they are learning, they are not going to perform as efficiently as they usually do. They're also going to make mistakes, possibly serious ones, in the early projects, usually due to unfamiliarity with the techniques and methods that the tools help to automate. These mistakes will not always be easy to spot and, once spotted, to correct.

The upshot of all this is a steep and extended learning curve, during which it's likely that performance and productivity will be at best equivalent to that achieved without the tools. Only after this learning curve effect has been removed can IS departments be expected to show measurable improvements in productivity. Only a few CASE users have reached this point so far, and the evidence indicates that it will take 12 - 18 months to bring a significant proportion of an IS department's development staff up the learning curve.

So if there are no quick gains in productivity from the adoption of CASE, are there benefits to be gained from improvements in the quality of information systems developed using CASE tools ? Once again, the problems posed by lack of a sensible baseline against which to measure hampers the argument. Generally, however, achieving significantly higher quality can be expected to involve more detailed analysis and design procedures, coupled with additional project management and control activities. It also implies the expanded involvement of users in the development process, and in the review and approval of work products. All this implies that more time and resources will have to be put into system development, and many of these resources are scarce and expensive. That's why we don't do things better now. It's not that the will and the expertise aren't there, its just that there is never enough of them. So can CASE make enough of a difference on the productivity side that resources can be released to focus on quality ?

The evidence so far is that it can, although it barely achieves a real difference during the initial implementation period. The consistency and completeness checking facilities provided by the leading CASE tools do make a significant difference, but only once IS staff understand how to use them effectively. The code and application generation capabilities of Lower-CASE and some I-CASE tools are also major contributors to improved quality, but only if the designs they work from have been correctly developed as solutions to user requirements.

In essence, we have to come up with a number of criteria against which to evaluate the effect of CASE, and to translate the measures of this effect into benefits that IS or user management will agree can and will be achieved. CASE alone won't deliver benefits to anyone. Only if managers and users agree to make use of the potential that CASE offers to improve some aspects of the systems development process will benefits be achieved, and even then, only after the use of CASE has become firmly established.

Critical Success Factors

Finally, lets summarise the critical factors in successfully implementing CASE in an organisation. Not necessarily in this order of importance, all the following are required:

- **Management Commitment**. The first lesson has to be that the adoption of CASE tools is not something that can be undertaken by the IS department alone. There is a temptation, however, to begin experimentation with CASE as an IS only activity, and to let others in the organisation become involved once the experiment has proved to be successful. When they are finally allowed to participate, users and user management treat CASE as "just another attempt by the IS department to spend our money on their toys" (this is an actual quote from the chief executive of a large insurance company, asked to expand a small IS pilot project from 5 users of CASE to over 100).

Organisations who have succeeded with CASE ensured that both IS management and senior user management knew what was going on right from the outset, and were prepared to support the implementation process publicly. This is usually a new and difficult role for IS departments, and generally they do it badly or not at all. If your IS staff can't or won't set up and run some such programme of management education, you'll need to get outside help to do so. If you omit this step, you'll find it much harder to get the use of CASE accepted. Once you have identified and agreed a sponsor, and set up a management education programme, it's time to take a look at the structure and management of the IS department, and start to get this into shape for effective control of the use of CASE.

- **Methodology**. No Methodology - no hope. In more than 4 years of involvement with CASE implementations I have yet to see an organisation successfully adopt CASE without already having a competent structured development methodology in widespread use. Quite a lot of organisations have tried, and have discovered a some stage in the implementation process that no one really understands what to do with the tools. They then have to stop or slow down their use of CASE while a suitable methodology is selected and introduced. Those organisations that never adopt and implement structured methods fail to implement CASE, or demote the tools to use as simple diagraming aids.

Note that buying a structured methodology product is not the same as implementing the method. There is just as much shelfware in methodology as there is in software and three feet of dusty manuals on a shelf, or a £0.5 million training programme does not mean that the method is being used. The UK is particularly prone to this situation. Methodologies are adopted, staff are trained and the result ? At best, structured documentation, at worst nothing at all to show for the investment.

- **Training**. Training is expensive, takes key staff away from essential work and never really seems to teach staff what they need to be productive on their return. So it gets skimped or skipped altogether. Since the leading CASE tools are always sold as easy to use, why spend the time and resources on expensive training courses ? Just install the tools, let the chaps play with them for a while, and away you go! Sound familiar? It should. I must have heard variations on this theme dozens of times from IS managers, prepared to spend tens or hundreds of thousands of pounds on tools, but little or nothing on the training needed to make effective use of them.

And training is needed. Development using CASE tools is sufficiently different from conventional development that IS staff can't usually work out how to use the tools to best effect unless someone shows them. They can then take the basic principles of CASE tool usage and adapt them to the needs of their own organisation. Without training, this process of learning and adapting to the use of CASE will take a long time and may never be achieved. Unless the learning process takes place, however, CASE tools will not achieve their potential.

- **Involving Users**. Most CASE tool developers and the majority of those adopting them have assumed that CASE is essentially for the support of professional IS developers. The tools generally support tasks and techniques that have been the preserve of IS analysts and designers, and offer little direct support for non-IS staff who may participate in projects. Modern structured methods, in contrast, stress the need to involve users, both as sources of information on business requirements and as active participants in project teams. If the benefits of user contribution are to be fully realised, they to must be able to understand the need for, and if necessary use, CASE tools to support their participation. In my experience, where users do receive encouragement and training, they take up the use of the tools just as fast, if not faster than professional development staff. It can be argued that their use is at a trivial level, since they do not really understand the techniques that are being automated by the tools, but that's not the users' perception. They see themselves as making a direct contribution, alongside and on a par with IS staff, and this strengthens their enthusiasm and support for the CASE-based development process. Provided that the extent of their contribution is effectively managed the overall performance of a mixed team of users and professionals supported by CASE tools can be significant. Just how far the principles of user involvement and direct use of the tools should be taken is still a matter of debate and of research efforts, both in the US and the UK. It is already evident, however, that users have a great deal to contribute to the implementation of CASE, and if they are prevented from participating, they will probably adopt a posture of active or passive opposition.

- **Selecting Appropriate Tools**. Just how easy it is to get IS staff and users started with CASE depends on which tools are selected, and what they are to be used for. In many ways, the selection of appropriate tools produces a dilemma:

  - The initial requirement is for tools that are easy to learn and can be productive quickly, addressing widely accepted problems and showing rapid payback. Such tools do exist, but are mostly limited in capability, and so reach the limits of their effective contribution relatively quickly

  - In the medium term, the requirement is for high functionality tools that cover most or all of the life cycle and support sophisticated users in complex problem solving environments

The leading tools try to address this dilemma by providing a simple to use user interface, that hides, but does not eliminate much more sophisticated functions and facilities. Nevertheless, someone adopting CASE for the first time must decide between:

  - Starting with a simple tool, and planning to replace it at a later stage with something more capable and sophisticated, with the consequent disruption, increase in acquisition costs (possibly including new hardware and software platforms), retraining requirements and implementation overheads

  - Starting with simple use of a more complex and capable tool, and actively managing the process of bringing more functions and facilities into effective use as user experience grows. This solves the disruption and duplication problem, but has consequences for training (an incremental training programme is needed) and requires much more management involvement in the process. It can also be frustrating for those users who want to move ahead faster than their managers are willing to allow

Both approaches have been tried in practice, with mixed results. The evidence suggests that organisations adopting the first approach reach the limits of their initial tools capability faster than they expect, but have considerable problems getting approval for the migration to a second tool. On the other hand, organisations adopting the second approach seem to reach a plateau in their use of the tools functions that is ahead of that achieved with simple tools, but well below the full capability of the selected product. Getting things moving forward again seems to pose significant difficulties.

One factor is, however, common in successful implementations. More than one tool is involved. The introduction of standards for interworking among CASE tools, particularly a standardised repository, will tend to promote the merits of multiple specialised tools rather than single vendor I-CASE products and further extend the tool kit concept.

- **Picking the Right Approach**. It's very common to find organisations starting their involvement with case without any clear idea of where they intend to go with their use of CASE tools. Developing a sensible CASE strategy is often something that they do after the initial experimentation, perhaps even after the initial implementation attempt. It makes a lot more sense, right from the start, to plan for the extent of CASE usage and the impact of a CASE implementation programme. Developing a CASE strategy can also save considerable effort in the investigation and experimentation stages by eliminating tools that are a poor match to the selected approach. Adopting CASE is no different from any other type of major project. It needs a definition of scope, of the approach to be adopted and of the selection criteria to be used. It's always cheaper to do this first, rather than trying to retrofit scope and approach to an existing situation.

Once a CASE strategy is in place, the IS department can concentrate on implementation tactics. This should involve developing a short and medium term implementation plan, not just planning the investigation and implementation stages. The implementation process is not a short term effort, and treating it as though it is will reduce the chances of success, or at least delay the process significantly.

- **Getting Help**. Getting all of these elements in the implementation process right, and keeping every key aspect progressing at a compatible rate is a major challenge to IS departments, already faced with significant pressures on budgets and staff resources. It makes sense, therefore, to supplement IS resources with external resources and expertise. Many organisations are reluctant to do this, however, for a variety of reasons:

  - It's expensive, and not necessarily value for money unless effective transfer of skills and experience take place

  - It is seen to reflect badly on the capabilities and competence of the IS department

  - Many of those offering help have no more experience with CASE than those they are trying to assist

Nevertheless there are very few examples of successful implementations that did not make use of external help, especially during the first few critical CASE-based projects.

- **Expectations**. Even if you get everything else right, it's essential to remember that CASE tools are just tools, and won't do anything for you unless they're used effectively. Even if they are used properly, they still won't do everything. All those involved with the introduction of CASE need to be reminded of this on a regular basis.

This may seem like a long list of things to get right, but changing the fundamentals of the system development process is not likely to be simple or straightforward. It's important to remember as well that you don't have to get all these things correct in one go or at the same time. What's critical is that you have them as objectives, and create a CASE strategy that works towards all of them. Then CASE will be a success for you. Leave any of them out and it probably won't.

CASE Tools and Software Factories

Erik G. Nilsson

Center for Industrial Research (SI)
Forskningsveien 1, P.O. Box 124, Blindern
N - 0314 Oslo 1
Norway

Abstract

The present paper addresses CASE tools as they are today, and what we believe will be the next generation CASE tools - Software Factories (or IPSEs - Integrated Project Support Environment, or ISDEs - Integrated Software Development Environments).

The paper first gives a definition of CASE tools, and investigates strong and week sides in todays CASE tools. One of the major drawback of todays CASE tools is the lack of integration between specification tools and construction tools. The paper describes four different techniques for such an integration, one of them being usage of a Software Factory architecture.

Then the paper gives a definition of Software Factories - integrated software development environments - , investigates who makes Software Factories, what is achieved by using Software Factories and describes one particular Software Factory - Eureka Software Factory (ESF).

ESF is a multinational, european research and development project that is developing a framework for integrated software development environments, and special environments for special application areas. ESF has a deep foundation in the industry. The paper describes the ESF project, the technical architecture used, and results so far.

Introduction

CASE tools have gathered much interest recent years. From being quite simple drawing tools, powerful ones with wide functionality have emerged. The interest in this kind of tools (and the tools themselves) come(s) mainly from the industry, not from academic circles. Thus, the topic CASE tools has become an area discussed among practitioners, not by academics. Because of this, there are not many general publications (at conferences or in scientific journals) treating CASE tools as a phenomena [HEDQ88, CASE89, BUBE88, NILS88, ROEV89b], but there exists quite a number of articles in computer magazines (like BYTE, Datamation, Computerworld, etc.), both on specific tools and on the field in general [BYTE89, COWO87, COWO88a, COWO88b, ELEC87, IEEE88, DAMA88, INWO88]. One of the reasons for the large interest among practitioners, is the huge amounts of available tools.

Within the field *Software Factories,* the situation is the other way around. There has been quite a lot of research done on integrated software development environments, but few (if any at all) available products exist. Because of this, the knowledge of and interest in such environments is not big among practitioners.

CASE Tools

In this section we take a closer look at CASE tools as they are today. We give a definition of our understanding of what a CASE tool is, we investigate week and strong sides, and we describe how an ideal CASE tool should be, as view from the user (i.e. primarily software developers). As the number of commercial available CASE tools are very high (at least three digits), we make this presentation quite general, without any references to specific tools. Because new tools are emerging all the time, making such references complete would be meaningless. Readers who are interested in specific tools should read[ROEV89b, HEDQ88 and COWO88a].

What is a CASE tool?

The term *CASE tool* has become a buzzword the last years. Linguisticly, the term *Computer Aided Software Engineering* could cover almost any tool that supports software engineering (even a compiler), and a lot of vendors indeed use the term in a very wide sense to be able to put the *CASE tool* label on their products.

The term is also used quite inhomogeneously by different people. From the beginning of *CASE tools,* the term denoted tools that support specification work, i.e. systems analysis and to some extent systems design. As *CASE tools* grew more popular, the meaning of the term "expanded" to cover tools for the all aspects of systems design, and also systems construction. This expansion of meaning is consistent with the semantic meaning of the word, but have also made it less precise.

The need for more precise concepts has lead to different prefixes and suffixes to CASE, *upper, middle, lower, toolkit, workbench* and *integrated* being the most commonly used. Some refer to *upper CASE* as tools supporting systems analysis, while *lower CASE* support all activities from systems design through systems construction and even systems installation. Others restrict *upper CASE* to the phases *before* systems analysis, i.e. corporate planning, strategy study, breakdown of goals, objectives, etc., and use *middle CASE* to denote tools supporting analysis and design, while *lower CASE* is tools supporting systems construction. A third usage, is to make the distinction between *graphical (or diagrammatic) tools* and *code generators, 4. gen. systems, and other non-graphical tools.* In this case, *upper CASE* is the diagrammatic tools, and *lower CASE* is the non-diagrammatic tools. Dividing it this way, puts the border between upper and lower CASE somewhere in the systems design phase. In this paper, we use this last definition of *upper* and *lower CASE* (we do not use *middle CASE).*

Some people make a distinction between *CASE toolkits,* supporting one phase of software development, and *CASE workbenches,* giving support across the software development process. This distinction is often quite fuzzy, and we do not use it in this paper.

Integrated CASE, or *I-CASE* is also used differently by different people. Some use it to refer to tools supporting all activities in software engineering in an integrated manner. Others use it to denote the integration mechanism, i.e. either a common data base (repository, data dictionary, encyclopedia, ...) or a tool (e.g. a software backplane). A third usage is tools that support a specific software development methodology (or life-cycle model). The term *I-CASE* is sometimes used synonymously with *IPSE - Integrated Project Support Environment* (by some people also used to denote Integrated Programming and Software Engineering). We will not use the term *I-CASE,* but rather use the term *IPSE, Software Factory* or *Integrated Software Development Environment (ISDE),* which we find more precise.

With this definition, upper CASE tools covers tools that support techniques like conceptual data modelling (e.g. Entity Relationship (ER) models, entity life-cycle history), structured analysis (e.g. data-flow diagrams, control flow diagrams, activity decomposition diagrams, activity dependency diagrams, state transition diagrams and flow-charts), and techniques like action diagrams, minispecs, pseudo code specification, prototyping, etc. Lower CASE include traditional 4. generation tools (i.e. application generators with tools for dialog design, screen painting, report layout specification, automatic data base design, code generation, etc.). Most CASE tools have a built-in data dictionary (or repository). While most CASE tools are specialized for business application (commercial data processing), some CASE tools for other application areas (like real time systems) have emerged the last years.

In this section we consider both upper and lower CASE tools, but we have the emphasis on upper CASE.

What is good about CASE tools?

Present CASE tools have many strong sides. The main benefit in upper CASE tools is the ability to support the human activities in specifying requirement, i.e. they give aids for documenting results from the requirement specification process. The people performing the specification work no longer need to use pen and paper in drawing their diagrams (and *edit* them), nor to develop their own data dictionaries. In that way they can use more time on creative work, not on tedious drawing work. Even more important, as a result of using these tools, the diagrams and the data dictionary are integrated. Many such tools have modules for automatic generation of documentation of the system being developed. In some tools there are also an integration with word processors, which makes documentation even more convenient.

Some tools also support a simple consistency check between different parts of the specification (different diagrams, information in the data dictionaries, etc.), e.g. between a data flow diagram and an ER diagram and their connected data dictionary specifications. Such a consistency check is f.ex. controlling that the content of data flows and data stores in the data flow diagram are specified in the ER diagram.

In addition, most upper CASE tools have facilities for code generation. These are often restricted to the ability of automatic generation of data base schemas (usually expressed in SQL), but some also support limited program code generation. Some upper CASE tools also offers prototyping tools, but it is seldom possible to use (parts of) the prototype (e.g. screen layouts) outside the CASE tool.

An organizational benefit from the use of CASE tools is a standardization of methodologies and techniques used in the organization.

Another feature supported by some upper CASE tools is the ability to do automatic normalization, but we do not consider this facility as being very important. We feel that doing a good job specifying the conceptual data model makes normalization unnecessary. Normalization is in fact only a control. It can never *produce* good data models or data bases.

The lower CASE tools usually have much more powerful code generation facilities than the upper CASE tools. This is partly due to the kind of information put into the tools, especially the level of detail. As more details are fed into lower CASE tools, code generation is more powerful. The lower CASE tools also usually have more powerful tools for prototyping and application development (e.g. report and screen layout specification), and the application development tools produce executable code, i.e. are integrated with the program implementation tools.

What is bad about CASE tools?

Unfortunately, CASE tools also have a number of weak sides. One drawback in most of todays upper CASE tools is that the users are forced to use the techniques / methodologies supported by the tools they use. This applies both to the visual appearance of the diagrams and the rules used in the techniques. This problem is sometimes referred to as *tool imperialism*. We do not claim that it is wrong to use *one* specific technique / methodology in an organization, but the choice should be done by the organization, not by the tool vendor.

Another problem is that some upper CASE tools are cleverly implemented tools based on bad techniques. The people developing the CASE tools sometimes have higher qualifications in implementing graphical user interfaces than they have in requirement specification techniques. Therefore, the choice of the underlying techniques are in some cases rather arbitrary. This is not as big a problem today as it was in the young days of CASE, but it still does occur.

Although most upper CASE tools have quite good user interfaces, especially if one compares them with other tools supporting systems development (e.g. most lower CASE tools), the user interface could be better in many tools. In our opinion, a common weakness in the user interface is too much use of *modes*. This is especially the case in MS-DOS and MS-Windows based tools (which many CASE tools are). One example of unfortunate use of modes is when you have to perform a special command (putting the tool in a special mode) for operations like moving objects, re-sizing objects and deleting objects. Such operations should be performed either by direct manipulation of the objects, or by selecting the objects and then performing an operation (preferably a keyboard shortcut, e.g. the rub-out key for deletion).

Of course, there is a trade-off when to use modes and not. Usage of modes f.ex. has the benefit of *open end* operations. It is also important to have *general* commands, i.e. dividing the operation and the operand. This minimizes the number of commands. In some CASE tools this is not the case, and one may experience long lists of commands like *create entity, create relationship, ..., move entity, move relationship, ...,* etc.

Another aspect of user interface is the choice of how the tools should enforce rules in the techniques. Many tools let the users do almost anything, and performs a check of the results afterwards. Other tools restrict the users while using the tools, making such a check - which may cause a lot of work for the user - superfluous. A good rule when designing user interfaces is that the user shall not be allowed to perform illegal operations.

Yet another aspect of user interface is the integration between diagrams and textual information in the upper CASE tools. This integration is often done by having a possibility to "explode" elements in the diagram, and thereby getting a screen layout for specifying detailed information. This solution is often due to lack of windowing capabilities in the CASE tools, and use of small screens on the monitors of the PCs running the tools. Combining diagrams and detailed information in compound screen layouts often yield a better user interface.

In addition to the bad user interface (usually terminal and character based with no use of graphics and direct manipulation), lower CASE tools also requires quite a lot of information to be supported by the user to be able to generate code successfully. The bad user interface is often due to the fact that many such tools are mainframe or mini-computer based. Therefore, they are often quite expensive, especially compared to upper CASE.

Most CASE tools (both upper and lower) are directed at developing new systems. Few support what most systems engineers spend most of their time doing, namely maintenance.

The major problem, though, is that the CASE tools are "islands", i.e. they fulfill their purpose in *some part* of the systems development process. As mentioned earlier, the upper CASE tools have some code generation facilities, and the lower CASE tools have quite good code generation capabilities. But unfortunately, that is not enough. As the development evolves, the information stored in the CASE tools are not changed to reflect the *actual* specification and implementation. The reason for this is mainly that the upper CASE tools have very little *connection* to the lower CASE tools, and even less to the program implementation tools, i.e. they can produce results for the lower tools, but they can not get changed specification in return. There is also a problem that upper and lower CASE tools sometimes have overlapping domains, so that one may have redundant specifications. This topic will be discussed in more detail below section *Integration between CASE tools and implementation tools.*

How should an ideal CASE tools be?

In our opinion, the ideal CASE tool should have a lot of features. The most important ones - in addition to those listed above under the heading *What is good about CASE tools?* - are listed below:

Upper CASE tools should be independent of techniques, i.e. they should support a number of techniques, also "dialects" of the same main technique. It should also be possible to *tailor* the tools, at least in four different areas:

(i) It should be possible to tailor the graphical interface for a technique, i.e. to change symbols, colors, the appearance of arrows, etc.

(ii) It should be possible to tailor the *meta model*, i.e. the schema of the data dictionary. If the user wants to document an additional aspect for every entity type, he should be able to add an attribute in the data dictionary to handle that aspect.

(iii) It should be possible to tailor the rules used in the techniques, e.g. to specify whether a relationship could have connected attributes, or whether n-ary relationships are allowed.

(iv) It should be possible to tailor the connection between different models, e.g. to specify which connections that should exist between data flows and data stores on a data flow diagram and entities and attributes in an ER diagram.

All these tailoring facilities should be easy to use, i.e. the upper CASE tools should have special *modules* for tailoring. These tailoring features (at least (i), (ii) and (iii)) are available in some existing CASE tools.

Lower CASE tools should have more graphical user interfaces, and should be based more on manipulation of objects in the systems to be developed. Usage of direct manipulation when f.ex. specifying screen layouts, would make such tools easier to use. This indicates that such tools should run on PCs or work stations, or at least have an interface from such machines. More general, lower CASE tools should run on the same hardware platform as the upper CASE tools, or even more preferable, the CASE tools should be portable.

Both upper and lower CASE tools should support reuse. Not only reuse of code, but also reuse of specifications and design.

All CASE tools should be integrated with implementation tools. (By *implementation tools* we mean tools for either writing code (editors etc.), or manipulation code (compilers, debuggers, test tools, etc.).) It is also important that the integration is done in such a manner that changes in the implementation more or less automatically are reflected in the CASE tool. In an environment with a 4. gen. tool that operates on the "model level", e.g. with concepts from the ER approach and abilities to produce all code automatically (such tools exist), this integration is achievable.

The ultimate goal would be that the distinction between upper CASE, lower CASE and program implementation tools become transparent. The user should operate in an integrated environment, which support all tasks in the software engineering process (also administrative tasks like project management), and the facilities offered by the environment reflect different tasks for the software engineer, not different underlying tools. Such environments are often referred to as IPSEs (Integrated Project Support Environment) or Software Factories. We denote such environment *Integrated Software Development Environments*. But before we take a closer look at such environments, we investigate different models for integrating different CASE tools and implementation tools.

Integration Between Specification Tools and Construction Tools

In this section we take a closer look at four different models for integration between specification tools (mainly upper CASE) and program construction tools (lower CASE and implementation tools). Looking at these four models, it is important to bear in mind the goal of the integration, namely that the user (i.e. the systems developer) should have a work environment where the distinction between the different tools is transparent, that the tools should support the different *tasks* the systems developer performs, and of course that there should be some sort for integration also on the data level [NILS90].

General remarks

One may claim that because specification tools and construction tools cover different phases and activities in a software development effort, there is no need for an integration on the *user* level. We claim that although there are separate phases, an integration on the user level is necessary. The reason for this is that the specification changes in the construction phase, often as a result of trade-offs done to make the implementation effort obtainable. Such changes in the specification should also be reflected in the documentation of the specification, i.e. in the different CASE tools.

The integration between CASE tools and implementation tools must be handled in a special manner in tools for automatic code generation based on specifications on "model level". As long as the "executable" specifications are expressed in terms of the models in the CASE tools, the integration with implementation tools become both a necessity and much easier. A necessity because it is the *specifications* that are altered when a change is issued (not the generated code), and much easier because one only operates on the specification level, and therefore do not need to bother much about the implementation tools.

Independent of which of the models below that are chosen, there is a need for *semantic integration* when different tools support the same problem domain. By semantic integration we mean that the different tools that are integrated have a conformal use of concepts. This is of extreme importance if different tools use the same data store, and is also important if they have different data stores, but common user interface. In the latter case, semantic inconsistencies could be handled by the integration mechanism in the user interface.

Model I: Integration using import and export

Integrating specification tools and construction tools by using import and export is the most common solution today. Most upper CASE tools have some code generation facilities, usually restricted to generation of data base schemas. I.e. this integration is usually a one-way data transfer *from* the CASE tool *to* the implementation tool. (The integration between lower CASE tools and implementation tools is often tighter). In addition to import and export facilities connected to the tools, various users have developed their own import and export program ("bridges"). Some of these have been distributed as freeware or shareware.

Very few (but some) upper CASE tools have the ability to transfer data the other way. (See figure 1 (next page)). The integration the other way could either be done by letting the implementation tool have a facility for producing input to the specification tools (on a special format) or by letting the specification tool have a feature for importing some data format that is easy to produce from the implementation tool. In the latter case, changes is the data base structure could be expressed in SQL, which the specification tool translated back to a conceptual data model, and merged with its existing conceptual data model. A few existing CASE tools have the possibility to import data from implementation tools (usually from the same vendor).

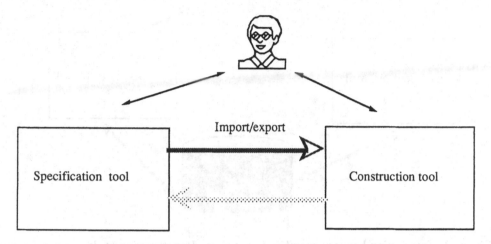

Figure 1 - How integration between specification tools and construction tools usually is done today

The process of translating from implementation level to specification level is sometimes referred to as *reverse engineering* [CASE88, NILS85], and is a more general way of transferring information from implementation tools to CASE tools (both upper and lower).

The advantage of this way of integrating specification tools and implementation tools is that it can be implemented without issuing big changes in the tools. The data transfer and data conversion can be handled by a separate tool (an "agent").

The disadvantages are many. It is often difficult to transfer data *to* the specification tools. This feature is essential if the integration is to be successful. The integration is in many extents "manual", i.e. one has to do special tasks and to run special programs to integrate. Integration should not be a special task that has to be performed every time something changes, integration should be done automatically. And as the integration task has to be manually triggered, there is a fair chance that one forgets to do it, or omit to do it because it is time consuming. The last disadvantage is that there is no user integration.

Model II: Integration using common data base

One way of making the integration between specification tools and implementation tools tighter is by using a common data base where the information is stored. In that way, data from the specification tool can be used by the implementation tool and vice versa (see figure 2 (next page)). This model requires either that one tool is able to read data stored by an other tool, or that one tools is able to write in the data store of an other tool. This kind of integration can also be used to interchange information between different CASE tools (upper and lower).

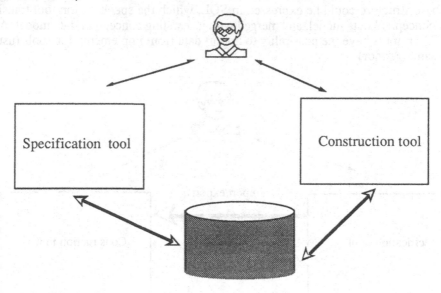

Figure 2 - Integration between specification tools and construction tools using a common data base

This kind of integration is often referred to as *the* future integration between different CASE tools, and between CASE tools and implementation tools. The emergence of different standard repositories (from different vendors and standardization bodies) and interchange formats (like EDIF - Electronic Design Interchange Format) give high expectations to a storage standard.

One advantage of this way of integrating specification tools and construction tools is that the tools are independent of each other as long as they are able to read and write in the agreed formats in the data base. This makes the total system modular and thereby flexible. An other advantage is that the integration could be *instant,* i.e. it is possible to implement the integration so that there is no need to manually trigger the integration.

One disadvantage is that a common data base requires much agreement between the vendors of the different tools and thereby also re-implementation of existing tools. To access a common data base, one has to use a general data base management system having a special subroutine interface. To adapt existing tools to such an interface (not all existing tools uses general data base management systems today) requires a lot of re-implementation. The vendors also have to agree on the data formats that shall be read and written in the data base. There will also be a problem when some tool support more or less information than what is possible to store in the standard repository (semantic integration). One important question is: should the common data base store the union or intersection of all information in all tools that should be integrated?

The key issue to the success of this type of integration is that one standard is commonly *accepted* by the different vendors (and users), and that the vendors conform to it. There are a number of commercial benefits for the vendors by doing so, but there are also a number of commercial drawbacks.

This solution may also cause integrity problems, especially if one tool is permitted to write in the data store of an other tool. The last disadvantage is that there is still no user integration.

Model 3: Integration using communication mechanisms

In this model, the tools are considered as processes connected to and communicating through a data network. The integration can be performed issuing some network service, e.g. file transfer (FTP) or remote procedure calls (RPC). To achieve a higher level of integration than in the models above, RPC is required. In that case, the integration is implemented by one tool requesting or supporting information from / to an other tool (see figure 3). This is done by initiation actions in the other tool. The tools may use their own data stores or a common one.

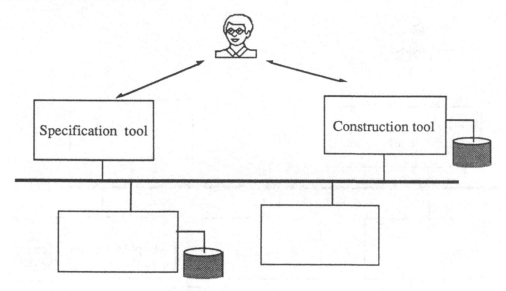

Figure 3 - Integration between specification tools and construction tools using communication mechanisms

This model requires a well defined interface and interaction protocols that the tools agree upon. The proposed EDIF-standard could be one such interface.

The advantage of this way of integrating specification tools and construction tools is that it enables integration in a very flexible manner. One tool may ask for some specific data, or it may start a function in an other tool. One may also use an "agent" to handle the communication. The integration may also be implemented so that it is "instant".

This model gives a form of "loose coupling" between the tools. Ideally, one tool can be exchanged with a new one as long as it offers functions that are equal to or a superset of the functions in the old one. An other advantage is that the responsibility for the data lay on each tool. To access or alter data in an other tool, a function must be activated, an thus integrity constraints may easier be fulfilled. It is also possible to access *derived* data that is not stored by the tools, but that can be accessed using a function.

One disadvantage is that the vendors of the different tools still have to agree upon quite a number of things (but not necessarily on a common storage format), and this may cause re-implementations in existing tools. An other disadvantage is that there still is no user integration. The CASE tools and implementation tools are still separate user tools.

Model IV: Integration using software factory architecture

This model [OFTE87] is to some extent quite equal to the previous one, but to some extent also quite different. The tools are still processes communicating through a network, but the different tools are now *services* issuing special functions. The user interface is handled by a special *user interaction component,* a tool that support the different tasks in a systems development process (see figure 4).

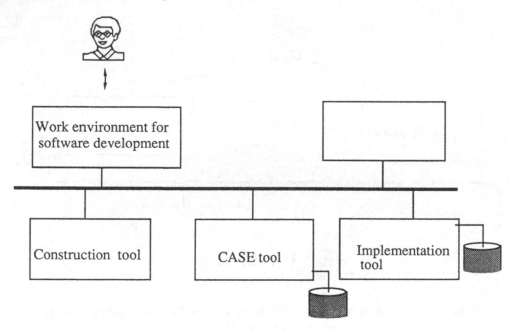

Figure 4 - Integration between specification tools and construction tools using a software factory architecture

The advantages in the previous model also apply on this model, but all the disadvantages do not. The vendors still have to agree on standards and protocols, but on an other level. The tools are now functional components issuing services to other tools, and much of the integration efforts are handled by the user interaction component. Therefore the different tools mainly have to be able to *respond* to certain functions, and only to a small extent themselves *issue* actions in other tools. The integration is no longer done on a tool to tool basis, but more on "global" level in the software factory.

The main advantage, though, is that there in this model is *user integration*. The distinction between the CASE tools and implementation tools (and other tools) are transparent. The user gets tools supporting his work, and the user interaction component handling his work environment issues the necessary functions in the service components. So that when the user perform some changes in the implementation phase, the changes in the CASE tool is performed automatically, i.e. the user has to perform all the changes required by the system, but he does not (and need not) know which changes apply to the implementation tool and which apply to the CASE tool.

The disadvantage of this model is that building the user interaction component is difficult. This kind of architecture requires that a lot of vendors agree on it, and offer their tools as functional components, with a well defined functional interface.

Other aspects of integration

There are a number of other aspects concerning integration between different CASE tools, and between CASE tools and other tools. We mention some of them briefly.

CASE tools should be integrated with tools covering tasks in the whole software engineering process, most important are project management tools and quality assurance. CASE tools may support those tools with valuable information in a more or less automatic manner, e.g. information on the degree of completion of different parts of the system that is developed.

An other aspect that covers the whole software engineering phase is the methodology, or life-cycle model that is used. The software engineering work may be much more structured if the tools support the life-cycle model. Such support is given in some existing CASE tools, i.e. tools from one vendor that support most software engineering activities. This kind of methodology support is sometimes referred to as *process control*. Related aspects are *requirement traceability* and *change control*.

A recent development trend is an integration between tools for software development and tools for hardware development.

An other resent trend is integration of artificial intelligence techniques and tools into the CASE tools. Such techniques and tools can be used both to check rules in the supported techniques, and to help the user in the *creative* part of the development work.

CASE tools (and other software engineering tools) should also cover a quite different aspect of integration, namely integration between different people. This covers both multi-user tools, and support for cooperation between different people cooperating in developing a system. This is sometimes referred to as *groupware*.

Integrated Software Development Environments

In the above section describing CASE tools, we pointed out some characteristics of an ideal CASE tool, which we denoted an Integrated Software Development Environment (ISDE). In this section we investigate ISDEs in more detail. We give a definition showing the main characteristics of ISDEs, we look at who makes such environments, and we point out what is achieved by using such environments. We use the term ISDE, because we feel that it covers the functionality of such an environment. The term Integrated Project Support Environment (IPSE) and Software Factory are sometimes used to denote the same type of environments.

Characteristics of Integrated Software Development Environments

An integrated software development environment is a collection of tools supporting the different tasks that must be performed while developing software. The tools must be integrated, also on the user level, i.e. there must be user environments for different user groups, consisting of user interaction components tailored to support a special task. Each user interaction component may use different service components (or tools) when operating.

An ISDE must give support for a wide variety of tasks, not only typical systems development tasks like requirement specification, analysis, design, implementation, testing and maintenance, but it must also support related tasks like project management, methodology support (process control), etc.

Furthermore, an ISDE must support all users or user roles in a software development team. Not only data processing roles like programmer, systems analyst, etc., but also more administrative roles like project manager, sales and support people, etc.

Because software development usually is performed in teams, an ISDE must support cooperation and communication among team members. This requires more powerful tools than traditional electronic mail.

Such an environment must be easy to change and to supplement when new and powerful tools emerge. This implies an architecture that supports reuse of old and new components, that the architecture is flexible and configurable, and that the environment operates in a distributed, heterogeneous environment. It must be possible to exchange an existing component with a new one, without having to do major changes in the other components in the environment. These characteristics point towards usage of object orientation [MEYE88].

Who makes Integrated Software Development Environments?

There are quite a number of research and developments efforts around, that aim at building ISDEs.

In the large european research and development programs, like ESPRIT, EUREKA and ALVEY, there are different projects that develop parts of or complete software development environments. One example of such a project is the Eureka Software Factory project. It is one of the largest of the european projects in this area. It will be described in more detail below.

There are also quite a lot of research and development efforts in this area in the US. These activities are performed by various universities, research institutes, governmental bodies (e.g. Department of Defense), and software vendors. Arcadia and CAIS are two examples of such project.

In addition, there are some development efforts conducted by large multi-national companies (like Alcatel) that develop integrated software development environments, and some CASE vendors also develop tools that have some ISDE functionality (e.g. Software BackPlane from Atherton Technology).

What is achieved by using Integrated Software Development Environments?

There are lots of benefits that may be achieved by using ISDEs when developing software. In this section we point of some of them.

The main benefit is *reduced costs and development time* in software development projects. Because the environment is integrated, both on the user level and on the tools level, there will be increased productivity in projects using ISDEs. Such an environment will also support reuse of code when developing new software. Furthermore, the integration issues higher quality in the software developed. All of this elements contribute to reduced costs and development time.

One will also achieve better cooperation between members of the development team, which also gives positive impact on quality, productivity and well-being.

The project manager will be offered better tools for estimating the costs of the project, and for monitoring the progress.

Eureka Software Factory (ESF), an Example of an Integrated Software Development Environment

Center for Industrial Research (SI) is participating in a project that will produce different elements of integrated software development environments - the Eureka Software Factory project (ESF). This project will produce an architecture and a framework for ISDEs, basic building blocks, general components, and a number of environments for different application areas (like business applications, real time applications, telecommunication systems, and embedded systems).

The participants in the project are large european companies, computer manufacturers, software houses, research institutes and universities. Figure 5 (next page) shows the different participants i 1989. (The consortium will change during the project).

The project has a 10 years horizon (1987-1996), and imply approximately 2400 man-years of work. The work is financed 50% by the industry and 50% by national government.

Goals of ESF

The main goals of ESF are *to produce an effective production environment for software* and *to facilitate the production of flexible and integrated applications for the end user*. These goals shall be achieved through a *top-down strategy* and focus on different users needs for *functionality* and *integration*.

ESF is meant to be a european answer to american and asian efforts on software engineering. It shall contribute to making european industry in general, and especially the software industry, more competitive. ESF shall be driven by the industry and oriented against products in a marketplace. The project shall use results from other research programs like Race, Esprit, Alvey and ESA.

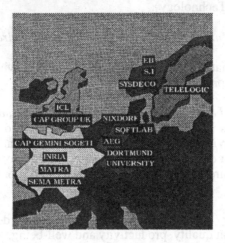

Figure 5 - The participants in ESF

Status in ESF

The project started in 1987 with a requirement specification phase. In 1988, a technical and administrative team was founded in Berlin, and a number of subprojects solving special problems and developing various components, was started. Most of the development work will be performed in subprojects. Also in 1988, a detailed architecture for ESF was developed. The first two milestones in the project were/are:

(i) In may 1989 a number of ESF demonstrators were developed to show different aspects of a software factory. The demonstrators were prototypes showing what can be achieved in the project. One of the ESF demonstrators is the *SI Team Environment (SITE)*, which is presented in more detail below.

(ii) In september 1990 the ESF mini is scheduled to be finished. The ESF mini is a first prototype of an integrated software development environment (or software factory), and will consist of components that are commercial products.

Later on (1991 - 1996) the first commercial software factories will be released.

The technological foundation of ESF

On the technological level, ESF shall produce guidelines, standards and products in various areas.

ESF has already defined an architecture for building software factories, which acts as a basic framework. The basic mechanisms and tools in this framework will also be produced. ESF will also develop methods for software design according to this framework.

ESF will develop components and production environments that will be parts of a software factory, and give standards and guidelines for how to produce software components that will conform to the ESF architecture [ESF89].

The goal of the ESF architecture is to be able to "compose" user environments tailored to the tasks that shall be performed by the user, to use common services in different user environments, to be able to change the user interface of the factory without having to change the service components, and to have different components on different computers (e.g. special purpose computers like data base machines).

To facilitate such an architecture, the components must fulfill certain requirements. It must be possible to access operations and data. There must be a well defined interface to the components (preferable a subroutine interface). There must be a possibility to track errors, it is not acceptable that the components present error-messages directly to the screen. There must be a possibility for the components to report changes, so that other components can act according to the changes. Last, but not least, there must be a clear distinction between the user interface and the functionality.

Figure 6 gives an overview of the principles of the ESF architecture.

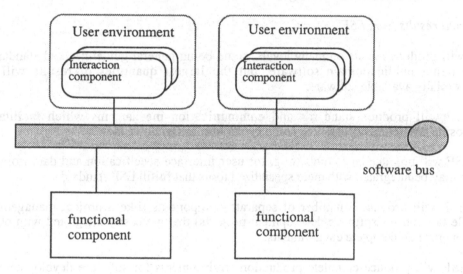

Figure 6 - The ESF architecture

Ideally, each component in this architecture is an implementation of an *abstract data type (ADT)* [GUTT77]. A data type is a set of values - its domain - and a set of operations by which its values can be manipulated. An *abstract data type* is a data type whose domain contain abstract values, i.e. values having an unspecified representation, and whose behavior is completely determined by the effects of the operations associated with the abstract data type. The semantics of each operation may be defined either informally, or by formal mathematical expressions.

The different components communicate through a *software bus,* which handles communication, data conversion, configuration, and a number of other services.

SITE - one of the ESF demonstrators

As our contribution to the ESF demonstrators in may 1989, Center for Industrial Research (SI) developed a prototype, *SITE - SI Team Environment,* which demonstrates a system that supports cooperation between a project manager and a programmer [SITE89]. The prototype covers functions like project planning, job definition, job assignment through electronic mail (with tools and documents integrated in the mail), personal work management, programming and documentation, progress reporting, and progress monitoring.

The prototype is implemented according to the ESF architecture, with different components on different workstations. The implementation is indeed heterogeneous, with components implemented in C, Lisp and Smalltalk. A number of existing components were reused in the implementation. The software bus were implemented using SUN RPC, extended with a specially developed update mechanism (in C).

The environment consist of five user interaction components (process support, job management, extended electronic mail, documentation and programming). These component use functionality in four service components (process model, unix mail, work context storage and document storage).

Expected results from ESF

ESF will produce results on many levels, some being general guidelines and standards, some being public domain software, but the largest quantities of results will be commercially available software.

(i) ESF will produce standards and communication mechanisms which facilitates composing environments based on components from different vendors.

(ii) ESF will produce basic tools (e. g. for user interface specification and data storage) which may be integrated with more specialized tools that fulfill ESF standards.

(iii) ESF will produce a number of separate components (like a project management module tailored for software development projects) that are easily integrated with other components into complete environments.

(iv) ESF will produce complete production environments for software development in special application areas. These environments will be adaptable to needs in the organization using them.

(v) Lastly - but maybe most important - ESF shall become a *market place,* where software developers may offer their tools and compose new tools, and where user organizations may buy just those tools or just the environments they need for their software development activities.

Conclusion

In this paper we have shown that CASE tools have a number of strong sides, but that they must be tighter integrated with each other and with implementation tools to be able to utilize their potential. We have presented different models for such an integration, and have shown that this integration is just the start of what is really needed to give support to the software development work, namely Integrated Software Development Environments (or Integrated Project Support Environments or Software Factories). I.e. environments that support all tasks in the software development - also the early phases where upper CASE tools have their benefits, and related activities like project management - and which integrate different tools, both on the user level and on the data level. The user interface of such environments must reflect the tasks the users perform, not the different tools that are used as service components.

We have pointed out that much work is done to produce such environments, and we have presented in more detail one of these projects, Eureka Software Factory. Hopefully, this project - and the other ones - will produce environments that will contribute to making software development an easier task in the future.

References

[BUBE88]   Selecting a strategy for computer-aided software engineering (CASE), SYSLAB, University of Stockholm, June 1988

[BYTE89]   CASE, In Depth Section (various authors), BYTE, April 1989

[CASE88]   CASE Outlook 1988. CASE tools for Reverse Engineering. CASE Outlook 2, 2, p. 1.

[CASE89]   Proceedings of The first Nordic Conference on Advanced Systems Engineering, Bjørn Nilsson (ed.), SISU, Kista, May 1989

[COWO87]   Tools of the trade: Is CASE really a cure-all?, Jim Huling, Computerworld, April 20, 1987

[COWO88a]   CASE product, Spotlight Section (various authors), Computerworld, June 6, 1988

[COWO88b]   What CASE can't do yet, Tony Percy, Computerworld, June 20, 1988

[DAMA88]   A Guide To Selecting CASE Tools, Michael L. Gibson, Datamation, July 1, 1988

[DAMA89]   Cutting Through the CASE Hype, Kit Grindley, Datamation, April 1, 1989

[ELEC87]   Integration is crucial to CASE's future, Tom Manuel, Electronics, September 17, 1987

[ESF89]   ESF Technical Reference Guide (version 1.1), Eureka Software Factory, 1989

[GIBS89]   The CASE Philosophy, Michael Lucas Gibson, BYTE, April 1989

[GUTT77]   Abstract Data Types and the Development of Data Structures, John Guttag, Communications of the ACM, Vol. 20, N. 6, June 1977

[HEDQ88]   Datorstödd programutveckling - CASE - i USA, Torbjörn Hedqvist and Jonas Persson, Swedish Attaché for Science and Technology, 1988 (In Swedish)

[IEEE88]   Automating software: proceed with caution, John Voelcker, IEEE Spectrum, July 1988

[INWO88]	Making a Case for CASE Tools in the Application Development Process, InfoWorld, January 11, 1988
[JONE89]	Why Choose CASE?, T. Capers Jones, BYTE, December 1989.
[MCCL89]	The CASE Experience, Carma McClure, BYTE, April 1989.
[MEYE88]	Object-Oriented Software Construction, Bertrand Meyer, Prentice Hall 1988, ISBN 0-13-629049
[NILS85]	The Translation of a Cobol Data Structure to an Entity-Relationship Type Conceptual Schema, Erik G. Nilsson, IEEE Proceedings of the 4th International Conference on Entity-Relationship Approach, Chicago, 1985
[NILS88]	CASE Tools are still too young to reach decadence, but we better watch out, Erik G. Nilsson, Position Statement at the 7th International Conference on Entity-Relationship Approach, Rome, 1988
[NILS90]	Aspects of Systems Integration, Erik G. Nilsson, Else Nordhagen and Gro Oftedal, Proceedings of the First International Conference, Morristown, April 1990 (In press)
[OFTE87]	The Use of Remote Applications from a Smalltalk Workstation, Gro Oftedal, Master Thesis, University of Oslo, 1987
[ROEV89a]	Analysis Techniques for CASE: a Detailed Evaluation, Rosemary Rock-Evans and Brigitte Engelien, Ovum Ltd, 1989
[ROEV89b]	CASE Analyst Workbenches: a Detailed Product Evaluation, Rosemary Rock-Evans, Ovum Ltd, 1989
[SHIE88]	Second Chance for Escape?, Gordon Shields, Computerworld,June 6, 1988
[SITE89]	SITE- SI Team Environment, How to Support Cooperation in Teams, Center for Industrial Research, May 1989

Selecting System Development Tools:
Some Experiences

REIMA SUOMI

LisSc(Econ)

Turku School of Economics and Business Administration

Sampo Insurance Company Limited

Abstract: Case-tool market is quite unstructured and not mature. It is no wonder that buyers are more than blurred. Several acquisitions have so far been based on false or insufficient data, which has led to lost money and other resources.

Some companies have even worsened their application backlogs because of unwise use of wrong case-tools. Experiences from real-life situations should contribute to the understanding of these problems considerably. This article tries in its part to fulfill this gap.

This article describes implications and results of two software selection processes in a Finnish insurance company. First, during year 1987, the company selected an application generator for mainframe use and for mainframe-based systems. During year 1988 this acquisition was followed up by a selection of a tool for system requirement analysis and description purposes (a case-tool) which should be based on PC's.

Both acquisitions were based on a very detailed process, the experiences of which are summarized here. This is done by the means of describing the phases every good selection process should include. For each phase, targeted results are described and reasons to go through the phase are served.

1. Introduction

The need to make systems work more efficient is today more urgent than ever before. Technology is evolving at a fast rate and old systems become outdated faster than ever. Updating and maintenance of old systems is becoming a major burden for most companies[1]. In addition, new, yet unseen, application areas such as artificial intelligence, inter-organizational information systems and new generations of decision support systems are emerging. One study [Martin 1982, referring to a study by IBM] has found out that the number of requests for new applications is increasing at a 45% yearly rate in enterprises. Another study [Case 1986] by U.S. department of defense found out that system work productivity will grow only 4 % yearly, whereas demand is growing at a pace of 12 % annually. Both new and old applications increase the total burden of system developers:

Figure 1:

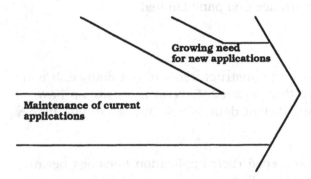

Growing need
for new applications

Maintenance of current
applications

The increasing amount of systems work needed

The industry and organizations have tried to solve this problem by various means in different times. Three distinctive periods seem to emerge:

1   development of methods
2   development of organization
3   development of tools

---

1   Common pitfalls in information system planning are summarized in a study by Lederer & Sethi [1989]

In the first instance, different kinds of techniques, methods and methodologies were developed in order to intensify and lead system work. Structured techniques, life cycle -oriented thinking and project organizations were children of this time. The main invasion of these techniques was in the beginning of the 1970's. The nature of the problems - they were mainly technical - allowed this kind of approach quite well.

During the late 1970's, winds of distribution and decentralization began to emerge. It was understood that the nature of the system development problems was mainly social and organizational, and the end users were tied to the processes. Information system development resources were assigned to the management of the basic business functions.

In the 1980's - after the invention of microcomputers - focus has turned to the different tools available for system development. Microcomputers were the needed technology which allowed cost-efficient and user-friendly tools to emerge to the tables of system developers as well as end users. This means that the methods have already established themselves - at least some of them - and that distribution is seen as an established method of organizing information technology and its development resources. New efficiency is sought from tools more eagerly than ever. According to a study by McClure [1988], the total market for front-end tools (case-tools) is up to 500 000 copies, for code generators at least 7 000. By 1987, a modest 2 percent penetration level was accomplished.

The classification of different tools for development of systems work would be an endless topic, here we will suffice ourselves with the view that these tools can be divided according to three dimensions:

1   front end tools - back end tools
      -front end tools are for logical development of the system,
      back-end tools for technical development
2   tools for professionals - tools for end-users
3   tools for individual use - tools for group use

Figure 2:

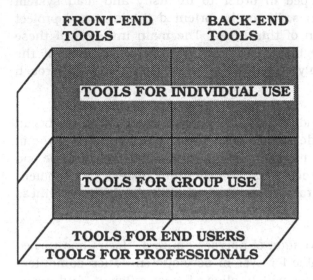

FRONT-END   BACK-END
TOOLS   TOOLS

TOOLS FOR INDIVIDUAL USE

TOOLS FOR GROUP USE

TOOLS FOR END USERS
TOOLS FOR PROFESSIONALS

Classification of system development tools

System development - especially the phase of coding - has always been
a manual, work intensive and error-prone phase of system development,
which has allowed few possibilities for making the work more efficient.

It has long been known that the elimination of these manual work
phases would be the key to more efficient systems work. The most
visible drawbacks of manual operations are:

-        the unbroken chain is spoiled: changes in one or other end are no
         more automatically transferred to the other end
-        the manual operations easily produce errors
-        yet only a small part of the total work is manual, the human
         worker must introduce her/himself to the whole chain of actions
-        the manual operations take time

The current automated techniques of software engineering and
automated tools did not anyway occur overnight, but needed time to
mature and lay on three basic innovations or approaches in system
development methodologies that have occurred during years:

<u>Figure 3:</u>

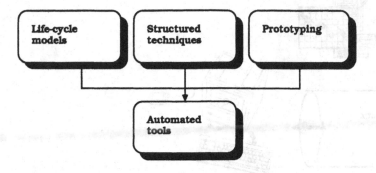

Approaches leading to automated tools

Life-cycle models laid the major theoretical but also practical view on how system development should be divided into phases. The major differentiation between logical and technical planning, implementation and maintenance is still valid today. The phases of coding and testing are beginning to fade away as new automated tools take hand of these phases.

Structured techniques provided the major tools for describing complex systems in quite a simple way. These techniques, however, need a lot of drawing and updating, a work that has become tolerable first now as we have new tools to be used. The future importance of the structured techniques is stressed for example in books by Martin & McClure [1985] and in an article by Yourdon [1986].

Prototyping approach brought in the innovation that systems should be made visible already when they are still under development. This is just the way new system development tools work: they allow to view not finished systems and make improvements and changes easy to make.

Nowadays it is also possible to get at least very near to the final mode: the users give their logical insight on how the system should work, and different automated tools will build up the working information system based on these logical descriptions:

Figure 4:

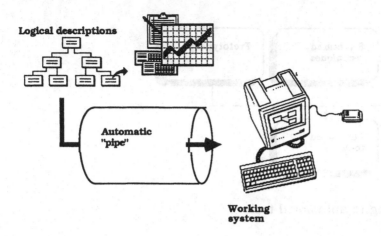

Logical descriptions

Automatic
"pipe"

Working
system

The ideal of systems work.

2. Methods: the tailoring and customer approaches

There seems to be two main approaches (in addition to the option of making all the needed programs self, which is hardly a cost-efficient method for most companies) for acquiring automated support for system development.

First, it is possible to buy a tool that covers up the whole lifecycle. Such products are usually closely tied to some particular methodology, and include all the major parts of a case tool: support for all the phases of the system work from strategic system portfolio planning to the maintenance of individual systems. The buyer of the tool enters a very close customership to the vendor, so the name customer approach.

Second, it is possible to buy a set of tools, each of which is especially designed to support one or a few of the phases of system development work. In such a way a set of state-of the art products can be selected, but the integration between the tools may be less than optimal. This approach necessitates a lot of tailoring work, so this name.

Within the tailoring approach, products in very many price categories can be found. In general, the case market seems to be in a play of decimals. There are three classes from which to select the tools:

1   full packages
-    include tools for analysis and design, implementation plus a method framework
-    price about 1 000 000 FIM
2   normal packages
-    include tools for analysis and design
-    price about 100 000 FIM
3   modular packages
-    include tools for some phases in analysis and design
-    price about 10 000 FIM

The differences of the tailoring and customer approaches from some critical viewpoints are discussed here:

The critical success factor for individual tools is their **connectibility**. Nearly all these tools have options for data input and output, and actually a link can always be programmed between two tools with quite a bearable effort. The trouble sets in when new versions of the products are introduced, and the tailored links must be programmed every time anew.

What is needed is different **standards** that link these products together. The trend seems to go to the same situation as is seen in other fields of information technology: there are official standards such as EDIF or IRDS, and then there are practical standards set up by dictionary/repository manufacturers. In this field, time will show which will be the effect of the new repository of IBM.

The organization which is to use these products must take into attention it **current investments**. If one can set up from an empty table, a total new system according to the customer approach may be the best solution. The trouble is just how to find the right product. When a total commitment can be foreseen, it should be to a product with future. No matter how small part of the total system development work the new tools covers, if links are to be built to other tools and work is to be based on this tool, future support from the vendor of the tool will most surely be needed. In addition to the vendor local importors and distributors must also be engaged to the product.

When current systems are highly usable and will surely need support also in the future, the tailored approach may be of use. When tailoring links between the system development software packages, links to current production systems can also be considered. The tailoring approach of stepwise nature also leaves room for slow replacement of current systems.

From the viewpoint of the required **new investments**, the tailoring approach seems to be easier to suffer: quite low initial investments will suffice. On the long run, the cost will anyway rocket. New software will be constantly needed (every workstation will usually require its own license), and the tailoring work going on in the organization can become a major burden. In addition, the ongoing education in small groups and during work can lower productivity more than a one-time total commitment to the education effort. The customer organization will usually have to tailor its own methods, and this will most surely also consume a lot of resources. The customer approach at its side usually means a million-investment right from the beginning, but with the sum usually an unlimited number of workstations is achieved (the programs supporting the whole life cycle usually reside on mainframes) and the method and education support is settled at the same time.

The customer approach usually means big influence from the side of the vendor. They tend to offer support, methodologies and consulting with the actual software package. The costs of these services very easily nearly double the price of the solution, if they are not included in the total package. In general, the costs of introducing a new tool include at least following parts:

- build-up of links to other tools
- build-up of links to system software
- build-up of necessary standards
- training of personnel on the use of the new product
- salaries of the personnel responsible for the product
- maintenance costs of the product.

In general, the acquirement of the tool should be based on mutual confidence. If too much pressure is applied from the side of the customer to the price or other terms of the agreement, this will produce later lower service levels. If the seller gets the price it has calculated will cover the expenses caused by the service, it will also be willing to give that service. Bargaining is always needed, but must not be practised into extremes. It must be remembered, that the price paid to the vendor is only a small part of the total expense, and good relations to the vendor can clearly lower other expenses.

What must be considered is own experience. If new methods of system work are really needed and investments in them seem anyway unavoidable, the customer approach with the acquirement of a complete methodology is reasoned. But if own methods and ways of doing things are well established and of state-of-the-art quality, there is no reason to abandon that investment and make a new. The tailoring approach with moderate investments seems to be a wiser approach.

The totality of the customer approach is the risk of this approach. Risk is here a way of assessing things, not absolutely a bad thing. With the customer approach, the results can be either very bad or very good ones. With the tailoring approach, risks are lower (investment is lower), but the possible outcomes are too only at a moderate level.

The differences between the two approaches are summed up in table 1:

Table 1:

Tailoring approach	Customer approach
Best tools for every phase of system work	Best support for total life cycle support
Methods can be tailored	Usually tightly tied to one method
Risk usually manageable	Big risk
Lot of tailoring work needed	Usually little tailoring work
Integration with current systems easier to achieve	Integration with current systems difficult to achieve
Can be built up in phases	Taken into use in one effort
Investment in small doses, total investment may be bigger	Big one-time investment, total investment maybe smaller
Learning by doing	Learning by vendor education
Commitment can vary	Total commitment needed
Suitable when current applications portfolio big	Suitable when current applications portfolio not big

Differences between the customer and tailoring approaches

The size of current applications portfolio must be taken into attention when the desired approach is selected. The introduction of a new comprehensive toolset tends to lead to a situation where the new applications and the old ones are very loosely coupled. The process of the introduction of the new tool leads to a situation where new systems are built with the new tool, but where very little support is given to the maintenance of the old application portfolio, which originally was the problem. So, an environment with established tools and applications and a lot of maintenance work seems to necessitate the tailoring approach. If there are only few old applications, a totally new generation of applications and methods is easier to begin.

3.   A stepwise approach to selecting software products

Published comments and descriptions on software selection processes leave behind a picture of a quite random process[2]. Many times not even the minimum trouble of a decent selection process is met, but the decision on software products to be used is based on some other factors such as:

-   one product, usually the one that seems to be the market leader, is picked up randomly
-   the product that is most eagerly marketed is selected
-   the product with the lowest start-up price is selected
-   a product sold or recommended by the hardware vendor or some major software vendor is selected
-   the personal relationships or attitudes of higher management dictate the product to be selected
-   the product that a competitor or mother or daughter company is using is adopted

These approaches however many times seem to result in failures. Reasons for failures stem from two sources: either from inside or from outside of the company selecting the software. The main reasons for outside reasons are the failures and shortcomings in the products, but

[2]   This in spite of the fact that there are many detailed descriptions how on how software tools should be selected [Gibson 1989, Lucas. & al 1988, Martin 1985, McClure 1988]

they are left unnoticed by the improper selection processes inside the company. These are caused by false assumptions and behaviors.

The usual mistakes made are summarized in table 2:

Table 2:

-too cumbersome and laborious use of the product
-mistakes and flaws in the product
-bad support for the product
-unplanned need for acquisitions
-bad reception of the selected product
-incompatibility with other software
-too heavy use of machine resources

Usual mistakes during a software selection process

During the selection process ideas and opinions about the tools to be selected have time to mature. In order to make the selection a real group work which produces confidence and engagement to the new product, the group responsible for the selection should have members from all the major interest groups of the new tool, as described in the figure:

Figure 5:

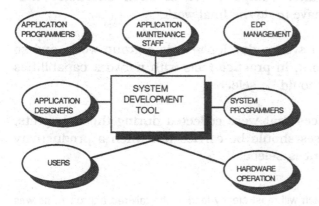

Interest groups of a system development tool

The time needed for the selection process should obviously depend on the planned useful life of the product to be acquired. If you are selecting a tool to be used for some months or perhaps a year, not much time can be spent on the selection. On the other hand, if you are selecting the backbone of your application development to be used for decades, a year seems a short time.

The author was responsible for selecting two major productivity tools for system development to one of Finland's biggest insurance companies. With the goal of automated system life cycle, the process was divided into two phases: first a back-end tool for code generation was selected, since this was the phase of most urgent need for help, and a year later a front-end tool to be joined in front of the back-end tool was selected[3]. The reasons for first selecting the back-end tool were:

- programming is nearest to maintenance, the area of biggest problems. It was hoped for that by automating code generation maintenance could be automated little by little.
- programming seems to be a quite structured task which could maybe be automated quite easily
- good programmers begin to be a scarce resource
- the tools used here were quite oldfashioned in the company (conventional third generation languages)
- testing of technical details is a time-consuming task, which can be eliminated by automated code generation

During the whole process it was clear that the tools to be selected would be for edp-professionals[4] only. The heavy transaction-processing applications of an insurance company are of such character that professionals will anyway have to do the final work.

The main idea was too that system development is a group work, and so tools allowing for group work, in practice tools with network capabilities and common data-bases, should be selected.

According to our experiences that were collected during those projects, at least the following phases should be carried out when a productivity tool for system development is selected:

---

3 This kind of stepwise approach will most clearly lead to the tailored approach, as was the output here

4 This is not to say that there were no projects to help end-users in the company, only one of the many edp-projects in the company is described here

Figure 6:

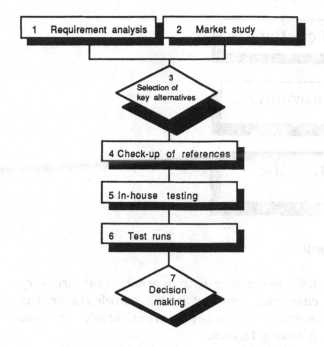

Phases of a proper software selection process

First a proper **requirement analysis** is needed. Goals stated in a general way are not enough: "efficiency for development work", "good user interface", "connections to application generator" are not detailed enough requirements. What is needed is a set of requirements that serve as a basis for concrete questions that can be answered "yes" or "no". An example of a requirement might be "an user interface with windows" and the concrete questions like "can at least three windows be open at the same time?", "can the size of the windows be changed?" and "is it possible to cut and paste graphical objects between the windows?".

The requirement analysis should be done with a wide group of people. As many opinions as possible should be acquired. What should be first is the need of the interest groups of the system, not for example the needs of the current hardware architecture or repository. Here, as in other fields of applications, we should focus first on the needs of the users and customers of the new tools, then we should select the best of the available technology bases for fulfilling this need, and first the third task should be the decision on the product.

Figure 7:

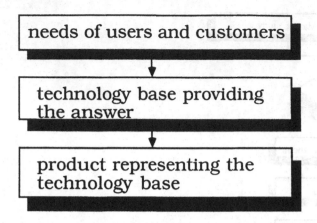

| needs of users and customers |
| technology base providing the answer |
| product representing the technology base |

Where to focus on which order

A **market study** is especially necessary with markets that are very dynamic like the current case-tool -market where knowledge on the market gets old pretty soon. A proper market study collects information on at least the following factors:

- products available (name, price, reductions, domestic users and users abroad (number of licenses and number of customers)
- distributors of the products (service available, market share, resources, other products distributed)
- vendors of the products (service available, market share, resources, other products supplied).

Data during the market study phase can and should be collected from journals, newspapers, product reviews, professional meetings, seminars, prospects of the vendors - and from hearsay too, which can be a very valuable source of knowledge.

Sooner or later the buyer will have to make a **selection of key alternatives**. The phases of the process from this point on tolerate only a limited number of alternatives, usually from two to four. Usually the key alternatives represent different technologies, and the best product representing each technology should be taken into further considerations.

Visits to reference companies are many times the most illuminating part of the process. What must be remembered is that they should be based on mutual trust and change of information, i.e. you will have to tell about your own intentions and results of the market study, too. In general, it must be remembered that companies that have acquired some products tend to stay behind them also when they are not quite satisfied. So, don´t let the discussion go on in a general level in the reference company, but try to get into the daily operations level. Ask, **how** is this and that task done, not **how well** the tool supports work in general.

In-house testing of the products is always needed. For example, current case-tools include thousands of details and it is impossible to get an impression on them based on demonstrations and short viewing. Usually the time to learn the usage of a case-tool is from one week to one month. First after this threshold it is possible to begin to do efficient work, work which first reveals the virtues of the product.

Case-tools can be best tested by building anew some old applications with the new tool. If you try to do too much at a time and design a completely new application you may lose your strength to the application, not to the test itself, which should be the most important thing in the selection process.

In-house testing gives some quidance about the user interface, the working methods with the tool, and similar technical aspects, but conclusions on the impact of the tool on the total productivity of the company can not be derived. System development tools mature first after they are properly istalled to the company, a process which can take years.

Test runs in own machines are needed in order to find out how much resources the software to be acquired needs. The resources to be looked after are consumption of CPU-time, input-output capacity and central memory. All are relevant in mainframes, central memory sizes can be very critical in micros. Exact figures - not to talk about comparisons between different products - are not available from vendors. Usage of resources should be tested in two different points, when

-       the product is used for building applications
-       the applications built with the products are used.

Decision making should be based on the results of all the phases of the selection process. Who are the decision makers depends on the organization, but usually they should be the managers who will be responsible for the future application of the tool and who must pay for it. Special care should be taken to beware strong managers who try to bypass the selection process and justify their own personal but unproven opinions.

Usually there is a tendency to give bigger value to the results gained most recently. Anyway, if all the other phases of the work have indicated results that are not in line with the results of the in-house tests, these results should also be taken into attention when making the final decision. On the other hand, when the process described here is followed, no bad products will ever come to the testing phase.

During the whole selection process, a lot of reports should be produced and circulated effectively. **The key activity is to engage the whole organization into a discussion about the alternatives**. This can only be gained by literal documents in an organization bigger than ten employees, and the application of literal material also gives the process the needed openness and rigidity. Special care should be taken when the decisions are documented: on which data they were based and who made them.

4.   Discussion

Productivity tools for software development are clearly needed. In addition, they are a clear product of logical developments in the field of system development. Organizations should familiarize themselves with these tools and try to use them in the best possible way. But there is no reason to do unargumented decisions as seems to be the trend today. By taking into attention some general and simple rules as presented here the organizations will be much better off.

Productivity tools for system development are a comparatively new phenomenon, and there is no reason to marvel at why the market is in such an unmature state as it is. In such a kind of market, possibilities of wrong actions are very high. Some of the major characteristics of the current markets seem to be:

- most companies have selected their tools in a random way, usually based on personal preferences of some managers
- the ideal of an automated life-cycle is still far from fulfilled: current tools are mainly used to support distinctive phases of the system work, integrating links are a rarely met
- a parade application seem to be analysis of conceptual modelling for data-bases[5], many companies have not at all used the tools for process planning
- the tools are difficult to learn, getting familiar with the structured methods involved is a hard task (as expected)
- some 30-40 back-end tools which necessitate a deeper commitment have been sold in Finnish market, front-end tools are acquired mainly for testing purposes in low quantities
- results from many pilot projects have been unsatisfactory, many products have been abandoned
- the main advantage of new system development tools seems to be that of improved quality, not that of efficiency
- some companies, however, had acquired considerable short-term gains in the form of saved work
- the tools remain islands of technology, no links to other software tools of organizations have been built
- no adjustments of system development methods has occurred because of the tools[6]

The whole situation of the market should become better if software buyers were more critical and capable of conducting thorough selection processes. So the whole market would be under a harder pressure and the best products would be selected from the mass sooner. Currently, the unmature state of the productivity tool market is inhibiting development.

The last advice is: begin work on system development tools such as application generators and case tools today. By beginning is meant interest on the issue, not a selection of a comprehensive tool right away. Usage of system development tools is not a metro train that passes by daily and to which you can jump whenever you want. It is hard work, and if you want results in a few years, you must take the drivers seat on the metro right now.

---

5 This fact is for example recognized by Yourdon who is to be considered one of the "Fathers" of structured techniques [Yourdon 1988].

6 This is considered to be one of the major failures of case-tool usage by Inmon [1987]

References:

Case, Albert F., Jr. (1986) Information systems development: principles of computer-aided software engineering. Prentice-Hall.

Gibson, Lucas Michael (1989) Implementing the promise. Datamation February 1./89, 65-67.

Inmon, Peter (1987) CASE no cure-all. Computerworld November 23./87.

Ledered, Albert - Sethi, Vijay (1989) Pitfalls in Planning. Datamation June 1./89, 59-62.

Gibson, Lucas Michael (1989) Implementing the promise. Datamation February 1.2/89, 65-67.

Lucas, Henry - Walton, Eric - Gingberg, Michael (1988) Implementing Packaged Software. MIS Quarterly December/88, 537-549.

Martin, James (1982) Application Development without Programmers. New Jersey.

Martin, James - McClure, Carma (1985) Diagramming Techniques for Analyst and Programmers. New Jersey.

Martin, James (1985) Fourth Generation Languages, Volume I, Principles. New Jersey.

McClure, Carma (1988) The CASE technical report. Extended Intelligence, Inc. Chicago.

Yourdon, Edward (1988) Case competition is all over the world. Software Magazine November/88, 53-60.

Yourdon, Edward (1986) What ever happened to structured analysis? Datamation June/86, 133-138.

Software Configuration Management for Medium-Size Systems

W. Reck, H. Härtig

German National Research Center For Computer Science (GMD)
Postfach 1240
5205 Sankt Augustin 1, West Germany

1 Abstract

Software configuration management for large real systems is an ugly task. For such systems large–scale software configuration management systems are necessary. Small systems don't need software configuration management except a way to backup. This paper describes a simple software configuration management system (called SCMB) for real medium–size systems.

SCMB obtains its simplicity from clearly separating revision control (i.e.maintaining sequences) from variant control (i.e. maintaining alternatives) and instrument elimination.

Center of SCMB is the variant control system VCS. VCS maintains variants and sets of variants using a *context free grammar*. The terminals and nonterminals of the grammar reemerge as names of *variant subsystems* of the hierarchally structured system.

Based on VCS, a common revision control system for modules, and a compiler, which is able to analyze the dependency structure of modules, the SCMB is used

- to check the *variant consistency* of the system.

- to generate configurations of the system according to a triple (revision, variant, instrumentation).

- to manage revisions of the *system*

This paper describes design, implementation, experiences and limitations of SCMB, which has been used for the development and maintenance of the BirliX operating system, consisting of 300 Modula-2 modules containing about 200000 lines of code.

KEYWORDS: software configuration management, revisions, variants, instruments, subsystem creation, conditional compilation, physical separation

2 Introduction

Software configuration management for large real systems is an ugly task. For such systems large—scale software configuration management systems are necessary. Small systems don't need software configuration management except a way to backup. This paper describes a simple software configuration management system (called SCMB) for real medium—size systems.

SCMB obtains its simplicity from clearly separating revision control (i.e.maintaining sequences) from variant control (i.e. maintaining alternatives) and instrument elimination.

As a system is continuously developed further, continuously new *revisions* of the system arise. Storing old revisions of a system is necessary to fall back on these if the further development becomes faulty, or if faults are reported for old revisions. The function of the software configuration management concerning revisions is to register and store changes as well as to designate (e.g. date, number) and to *identify* revisions. Essentially, revision management is done by managing sequences.

Variant management is done by managing alternative realizations of the same concept. Variants of a system appear if the system is designed for different target systems or/and for different user interfaces. Since some parts of a system — the *common base* — are valid for all variants, some parts are valid only for some variants and some parts are valid only for one variant, the software configuration management has to enable the creation of any set of variants. Like revisions, variants need to be identified. At the time of system design often not all target systems or user interfaces are known in advance. That means some variants are created though they are not expected to occur. Therefore the software configuration management should supply ways to easily add one or more variants.

Instruments support debugging and tuning a system. As mistakes are made during the development of a system, instruments are necessary to find them. The function of the software configuration management concerning instruments is to eliminate (parts of) them if they are not needed, e.g. for efficiency reasons.

To avoid making manual mistakes the software configuration management must be able, to generate *automatically* an executable system for one *configuration*. A configuration of a system designates the software for one revision in one variant and with certain instruments.

3 Related Systems

Generally revisions of modules (or, more general, documents) are managed using text differences. Examples are RCS [Tic85] and Jasmine [MW86].

Variant management in known systems is mixed up usually with either revision control or automatic recompilation issues. Both approaches have inherent disadvantages:

Revision control systems support the appearance of variants by allowing alternative sequences of revisions. Whenever a change is affecting one variant only, an additional revision is created for the respective sequence. Thus, if a change affects the common base of some variants, all alternative sequences of revisions must be changed. This finally leads to the concept of 'merge'. Since merges in systems based on text differences can be handled by text differences only, i.e. without semantic knowledge, they can hardly (or not at all) be done automatically.

Automatic recompilation systems such as Make [Fel83] use dependency descriptions of a set of modules to produce object code. Make supports variants by allowing multiple dependency descriptions with several entry points ('targets'). The dependency descriptions are also used to identify the common base of variants. The problems caused by this approach are result from the fact, that the variant structure is hidden somewhere in a much more powerful and dedicated data structure. Manual or automatic checks of any sort of variant consistency is very difficult. Changes in the variant structure may cause a large number of changes in the remaining dependency descriptions, which could be omitted in appropriate high level variant management systems. In this sense, Make can be considered as 'assembly language for variant management'.

SCMB avoids these disadvantages by clearly separating management of sequences, alternatives and instruments. To manage variants, a simple and efficient variant control system − called VCS − has been built. Together with RCS, which is used for revision control only, and conditional compilation for instrument elimination, an executable system can be generated according to a triple (revision, variant, instrumentation).

4 Variant Management

The essential function of variant management is to *identify* a variant of a system. To identify a variant several decisions have to be made on different levels of abstraction. In the case of an operating system, a top level decision can be: 'it is for a single processor machine, not for a multi processor machine'. A decision of the next lower level of abstraction can be: 'it is for a Motorola processor, not for an Intel or a VAX processor'. Finally a decision on the lowest level can be: 'it is for a SUN machine, not for a PCS or a Macintosh machine'.

That hierarchy of decisions can be expressed by the productions of a *context free grammar*. To this end variants are represented by terminals, decisions by productions. The *language* described by the grammar is the set of variants. In the example above,

- terminals, i.e. variants, may be denoted

SUN3.T
PCS.T
MAC2.T
IBM.T
SIEMENS.T
SEQUENT.T

- nonterminals may be defined as

START == Single.N | Multi.N
Single.N == SingleMC680x0.N | SingleIntelx86.N
SingleMC680x0.N == SUN3.T | PCS.T | MAC2.T
SingleIntelx86.N == IMB.T | SIEMENS.T
Multi.N == SEQUENT.T

Describing the variant structure of a system by a context free grammar is independent of how different variants are textually represented. Different variants can be represented inside one module (conditional compilation) or in different modules (physical separation) or by text differences.

Since SCMB strictly separates different software configuration management problems and because conditional compilation must be used for instrument elimination (see chapter 5), different variants are represented in different modules. The decision where an alternative of a variant dependent module is laid down in the system, had been influenced by the hierarchally structure of the BirliX operating system [HKK*90]. BirliX has been built using a 'stepwise refinement procedure', where modules are laid down in different subsystems. Each subsystem consists of a specification and an implementation. A specification consists of a single module, while an implementation consists of a single module or several modules in a subsystem of the next lower level of hierarchy. While a specification is variant independent, an implementation may be variant dependent. Now different variants of an implementation are laid down in different subsystems too. The name of a such a subsystem, called *variant subsystem*, is a terminal or nonterminal.

For example, the topmost subsystems of the BirliX operating system are Nucleus, MemoryManagement, InnerKernel and OuterKernel. The Nucleus consists of subsystems Processes, Synchronization, Scheduler, and so on. Since scheduling on a single processor machine is partially different from scheduling on a multi processor machine, the subsystem Scheduler consists of variant subsystems Single.N and Multi.N. That is one implementation of the scheduler is valid for variants SUN3.T, PCS.T, MAC2.T, IBM.T and SIEMENS.T (derived from Single.N), the other is valid for variant SEQUENT.T (derived from Multi.N).

Figure 1 shows a cut of the *source tree* from the just mentioned example. The source tree is that data structure which contains the modules of a system in all variants with all revisions and with all instruments.

Variant dependent implementations and their specification form a *variant switch*. A variant switch represents a production of the context free grammar. The specification represents the left side of the production, because the specification is valid for all variants (terminals) which can be derived from the nonterminal on the left side of the production. Each implementation represents a terminal or nonterminal on the right side of the production, because the name of the corresponding variant subsystem is such a terminal or nonterminal. In figure 1, the single variant switch represents the production
START == Single.N | Multi.N .

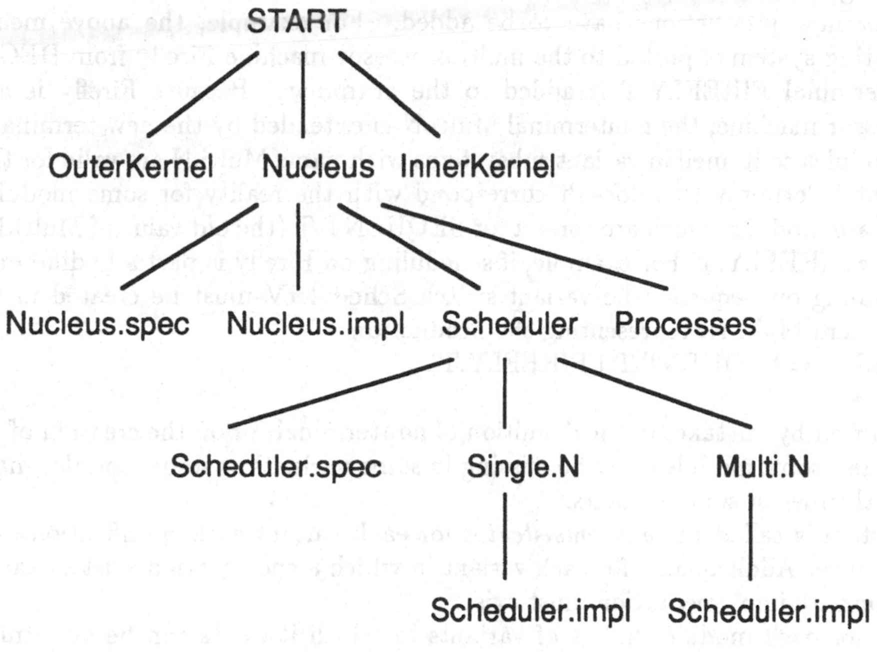

Figure 1: Hierarchally structured source tree with variant subsystems

A consequence of the described concept is, that variant switches are as important as 'normal' subsystems. If only a small part of an implementation is variant dependent, the variant dependencies receive an own variant switch. The specification of the variant switch defines the interface of the variant dependencies. For example, if only a small part of the subsystem Scheduler is variant dependent, variant switch SchedulerV is created. Then the modules Scheduler.spec, Scheduler.impl and SchedulerV.spec are laid down in the subsystem Scheduler, and one implementation SchedulerV.impl is laid down in the variant subsystem Single.N, the other in Multi.N.
The alternative to the creation of a new variant switch is the existence of several very similar implementations. This alternative has the disadvantage that changes at the variant independent part may be neglected in some implementations. This disadvantage exists in systems like RCS which control variants with the aid of text differences.

As mentioned in chapter 2, the software configuration management has to enable the creation of any set of variants, because the common base of the systems is valid for all variants, some parts are valid only for some variants and some parts are valid only for one variant. Naturally, all terminals derived from one nonterminal form a set of variants.

New subsets of variants are defined by defining new nonterminals using existing nonterminals and terminals.

A new variant arises, if e.g. an operating system is ported to another target system. With respect to the grammar, adding a new variant means adding a new terminal to the grammar. Some existing productions (nonterminals) have to be redefined, and/or new productions have to be added. For example, the above mentioned operating system is ported to the multi processor machine Firefly from DEC. Then the terminal FIREFLY.T is added to the grammar. Because Firefly is a multi processor machine, the nonterminal Multi.N is extended by the new terminal. Now all modules contained in variant subsystems with name Multi.N are valid for the new variant. Certainly this doesn't correspond with the reality for some modules, i.e. there are modules which are correct for SEQUENT.T (the old value of Multi.N), but not for FIREFLY.T. For example, if scheduling on Firefly is partially different from scheduling on Sequent, the variant switch SchedulerV must be created in variant subsystem Multi.N, representing the production
Multi.N == SEQUENT.T | FIREFLY.T

Caused by mistakes in the definition of nonterminals or on the creation of variant switches, some modules may be missing in some variants or some modules may exist several times in some variants.

A system is called *variant consistent* if for each variant each specification exists at most once. Additionally, for each variant in which a specification exists, exactly one appropriate implementation must exist.

Since for each module the set of variants in which it exists can be determined by traversing the source tree, the variant consistency can be checked automatically.

The automatic generation of an executable system according to a triple (variant, revision, instruments) is done in the following way. The source tree is traversed and the specified revision of each module, which is valid for the specified variant, is moved into a so called *compilation library*. Finally the Modula−2 compiler is required to compile (with the specified instrumentation) and link all modules. Because the Modula−2 compiler analyzes the dependencies between modules, no extra 'make' is necessary.

Note that VCS doesn't presume that modules containing a specification are compilation units as in Modula−2 [Wir83]. A specification may be any kind of document.

5 Instrument Elimination and Revision Management

As solution for the instrument elimination problem the conditional compilation suggests itself. A manual instrument elimination comes not into question, because most systems are developed further and serviced continuously and the instruments are used again and again. If the used compiler doesn't know conditional compilation, the use of a preprocessor is an equivalent alternative.

When generating an executable system, the compiler is called with the specified instrumentation and compiles all modules with that instrumentation. Of course, instruments which are not specified are not compiled but eliminated.

That conditional compilation must be used for instrument elimination is a strong reason for not using conditional compilation to solve the variant mangement problem. Otherwise instrument elimination and variant management would be interlocked, and the problem of nested conditional compilation would arise.

Each module may exist in any number of revisions independently of the variants. Thus all revisions of a module are valid for the same set of variants.

SCMB uses RCS to maintain revisions of single *modules*. But as import as maintaining the revisions of single modules, is maintaining revisions of the *system*. When identifying a configuration of the system according to a triple (variant, revision, instrumentation), the revision component must be applicable to each module. Revision numbers of modules can't be used because different modules are checked in different often and thus their revision numbers diverge too much.

To solve the problem, SCMB maintains a 'reference tree' and supports *complex updates* of the 'reference tree'. A complex update consists of several modules, changed in 'private trees' of possibly several software engineers. Each update of the 'reference tree' is assumed to be tested in a compilation library. Then the *date* and a short description of each update is stored in a special file. Each date in the special file defines a revision of the system, because it is applicable to each module. In RCS, specifying a date denotes the first revision which is as old as or older than the specified date.

When generating an executable system according to a triple (variant, revision, instrumentation), the revision component is always a date, in general the current date. When falling back on an old revision of the system, a date is selected which is stored in the special file. The short descriptions in the special file can be used to select the right date.

6 Experiences

The development of the BirliX software configuration management system began with VCS, because early in the development of BirliX multiple variants were needed. The mistake, which occurred most frequently at this time, was that after changes modules were copied to the wrong place in the reference tree ('update mistake').

Thus some modules existed in an old and in a new revision (at this time no revision management was in use) which led to compilation or runtime errors. To recognize the update mistake early, the variant consistency of the system was defined and checked periodically. Since this checking had sometimes been neglected, it was included into the automatic generation of an executable system. Since RCS is used, each software engineer has to use an uniform update tool. A module is checked in only if it just exists. Otherwise the user of the tool is asked whether he didn't make a mistake. In this way the update mistake is recognized at the earliest possible time.

The automatic generation of an executable BirliX system requires 40 minutes on a SUN3/260. 10 minutes of that are used to check the variant consistency, to eliminate the old compilation library, to check out the needed modules and to build up the compilation library. The remaining 30 minutes are required for compilation (and linking). The Modula−2 compiler MOCKA (developed at GMD Karlsruhe) compiles up to 15000 lines per minute, but slows down with the number of IMPORT statements. If the 'reference tree' is not on the same machine as the compilation library, the automatic generation requires 50 minutes.
Consistency checking (written in Modula−2) requires 1 minute.

The described software configuration management system provides advantages taking into account a number of limitations.
The advantages include an efficient way to maintain variants. Its simple and clear conceptual model makes it acceptable for the users. The structure of a source tree is easy to read. Problems arising with 'merging' are avoided.
The limitations are

- VCS can't be adapted to existing systems. If variants have not been built according to the described model, the system has to be adapted to VCS.

- maintaining various revisions concurrently, as needed for large and extensive systems, is not supported. It's an unanswered question, whether this function can be incorporated into SCMB without giving up its simplicity.

- a hierarchally structured system design is presumed. That implies, that unimportant but variant independent modules (e.g. string operations) are laid down in high level subsystems of a source tree (i.e near the root), because low level subsystems are often variant dependent.

7 Future Work

The next tasks concerning SCMB are

- to analyze how the existing theoretical knowledge about formal languages can be used to prove and extend its power.

- to analyze whether it is applicable for general document management.

- to compare the power of VCS with systems like shape [AM88], which use *attributes* to deal with variants. At a glance, both models seem to have the same power. Since in 'attributive systems' a set of attributes is used to define a variant, a set of attributes corresponds to a terminal (i.e. variant) in VCS. Single attributes seem to correspond to nonterminals.

References

[AM88]   Andreas Lampen Axel Mahler. shape - a software configuration management tool. In *International Workshop on Software Version and Configuration Control*, pages 228–243, Grassau, January 1988.

[Fel83]   Stuart I. Feldman. MAKE - A Program for Maintaining Computer Programs. *Proc. of the SIGPLAN 83 Symposium on Programming Language Issues in Software Systems*, 18(6):1–13, June 1983.

[HKK+90]   H. Härtig, W. Kühnhauser, O. Kowalski, W. Lux, W. Reck, H. Streich, and G. Goos. The Architecture of the BIRLIX Operating System. In *11. ITG/GI Fachtagung Architektur von Rechensystemen*, Munic, March 1990. VDE Verlag.

[LS79]   B. Lampson and E. Schmidt. Organizing Software in a Distributed Environment. *Software - Practice and Experience*, 9(3):255–265, March 1979.

[MW86]   Keith Marzullo and Douglas Wiebe. Jasmine: A Software System Modelling Facility. *Communications of the ACM*, 22(1):121–130, December 1986.

[Tic85]   Walter F. Tichy. RCS - A System for Version Control. *Software - Practice and Experience*, 15(7):637–654, July 1985.

[Wir83]   N. Wirth. *Programming in Modula-2*. Springer Verlag, 1983.

Automated Support of the Modelling Process:

A view based on experiments with expert information engineers[1]

G.M. Wijers[2,3] and H. Heijes[2]

[2]Delft University of Technology
Faculty of Technical Mathematics and Informatics
Department of Information Systems
P.O. Box 356, 2600 AJ Delft, The Netherlands

and

[3]SERC
P.O. Box 424, 3500 AK Utrecht, The Netherlands

Abstract

A trend can be discerned clearly indicating that current developments in methodologies concentrate on an ongoing structuring and integration of modelling techniques. Automated support is the prime mover of this trend. In this article it is argued that a lack of explicit knowledge about the process of model construction has resulted in problems with CASE-tools concerning adequate support in the form of verification and navigation. We present a view on modelling processes which has been applied in experiments with expert information engineers. The key concepts of this view are strategy and natural level of consistency. It is argued that adequate support can be realized for navigation and verification on the basis of (1) knowledge about tasks and decisions part of a strategy and (2) knowledge about the natural level of consistency of tasks. The experiments with expert information engineers have been performed as part of the realization of a knowledge acquisition approach for modelling knowledge. From each expert we have been able to extract detailed knowledge about the modelling process studied. The last part of this paper describes an architecture of modelling support systems, as well as a prototype that is capable of supporting the presented aspects of modelling processes.

[1]This research is partially funded by the Dutch User Group of Structured Development Methodologies (in Dutch the NGGO), BSO/Rotterdam AT, Hightech Automation, Nixdorf Computer and Unisys Nederland.

1. Introduction

Within the field of information systems no one doubts that it is irresponsible to develop systems on an ad-hoc basis. While many reasons exist for the interest in methodologies systematizing the development process, most of these are concerned with issues of quality of the information system and productivity of the development process (see also Blokdijk (1987) and Sol (1985)).

A trend can be discerned clearly indicating that today's developments in methodologies concentrate on a further structuring and formalizing of the necessary development products (Martin (1986)). The ultimate goal of these so-called engineering-like methodologies is to offer a coherent, integrated set of techniques that covers the entire development process.

Increased complexity of applications, improved verification possibilities, documentation, communication and standardization are among the explanations used for the above mentioned trend. In our view automated support is the prime mover of the ongoing formalization. Martin (1986) states that engineering-like methodologies could not have even existed before 1983 because they depend on automated tools.

According to Butler Cox (1987) and Yourdon (1986) experience with the use of structured techniques such as entity-relationship diagrams, dataflow diagrams and structured English has shown that them to be tedious and time-consuming, and even impractical if they are not supported by automated tools. It is our assumption that automated support will facilitate and increase the use of structured techniques in the first phases of the information systems development process.

Automated support tends to pay less attention to the modelling process than to the modelling techniques (Knuth (1986), Lockemann (1986), Potts (1989)). In particular (but not exclusively) in the first phases of the development process, modelling is a complex problem solving process in which iteration, incompleteness, heuristics, etc. are important characteristics. Today's tools do not support these characteristics explicitly, and for this reason they are merely used as drawing and reporting tools instead of as modelling support tools (NGGO (1989)).

A similar observation can be made on methodologies in general: although most methodologies prescribe tasks to be performed and the sequence of these tasks, very few methodologies offer detailed guidelines how to perform the various tasks and, more important, how to determine the quality of the development products, i.e. the models. Quality is dependent on the competence of the information engineer (Bubenko (1986)).

In our opinion, quality will not be achieved only by specifying the ultimate products. In particular, knowing where to start, how to continue, what to look for, and when to finish - in other words a clear strategy - will largely contribute to the quality of the information system and the productivity of the development process. In this article we report on our study of the modelling process of experienced information engineers as part of an approach to increase existing modelling knowledge. A new architecture of automated tools is presented that reflects both the characteristics of the modelling process and the products of the modelling process.

The main purpose of this architecture is to reduce the dependency of the quality of information engineers, and to introduce more of their capabilities into a modelling support system. It is our philosophy that automated support should be a support environment in the sense that it supports the user in his or her modelling process. Support is achieved by offering guidance based on an explicit strategy as extracted from expert information engineers and by giving advice on (probably) correct or incorrect model structures.

The remainder of this article is organized as follows: In section 2 we introduce a framework for methodologies that we use to describe an approach for information systems development by distinguishing between a way of thinking, a way of modelling, a way of working, a way of control and a way of support. In section 3 we will use this framework to describe some of the problems occurring in the automated support of the way of modelling and the way of working. It is argued that these problems can be solved by a better understanding of the modelling process. Section 4 is related to our model of the modelling process that we have used in the analysis of the experiments performed to gain more insight in the process of model construction. Section 5 highlights some aspects of the experiments as they are performed with expert information engineers and in section 6 some major results concerning the modelling process are presented.

Section 7 includes the description of the new architecture of modelling support systems for which we are developing a prototype by now. At a global level the distinction between inference engine and modelling knowledge is important. Also, in section 7 we will describe the mechanism of the workbench shell in more detail. Finally, section 8 contains our conclusions, as well as some directions for future research.

2. Understanding information systems development methodologies

In the development of information systems, a major problem is that development is too complex to be handled straightforwardly. We need some means to handle this complexity. Constructing models of the problem constitutes such means. By the use of a model it is possible to focus on certain aspects of the development process. Modelling is a prerequisite for the information engineer to understand the area under consideration by making certain aspects of that area explicit in a simplified and understandable way. In the development of information systems there are many different aspects and interrelated (problem) areas which have to be dealt with. Thus, a series of models is usually needed to represent all these aspects within the development process. This series of models is defined to be the way of modelling (i.e. the models which have to be constructed and their interrelationships).

2.1. Way of modelling

In all methodologies models are used: models of (part of) reality, models of the organization or business system, models of the information system (or parts of it) in its final form or in intermediate stages, etc. Some models are rather sketchy and informal, others are highly formalized. Some models may be introduced only occasion while little reference is made to them; others are used extensively. Some models are rather isolated, others are intricately related.
The way of modelling of a methodology describes the network of its models, i.e. the models, their interrelationships and, if present, a detailed description of the model components and their relationships. More specifically the way of modelling:

- describes the models used
- describes the components and their relationships within the models used
- describes the relationships between the models used

There are methodologies that introduce models with little instruction, other methodologies offer algorithms, or at least explicit procedures, to construct a specific model or to verify it. Yet other methodologies give informal but practical suggestions to obtain a model. Therefore it is sensible to distinguish between the 'way of modelling' and the 'way of working' of a methodology.

2.2. Way of working

The way models are being constructed is put into practice in the way of working. The way of working includes the means a methodology offers to create, handle and use models at an operational level. The way of working describes how the work is structured. More specifically, it:

- offers tasks and task definitions at the operational level
- offers a task structure
- includes procedures
- includes informal suggestions
- defines its relationship with the way of modelling

2.3. Way of control

The way of control is in essence related to the control of time, costs and quality of the I.S. development process and its products. It comprises the means a methodology offers to handle models at a managerial level. Typical tasks of controlling a project are:

- setting up a project organization
- splitting up the project into well-defined parts
- defining decision points and control points

It will be clear that the way of control on the one hand and the way of working and the way of modelling on the other hand mutually interact and are dependent on each other. This is the reason why we present them together in figure 1. The way of working constitutes the process-oriented operational aspect of a methodology. The way of modelling constitutes the product-oriented operational aspect of a methodology. The way of control is concerned with managerial aspects.

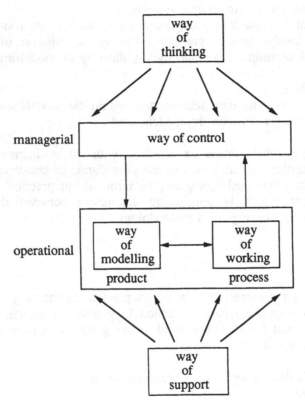

Figure 1. Framework for methodologies

It appeared, see Seligmann (1989), that methodologies can be described quite satisfactory by distinguishing between a way of modelling, a way of working and a way of control. However, for really understanding a methodology it is necessary to know its underlying philosophy or way of thinking used to look at organizations and information systems (Sol (1983), Kensing (1984)). The importance of the way of thinking is reflected in figure 1.

2.4. Way of thinking

The philosophy or Weltanschauung behind a methodology is often overshadowed by or implicit in the techniques and methods embedded in that methodology. These hidden assumptions, however, are of great influence on the ultimate appropriateness of methodologies to certain information systems development problems. In fact, features which are considered to be important to the process of constructing models and to the models themselves, depend on the underlying way of thinking.

The major characteristics of a methodology (be it that they surface only implicitly, e.g. through the character of the network of models, or also explicitly through expository writing), are handled in the 'way of thinking'. In the way of thinking we present basic (implicit or explicit) assumptions and viewpoints of a methodology as regards information systems, their relationship with the environment and their components.

In the way of thinking we describe the major perspectives of a methodology on the following subjects:

- what is an information system
- what is the function of an information system (see environment)
- what are the components of an information system
- what constitutes the environment of the system
- what are the components of the environment
- what are the major characteristics of the components of both the information system and the environment (i.e. a larger system)

2.5. Way of support

In a complete methodology one can argue that complete knowledge exists about which models have to be constructed and in which sequence they have to be constructed. Even then, the development of information systems has to be supported by tools that facilitate the development process. Only a few years ago typical tools were word processors, editors, compilers, stencils, wipe-boards, etc. Today CASE-tools are considered to be an important component of the way of support.

3. Automated support

As stated in section 2 the way of support includes the so-called CASE-tools. These tools should support the way of modelling, the way of working and the way of control in the best possible way. This means that we believe that the usefulness of tools is directly related to the level of integration with the other "ways" of a methodology. If a tool is not truly integrated with the other "ways", it will never become anything more than a documentation aid, see Wijers (1987). A mismatch between modelling process and CASE-tool constitutes an inefficient and ineffective support.

CASE-tools offer editors to support the specification of models. All models are stored in a central dictionary, an encyclopedia, a design database or whatever it may be called. If a model has been fully specified it can be verified by the application of verification rules. Most tools offer the possibility to decompose diagrams; some offer the possibility to integrate models as well. Automatic transformation from a given model to successive models is possible in only some cases.

More general characteristics of current CASE-tools can be found in Bubenko (1988) and NGGO (1988). We will focus on problems that arise when CASE-tools are applied while there is a lack of knowledge about the process of model construction.

3.1. Problems in verification

A problem in offering verification possibilities in CASE-tools is the choice between "a priori" verification and "a posteriori" verification. A priori verification is realized by offering support in which it is impossible to specify incorrect models. For example, IEW only records relationships between entity types in which both roles are named.

A posteriori verification is realized by offering support in which all specifications are allowable and in which only on request verification rules are applied. In general, a posteriori verification is favorable because a priori verification might conflict with the desired way of working of an analyst. However, in the specification of a relationship between entity types, for example, nobody notices the restriction that each relationship has to be drawn between two entity types.

Too strong a priori verification burdens the designers creativity and exploration possibilities. Only a posteriori verification might result in illogical and unsound models because too little guidance was offered in course of the modelling process. A correct trade-off between a priori and a posteriori verification is defined as supporting a natural level of consistency.

3.2. Problems in navigation between various models

Some models have to be constructed before others. For example, an action diagram is made for an already specified process in a dataflow diagram. Other models might be developed in parallel or in an iterative way, such as dataflow diagrams and entity relationship diagrams. Also, models of the same model type are specified in a certain order. One could think of a top-down or a bottom-up approach.

Many CASE-tools, such as SDW, Blues and Excelerator, are very modular in the sense that they offer separate editors for each type of model. By consequence, these tools do not offer any navigation between model types. Other tools, such as IEF and IEW, are more integrated towards the phases of the life cycle. In these tools navigation between model types is realized in some way or another.

In this section we have focussed on problems that arise because there is a lack of knowledge of the process of model construction. Other possibilities to improve the quality of support might be found in the introduction of domain knowledge in CASE-tools, see Falkenberg (1988), Loucopoulos (1989) and Puncello (1988). In our opinion the introduction of domain knowledge will not solve the problem that CASE-tools offer support that does not correspond with a natural way of working. For this reason, we find that priority should be given to process support above domain knowledge support.

4. The process of modelling

In section 2 we have defined the process of modelling to be the way of working. The way of working represents the operational process-oriented aspect of a methodology. We have defined it in terms of tasks that have a sequence which can be coordinated by decisions, whereas each task can be decomposed into sub-tasks and decisions, see also Bots (1989). In this section we will interrelate the way of modelling and the way of working by relating models, model components, tasks and decisions. The basis of this integration of the way of modelling and the way of working is illustrated in the base model of figure 2.

If we look at the way of modelling we can distinguish models, model components, and relationships between model components. Models can in turn consist of sub-models and model components can be represented in more detail by a model. We have abstracted this into the view as presented in figure 2 in which a modelling concept, i.e. a model or model component, is related to other modelling concepts, and might be further specialized into more specific modelling concepts.

If we look at tasks in the process of modelling, we assume that information engineers work with certain (interrelated) concepts in a task, i.e. create instances of these concepts, and that this task is performed at a given natural level of consistency. In other words, using the terminology of section 3, each task has a corresponding set of a priori and a posteriori rules. On the one hand certain conventions (a priori rules) have to be respected within a task, on the other hand a result has to be realized within a task (a posteriori rules). As part of achieving the desired result, the task can of course be further refined into sub-tasks and decisions. A decision is made in order to define the subsequent course of action. The likelihood of one of the alternative courses is based upon one or more decision rules. If no alternatives exist the termination of one task results in the start of the subsequent one.

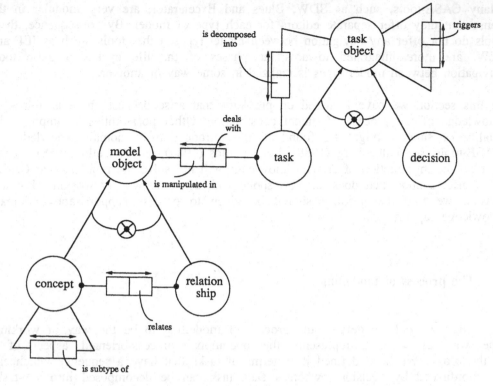

Figure 2. Base model for the modelling process

In order not to complicate figure 2, we have not included explicitly the notions of a priori rule, a posteriori rule and decision rule. Furthermore we have not included that we distinguish simple tasks (or procedures) from composed tasks, see section 7, and that specific information sets can be defined in order to accomplish explicit information passing.

With regard to the coordination of tasks we stress the importance of the relationship "triggers" between task objects, because it enables specification of a sequence of tasks, a choice between tasks and parallelism between tasks, see figure 3. Iteration is accomplished by a decision through which one can return to a previous task.

This so-called task structure is a description of the possible flow of tasks in the way of working. It represents the strategy and direction in the modelling process. Decisions are mostly made based on incomplete knowledge and there always is some doubt as to which alternative should be selected, see Bots (1989). Therefore a choice made at some point in time for one of the alternatives sometimes may have to be reconsidered at some later instant. The task structure only represents the primary flow of tasks.

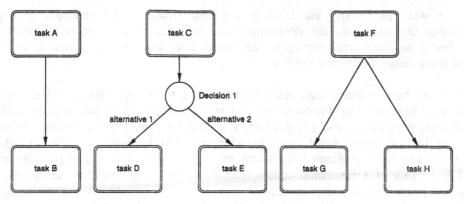

Figure 3. Sequence, choice and parallelism in the way of working

5. Experiments with expert information engineers

Over the past 18 months we have performed three experiments with expert information engineers. As we put forward in section 1, quality depends on the competence of the information engineer. Quality cannot be achieved only by having knowledge about the ultimate products. Knowing where to start, how to continue, what to look for and when to finish does contribute to the quality of the ultimate information system. In the experiments we were particularly interested in the extraction of a detailed understanding about (1) the flow of tasks, (2) the kind of concepts used within and across each task, and (3) the natural level of consistency for each task. As part of the experiments we applied our view on modelling as presented in section 4. Being able to extract detailed modelling knowledge provides a starting point in integrating this knowledge into automated tools, see section 7.

We have investigated for each expert which tasks he performs, with which concepts he works within a specific task, how each task is decomposed, which decisions are taken as part of a task, which decision rules can be distinguished, and which goals he expects to achieve in each task. As for the modelling concepts, we have investigated further specializations of concepts, applicable "a priori" rules and relationships between modelling concepts, in particular those across task boundaries.

5.1. Experiment construction

In Kidd (1985), Hart (1986) and Slatter (1987) various elicitation and formalization techniques are explained together with their useability concerning different types of knowledge.

Since we were particularly interested in the task structure, the concepts an expert uses within the tasks, and the decisions he or she makes to go to other tasks, we have chosen to use verbal protocols, structured interviews and focussed interviews, see for more detail Ledderhof (1989).

Experts have been selected with respect to the two following criteria: (1) the expert should have been working for more than 10 years in the field of information analysis or information planning, and (2) the expert should be considered a leading authority in his or her company. After some introductory conversations with the expert, an experiment has been performed in which he had to construct a global information model consisting of a functional decomposition, one or more dataflow diagrams, and one or more entity-relationship models.

Figure 4 shows a photograph of one of the experiments. An important reason to use an experiment environment as shown in this figure is that the expert is separated from the user by a sound-proof wall in order to allow the expert to think aloud as much as possible.

Figure 4. A photograph of one of the experiments

Communication with the user is realized by computer and video connections. Details concerning the above experiment environment can be found in Ledderhof (1989).

5.2. Experiment analysis

Analysis has been performed in three steps: (1) making transcripts of the sessions, (2) clustering the transcripts into tasks and defining the concepts within each task, and (3) formalizing the task clusters and concept lists into the notions as presented in section 4. As part of this formalization step we have extensively used two diagramming techniques, namely task structure diagrams, see Bots (1989), to represent tasks, decisions, their trigger relationship and task decompositions, and NIAM models, see Nijssen (1989), to represent the modelling concepts, their specializations, their relationships and some of the most important rules.

6. Results of experiments

In view of this paper, we will only highlight some of the conclusions based on our experiments. The conclusions are all related to the overall conclusion that by using the view on modelling as presented in section 4 together with the knowledge acquisition approach as described in section 5, a detailed understanding of a modelling process can be achieved. In this paper we will focus on those results that are related to the extracted strategies and their inherent decisions, the natural level of consistency concerning tasks and the specializations of modelling concepts found.

6.1. Strategy in task structures

In section 4 we have mentioned the coordination between tasks. All three experts appeared to have quite a different strategy. In paragraph 5.1 the overall task of the experts was described as the construction of a global information model consisting of a function decomposition, ER-models and dataflow diagrams. Each expert appeared to have his own preferred technique. The first focussed on ER-models, the second on dataflow diagramming and the third on functional decomposition. The most intriguing fact was that all three used various arguments and practical examples to explain their preference. Another aspect of strategy is that of flexibility. Although there was a preferred strategy all experts had alternative paths in their strategy. Figure 5 shows a strategy of one of the experts.

The tasks presented in the strategy of figure 5 are all further decomposed into sub-tasks and decisions. At more detailed levels in the task structure we found two typical patterns.

Division
In the experiments we often found a strategy similar to the divide-and-conquer principle. For example, a trigger analysis is made for each external trigger, an ER-model is constructed for each dataflow diagram, a market potential is defined for each product group. In order to realize this strategy, the select procedure appeared to be very important. A selection is made in order to do something specifically for that selection.

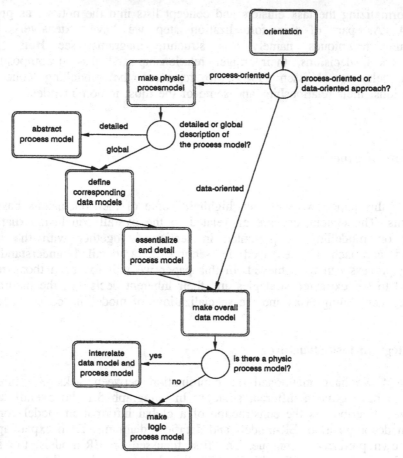

Figure 5. An example of a strategy

Integration

A consequence of division is that we also observed various integration tasks,
such as: make a complete data model based on the existing partial models.

Particularly in relatively small tasks, decisions what to do next are heavily influenced
by previous tasks. For example, it appeared to be most natural to define directly the
relationships for the last entity and not to continue with the definition of new
entities. So, the decision to add a relationship is heavily influenced by the creation or
identification of an entity. In our formalism an information set "the last entity" is
defined and on the basis of that information set a decision rule can increase the
likelihood of the task "define a relationship".

Generally, information about already defined concepts is widely used across task
boundaries. Sometimes an already defined concept can be directly used in new
models (for example, in an integration step or in dataflow diagramming after
functional decomposition), in other cases we were able to express heuristic decision

rules such as: "if there is a model construct X, then there is probably a model construct Y".

6.2. Natural level of consistency

In section 4 we introduced the concept of natural level of consistency of tasks. A correct trade-off between a priori rules and a posteriori rules for a task constitutes a natural level of consistency for that task. Both a priori and a posteriori rules appeared to be very important. Examples are thoughts such as "I think we also need something like a payment", "Do I have external parties?". In general, we see that a task is finished if the expert does not have explicit expectations anymore, i.e. if the natural level of consistency is reached, and - very important - if the user has nothing more to add. With regard to the natural level of consistency, refinement is very important. Refinements occur when additional concepts (new expectations) are used within a certain model or stronger verification rules are applied. For example, an entity-relationship model is further refined with respect to optionality of relationships. Another example in ER-modelling is the fact that finally all relationships have a cardinality, but not in the first version of the model.

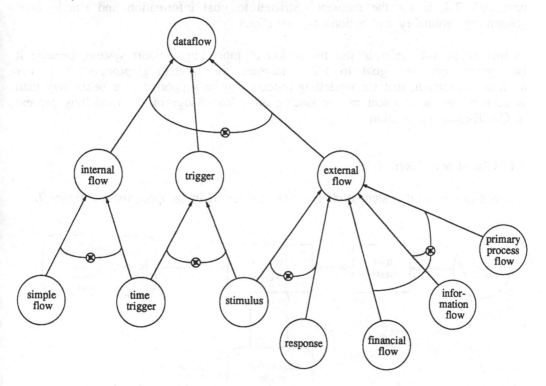

Figure 6. A specialization of the concept "dataflow"

6.3. Finer categorization of concepts

During the analysis of the experiments it appeared to be very well possible to further specialize important concepts part of the diagramming techniques used within the experiments. For each expert the preferred technique appeared to be the most specialized one. In figure 6 we show an example of a finer categorization of the concept "dataflow".

7. An architecture of modelling support systems

In the previous sections we have presented some typical results of our experiments. In all, these results have indicated that our approach indeed leads to a better and detailed understanding of the modelling processes analyzed. In this section we will present our developments up till now concerning automated support of modelling processes as observed in the experiments. For the moment a prototype is available supporting the concept of task agenda, see paragraph 7.3. Intelligent support, see paragraph 7.4, is for the moment restricted to goal information and simple rules concerning cardinality and optionality restrictions.

In this article we prefer to use the notion of modelling support system, because it has never been our goal to fully automate the modelling process. It is our assumption, though, that the modelling process can be supported in a better way than is achieved at the moment by introducing more knowledge of the modelling process in CASE-tools, see section 3.

7.1. Global architecture

A modelling support system itself consists of three main components, see figure 7.

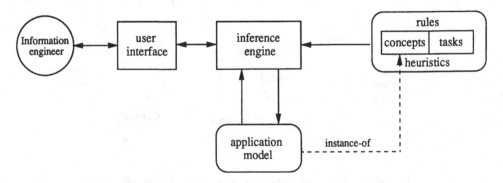

Figure 7. The global architecture of a MSS

First of all, the knowledge of the modelling process of a methodology should be available. Modelling knowledge is structured into:

- Knowledge of tasks
- Knowledge of concepts and relationships used in tasks
- Rules governing the applicability of tasks and concept structures

Secondly, there is the inference engine which operates according to the modelling knowledge specified. The inference engine is a kind of mechanism that presents the information engineer with allowable tasks at a certain moment in time. User interface problems are not considered to be part of the inference engine or the modelling knowledge but have of course to be taken care of in a modelling support system.

The third component is called the application model. The application model consists of all the information specified by the information engineer about a specific application. The items stored in the application model are instances of the concepts and relationships part of the modelling knowledge.

The inference engine, as stated above, operates on knowledge about a specific modelling process. This knowledge is specified using a language called *Methodology Representation Language* (MRL).

This language offers the possibility to specify:

- a task structure
- a concept structure
- decision rules
- a priori rules
- a posteriori rules
- unstructured information for goal facilities

A specific program generates a third generation language source file (Object Oriented Turbo Pascal 5.5) out of a MRL-specification. Linking this source file to the source code of the inference mechanism and the general user interface routines will result in a modelling support system for a specific modelling process.

7.2. Three levels of abstraction

In order to fully understand our architecture as described above, it is important to see that three levels of abstraction can be discerned when an information engineer is working with a specific modelling support system, see figure 8.

At the first level (the application level) case-specific data is specified. Case-specific data is, for example, an organization called *"my_Company"*, which has a *sales department*, a *production unit*, etc.

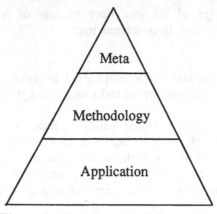

Figure 8. Three levels of abstraction

At the second level (the methodology level) models and model components are defined which are used to represent the case-specific data in a more or less structured way. A possible type of model is a *Functional Decomposition Diagram* ("my_Company") describing *Business Functions* ("Sales", "Financial management", "Production", etc.).

The third level (the meta level) is concerned with structuring the methodology level in task structures, concept structures and additional rules. For example, the analysis of the construction of a functional decomposition results in the *concepts* ("FD-Diagram", "Business Function", "Business Process") and the *task* ("Make a Functional Decomposition Diagram") and the *rule* ("Each Business Function has to be part of a FD-Diagram").

When an information engineer is working with a modelling support system, he is defining models at the application level. These models are instances of the kind of concepts defined at the methodology level. When we are developing a specific modelling support system for a specific methodology, we define a methodology using MRL. MRL can be placed at the meta level.

7.3. Mechanism of the inference engine

Knowing the difference between the application level and the methodology level, it will be clear that the inference engine offers the information engineer a task structure allowing him to enter specifications at the application level. The task structure is offered by presenting a *task agenda,* see Bots (1989).

In the task agenda, see figure 9, all the tasks presented are part of a higher level task or of the top task in the hierarchy of tasks. A task in the task agenda is either a most likely task, an executable task, or a non-executable task, depending on the current state of the modelling process.

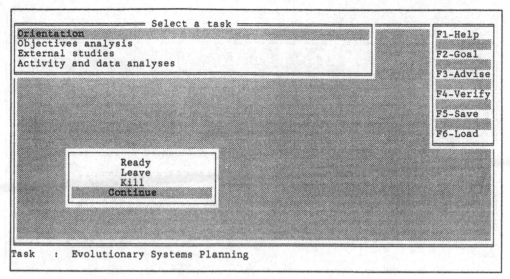

Figure 9. Screen dump of an example of a task agenda

Executing a most likely or executable task will result either in a new task agenda or in the execution of a simple task (procedure). Manipulation of concepts or relationships is realized by procedures. There are four types of standard procedures: create, select, modify and delete. Procedures always behave in accordance with the "a priori" rules of the corresponding task. In addition it should be possible to specify non-standard procedures, the so called *User-Defined-Procedures (UDP's)*. An example of an UDP is the procedure "move". In the current prototype UDP's cannot be defined.

7.4. Intelligent support

At each moment in the modelling process the information engineer might be supported by the modelling support system. Three ways of support are realized: goal information, advice, and verification.

Goal information
> The information engineer may ask for information about the goal of a (simple) task. The reason why a task has to be performed and what its result should be is explained, see figure 10.

Advice
> Based on (heuristic) decision rules, the inference engine is able to deduce likely or unlikely model structures concerning the model the information engineer is working on. Part of these rules are suggestions for various ways to implement the likely model structures or to correct the unlikely model structures. If the information engineer decides to follow up a specific advise, the inference engine will execute the appropriate task.

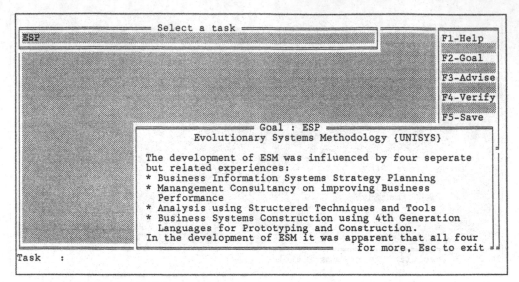

Figure 10. Screen dump of an example of goal information

Verification
Verification checks the "a posteriori" rules. Besides explicit request for verification, verification is automatically performed when the information engineer decides to finish a task. A task is only considered to be finished if the task result is consistent with the "a posteriori" rules.

8. Conclusions and future research

In this article we have argued that a lack of knowledge about models and modelling processes has resulted in problems with CASE-tools concerning verification and navigation. A more process-oriented view on modelling is presented in which the notions of strategy and natural level of consistency are important. A knowledge acquisition approach has been formulated in order to extract detailed modelling knowledge. Protocol analysis is an important part of this approach. This approach has been applied to three expert information engineers. These experiments with expert information engineers have resulted in a better understanding of the modelling processes analyzed.

Diagrams constructed by experts appeared to contain more concepts than that there could be represented externally or explicitly. In other words, the known modelling concepts could be specialized into more specific concepts. In general, the modelling process gradually changed from informal to formal and we noticed that the natural level of consistency changed from a heuristic nature into a more strict nature. In order to maintain a limited span of control, division and integration appeared to be important notions in the way of working.

In the architecture of modelling support systems we have implemented as much as possible our notion of "intelligent" support, which means support based on explicit knowledge of the modelling process. We have introduced the notion of task agenda. Based upon this notion it is possible to offer a strategy in a flexible way, to specify models at the application level in terms of procedures, to implement a functionality for the finer categorization of concepts, to divide and integrate models, to perform iterations, to re-use concepts across task boundaries, and to fire rules for advice and verification. A prototype is available supporting the concept of task agenda including intelligent support by goal information and simple rules based on cardinality and optionality restrictions. Future developments with regard to the prototype will, among other things such as more complex rules, be concerned with improvement of the user-interface.

In the SOCRATES project, see Hofstede (1989), further research is performed concerning knowledge representation of modelling knowledge, modelling knowledge acquisition and modelling support systems. The SOCRATES project will deliver a completely implemented MSS architecture as it is presented in this article.

References

Blokdijk, A. and P. Blokdijk, *Planning and Design of Information Systems*, Academic Press, London, England, 1987.

Bots, P.W.G., *An Environment to Support Problem Solving*, Ph.D. Thesis, Delft University of Technology, Delft, The Netherlands, 1989.

Bubenko jr, J.A., "Information System Methodologies - A Research View", in T.W. Olle, H.G. Sol and A.A. Verrijn-Stuart (Eds.), *Information Systems Design Methodologies: Improving the practice*, North-Holland, Amsterdam, The Netherlands, 1986, pp.289-318.

Bubenko jr, J.A., *Selecting a Strategy for Computer-Aided Software Engineering (CASE)*, Report No.59, SYSLAB, University of Stockholm, Stockholm, Sweden, 1988.

Butler Cox, *Using System Development Methods*, Research Report 57, Butler Cox Foundation, London, England, 1987.

Falkenberg, E.D., H. van Kempen and N. Nimpen, "Knowledge-Based Information Analysis Support", in R. Meersman and C.H. Kung (Eds.), *Proceedings of the WG2.6/WG8.1 Working Conference: The role of A.I. in databases and information systems*, Guangzhou, China, 1988.

Hart, A., *Knowledge Acquisition for expert systems*, Kogan Page, London, England, 1986.

Hofstede, A.H.M. ter, T.F. Verhoef, S. Brinkkemper and G.M. Wijers, *Expert-based support of Information Modelling: A Survey*, Report RP/soc-89/7, SERC, Utrecht, The Netherlands, 1989.

Kensing, F., "Towards Evaluation of Methods for Property Determination", in The.M.A. Bemelmans (Ed.), *Beyond Productivity: Information Systems Development for Organizational Effectiveness*, North-Holland, Amsterdam, The Netherlands, 1984, pp.325-338.

Kidd, A.L., *Knowledge Acquisition for Expert Systems: A Practical Handbook*, Plenum Press, New York, New York, 1987.

Knuth, E., J. Demetrovics and A. Hernadi, "Information System Design: On conceptual foundations", in H.J. Kugler (Ed.), *Information Processing 86*, North-Holland, Amsterdam, The Netherlands, 1986, pp. 635-640.

Ledderhof, H.J.A., *Structured Analysis in de praktijk: Hoe gebruikt een expert het?*, Master's Thesis, Delft University of Technology, Delft, The Netherlands, 1989.

Lockemann, P.C. and H.C. Mayr, "Information system design: Techniques and software support", in H.J. Kugler (Ed.), *Information Processing 86*, North-Holland, Amsterdam, The Netherlands, 1986, pp. 617-634.

Loucopoulos, P. and R.E.M. Champion, "Knowledge-Based Support for Requirements Engineering", in *Proceedings of the 1st Nordic Conference on Advanced Systems Engineering*, Kista, Sweden, 1989.

Martin, J., *Information Engineering Volume 1: Introduction to Information Engineering*, Savant Research Studies, England, 1986.

NGGO, *Computer Ondersteuning van Gestructureerde Ontwikkelingsmethoden, een inventarisatie van tools*, NGGO, Amsterdam, The Netherlands, 1988.

NGGO, *Ervaringen met tools*, NGGO, Amsterdam, The Netherlands, 1989.

Nijssen, G.M. and T.A. Halpin, *Conceptual Schema and Relational Database Design: A fact oriented approach*, Prentice-Hall, Englewood Cliffs, New Jersey, 1989.

Potts, C., "A generic model for representing design methods", in *Proc. of the 11th Int. Conf. on Software Engineering*, Pittsburgh, Pennsylvania, 1989, pp.217-226.

Puncello, P.P., P. Torrigiani, F. Pietri, R. Burlon, B. Cardile and M. Conti, "ASPIS: A Knowledge-Based CASE Environment", *IEEE Software*, March 1988, pp.58-65.

Seligmann, P.S., G.M. Wijers and H.G. Sol, "Analyzing the structure of I.S. methodologies, an alternative approach", in *Proceedings of the First Dutch Conference on Information Systems*, Amersfoort, The Netherlands, 1989.

Slatter, P.E., *Building expert systems, cognitive emulation*, Ellis Horwood, Chicester, England, 1987.

Sol, H.G., "A Feature Analysis of Information Systems Design Methodologies: Methodological Considerations", in T.W. Olle, H.G. Sol and C.J. Tully (Eds.), *Information Systems Design Methodologies: A Feature Analysis*, North-Holland, Amsterdam, The Netherlands, 1983.

Sol, H.G., "Kennis en ervaring rond het ontwerpen van informatiesystemen", *Informatie*, Vol.27, No.3 (1985).

Wijers, G.M. and H.G. Sol, *Intelligent development environments for information systems*, Report 87-05, Faculty of Technical Mathematics and Informatics, Delft University of Technology, Delft, The Netherlands, 1987.

Wintraecken, J.J.V.R., *Informatie-analyse volgens NIAM*, Academic Service, Den Haag, The Netherlands, 1985.

Yourdon, E., "What ever happened to structured analysis", *Datamation*, June 1986, pp.133-138.

Software Process Modelling in EPOS

Reidar Conradi,*

Anund Lie, Espen Osjord, Per H. Westby,
Norwegian Institute of Technology, Trondheim, Norway

Vincenzo Ambriola, Univ. of Pisa and Udine, Italy
Maria Letizia Jaccheri, TecSiel, Pisa, Italy
Chunnian Liu, Beijing Polytechnic Univ., Beijing, P.R. China

Presented at CAISE'90, Kista, Stockholm, Sweden, May 8-10 1990.

Abstract

EPOS[1] is an *instrumentable, kernel* Software Engineering Environment
(SEE). It consists of facilities for management of versioned **products** (configurations) through file-based workspaces attached to a versioned DBMS. EPOS
will also manage the associated software development **processes** (tasks), being the subject of this paper.

The **EPOS-OOER** semantic data model can describe deriver tools, human actors, tasks and subtasks, projects, and triggers/notifiers; as well as
normal software products. EPOS-OOER incorporates object-oriented ERA
modelling, extended with tasking (PRE, POST, CODE) and simple type constructors (FORMALS, DECOMPOSITION). Customization is done through
versioning of task types in project-specific workspaces.

Static task knowledge is expressed by types and subtyping, and is used
for reasoning, planning, scheduling and execution of activities. Dynamic task
knowledge is expressed by a *versioned* task network with a horizontal (temporal) and a vertical (decomposed) dimension. Tasks are connected to products
by normal relationships.

Keywords: Object-Oriented ERA Model, Planning, Software Configuration Management, Software Process Management.

*Address: Division of Computer Systems and Telematics (DCST), Norwegian Institute of Tech-
nology (NTH), N-7034 Trondheim, Norway. Phone: +47 7 593444, Fax: +47 7 594466, Email:
conradi@idt.unit.no.

[1] EPOS, Expert System for Program and ("Og") System Development, is supported by the Royal
Norwegian Council for Scientific and Industrial Research (NTNF) through grant ED0224.18457.
Do *not* confuse with the German real-time environment of the same name [Lem86]!

1 Introduction

Experience with SEEs indicates that an *open* architecture is crucial to avoid strait-jacketing effects. Both new and old tools must be accommodated, and relevant company or project policies should be explicitly stated, enforced, reasoned about – and changed. This puts high demands on the expressivity and flexibility of the underlying formalism.

A software product is described by many interrelated and evolving software components. A software configuration management (CM) tool is therefore needed to control the evolution of such systems. Most CM tools are marginally aware of the underlying software processes and their management (PM). Such a development process is often described in terms of the product (*what*), while the process (manual or automatic) can specify *how* and *why* a version of a product is constructed. In other words: the CM and PM areas should be integrated. Much work has recently been spent on PM in order to understand, model, execute ("enact") and record the operations performed on a product. Such operations or processes range from simple tool invocations to high-level design and project-related activities performed by human actors. A perpetual argument in the PM area has been human creativity vs. automation [Leh87].

Several *generic* or meta-models for PM have been introduced. These can be *instantiated* or customized into a more *specific* process model, e.g. a waterfall, spiral or project-specific model. This puts high demands on the dynamics and generality of the underlying type system.

The EPOS PM approach is to integrate:

- Static process programming as in ARCADIA [TBC*88] and IPSE 2.5 [OR86].
- Dynamic (sub)contracts as in ISTAR [Dow87].
- Rule-based reasoning as in MARVEL [KF87] and ALF [B*89],
- Networked tasks with dynamic triggering à là OSMOSE (Petri net model) [DGS89], and to some extent PCMS [HM88] and NOMADE [BE87].
- Subtype refinement as in Process-Oriented CM [BL89].

Some more high-level structuring is needed, but we are only describing the kernel facilities and basic type system.

The ensuing sections of this paper are as follows. First the EPOS architecture and basic CM model of EPOS are summarized. Then the overall PM model and the associated Activity Manager are presented. Then follows a more formal treatment of our object-oriented ER model, EPOS-OOER, with emphasis on PM-relevant type properties, type constructors and project-specific versioning. Lastly, some present problems and ideas on future work are given.

2 EPOS Background

2.1 EPOS Architecture

The main EPOS components are:

- A semantic data model, *EPOS-OOER*.
- An advanced *CM system*, p.t. on top of the INGRES relational DBMS [SWKH76].
- An *Activity Manager* and *Planner* for PM support. The Activity Manager includes a *Builder*.
- A set of EPOS support tools, such as a *Product Editor* and a *Maintainer's Assistant*.
- A *User Interface*, based on the X Window System.
- *Local, checked-out workspaces* or configurations (files, databases in special formats), accessed by misc. *programming tools*.

EPOS will run on Unix workstations, using INGRES, X Windows, C++, and Prolog. See [CDrG*89] for more details.

2.2 Change-Oriented Versioning and Related CM

We have adopted the *change-oriented* model (COM) to versioning [Hol88] [LDC*89] [LCD*89]. Here, a *functional change* involving several (related) components is described by a single, *global option*. COM resembles and generalizes conditional compilation, and is fundamentally different from more conventional, *version-oriented* models (VOM). Most most database (DB) items can be **uniformly versioned** from a technical point of view. Some COM concepts are:

- *Option*: Essentially a boolean variable to describe a functional change (external property), such as MachineSun or BugFixCommandA. It is not an object attribute as in VOM, rather a non-versioned(!) entity with its own attributes: DateTime, Validity, Name, etc.
- *Validity*: Boolean expression over options to describe valid combinations of options. It corresponds to attribute constraints in VOM.
- *Fragment*: Basic information item, such as a relational tuple or a text line.
- *Visibility*: Boolean expression attached to each fragment of VersionedObj instances.
- *Version*: It consists of all fragments where the visibility evaluates to True for the given version-choice. A version is not an instance itself, but the result of a functional evaluation!
- *Version-choice*: A set of (option,value) bindings to describe which version an application task wishes to see. A version-choice is *complete* if a unique version of the DB is produced.
- *Version-description*: High-level DB query, that maps to a low-level *version-choice*, which defines a specific *version-view* or version of the DB.
- *Product-description*: Tuple of (Root objects, ER types), that maps to a *product-view* or product *closure* on the DB. The product is described by SysBody and similar entity

111

types. Note, that all DataEntity instances have a long Contents field, represented by an external file.

- *Config-description*: *Generic* (Product-description, Version-description), that maps to a *config-view* closure on the DB.
- *Specific, primary configuration*: a config-view to be used as a *workspace* by developers or tools.
- *Specific, derived configuration*: can be produced by the Builder as *Deriv-Config := Build(Product-view(Version-view(DB)))*.
- *Change job*: An edit-update *task* that controls a long *transaction* associated with a workspace, thus linking CM to PM.
- *Ambition*: A non-complete version-choice associated with a change job. It identifies the set of version-choices where new changes are going to be visible.

To interface old tools, the only viable solution is to *check-in* and *check-out* local workspaces of files and related DB information. This corresponds to the *copy-modify-merge* paradigm in NSE and PACT [Sun88] [Bul87]. An example of two coordinated workspaces is shown in figure 1. Here, workspace WS_1 belongs to Project P_C. This is a subproject of project P_A that controls workspace WS_2. Each

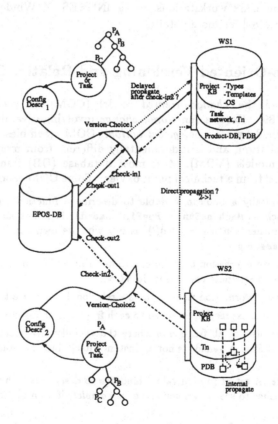

Figure 1: Central DB with checked-out workspaces, WS_i

workspace or configuration is controlled by a change job and its configuration description. A workspace is divided in three: product DB, task network, and project knowledge base (KB, with types and various other descriptions).

3 PM in EPOS

3.1 General Demands for Generic PM Support

Our goal is a common, system-interpretable formalism to describe software development processes. The model must cover:

- Deriver *tools*: their description (pre/post-conditions, inputs/outputs, tool switches) and aggregation.
- *Human actors* in an open-ended way.
- "Active" relationships to express change propagation by triggers.
- Chained tasks for *horizontal* life-cycle phases, revision lines, or derivation graphs.
- Subtask hierarchies to describe *vertical* work decomposition.
- Complex interactions between tasks and tools/users.
- Special project tasks to control workspaces with project-specific information (e.g. types).

3.2 A Survey of the PM Model

Our activation mechanism is coarse-level and mainly *descriptive*, based on PRE- and POST-conditions in types. Such conditions seem to flexibly express the activity rules for PM. They are also well-suited for *static*, forward and backward reasoning without executing the CODE.

The CODE associated to a task instance is responsible for causing its POST-condition to become True, and thus cause ("fire") other PRE-conditions to become True etc. The POST/PRE coupling therefore serves as a *dynamic synchronization mechanism*. The CODE of a task may re-execute, repeating the PRE/POST pattern above.

The experience with unrestricted "firing" of unbound rules and *triggers*[2] in databases, AI applications, and syntax editors [HN86] made us sceptic to such solutions. In our case, direct task communication is limited to relationship-connected *neighbor tasks* (4.5.1), and can thus describe traditional message passing and *notification*. Note the analogy with Petri nets [Rei85]. Note also that task execution can occur at any network node, not only at the leaves – cf. ISTAR. This distinguishes the network from a finite state machine, where only one node at a time is active.

---

[2] We may, of course, consider a task with a PRE-condition and an imperative CODE as a "trigger", with syntax IF — THEN — . Note also, that the EPOS *task type* corresponds to a conventional AI *rule*.

Dynamic subtask creation allow for considerable freedom in organizing the software work, and alleviates the limitations of static CODE in instantiated tasks. There are FORMALS and DECOMPOSITION properties (constraints) to regulate the *structure* of the task network.

3.3   The Activity Manager and Planner

Management of task types and instances is done by the EPOS *Activity Manager (AM).* and its associated Planner [Mul89] [LC89]. High-level or more complicated tasks must be delegated to human actors. Generally, we will have a high-level *goal* to achieve, and a product DB and a project KB as the starting point.

The relations between the Activity Manager and types, tasks and products are shown in figure 2:

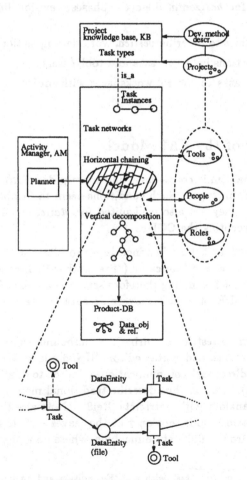

Figure 2: **AM and data**

The Activity Manager consists of:

- A *Type Manager (TM)* to construct and modify specific `TaskEntity` subtypes. The TM cooperates with a project manager or another meta-user.

- An *Instance Manager (IM)* to dynamically create, edit, and delete task instances; and to manage horizontal and vertical composites of such. The FORMALS and DECOMPOSITION information from task types will be used to automatically construct new and type-validated task structures.

  The IM cooperates with the Planner or a user to handle simple tasks (tool activations), and with a meta-user for more complex tasks (e.g. projects).

- An *Execution Manager (EM)* to interpret, execute, control and record task instances – while obeying the static task knowledge. E.g., tools must be called correctly, with dynamic checking of parameters if necessary.

  The EM cooperates with tools, users, the Builder (an EM component), and the Planner. Possible error situations must be monitored for alternative actions, and may include replanning and re-execution.

The Planner will:

- Offer *product-level* assistance such as construction of the empty derivation graph – a *plan* – for the Builder, cf. [HC88]. The plan may be *incomplete*, and a `TaskState` attribute of the planned tasks may reflect this.

- To some extent offer *project-level* assistance about task or work decomposition, work plans, etc.

- Utilize *static*, method-specific type knowledge about legal task communication and combination patterns. This is expressed by PRE, POST, FORMALS and DECOMPOSITION properties. This knowledge will be combined with information from the product DB. Only the non-temporal aspects of PRE- and POST-conditions will be considered, excluding comparison of `DateTime` timestamps, or scheduling rules like `<Compile between 24:00 and 06:00>`.

- Replan upon execution failures.

- Assess the impact of changes.

- "Learn" by putting generalized PM types back into the KB.

The Planner will borrow ideas from MARVEL, the AGORA PLANNER [BLA88], the domain-independent IPEM [AS88], and case-based planning.

4 EPOS-OOER, The Semantic Data Model

A common, semantic data model for CM and PM is sought, since there is much interaction between the two areas. **EPOS-OOER** represents a unification of ER [Che76] and *object-oriented* (OO) modelling, and allows general subtyping. The use of low-level pointers instead of general relationships in OO models has been remedied [Rum87]. From semantic network models we have been inspired by uniform handling of entities and relationships [TL82].

4.1 Available Type Properties

Multiple subtyping is specified through SIMULA-style prefixing. We will not define the *schema* notation formally, as the examples should be self-explanatory. The repertoire of type properties is explained in the following sections.

4.1.1 DOMAINS and ATTRIBUTES

Attributes belong to given domains, and represent passive *variables* or active *PRO-Cedures* (methods). Domains are declarable, and include scalars, text strings, pointers (REFs, see below), PROCs, and pre-defined ones like Bool. A REF-value is the value of the ObjId attribute of the referred object (see RootER type below). REFs are restricted to non-PersistentObjs, temporary PROC parameters, and access functions for CONNECTION data (4.1.2). In task types externally callable PROCs are constrained to functions without side-effects, i.e. functional attributes. Initialization is provided by = <init-value>. CONST means read-only or system-maintained variables.

Inheritance means that the supertypes' global attributes and domains are inherited into the subtypes. Multiple names in the supertypes are resolved by bottom-up, left-right search. A local name will always hide or overload the global one.

An example of a type definition with domains and attributes is:

```
TYPE RootER =                            % No prefixing supertypes.
DOMAINS
  DT = String;                           % A domain definition.
ATTRIBUTES
  % Four system-maintained attributes:
  ObjId   : CONST <64-bits> = ...;       % Unique and immutable.
  TypeId  : CONST 'REF TYPE' = ...;      % 'Is-a' relationship.
  DateTime: CONST DT         = ...;      % Create time.
  Primary : CONST Bool       = ...;      % Prim/Deriv?
  New     : PROC (--)=--;                % In meta-type?
  Delete  : PROC ()  =--;                % Similarly.
  Read    : PROC (--)--=--;              % On attrs also
  Write   : PROC (--)=--;                % Make version?
  Select  : PROC (--)=--;                % Very general.
  ---
END-TYPE RootER;
```

4.1.2 CONNECTION

Types with no CONNECTION property are implicitly called **entity** types. Inversely, a CONNECTION implicitly identifies a *binary* **relationship** type, that connects two entity types[3]. Only single type inheritance is allowed at the user

---

[3]In ER terminology, *roles* should have been used here. – And the debate whether relationships should have identity and TypeId or not, is still going on!

level, starting from the Relationship type below. Inheritance may constrain cardinalities and related entity subtypes, and may rename the access functions.

An example of a basic relationship type is:

```
VersionedObj, PersistentObj, GenRelationship TYPE Relationship = % NB!
CONNECTION
   Acc1 : Entity1(l1..u1) <-> Acc2 : Entity2(l2..u2);
   % Defines a binary relationship between Entity1 and Entity2
   % with access functions Acc1 and Acc2, and
   % with cardinalities l1..u1:l2..u2 - or u1:u2 in short.
   % ui = * means unbound cardinality, and SEQ after ui means ordering.
   % NB: The suffixes in Entity1 and Entity2 only serve to distinguish
   %       these from one another!
   %       Also, li = 0 and ui = * at this general type level!
ATTRIBUTES
   Closure: PROC (--)=---;     % Special DB op.
   ---
END-TYPE Relationship;
```

Named access functions (Acc1 and Acc2 above) are implicitly available to the "related" entities, but formally defined in the connecting relationship type. Assuming a cardinality of *:1, Acc1 could be defined in Entity2 with domain 'SET(REF Entity1)'. With a cardinality 1:*, the domain of Acc1 could be 'REF Entity1'. "CONNECTION data" may be stored inside the related DB entities as pointers or sequences of such for reasons of efficiency.

A short-hand notation for simple relationship types, implicitly prefixed by Relationship is offered:

```
RELATIONSHIP-TYPE
   RelType = Acc1 : Entity1(l1..u1) <-> Acc2 : Entity2(l2..u2);
```

4.1.3 CODE

This is a piece of program code expressed in an imperative programming language, executed by the Activity Manager. CODE is primarily used in TaskEntity types, but may be used for initialization of non-tasks. However, such instances are not "active" tasks in the OO sense.

The CODE language is *not concurrent*, as all triggering is implicitly expressed by PRE- and POST-conditions. The CODE language is a restricted Unix shell language. STOP means task termination. Shell variables such as $<name> can be accessed. Into(AccFunc,X) means insertion of X into a relationship. INNER means execution of the subtype's CODE. It will be appended in the CODE part, if missing. Type inheritance implies concatenation, using SIMULA's INNER mechanism.

117

4.1.4 PRE- and POST-conditions

As mentioned, a task waits for its PRE-condition to become True before (re-)activation of its CODE part. After each activation, the POST-condition must be fullfilled. PRE and POST are intended for task types, but can be envisaged as initialization and termination constraints elsewhere. Type inheritance is by conjunction ($\wedge$), starting from True in the TaskEntity type.

PRE- and POST-conditions are formulas in first-order predicate logic, with the following predicates and functions:

```
ALL(x:accfunc!cond)     True, if valid for all x
SET(x:accfunc!expr)     set of all expr's
CLOSURE(accfunc)        closure from curr.obj (def. in Relationship)
CLOSURE(x,accfunc)      closure from x obj
NOTIFY(set)             DB change-message
t1 SUBTYPE_OF t2        subtype test
set1 IN set2            subset member test
x WITHIN (.values.)     scalar range test
MIN(values),MAX(--)     minimum, maximum
ANDIF, ORELSE           McCarthy and/or
```

For technical reasons, the PRE-condition is split into two parts: PRE_STATIC used by the Planner and PRE_DYNAMIC used by the Execution Manager. We have not yet found it necessary to split up the POST-condition similarly.

The PM types (4.5) contain examples of PRE- and POST-conditions.

4.1.5 FORMALS and DECOMPOSITION constructors

Both specify simple type templates, and are restricted to TaskEntity type and subtypes. Type inheritance rules are as for attributes, although we have considered various schemes of subtype-constraining semantics [CW85].

FORMALS constrains the indirect, *horizontal chaining of tasks*, i.e. the legal types of actual task parameters. These parameters are expressed by the GenInputs and GenOutputs relationships between TaskEntity instances and their inputs and outputs (4.5.1).

An example of a FORMALS specification is:

```
TaskEntity TYPE TaskX =
FORMALS
  a:C_Source * $b:C_Include -> c:DerivEntity
```

This means that TaskX instances take one input of type C_Source and a variable number of inputs of type C_Include (because of the starting $-sign in the parameter name), and produce one output of type DerivEntity – or subtypes thereof for all these types. All parameter types must be subtypes of Entity, i.e. no relationships can be processed by tasks. The default FORMALS specification is:

```
$in:Entity -> $out:Entity
```

i.e. no constraints at all. CHECK_IN_FORMALS and CHECK_OUT_FORMALS
predicates are available for use in PRE/POST-conditions, see Sec. 4.5.1.

DECOMPOSITION constrains *vertical task breakdown*, i.e. the SubTasks relationship between parent and children tasks (4.5.1).

An example of a DECOMPOSITION specification is:

```
TaskEntity TYPE TaskY =
DECOMPOSITION
   CHOICE(SEQ(ta:T1,tb:T2), PAR(tc:T3,td:T4), tseq:REPERTOIRE(T5,T6,T7));
```

This means that possible children of TaskY instances may be either instances of
T1 and T2 executing in sequence, instances of T3 and T4 executing in parallel, or
any number of instances of T5/T6/T7 executing in parallel (PAR is implicit). The
default is REPERTOIRE(TaskEntity), i.e. no constraints.

The Activity Manager and Planner uses DECOMPOSITION for automatic generation of children tasks after creating a parent task, and so on. To avoid redundancy
with Into(Children, NEW TaskEntity(...)) in the CODE part, the DECOM-
POSITION should be empty, if the parent task explicitly generates or kills its
children tasks. In case of a SEQ specification, synchronization of children tasks
will be checked and possibly enforced by the Planner.

4.1.6 EXECUTABLE

This identifies the *logical* name of the associated OS-tool of a deriver task. Such a
tool can be considered an "external" PROC, possibly shared by many similar task
types. Upon workspace initialization, a "soft link" between the *type* object(s) and
the selected Executable *instance* will be established.

4.1.7 INVARIANT

This is a formula in first-order predicate logic, specifying an assertion over certain
DB instances. It should always be True. Type inheritance is by conjunction ($\wedge$).
Sec. 4.5.5 contains an example of an INVARIANT.

4.2 Pre-defined Types

A type semi-lattice of some of the *pre-defined* types is shown in figure 3, with the
system-defined ones above the dotted line:

For a real project, all the main types have much more subtypes than indicated.

119

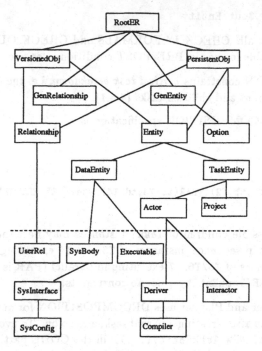

Figure 3: EPOS type semi-lattice

4.3 General Comments on EPOS-OOER

DB *instances* of any type can be created, by NEW Type(List of <AttrName = Value>). Entity instances are often called "objects".

The types are represented as normal DB objects or TypeDescrs (4.4), available for dynamic interpretation. There are no meta-types.

The non-PROC ATTRIBUTES and CONNECTION part of EPOS-OOER is called the *CM-part*. The rest is called the *PM-part*, since such properties are stored at the type level and are implemented by the Activity Manager. This PM-part can be *versioned* (4.6).

Note, that EPOS-OOER is not quite "unified": There are limitations on the use of pre-defined types as supertypes. E.g. PersistentObj and VersionedObj (2.2) mostly serve as *keywords*, GenRelationship subtypes are restricted to simple inheritance, and Option cannot be used as a supertype at all. Type properties beyond domains and attributes are only relevant for TaskEntity subtypes.

An alternative conceptual base would have been more specialized type categories – DATAENTITY, RELATIONSHIP and TASKENTITY – and a more closed data model.

4.4 On Task / Tool modelling

The OO ERA modelling in EPOS-OOER follows conventional patterns. The problem has been the modelling of tasks and tools, where the solutions have changed fundamentally over the last year. We will repeat the relevant arguments and rationale for the uninitiated reader.

The main PM type is now `TaskEntity` (4.5.1). A `TaskEntity` instance describes a potentially *active* process or task. Its CODE part may execute its own program, and indirectly that of its children. The low-level, more specialized `Deriver` tasks may directly call *passive* OS-tools, so-called `Executables`, through a procedural envelope with given file parameters. Static tool aggregation is done by DECOMPOSITION of associated task types. Versioning of OS-tools is done by the normal CM mechanisms, and versioning of task types is explained in Sec. 4.6.

We have also had problems in modelling formal parameters and task/tool templates. Both these imply *type-level* "relationships" or constructors to express constraints, which are not easily expressible in an ER framework:

- *Formal parameters* were initially expressed by ad-hoc `ProcInputs` and `ProcOutputs` *"meta-relationships"* to connect a `TaskEntity` *type* with its legal input and output *types*. The type information of such formal parameters could then be matched against the types of the actual parameters.

  It remains a problem to compactly express *shared* formal parameters between similar deriver tasks. We may need a separate *signature* type ("arrow" type) for this.

- *High-level templates* for task/tool aggregates and task networks may assume *type composites* at the meta-level.

Instead of having a more sophisticated type apparatus on the *meta-level*, we have introduced the FORMALS and DECOMPOSITION properties. However, we have no separate `Template` type to describe more generalized type composites.

FORMALS and DECOMPOSITION are internally implemented by system-maintained "shadow types", `TypeDescrs`, at the *instance level*. Such `TypeDescrs` facilitate, in principle, any kind of *high-level typing* through arbitrary type relationships or *constructors*[4].

Some more technical arguments have been:

- An EPOS `Deriver` task is an abstraction of an activation of a real *OS-tool*. Such an OS-tool is called by issuing a command line (a script) to the OS, with proper tool name, tool switches and file parameters.

- Tool *envelopes* are needed to hide OS details and to provide project instrumentation and error treatment.

- Tools cannot be expressed as traditional OO "methods" (PROCs) in such types. This is because the tools may be shared by several task types and

---

[4]EPOS-OOER only supports ''Subtype_Of'', FORMALS and DECOMPOSITION type constructors.

possibly independently produced and versioned by the surrounding OS – cf. EXECUTABLE property and next item.

- *Tool switches* cannot easily be modelled by traditional parameters, due to varying number and special semantics. E.g., some switches cause extra output to be produced, so that different "deriver variants" must be defined with appropriate FORMALS[5]. Centralized control over default tool switches is also desirable.

- Tool *aggregates* are needed to hide details, using DECOMPOSITION to express super-tools.

- Lastly a reminder: We do *not* want to model *all* the "hairy" semantics (to put it mildly!) of the OS-tools. Only the essential parts for basic tool management need be covered.

There are *three* different task/tool breakdowns, all N:M:

- The static type semi-lattice.
- Static task/tool type aggregates through the DECOMPOSITION constructor.
- Dynamic decompositions of task instances through a SubTasks relationship, obeying the DECOMPOSITION constraints.

4.5 The main PM Types

4.5.1 The TaskEntity Type

TaskEntity has an Actor subtype (4.5.2) to execute an interactive or automatic tool, a Project subtype (4.5.5), and more specialized subtypes.

As mentioned, the CODE in a task instance is executed when the PRE-condition evaluates to True. A task serves as a *coroutine* – with an implicit, embedding loop around the outermost CODE part. The task execution environment is assumed to be cheap – probably co-routines in the Activity Manager, plus forking of real OS processes to execute OS-tools.

The TaskEntity definition is:

```
Entity TYPE TaskEntity =
DOMAINS
  TaskStates = ENUM(Created, Initialized, Waiting, Ready,
                    Active, Terminated, Deletable);
  Eagerness  = ENUM(Busy, Periodic, Opportunistic, ..., Seldom, Lazy);
ATTRIBUTES
  TaskState :      TaskStates = Created;
  BatchTool :CONST Bool = ...;                     % Deriver?
  Parallel  :CONST Bool = True;                    % PARallel?
PRE
  CHECK_IN_FORMALS(Inputs)                         % Type-check inputs.
```

---

[5]Indeed, the Unix CC-compiler may be used both as a pre-processor, compiler, linker, assembler, ... – and with different FORMALS within these categories!

```
CODE % Coroutine:
% DO                                            % Implicit DO.
   <Initial CODE part>;
   INNER;
   <Final CODE part>;
% OD;                                           % Implicit OD.
POST
   CHECK_OUT_FORMALS(Outputs)                   % Type-check outputs.
   AND ALL(o:Outputs ! o.Primary = NOT BatchTool) % Deriver condition.
   AND ('Success' OR 'Failure')                 % Outcome predicate.
END-TYPE TaskEntity;

RELATIONSHIP-TYPE
   SubTasks  =Parent   :TaskEntity(0..*) <-> Children:TaskEntity(0..*SEQ);
   GenInputs =GInNode  :TaskEntity(0..*) <-> Inputs  :Entity(0..*SEQ);
   GenOutputs=GOutNode:TaskEntity(0..*) <-> Outputs :Entity(0..*SEQ);
```

Name attributes of `GenInputs` and `GenOutputs` actual parameters are omitted for sake of clarity.

4.5.2 The Actor Type

`Actor` is a trivial `TaskEntity` subtype; not shown. It has two subtypes, an `Deriver` (4.5.3) and `Interactor` (4.5.4).

4.5.3 The Deriver Type

As mentioned, the `Deriver` type represents a deriver tool. Its CODE part is a shell script to prepare, activate, control, and record an OS-tool activation. This is done through "INNER"-subtyped *envelopes* of Pre/Post-Actions. Such actions may include "invisible" control and accounting functions, as in GENOS [GEC87]. The logical name of the OS-tool is given by the EXECUTABLE property. *Default* tool switches will be provided from the global `CurrProject`. *"Crucial"* tool switches, affecting the FORMALS, are contained in a local `DeriverSwitches` attribute. This attribute and the `matcher` PROC attribute (see 5.1.1) will be redefined by subtypes.

A `Deriver` definition with a *busy* rebuild rule is:

```
Actor TYPE Deriver =
ATTRIBUTES
   Analyzed       : DateTime;           % Last derivation.
   DeriverSwitches: String = 'xx';      % Redefined in subtypes.
   Matcher: PROC () = ---;              % Make derivation graph.
   TooOld : PROC () Bool =
   BEGIN
      MAX(SET(i:Inputs  ! i.DateTime)) > % Checking timestamps within
      MIN(SET(o:Outputs ! o.DateTime))   % a configuration.
   END TooOld;
```

```
PRE                           % Busy build in local config:
  TooOld() AND CurrProject.Rederiv_Policy() = Busy
EXECUTABLE 'xx'               % Redefined in subtypes.
FORMALS    ---                % The same.
CODE
  <Check derivation cache>;
  <PreAction>;                % Shell script.
  Call-OS-Tool(<EXECUTABLE-name>,
          DeriverSwitches, CurrProject.DefaultSwitches,
            <file parameters>);
  INNER;                      % Extra subtype actions.
  <PostAction>;               % Shell script.
  <Update derivation cache>;
  <Assemble product statistics>;
  <Report to PM recording tool>;
POST
  <Extra assumptions on output parms> AND <Success and failure modes>
END-TYPE Deriver;
```

A coarse description of success and failure modes must be supplied. Note, that each project may define its own rederivation policies (PRE-conditions) or CODE parts.

A deriver is typically a compiler, link editor, text formatter etc. We can envisage a `Compiler` subtype, with a `CC-Compiler` subtype of this etc.

4.5.4 Interactor Type

`Interactor` is an `Actor` subtype representing an interactive tool activation, coupled to a `Role` instance. The `Interactor` definition may look like:

```
Actor TYPE Interactor =
PRE
  <Input changed>
CODE
  <Call some role/tool pair, e.g. a Maintainer + Assistant>;
END-TYPE Interactor;
```

A `Role` represents a "canonical" person, emphasizing authorization, job position, and general project attachment. The `Role` will again be connected to specific `Person(s)`, having responsibility of certain software components.

4.5.5 Project Type

`Project` is a `TaskEntity` *subtype* to emphasize the productive aspect. A project specifies a *project KB* connected to a workspace. A new project instance, e.g. `CurrProject`, may be created in the workspace of its parent project. The new project will inherit the parent's workspace, and in addition create a *nested*

124

workspace of its own. In principle, the project KB can be changed on-the-fly! See Sec. 4.6 for binding mechanisms to achieve flexible project tailoring.

The project KB should contain the following information:

- A *config-description* (2.2) for the current DB transaction in the local workspace. This may include a traditional DB view, with rights and capabilities.

- A *coarse OS description*: specific or low level OS-tool information, such as file bindings, environment flags, default OS-tool set including tool switches (e.g. `-I <directory_name>` to compilers), ...

- *Subprojects*, and allocation of *persons and resources* – as in ISTAR.

- *Project-specific rules and policies*, through various PM types, task/tool templates, invariants, project-pervasive attributes, ...

Ex. Project policies for *CurrProject* = ProjectX.

```
Project TYPE ProjectX =
ATTRIBUTES
  DefaultSwitches : String;                          % Used above.
  Rederiv_Policy  : PROC () Eagerness = BEGIN Busy END Rederiv_Policy;
PRE
  ProjectAccount <> NIL AND ProjectLeader <> NIL  % Def. elsewhere.
CODE
  <Create subtasks>;
POST
  ---
DECOMPOSITION
  REPERTOIRE('Approved-task-types')                  % Special INVARIANT.
INVARIANT
  % Expresses policies: All documents created shall bef of (sub)types
  % approved by the project.
  ALL(x:CLOSURE(Children).Outputs
        ! x.TypeId SUBTYPE_OF 'Approved-document-types')
END-TYPE ProjectX;
```

4.5.6 Executable Type

This is a `DataEntity` subtype, and specifies `BinaryProgs`, `ShellScripts`, or other OS-tools.

4.6 Project Customization of Typing

Some possible binding mechanisms are:

- *Static inheritance* in the task type hierarchy, i.e. project-specific *subtyping*. This may lead to a proliferation of subtypes and mutual constraints on correct subtype selection, cf. option validities and figure 4.

- *Type parameterization* and instantiation of generic project types, as an alternative to subtyping.

- Project *versioning*: a generalization of subtyping, which is easy to achieve in our COM model from a technical point of view. However, we want essentially non-versioned types/DB-schemas to prevent a semantic explosion of sub-universes in the DB [SZ86].

- *Dynamic inheritance* in the task instance hierarchy, or along any given relationship.

- *Dynamic instrumentation* of the Activity Manager through special couplings to CurrProject, cf. CurrProject.Rederiv_Policy used by the Builder.

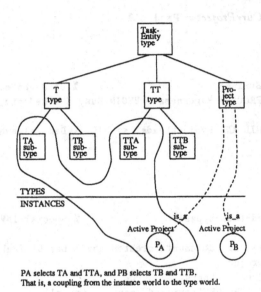

PA selects TA and TTA, and PB selects TB and TTB.
That is, a coupling from the instance world to the type world.

Figure 4: Consistent choice/version of subtypes

The EPOS solution is to use the system-maintained TypeDescr instances (4.4) to express limited *type versioning* within the workspace of a project, i.e. of the PM-part only. This guarantees some minimum DB stability.

A comment on the EPOS model of type versioning: It may seem primitive to let a set of *boolean* or scalar options "parameterize" our type system. However, we want to version an *entire* collection of types and other control information at the same time. Alternative approaches with sophisticated type parameters in addition to subtyping (cf. Eiffel [Mey88]) are more complex but still insufficient. In contrast, our scheme uses the *existing* versioning and workspace mechanisms in EPOS, i.e. it has a low human and computer cost.

5 Applications of the PM Model

5.1 Active Relationships, Derived Objects and the Builder

5.1.1 Active Relationships and the Derivation Graph

An intuitive modelling of "active" relationships is to associate triggers (rule-coupled tools) with relationship types. Since we do not allow *n-ary* relationships with possible task decomposition, we must insert extra task entities between the "N:M"-related objects, see next paragraph.

The conversion from a *dependency* graph with "pure" relationships to a *derivation* graph with inserted task nodes is *language-specific*. It is taken care of by the matcher PROC in the Deriver subtypes. For instance, GenInputs in a derivation graph must represent the *transitive closure* of the relevant inputs for programming languages like C, Pascal and Fortran (large, but shallow graph). That is, the Deriver step to compile a C-program X.c will require the "body" file X.c, the "interface" file X.h, and *all* .h files that these two files transitively include. This closure is not necessary for languages like Ada and Modula, having separately compiled interfaces (smaller, but deeper graph).

5.1.2 Derived Objects

Derived objects are different from *primary* objects. A derived object of type Entity is stored as a versioned, functional DerivResult "attribute" in an instance of DerivEntity type (not defined here). This instance represents a possibly empty version group of derived objects. Different tools operating on the same input objects must be described by *different* derived objects and derivation graphs.

When requested by an application, the versioned DerivResult attribute may be regenerated, using the available derivation graph. This corresponds to *lazy* build. The DerivResult attribute identifies the derived output, its inputs, and tool version and tool switches used. There is an accompanying, versioned DateTime attribute.

The set of non-empty versions of the DerivResult attribute can be treated as a global *cache* of derived objects, and is subject to user policies for deletion; see ODIN [Cle88]. It is important to *share* attribute versions between configurations – i.e. smart recompilation! – by "increasing" attribute *visibilities* [Lie89].

5.1.3 The Builder

The *Builder* operates in the current or LOCAL workspace (2.2). It is really a part of the Activity Manager, which also has created or planned the derivation graph of task objects. An example of a derivation graph is:

The Builder will generate a complete, derived configuration – upon explicit re-

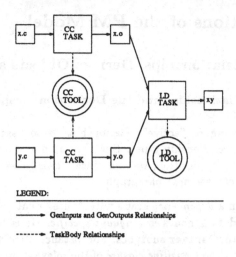

LEGEND:

⟶ GenInputs and GenOutputs Relationships

------▶ TaskBody Relationships

Figure 5: A derivation graph

quest (*lazy*, backward chaining), or when triggered by project-specific rules (*busy*, forward chaining). Error handling is difficult, e.g. to interpret compilation errors sensibly. Suppose that we want to nightly rederive the outdated objects, caused by DB-changes in the LOCAL workspace:

```
Deriver TYPE LocalDeriver =
PRE                              % Note PRE-concatenation by subtyping.
  NOTIFY(Inputs) AND (Inputs IN LOCAL) AND
  ClockTime() WITHIN (.24:00 .. 06:00.)
---
END-TYPE LocalDeriver;
```

Such a policy could also have been defined in CurrProject.Rederiv_Policy (4.5.5).

5.2 Subtasking and Task Sequencing

The task-subtask hierarchy, as illustrated in figure 6, covers many different purposes.

Projects fit nicely into the task hierarchy due to the definition of Projects as a TaskEntity subtype. This implies that projects may be decomposed into subprojects, and that they have a limited lifespan.

Task transition chains can be used to describe phases or revisions of software components at a more detailed level:

- Horizontal life-cycles, such as (Requirements, Specification, Design, Implementation, Testing, Release, Delivery).

- Revision lines, such as edit, review and test operations on individual objects within a lifecycle phase. Status attributes with values such as (Initial, Experimental, ..., Finished, Integrated, Approved) are suitable for composites like a configuration.

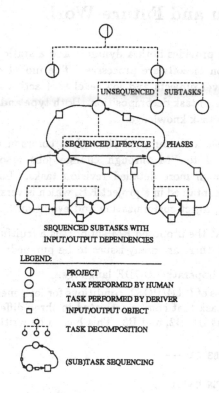

LEGEND:

○	PROJECT
○	TASK PERFORMED BY HUMAN
□	TASK PERFORMED BY DERIVER
▫	INPUT/OUTPUT OBJECT
⋮	TASK DECOMPOSITION
	(SUB)TASK SEQUENCING

Figure 6: General Subtasking

Below is an example of task modelling of a development task, with 5 subtasks of the requirements specification phase:

```
Project TYPE DevelopJob =
PRE                                            % Assumes existence
  Parent <> NIL ANDIF                          % of InformalReqSpec.
  Parent.InformalReqSpec.Status >= Experimental % Note '>='.
CODE
  ---
POST
     ALL(    rt:Children ! rt.TypeId SUBTYPE_OF ReqTask
        ANDIF rt.Status >= Approved)
  AND
     ALL(    tt:Children ! tt.TypeId SUBTYPE_OF TestTask
        ANDIF tt.TestLog.Status >=Approved)     % TestLog=produced doc.
  AND
     ALL(    dt:Children ! dt.TypeId SUBTYPE_OF DeliverTask
        ANDIF dt.Status = Finished)
```

```
DECOMPOSITION
  SEQ(ReqTask, ImplTask, TestTask, ReleaseTask, DeliverTask)
END-TYPE DevelopJob;
```

6 Conclusion and Future Work

The EPOS PM model provides both a dynamic and a static view of description, planning and execution of software processes. The model covers deriver tools, human actors, high-level projects and low-level tool activations, task transition networks, and project and task decomposition. Both type and instance hierarchies can be used to express task knowledge.

The CM and PM areas are connected through a common data model, EPOS-OOER. CM is coupled to PM through change jobs associated with config-descriptions, and through more detailed revision tasks. Likewise, PM-relevant control information is contained in a project KB, which is versioned (i.e. controlled by CM) to allow easy project customization and evolution.

All in all, we think that the proposed PM support is a fruitful basis for continued work in the area. Still, there are many issues to be pursued:

- A more powerful, imperative CODE language.
- The well-suitedness of PRE/POST-conditions for for general task synchronization. Consider a task that can be activated in three different ways, identified by PRE-conditions B1, B2, and B3. This has to be written as:
  ```
  PRE
    B1 OR B2 OR B3 OR ---
  CODE
    IF      B1 THEN Code1
    ELSEIF B2 THEN Code2
    ELSEIF B3 THEN Code3
    ELSE ---;
  ```
- More high-level type templates for task/tool patterns. See e.g. [ENE87] on graph grammars.
- A more generic and possibly dynamic data model, to avoid proliferation of trivial subtypes each time e.g. a new programming language is added. This resembles versioning of task types according to the current project.
- Better formalization of projects, and their workspaces for long transactions.
- Overall methodologies for project and process modelling.
- Better modelling of CASE-like meta-tools with internal tool policies.
- Planning: heuristics, intertwined planning and execution, knowledge representation, and KB support.
- Industrial scenarios and trial use.

Only a prototype EPOS implementation will be built in Trondheim, and only of the basic CM and PM system. On the other hand, CM has high priority within our industrial partners, Sysdeco and Veritas Research, so that future industrialization seems assured.

Acknowledgements

Thanks to P. Lavency et al. from Philips Research in Brussels on PM, and to J. Müller from the Techn. Univ. of Karlsruhe on the Planner design.

References

[AS88]   José A. Ambros-Ingerson and Sam Steel. Integrating planning, execution and monitoring. In *Proc. of AAAI'88*, pages 83-88, 1988.

[B*89]   K. Benali et al. Presentation of the ALF project. In *Prelim. Proceedings from Int'l Conf. on SDEF, Berlin, 9-11 May 1989*, page 23 p., May 1989.

[BE87]   Noureddine Belkhatir and Jacky Estublier. Software management constraints and action triggering in the ADELE program database. In *[NS87]*, pages 44-54, 1987.

[BL89]   Yves Bernard and Pierre Lavency. A Process-Oriented Approach to Configuration Management. In *[IEE89]*, 1989. 14 p.

[BLA88]   Roberto Bisiani, F. Lecouat, and Vinzenco Ambriola. A Planner for the automation of programming environment tasks. In *Proc. of the 21st Annual Hawaii International Conference on System Sciences*, pages 64–72, Hawaii, USA, January 1988.

[Bul87]   *PACT: The initial PACT Environment*. Bull, Louveciennes, France, September 1987.

[C*89]   Reidar Conradi et al. *EPOS Day Compendium – 1 Nov. 1989*. Technical Report, DCST, NTH, Trondheim, Norway, October 1989. NTH, 23 Oct 1989, 174 p.

[CDrG*89] Reidar Conradi, Tor Martin Didriksen, Bjørn Gulla, Håvard Eidnes, Even-André Karlsson, Anund Lie, Per Harald Westby, Svein Olav Hallsteinsen, Per Holager, and Ole Solberg. Design of the kernel EPOS software engineering environment. In *Proc. from Int'l Conf. on System Development Environments & Factories, Berlin*, May 1989. 16 p., Rev. Oct. 1989. Forthcoming as a Springer LNCS.

[Che76]   P. P.-S. Chen. The entity-relationship model — towards a unified view of data. *ACM Transactions on Database Systems*, 1(1):9–36, March 1976.

[Cle88]   Geoffrey M. Clemm. The Odin specification language. In *[Win88]*, pages 144-158, 1988.

[CW85]   Luca Cardelli and Peter Wegner. On Understanding Types, Data Abstraction, and Polymorphism. *Computing Surveys*, 17(4):471-521, 1985.

[DGS89]   Wolfgang Deiters, Volker Gruhn, and Wilhelm Schäfer. Systematic development of software process models. In *Carlo Ghezzi, John A. McDermid (Eds.): Proc. of ESEC'89 – the 2nd European Software Engineering Conference '89, Warwick, UK*, September 1989. Springer Verlag LNCS 387, p. 100-117.

[Dow87]   Mark Dowson. ISTAR and the contractual approach. In *Proc. of the 9th ACM-SIGSOFT/IEEE-CS Int'l Conference on Software Engineering, Monterey, CA, USA*, pages 287-288, April 1987.

[ENE87]   *Proc. 3rd Int'l Workshop on Graph Grammars and their Application to Computer Science*, Warrenton, VA, USA, 1987.

[GEC87]   *GENOS, GEC Software's IPSE*. GEC Software, London, UK, May 1987.

[HC88]   Dennis Heimbigner and Steven Crane. A graph transform model for configuration management environments. In *[Hen88]*, pages 216–225, 1988.

[Hen88]   Peter B. Henderson, editor. *Proc. of the 3rd ACM SIGSOFT/SIGPLAN Software Engineering Symposium on Practical Software Development Environments* (Boston, 28-30 Nov 1988), *257 p.*, November 1988. In ACM SIGPLAN Notices 24(2), Feb 1989.

[HM88]   Tani Haque and Juan Montes. A Configuration Management System and more (on Alcatel's PCMS). In *[Win88]*, pages 217-227, 1988.

[HN86]   A. Nico Habermann and David Notkin. GANDALF: software development environments. *IEEE Transactions of Software Engineering*, SE-12(12):1117–1127, December 1986. (Special issue on GANDALF).

[Hol88]   Per Holager. *Elements of the Design of a Change Oriented Configuration Management Tool*. Technical Report STF44-A88023, 95 p., ELAB, SINTEF, Trondheim, Norway, February 1988.

[IEE89]   IEEE/ACM, editor. *Proc. of the 11th International Conference on Software Engineering*, Pittsburgh, USA, May 1989.

[KF87]   Gail E. Kaiser and Peter H. Feiler. An architecture for intelligent assistance in software development. In *Proc. of the 9th ACM-SIGSOFT/IEEE-CS Int'l Conference on Software Engineering, Monterey, CA, USA*, pages 180–188, April 1987. (on MARVEL).

[LC89]   Chunnian Liu and Reidar Conradi. Planning Software Development Processes in EPOS. October 1989. In [C*89].

[LCD*89]   Anund Lie, Reidar Conradi, Tor M. Didriksen, Even André Karlsson, Svein O. Hallsteinsen, and Per Holager. Change Oriented Versioning in a Software Engineering Database. In *Proc. of 2nd Int'l Workshop on Software Configuration Management, Princeton, USA*, October 1989. ACM SIGSOFT Engineering Notes, Vol. 17, Number 7 (Nov. 1989), pp. 56-65.

[LDC*89]   Anund Lie, Tor M. Didriksen, Reidar Conradi, Even André Karlsson, Svein O. Hallsteinsen, and Per Holager. Change Oriented Versioning. In Carlo Ghezzi and John A. McDermid, editors, *Proc. of ESEC'89 – the 2nd European Software Engineering Conference '89, Warwick, UK*, pages 191–202, September 1989. Springer Verlag LNCS 387.

[Leh87]   M. M. Lehman. Process models, process programming, programming support. In *Proc. of the 9th ACM-SIGSOFT/IEEE-CS Int'l Conference on Software Engineering, Monterey, CA*, pages 14–16, March 1987. (Response to an ICSE'9 Keynote Address by Leon Osterweil).

[Lem86]   P. Lempp. Integrated computer support in the software engineering environment EPOS – possibilities of support in system development projects. In *Proc. 12th Symposium on Microprocessing and Microprogramming, Venice*, pages 223–232, North-Holland, Amsterdam, September 1986.

[Lie89]   Anund Lie. *Outline Design of the EPOS Database*. Draft, DCST, NTH, Trondheim, Norway, April 1989.

[Mey88]   Bertrand Meyer. Eiffel: a language and environment for software engineering. *The Journal of Systems and Software*, 199–246, 1988.

[Mul89]   Jürgen Müller. *Process Management Using AI Planning Techniques*. Technical Report 29/89, EPOS report 86, 117 p., DCST, NTH, Trondheim, Norway, June 1989. (MSc Thesis).

[NS87]   Howard K. Nichols and Dan Simpson, editors. *Proc. of the First European Software Engineering Conference* (Strasbourg, Sep 1987), LNCS *289* Springer Verlag, 404 p., September 1987.

[OR86]   Martyn A. Ould and Clive Roberts. Modelling iteration in the software process. In Mark Dowson, editor, *Proc. of the 3rd International Software Process Workshop*, Breckenridge, Colorado, USA, November 1986.

[Rei85]   Wolfgang Reisig. *Petri Nets – An Introduction*. Springer-Verlag, 161 p., 1985.

[Rum87]   James Rumbaugh. Relations as semantics constructs in an object-oriented language. In *Proc. of the ACM SIGPLAN Conference on Object-Oriented Programming Systems, Languages and Applications (OOPSLA'87)*, pages 466–481, Kissimmee, Florida, October 1987. In ACM SIGPLAN Notices 22(12), Dec 1987.

[Sun88]   *Network Software Environment: Reference Manual*. Sun Microsystems, Inc., 2550 Garcia Avenue, Mountain View, CA 94043, USA, part no: 800-2095 (draft) edition, March 1988.

[SWKH76] Michael Stonebraker, E. Wong, P. Kreps, and G. Held. The design and implementation of INGRES. *ACM Trans. on Database Systems*, 1:189-222, 1976.

[SZ86]   Andrea H. Skarra and Stanley B. Zdonik. The management of changing types in an object-oriented database. In *Proc. of the ACM SIGPLAN Conference on Object-Oriented Programming Systems, Languages and Applications (OOPSLA'86)*, pages 483–491, Portland, Oregon, 1986. In ACM SIGPLAN Notices 21(11), Nov 1986.

[TBC*88]   Richard N. Taylor, Frank C. Belz, Lori A. Clarke, Leon Osterweil, Richard W. Selby, Jack C. Wileden, Alexander L. Wolf, and Michael Young. Foundations for the Arcadia environment architecture. In *[Hen88]*, pages 1–13, 1988.

[TL82]   Dionysios C. Tsichritzis and Frederick H. Lochovsky. *Data Models*. Prentice Hall, 343 p., 1982.

[Win88]   Jürgen F. H. Winkler, editor. *Proc. of the ACM Workshop on Software Version and Configuration Control* (Grassau, FRG, 27-29 Jan 1988), *Berichte des German Chapter of the ACM, Band 30, 466 p.*, B. G. Teubner Verlag, Stuttgart, 1988.

A Communication Oriented Approach to Conceptual Modelling of Information Systems

Jan L.G. Dietz

University of Limburg
Faculty Economics and Business Administration
P.O.Box 616, 6200 MD Maastricht, The Netherlands

Abstract

Informata are introduced as a subclass of information systems. The SMARTIE framework is presented which supports the conceptual modelling of informata. The core of the framework is an automaton, which can be viewed as a generalization and an extension of the finite state machine, but which also draws on results of language philosophical research. A model of a system in this framework is called a communication model, as opposed to the conventional process model. Several techniques supporting the modelling and the specification of systems in the SMARTIE framework are presented. To demonstrate the practical applicability of the modelling principles, a traffic control system is taken as an example.

1. Introduction

The term "information system" is widely used nowadays to denote quite diverse things. E.g. an inventory control system is called an information system, but the particular way in which a marketing department of a company organizes the fulfillment of its information needs is also called an information system. Because not everything presented in this paper applies to all information systems, a subclass is delimited, which we prefer to call informata (singular: informaton).

An *informaton* (from *info*rmation and auto*maton*) is an information generating system, the operation of which is discrete and (potentially) completely specified. Non-determinism is allowed. Discrete means that only discrete information items are taken as input, and that the number of items generated in any finite time interval is finite. Although mostly informata are implemented using artefacts (computers), the incorporation of human beings is not excluded, provided their behaviour is prescribed and bounded to this prescription. For the remainder of the paper, the words "system" and "informaton" are considered to be synonym.

An informaton may be conceived to consist of a number of information producing units, which communicate by sending messages to each other. A model of a system in this respect is called a *process model*. A well-known process modelling technique is the DFD technique [5,12]. While this technique effectively supports the development of process models, it is not very well suited (and indeed is never meant to be) for the development of models at a higher conceptual level, at which the essential aspects of the communication between the units is abstracted from the particular way in which it is implemented. We will call this type of model *communication model* . The difference in abstraction level between a commmunication model and a process model of a system is comparable to the difference between a conceptual model and an internal model of a data base. The practical significance of a communication model is twofold.

Firstly, it describes the essential features of the communication relationships between units, such that there is precisely one communication model of every system, whereas there may be several process models corresponding to one communication model [3].

Secondly, it differentiates between pragmatic meanings of messages, as will be explained hereafter.

The communication between human beings by means of natural language is extensively studied in language philosophy, notably in [1] and [10]. One of the challenging outcomes of these studies for the field of informatics is that messages convey inseparably two things at the same time: the propositional *content* and the pragmatic *function* (effect, purpose). As an illustration, consider the next example messages:

1: "Mr. Smith wants to book a flight to Toronto"
2: "I will book a flight to Toronto for Mr. Smith"
3: "A flight to Toronto has been booked for Mr. Smith"
4: "Is there a booking of a flight to Toronto for Mr. Smith?"

The propositional content of all four messages is the same, viz. the booking of a flight to Toronto for Mr. Smith. However, their pragmatic functions are different. Message 1 conveys a *request*. The essence of a request is that the sender attempts to get the receiver to act in such a way that the proposition becomes true. Message 2 conveys a *promise*, the essence of which is that the sender commits himself to act in such a way as to make the proposition true. Message 3 conveys an *assertion*. The essence of an assertion is that the sender commits himself to the truth of the proposition. Message 4 conveys a *question*, the essence of which is that the sender attempts to elicit from the receiver as many information as is needed to conclude the truth or falseness of the proposition.

Several more pragmatic categories are distinguished in language philosophy.

However they are not relevant for our purposes, with the exception of one, viz. the *declaration* . Examples of declarations are "I herewith baptize you John" and the whistle-signal of the referee indicating the end of a soccer game. The difference between an assertion and a declaration is that an assertion is based on observing a situation while a declaration creates a situation itself. Messages of the declaration type illustrate pre-eminently that to a large extent the world is being made by language [1]. Searle distinguishes in this respect between 'brute facts' and 'institutional facts' [10].

Building on these language-philosophical basic outcomes we make two simplifications, which seem to be legitimated by our modelling purposes.
The first simplification concerns requests and promises. We assume the promise to grant a request implicit. In other words, the receiver of a request has not the option to refuse. The combination of a request and the corresponding promise is called an *order* . We envisage a collection of orders between two communicating actors, to which the sender can make changes. The receiver is compelled to execute these orders in due time.
The second simplification is that we assume the question related to an assertion implicit. The combination of a question and the corresponding assertion is called a *statement* . Furthermore, we envisage a collection of statements between two communicating actors, to which the sender can make changes. The receiver is able to inspect the contents of the collection at any time.
Although informata do not communicate in the way human beings do, one can take advantage of the language-philosophical analysis of communication acts in describing the communication between informata by distinguishing also between statements and orders.

In this paper a framework, called the SMARTIE framework, and some suitable techniques are presented for the development of communication models. In section 2 the basic characteristics of the framework are presented. Section 3 deals with the specification of the behaviour of a system, whereas the modelling of system structure is discussed in section 4. Section 5 contains a short evaluation of the presented material and some conclusions. As an illustrating example informaton throughout sections 3 and 4, a simple traffic control system is used. The next narrative description applies to it.
There is a simple road crossing having in each of the four directions traffic lights, as depicted in figure 1. The light signals in two opposite directions are identical.
In each direction a recurrent pattern of light signal changes can be observed :
...green - yellow - red - green - yellow .... These patterns are called cycles. Thus, there are only two different cycles in our example, called C1 and C2 (cf. figure 1). At any moment a cycle is in a particular phase (green, yellow or red). A more detailed description of a cycle as well as of the interdependencies between C1 and C2 is depicted in figure 2.
At some distance in front of a traffic light there is a traffic sensor. Every time a car passes such a sensor a signal is produced. If a car stops (for instance because the light is yellow or red) it covers the sensor, thus making it impossible for other cars to pass it.

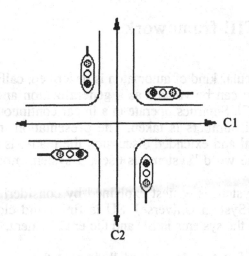

Figure 1. Picture of a simple road crossing with traffic lights

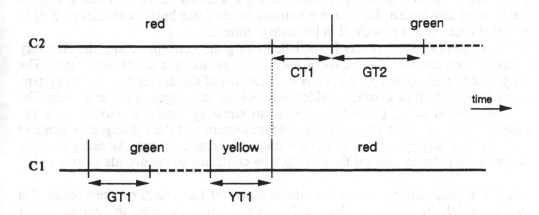

Figure 2. Cycles and their interdependecies

It takes a particular amount of time for a cycle to clear the crossing. From figure 2 it can be read that after cycle C1 goes into its red phase it takes CT1 (Clear Time) time units before cycle C2 goes into its green phase.

A green phase has a minimal duration of GT (GreenTime) time units. It is however prolonged always if there is no traffic asking to pass in the other cycle. The prolonged green phase is indicated in figure 2 by a dashed line.

Contrary to a red phase and a green phase, a yellow phase has a fixed duration. In figure 2 it is denoted by YT (YellowTime).

2. The SMARTIE framework

In this section a particular kind of automaton is described, called SMART automaton or smartie. A smartie can be viewed as a generalization and an extension of the finite state machine [7]. Smarties operate in a linear continuous time dimension, for which the set of real numbers is taken. The presentation in this paper is rather informal. For a formal and extended discussion the reader is referred to [3]. From now on, wherever the word "system" is used, a system modelled as a smartie is meant.

The operation of a system is easiest explained by considering the universe of all systems, called SU (System Universe). SU is finite and closed, so there are no relationships between the systems in SU and the environment.

The communication of statements is modelled using the concept of state. At every moment a system is in a particular state. A *state* is a set of propositions. The propositions p contained in a state are elements of the *state base* of the system, being the set of all propositions which may belong to a state of the system. The communication of a statement by a system to some system(s) is modelled as the generating of the statement $S(p)$ by the sending system and the subsequent change of the state of any system for which p belongs to the state base. A statement $S(p)$ is actual at time t if p is contained in the state at time t.

The communication of orders is modelled using the concept of agenda. At every moment a system has a particular agenda. An *agenda* is a set of pairs <p,t>. The propositions p contained in an agenda are elements of the *action base* of the system, being the set of all propositions which may belong to an agenda of the system. The communication of an order by a system to some system(s) is modelled as the generating of the order $O(p,t)$ by the sending system and the subsequent change of the agenda of any system for which p belongs to the action base. An order $O(p,t)$ is actual at the point in time t if the pair <p,t> is contained in the agenda at time t.

The set of propositions constituting the contents of the orders on the agenda of a system, which are actual simultaneously at some time t, is called the *action* for the system at time t. If there is a non-empty action, the system performs a *transition*, resulting in the production of a, possibly empty, finite set of statements, and a, possibly empty, finite set of orders.

The produced set of statements is called the *mutation* of the system. The contents of these statements are elements of the *mutation base*, which is the set of all propositions the system is able to generate as content of a statement. The generating of a statement instantly changes the state of any system for which the contained proposition belongs to the state base.

The produced set of orders is called the *reaction* of the system. The contents of these orders are elements of the *reaction base*, which is the set of all propositions the system is able to generate as content of an order. The generating of an order instantly changes the agenda of any system for which the contained proposition belongs to the action base.

The performance of a transition consists of the evaluation of a partial function, called the *transition base* of the system. A transition base can be denoted as a set of transitions <a,s,m,r>, where a is an action, s is a state, m is a mutation, and r is a reaction. For every pair <a,s> there is precisely one transition in the transition base. A transition <a,s,m,r> is said to be effectuated if the action of the system equals a and the state equals s. The effectuation yields a mutation m and a reaction r.

Below, a formal definition of the behaviour of a system is presented. In this definition, the powerset of a set X is denoted as $\wp X$, and the set of positive real numbers is denoted as $\Re^+$.

definition 1

The *behaviour* of a system is defined by a tuple $< S, M, A, R, T >$, where:

S : a set of propositions, called the *state base* ;
M : a set of propositions, called the *mutation base* ;
A : a set of propositions, called the *action base* ;
R : a set of propositions, called the *reaction base* ;
T : a partial function, called the *transition base* :
$$T \in \wp A * \wp S \rightarrow \wp(R * \Re^+) * \wp M;$$

Sometimes it appears more convenient to define T as $< TR, TM >$, where:

$$TR \in \wp A * \wp S \rightarrow \wp(R * \Re^+), \text{ called the } reaction\ function;$$
$$TM \in \wp A * \wp S \rightarrow \wp M, \text{ called the } mutation\ function;$$

(end definition 1)

Note that S,M,A and R may intersect in any way, as is illustrated in figure 3.

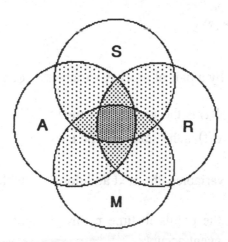

Figure 3. Illustration of the possible intersections of S,M,A and R

The performance of a transition is called an *event*. A sequence in time of events is called a *process* [3]. A process can be described fully by only two process variables. At a point in time t these variables are defined as the agenda and the state at time t. All other variables, which may be of interest, can be defined in terms of these two.

Below, a formal definition of the process of a smartie is provided. In this definition, the set of real numbers is denoted as $\Re$, and the set of natural numbers as $\aleph$.

definition 2

A *process* of a smartie is defined by a tuple $< S, M, A, R, T, I, E >$, where S, M, A, R and T are defined in conformity with definition 1, and where

$I = < IT, IS, IA >$, called the *initial conditions*, with

IT :   the *initiation time*, i.e. the start time of observing the process; $IT \in \Re$;

IS :   the *initial state*, i.e. the state at time IT; $IS \in \wp S$;

IA :   the *initial agenda*, i.e. the agenda produced internally before IT; $IA \in \wp(A * \Re)$;

$E = < ES, EO >$, called the *external influences*, with

ES :   the *external statements*; $ES \in \wp(S * \Re)$;

EO: the *external orders*; $EO \in \wp(A * \Re)$;

A *process* is described by a pair of process variables $< \phi, \sigma >$, where:

$\phi \in \Re \rightarrow \wp(A * \Re)$; $\phi(t)$ is the *agenda* at time t ;
$\sigma \in \Re \rightarrow \wp S$; $\sigma(t)$ is the *state* at time t;

In order to define these variables, the next additional variables are introduced :

$\tau \in \aleph \rightarrow \Re$;   the points in time τ_n are the only moments at which an event occurs; τ_n is a shorthand notation for $\tau(n)$;

140

$\mu \in \mathfrak{R} \rightarrow \wp M$;　　　　$\mu(t)$ is the *mutation* at time t;

$\alpha \in \mathfrak{R} \rightarrow \wp A$;　　　　$\alpha(t)$ is the *action* at time t;

$\rho \in \mathfrak{R} \rightarrow \wp(R * \mathfrak{R})$;　$\rho(t)$ is the *reaction* at time t;

The process variables can now be defined as follows:

$\tau_0 = IT$;

$\tau_{n+1} = \min \{ t \mid t > \tau_n \wedge \exists x : <x,t> \in ES \cup \phi(\tau_n) \}$;

$\phi(\tau_0) = IA \cup EO$;

$\phi(\tau_{n+1}) = \phi(\tau_n) \Delta \{ <x,t> \mid <x,t> \in \rho(\tau_{n+1}) \wedge x \in A \}$;

$\sigma(\tau_0) = IS$;

$\sigma(\tau_{n+1}) = \sigma(\tau_n) \Delta (\{ x \mid <x,\tau_{n+1}> \in ES \} \cup (\mu(\tau_{n+1}) \cap S))$;

$\mu(\tau_{n+1}) = TM(\alpha(\tau_{n+1}), \sigma(\tau_n))$;

$\alpha(\tau_{n+1}) = \{ x \mid <x,\tau_{n+1}> \in \phi(\tau_{n+1}) \}$;

$\rho(\tau_{n+1}) = \{ <x,t> \mid <x,t-\tau_{n+1}> \in TR(\alpha(\tau_{n+1}), \sigma(\tau_n)) \}$;

For $\tau_n < t < \tau_{n+1}$ holds: $\sigma(t) = \sigma(\tau_n)$; $\phi(t) = \phi(\tau_n)$; $\alpha(t) = \mu(t) = \rho(t) = \emptyset$;

(end definition 2)

The next event time τ is the next point in time at which an external statement or an external order or an internal order becomes actual.

The agenda ϕ is changed at a time τ by taking the symmetric set difference of the current agenda and the reaction ρ at time τ, as far as the elements of ρ belong to the action base. Initially the agenda contains the internally produced initial agenda and the external orders.

(Note. Actually, a change of the agenda is either the addition or the removal of an order. Consequently it would be necessary to distinguish between produced additions and produced removals, and to choose appropriate operations to deal with them. However, the symmetric set difference operation (denoted by Δ) appears to be a more convenient and elegant operation. The advantage of it is that adding and removing orders in order to arrive at the new agenda are performed in one go. The symmetric set difference of sets A and B is defined as: $A \Delta B = (A \setminus B) \cup (B \setminus A)$. End note.)

The state σ is changed at a time τ by taking the symmetric set difference of the current state and the union of the external mutation and the internal mutation, the latter as far as the propositions belong to the state base. Initially, the state is equal to IS.

The mutation μ at a time τ is the result of the application of the function TM to the actual action and the current state. At a time t between two successive points in time τ, $\mu(t)$ is empty.

The action α at a time τ is the set of propositions, which are the contents of the actual orders. At a time t between two successive points in time τ, $\alpha(t)$ is empty.

The reaction ρ at a time τ is the set of orders produced at that time. At a time t between two successive points in time τ, $\rho(t)$ is empty.

Because of the distinction between the communication of statements and the communication of orders, we accordingly distinguish between two kinds of influencing between systems, called conditioning and directing.

A system 1 is said to *condition* a system 2 if M1 and S2 do have a non-empty intersection. If this is the case, then every statement belonging to this intersection, produced by system 1, will change the state of system 2 instantly.

A system 1 is said to *direct* a system 2 if R1 and A2 do have a non-empty intersection. If this is the case, then every order belonging to this intersection, produced by system 1, will change the agenda of system 2 instantly.

The distinctive difference between conditioning and directing is that directing implies the triggering of a system to perform a transition, whereas conditioning does not do this. A system takes notice of communicated statements, i.e. of a state change, at some later point in time, namely when it is triggered and consequently needs to inspect its state.

3. Behaviour specification

The *specification* of the behaviour of a system consists of the specification of its five defining components: the state base S, the mutation base M, the order base A, the reaction base R, and the transition base T. The components S,M,A and R are specified by means of a proposition table, the component T is specified by means of a transition table.

3.1. The proposition table

First order logic appears to be a suited vehicle for expressing propositions, although there are alternative ways of specification. The advantage of logic is that it is well-defined and almost universally known. The major barrier to the use of logic seems to be the traditional Peano-Russell notation. Fortunately, friendlier and in some ways better notational forms are emerging (cf. [11]). The introduction of logic in this paper is rather informal. So a basic knowledge of first order languages (cf e.g. [9]) is assumed. A thorough discussion of the specification of systems can be found in [6].

A proposition is represented in first order logic by a ground atomic formula, or *atom* for short. By means of the usual logical operators (non-elementary) formulas can be composed out of atoms. Examples of atoms are:

flight_booking(toronto, mrs. adams, 890721)
cust_order(smith, bicycle, 20)

If the constants in the argument list of an atom are replaced by variables, the atom becomes an *atom type*. Atom types thus represent proposition types. A substitution of the variables of an atom type by constants yields an atom. The resulting atom is called an *instantiation* of the atom type. Analogously we distinguish between formulas and *formula types*.

Propositions are defined by means of a *proposition table*. Such a table contains an enumeration of atom types, and an indication as to which base(s) the propositions represented by their instantiations belong. Because the action base, the reaction base, the state base and the mutation base of a system may overlap in any way, several base indications may apply to the same atom type. Furthermore, a proposition table contains a narrative description of the meaning of the propositions.

Figure 4 shows the proposition table for the traffic control example. In the column "base" the base(s) are indicated to which the instantiations of the proposition types belong: A refers to the action base, S refers to the state base etc..

PROPOSITION TABLE		SYSTEM : traffic control
base	**atom type**	**semantics**
S	clear_time(C,CT)	the time neode to clear cycle C Is CT
S	green_time(C,GT)	the (standard) green time for cycle C is GT
A	let_pass(C)	a car has passed a traffic sensor in cycle C
S,M,A,R	phase (C,CLR)	the phase of cycle C is CLR (red, yellow or green)
S	yellow_time(C,YT)	the yellow time for cycle C is YT

Figure 4. Proposition table of the traffic control system

3.2. The transition table

The transition base T is specified by means of a *transition table*. Such a table comprises a set of *production rules*, each consisting of a data part and a facta part. (Note. 'Data' means 'what is given' and 'facta' means 'what is made or done'.)

The data part is further subdivided into an action part and a state part, both containing a formula type. The atom types, which figure in the action part represent proposition types, the instantiations of which are elements of the action base. The atom types, which figure in the state part represent proposition types, the instantiations of which are elements of the state base. A time reference may be added to an atom type in the state part, denoted by a negative number between rectangular brackets.

The facta part of a production rule also consists of two parts: the mutation part and the reaction part, both also containing a formula type. The atom types, which figure in the mutation part represent proposition types, the instantiations of which are elements of the mutation base. The atom types, which figure in the reaction part represent proposition types, the instantiations of which are elements of the reaction base. To every atom type in the reaction part a positive time delay is added between rectangular brackets.

The substitution of the variables in all atom types of a production rule by constants is called an *instantiation* of the rule. This takes place when the rule is *executed*, as a consequence of a triggering of the system. In order to guarantee that the atom types in the facta part can be instantiated, it is necessary to require that every variable in the facta part also figures in the data part.

The meaning of a production rule is based on the truth values of the constituent parts. The truth value of the action part is logically derived from the action at the time of execution. The truth value of the state part is logically derived from the state immediately before the execution. If a time reference is added to an atom type, a true instantiation yields the point in time at which it was added to the state. The truth value of the data part is the conjunction of the truth values of the order part and the state part.

The meaning of a production rule can now be defined as follows: if and only if the truth value of the data part for a given instantiation is true, the truth of the facta part is enforced.

The triggering of a system generally causes a number of parallel executions of production rule instantiations.

Firstly, there may be a number of true instantiations of the same rule. This may have two reasons. One is that there are two or more simultaneous actual orders of the same type. For instance, there may be two simultaneous orders of the type "let_pass(C1)", and even also at the same time one or two orders of the type "let_pass(C2)". The other reason is that the state part may contain variables, which do not figure in the action part. In that case, every substitution of these variables yielding a true state part, results into a separate instantiation of the rule.

Secondly, there may be true instantiations of two or more rules. For instance, there may be a "let_pass(C)" order and a "phase(C,CLR)" order at the same time.

Figure 5 shows the transition table for the traffic control system (for the sake of simplicity, only half of it is shown; by exchanging C1 and C2 the other half is got). A conjunction of formulas is denoted by a ",", and a disjunction by a ";". Negation, expressing the removal of a proposition, is denoted by "¬". For the denotation of constants and variables, the Prolog convention (cf. [2]) is adopted. The specification is considered to be self-explaining. Note that the occurence of an order "let_pass(C1)" leads to the execution of three rules, only one of which can succeed.

TRANSITION TABLE		PROCESSOR : traffic control	
DATA		FACTA	
action	state	reaction	mutation
let_pass(C1)	phase (C1, red), phase(C2,green)[-T], green_time(C2,GT2)	phase(C2,yellow) [+max(ε,GT2-T)]	
let_pass(C1)	phase(C1,red), phase(C2,red)[-T], clear_time(C1,CT1), green_time(C2,GT2)	phase(C2,yellow) [-T+CT1+GT2]	
let_pass(C1)	phase(C1,yellow)[-T], yellow_time(C1,YT1), clear_time(C1,CT1), green_time(C2,GT2)	phase(C2,yellow) [-T+YT1+CT1+GT2]	
phase(C2,yellow)	phase(C2,green), phase(C1,red), yellow_time(C2,YT2)	phase(C2,red)[+YT2]	¬phase(C2,green), phase(C2,yellow)
phase(C2,red)	phase(C2,yellow), phase(C1,red), clear_time(C2,CT2)	phase(C1,green)[+CT2	¬phase(C2,yellow), phase(C2,red)
phase(C1,green)	phase(C1,red)		¬phase(C1,red), phase(C1,green)

Figure 5. Transition table of the traffic control system

As an example we will elucidate the meaning of an instantiation of the first rule. It says that if a "let_pass" order is actual in cycle C1, and if at that time C1 is in its red phase and cycle C2 is in its green phase, then an order is generated which will try to change the phase of C2 to yellow. The moment at which this order will be actual depends on whether the green phase of C2 is prolonged or not. If it is, the order will be actual immediately (i.e. after the smallest possible amount of time ε). If it is not prolonged, it will be actual after the standard greentime of C2.

4. Modelling system structure

As we have seen, a system 1 and a system 2 communicate if there is a non-empty intersection of A1 and R2 or of A2 and R1, or if there is a non-empty intersection of S1 and M2 or of S2 and M1. The first case is called directing and the second one is called conditioning.

The communication relationships between systems can be made more intelligible if a set of systems is modelled as a smartienet. A *smartienet* is a network consisting of three kinds of components: processors, banks and channels. Four kinds of links are distinguished between these components. A smartienet provides a mechanical interpretation of the communication between systems.

The smartienet representation of a system consists of a processor (the kernel of the system) and a number of connected banks and channels. Figure 6 exhibits the symbolic representations of the components of a smartienet. A graphical representation of a smartienet using these symbols is called a *Communication Structure Diagram (CSD)*.

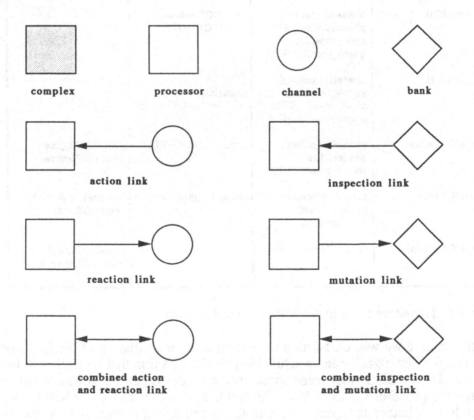

complex	processor	channel	bank

action link

inspection link

reaction link

mutation link

combined action
and reaction link

combined inspection
and mutation link

Figure 6. The components of a smartienet and the corresponding graphical symbols

Processors are executers of transitions. A processor represents the transition mechanism of a system. The operation of a processor therefore is defined by the system's *transition base*.

Banks serve to communicate statements. To this end, they are able to store statements (to be precise: the statements' contents are stored). The set of stored statements at some moment, is called the *contents* of the bank at that moment. The contents of a bank is updated and inspected by processors. A bank is defined by its *storage base* , which is the set of all propositions it is able to store as content of statements. The storage bases of the banks in a smartienet are disjoint.

Channels serve to communicate orders. To this end, channels are able to store orders (to be precise: pairs <p,t> are stored, where p is the order content and t the order time). The set of stored orders at some moment, is called the *contents* of the channel at that moment. The contents of a channel is updated and inspected by processors. When an order becomes actual the contained proposition is 'emitted'. A channel is defined by its *emission base*, which is the set of all propositions it is able to emit as content of orders. The emission bases of the channels in a smartienet are disjoint.

The being disjoint of the storage bases, the emission bases and the transition bases (cf. section 3) illustrates the conceptual quality of the smartienet. The important thing at the conceptual level is to discover and to show the essentially different kinds of communication among systems. Whether one chooses, for good reasons, to implement a transition base by means of multiple identical information processors, or to allow duplicate messages and data files for the implementation of channels and banks, is irrelevant from the conceptual point of view.

The reaction base of a system is equal to the union of the emission bases of its reaction channels. The action base of a system is equal to the union of the emission bases of its action channels. The action for a system at some moment consists of the union of the propositions emitted simultaneously by its action channels.
It is possible that a channel is action channel and reaction channel of a system as well. This case is called *self-directing* : the system is able to cause its own future transitions. In this way, for example, periodic activities can be modelled.

The mutation base of a system is equal to the union of the storage bases of its mutation banks. The state base of a system is equal to the union of the storage bases of its inspection banks. The state of a system at some moment consists of the union of the contents of its inspection banks.
It is possible that a bank is inspection bank and mutation bank of a system as well. This case is called *self-conditioning* : the system is able to inspect statements, which are produced by itself. (Note. Self-conditioning is the classical concept of the (internal) state of a system. End note.)

The CSD's of the conditioning and directing relationships between systems are pictured in figures 7. Processor 1 and processor 2 are the kernels of respectively a system 1 and a system 2. Channel c is called a *reaction channel* of system 1 and an *action channel* of system 2. Bank b is called a *mutation bank* of system 1 and an *inspection bank* of system 2.

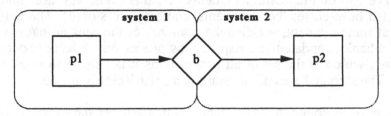

conditioning processor p1 conditions processor p2 through the interface bank b

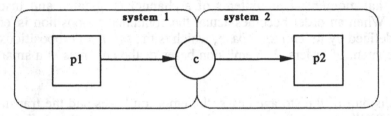

directing: processor p1 directs processor p2 through the interface channel c

Figure 7. The conditioning and directing relationships between systems

Figure 8 shows the CSD of the traffic control world. A world is defined as a system plus its environment. The environment of a system consists of the systems with which an interface exists. Two environmental systems are identified : "traffic" and "traffic control supervisor". The latter should be understood as the responsible person or organizational function. The system "traffic" directs the system "traffic control" by means of "let_pass" orders. The traffic control supervisor conditions traffic control by stating global control parameters like e.g. the duration of the yellow period. Traffic control conditions the traffic with respect to the phase each of the cycles is in. Apparently, it also uses this information for its own operation. The traffic control system directs itself through the local channel "phase changes".
The bank "parameters" contains statements of the type clear_time(C,CT), green_time(C,GT) and yellow_time(C,YT). The bank "phase" contains statements of the type phase(C,CLR).
The channel "let_pass" contains orders of the type let_pass(C) and the channel "phase changes" contains orders of the type phase (C,CLR).

The conceptual level of the SMARTIE modelling approach is apparent from the diagram of figure 8. For instance, the conditioning relationship from "traffic control" to "traffic" and to itself through the bank "phase" does not say anything, even not for the logical level, about how appropriate information flows, processes and stores should be designed in order to realize this relationship. A similar remark holds for the directing relationship between these two systems through the channel "let_pass". Of course, one is inclined to imagine respectively traffic lights and sensors in the road surface. However, it is important to realize that such imaginations are not suggested in any way by the smartie model or by the graphical expression of its structure in the form of the CSD in figure 8.

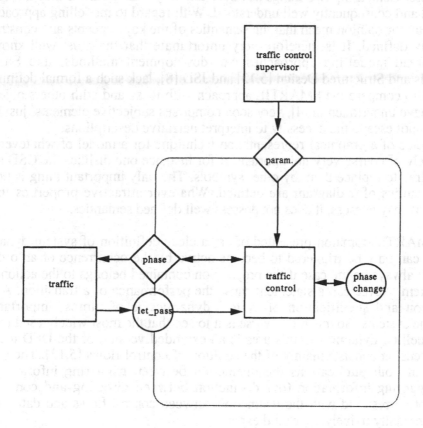

Figure 8. CSD of the traffic control world

5. Evaluation and conclusions

We have presented, be it in a concise way, the SMARTIE approach to systems modelling, and we have elaborated to some extent the specification of the behaviour of an informaton and the modelling of its structure.
It has been demonstrated that the modelling approach produces system models, which can rightly be called conceptual according to the definition of communication models provided in section 1. The clear distinction between conditioning and

directing as two essentially different kinds of communication between systems appears to lead in an almost natural way to true conceptual modelling. Discussions with many professional systems analists and designers affirm this.

A convincing way of introducing a new method or approach is to compare it with existing ones, especially well-known ones, and to reveal in doing so its strength and weakness. Comparing two things however can only make sense if they are both well defined and consequently well understood. With regard to modelling approaches this should to our opinion mean that the semantics of the key concepts and constructs are formally defined. It is therefore very unfortunate that the most well-known and widespread modelling approaches c.q. development methods, like Structured Analysis and Structured Design [5,12] and JSD [8], lack such a formal definition. An attempt to compare the SMARTIE approach with these and with others objectively, as we have undertoken in [4], very soon comprises subjective elements, just because one can not escape the necessity to interpret narrative descriptions.
The choice of a graphical representation technique for a model of whatever type is ultimately of course very unimportant. If for instance one dislikes the CSD symbols one is free to replace them by other symbols. The only important thing is how well the semantics of a diagram are defined. Whatever attractive properties the DFD technique may possess, it does not possess well defined semantics.

The SMART automaton presented offers a clear definition of system dynamics: a system can only be triggered to become active by the occurrence of an order, and this will always be the case if the proposition contained belongs to the action base of the system. Never can a statement cause the performance of a transition. A precise definition and specification of system dynamics is of utmost importance for real-time systems. So much the worse is it to see that the most widely used technique for modelling dynamics in this area is an extended version of the DFD technique. The extension consists mainly of the addition of control flows [5,12]. The sad thing is that in both publications the distinction between triggering information and non-triggering information (our distinction between directing and conditioning) does not correspond with the distinction between control flows and data flows, as one, apparantly naively(?), would expect.

The development of a practical method for the modelling and specification of systems is subject of current research. Future research topics include the formal derivation of system properties, and the development of suitable tools. Presently, only a prototype of a behaviour simulator in Prolog is available.

References

1. Austin, J.L., *How to do things with words*,
    Harvard University Press, Cambridge MA, 1962.

2. Bratko, I., *Prolog Programming for Artificial Intelligence*, Addison-Wesley Publ. Comp., 1986.

3. Dietz, J.L.G., A communication oriented approach to conceptual systems modelling, in: *Proceedings of the Int. Working Conf. on Dynamic Modelling of Information Systems*, Noordwijkerhout, The Netherlands, april 1990.

4. Dietz J.L.G., Houben, G-J., *A new system concept for conceptual systems modelling*, Research Paper, Eindhoven University, Netherlands, Dept. of Informatics, 1987.

5. Hatley, D.J., Pirbhai, I.A., *Strategies for Real-Time System Specification*, Dorset House Publishing, New York, 1987.

6. Hee, K.M. van, Houben, G-J., Dietz, J.L.G., Modelling of discrete dynamic systems; framework and examples, in: *Information Systems*, vol 14, no. 4, 1989.

7. Hopcroft, J.E., Ullman, J.D., *Introduction to automata theory, languages, and computation*, Addison-Wesley Publ. Comp., Inc., 1979.

8. Jackson, M., *System development*, Prentice-Hall International, 1983.

9. Lloyd, J.W., *Foundations of Logic Programming*, Springer Verlag, New York, 1984.

10. Searle, J.R., *Speech Acts*, Cambridge University Press, Cambridge, 1969.

11. Sowa, J.F., *Conceptual structures: Information Processing in Mind and Machine*, Addison-Wesley Publ. Comp., 1984.

12. Ward, P.T., Mellor, S.J., *Structured Development for Real-Time Systems*, Prentice-Hall Inc., 1985.

CORRECTION OF CONCEPTUAL SCHEMAS

C. SOUVEYET*,   C. ROLLAND**

*   Laboratoire MASI, Universite Pierre et Marie Curie
    4 place JUSSIEU, 75235 PARIS, FRANCE
    Fax : + 33-1-46-34-19-27

** Universite de la Sorbonne
    17 rue de la Sorbonne, 75231 PARIS cedex 05, FRANCE

Abstract :

This paper presents the interim results of a research project
aimed at the prototyping of an automatic tool, *Rubis*, to aid in
the development of,   validate and correct the conceptual
specification of information systems.

The Rubis systems allows a designer to specify an information
system using the Proquel language and to subsequently execute
the specification in order to prototype the design.

We present the control rules which enable the diagnosis of the
final specification, called an *R-Schema*, and describe the help
available to assist the designer in correcting mistakes and
anomalies detected during the diagnosis.

I Introduction

In this paper we introduce an environment called Rubis [ROL88] [LIN88b], which aims to aid the designer in designing information systems. The Rubis system provides the designer with:-

a model and associated high level development language, Proquel, to aid in the development of the specification of the R-Schema, specifying the static, dynamic and temporal aspects of the information system,

functions to determine the correctness of the R-Schema by running various checking rules on it, called the *Validation Module*

functions to assist in the correction of any errors highlighted by the checking phase, called the *Correcting Aid Module*

a prototyping mechanism allowing the execution of the specification on test cases, thus validating the dynamic aspects of the application. This is seen as an aid in improving the dynamic aspect of the final application,

various interfaces to modules implementing the above functions.

The paper is structured as follows:-

Part II discusses the Rubis architecture and functionality

Part III discusses the checking rule architecture, the checking rule taxonomy and the control levels used in checking the correctness of the R-Schema

Part IV discusses the Correcting Aid Module.

We conclude with a conclusion in Part V.

II Rubis Architecture and Functionality

As shown in figure 1, the Rubis system has four components as follows:-

1. The R-Schema: it describes the information system, and is stored in the Meta-base.

2. The R-Schema design interfaces: the Menu Interface, the Graphical Interface and the Proquel Interpreter.

3. The prototyping tools: the Application Monitor, the Event Processor, the Temporal Processor, and the Proquel Interpreter.

4. The validating tools:the Validation Module and the Correcting Aid Module.

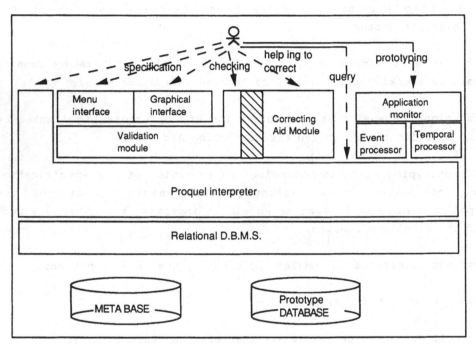

Figure 1 : Architecture of the Rubis system

II.1 The R-Schema

The R-Schema is based on the model used in the Remora methodology [ROLL.82] [ROLL.87], and describes both static aspects (structure) and dynamic aspects (behaviour) of the application. It is stored in relational form [COD.70] in the Meta_base, and is the focal point of interaction between the designer and the Rubis system.
The static aspects are modeled using objects, representing entities or entity associations in the real world (e.g. client, invoice, loan, etc.), and integrity constraints associated with these objects.

The constraints are classified in different classes; referential constraints, cardinality constraints, and domain constraints.

The _dynamic_ aspects are modeled using :
- _operations_ which represent elementary actions on an object (e.g. add a new client, modify an order, etc.),
- _events_ which represent elementary state changes in the system at which time some _operations_ must be triggered (e.g. when an order arrives, insert the order into the database, reserve the requested goods, prepare the delivery, etc.). The state change description of an object is defined in the _event predicate_.

A distinction is made between _external events_, which model the arrival of a message from the real world, _internal events_, which model elementary state changes of an object, and _temporal events_, which represent temporal conditions under which certain processing is triggered.

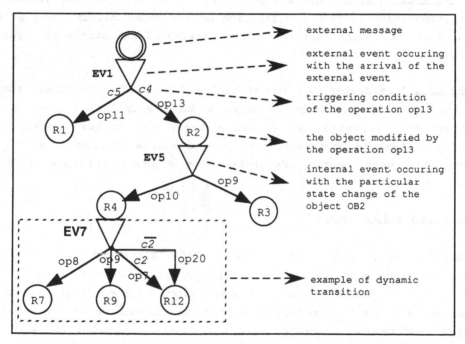

Figure 2 : a representation of a dynamic graph

The _Temporal aspects_ of the application are modeled using the temporal functions and types of the Rubis Temporal Model [NOB.88].
The R-Schema is therefore a collection of relations, events, and

operations defined for an application using Proquel specifications. The content of the R-Schema can be illustrated using a graph (Fig 2). Such a representation introduces the *dynamic transitions* of the application, showing their sequences and precedences. A dynamic transition is composed of (1) an event, (2) all operations triggered by the event, and (3) all references to objects modified by these operations. This corresponds to an elementary database transaction, since by definition a Rubis dynamic transition is atomic and must maintain database coherency across database coherency across database changes.

II.2 Design Tools

The Menu Interface allows the insertion, modification and deletion of different components of the R-Schema. Components are manipulated by the designer filling in forms during the specification process.

The Graphical Interface gives a great freedom to the designer during the acquisition stage of the specification of the R-Schema. It integrates a Graphical Editor which facilitates the drawing of the static and dynamic schemas.

The Proquel Interpreter is a design tool and a prototyping tool. Proquel [LIN.88a] is a specification language, a data manipulation language and a programming language. As a design tool, the Proquel Interpreter provides statements to insert, modify, and delete components of the R-Schema. The next section describes the Proquel interpreter as a prototyping tool.

II.3 Prototyping Tools

The Application Monitor allows the definition of the end-user interface. It automates the generation of data input screens, corresponding to each external event defined by the designer, from the specification text of these events. This text serves to specify the structure of the received message, and hence it may be used as a specification of the end-user screen. The associated event generated screens allow for the inputting of data test cases to test the correctness of the R-Schema behaviour.

The Temporal Processor manages all temporal aspects of the application, including :

-handling attributes of type 'TIME' (timestamps, dates, chronological order, calendar conversion, etc..),
-historical processing,
-evaluating expressions using temporal functions and types,
-automatic recognition of temporal events (absolute dates, periodic events, events times relative to other events, etc..).

The Event Processor drives the prototype. It facilitates the execution of the R-Schema by sequencing and synchronizing dynamic transitions, including :
-handling instances of external and temporal events,
-evaluating the triggering conditions of operations,
-controlling the execution of operations when the triggering condition is satisfied,
-recognition of internal event instances,
-managing the transaction aspects of the application.

The Proquel Interpreter is viewed here, as a prototyping tool. It is used by each of the other modules, but in particular by the event processor for the execution of operation, condition, and event predicate texts.

The relational DBMS [BOUF.86] is the foundation of the Rubis system. It manages the relations in the prototype database as well as the relations in the Meta-base containing the R-Schema.

II.4 The Validation Tools

The Validation Module performs the validation of the R-Schema, detecting situations which are either incorrect or probably incorrect.

The Correcting Aid Module aids the designer to correct the anomalies detected by the Validation Module.

R-Schema diagnosis requires a set of checking rules, which are presented in the next section. We, then describe two other aspects, the strategy used in anomaly detection, and the help provided to the designer in correcting these anomalies.

III The Checking Rules

The Validation Module is based on the set of checking rules to control the correctness of the R-Schema.

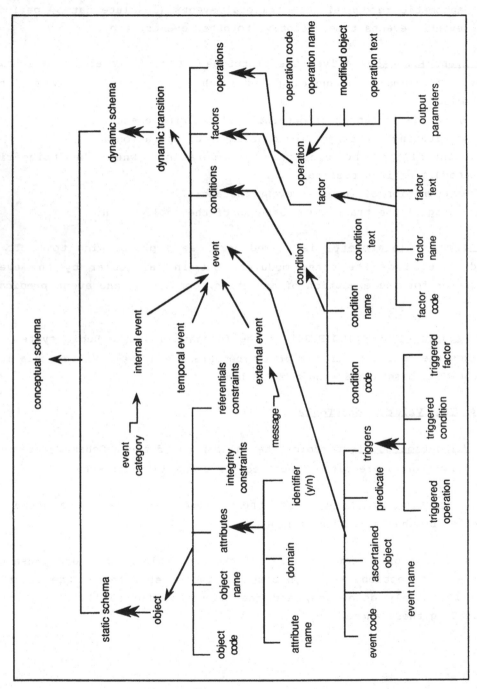

Figure 3 : Meta-Base design

The checking rule can be viewed as a predicate which must be satisfied by the R-Schema. In this section, we present the taxonomy of these rules, the implementation of them and the control levels at which they belong.

III.1 The Checking Rules Architecture

The aim of this architecture is to provide the Validation Module with the sequence of control rules to be checked at the requested level explained below (cf section III.4).

The strategy, we have chosen, is to model the static aspects of all components to be controlled and to associate to each component the set of checking rules which validate it. We have used on one hand, the aggregation, generalization and association constructors of semantic models [BRO.82] [BRO.83] [CAU.88] to model the static aspects of the R-Schema, whilst on the other hand, we have used the "encapsulation" notion defined in the object-oriented approach [PIN.88], to associate the checking rules to the component which they validate. The figure 3 illustrates the principal static part of the Meta-base which is checked.

For each constructor (aggregation, generalization and association), we define a checking rule strategy. Consequently, this hierarchical organization of components implicitly defines the control execution order. We illustrate this mechanism by an example of an "aggregate" component.
Consider the sub-set illustrated by the following figure :

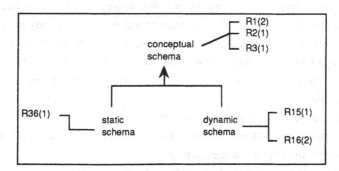

Figure 4 : representation of an aggregate component

This defines the component "conceptual schema" as an aggregate of two components "static schema" and "dynamic schema".

On the "static schema", we take the control rules which validate the static part without reference to the dynamic part. For instance, rule R36 is a method attached to "static schema" which expresses that **"when two objects have the same identifier, we must integrate both objects attributes in the only one object"**.

On the "dynamic schema", we take the control rules which validate the dynamic part without reference to the static aspects. For instance, the rules R15 and R16 express respectively that **"Each dynamic transition of an internal event must depend chronologically on an dynamic transition of an external or temporal event"** and **"When two dynamic transitions of internal events ascertain state changes of the same object, their predicates must be exclusive"**.

On the "conceptual schema", we take the rules which validate the relationship (or reference) between "static schema" and "dynamic schema". For instance, the rules R1, R2 and R3 are attached to "conceptual schema". The expression of these rules are :

R1 : **"Each object in the "static schema" must also exist in the "dynamic schema".**

R2 : **"Each object on which an event is ascertained, must be defined as an object in the static schema".**

R3 : **"Each object modified by an operation must be defined as an object in the static schema".**

The execution order of controls for "conceptual schema" is simply deduced from the component structure. We execute the control attached to the "static schema" and the controls attached to the "dynamic schema" in any order and when the components are correct, we execute the control of "conceptual schema" to validate the cross-references between "static schema" and "dynamic schema". We illustrate this mechanism by the following example.

If we define the following R-Schema :

-The objects OB1, OB2 and OB3 are described, but OB1 and OB2 have the same identifying attribute,

-Two events EV1 and EV2 are defined. EV1 is an external event which triggers the operation OP1 and EV2 is an internal event which ascertains the state change of the object OB2 and triggering the operation OP2.

-Two operations OP1 and OP2 are defined and they modify respectively OB1 and OB4.

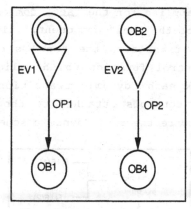

Figure 5 : The dynamic part of the R-Schema

The validation of the "conceptual schema" at level 2 will occur as follows:

We apply the rules attached to the components of the conceptual schema". Rule R36 is not respected on the "static schema" because OB1 and OB2 have the same identifying attribute and the rule R15 is not respected because the internal event EV2 does not depend on an external or temporal event. So, the "conceptual schema" is incorrect. If we correct this schema as follows :

-the event EV2 ascertains the state change of the object OB1, then the R-Schema satisfies rule R15,

-the changing of the identifying attribute of the object OB2 implies that it becomes different from the identifying attribute of OB1, then the R-Schema satisfies rule R36.

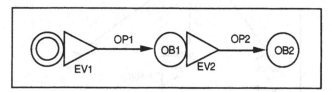

Figure 6: Graphical representation of the corrections

When we re-run the checking of the R-Schema, an error is detected by rule R3 because the operation OP2 modifies the object OB4 which is not defined as an object in the static part. If we correct the definition of the operation OP2 for modifying the object OB3, the "conceptual schema" becomes correct.

A similar approach, is applied for the "set" component and the "generic" component. In the case of the "set" component, illustrated by the figure 7, the checking module translates the "set" structure by on the one hand, the iterative control function which validate each set members (for instance, we check each "dynamic transition"), and on the other hand, the execution of controls attached to the "set" component (for instance, we check the correctness of "dynamic schema").

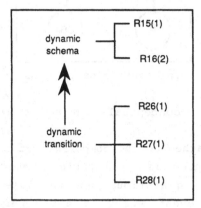

Figure 7 : Schema of a set component

The case of a "generic" structure, illustrated by figure 8, is more complex.

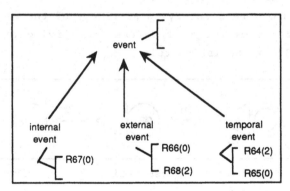

Figure 8 : Schema of a generic component

We attache to the "specialized" component the rules which allow the validation of :

    -its own components,

    -the relationships between them,

    -the relationships between the components of the "generic" item and the components of the "specialized" item which corresponds to it.

This structure is translated by a checking function which first runs the controls attached to the "generic" component (e.g. we check the component "event") and then the controls attached to the "specialized" component which corresponds to it (e.g. we check the "specialized" component "internal event" or "temporal event" or "external event").

The advantages of this architecture are :
  -it provides a control triggering strategy which is systematic and modular,
  -Rubis model extensions or Meta-base improvements are easily integrated into the Validation Module as a direct result of the flexible representation.
  -the performed controls are independent of what interface is used to input the part of R-Schema, so the Rubis architecture can integrate new interfaces without any modification of the Validation Module.

III.2 Rule Taxonomy

We distinguish four rule classes :
  - conformance rules,
  - consistency rules,
  - completeness rules,
  - accuracy rules.
This taxonomy is similar to that found in TODOS [PER.88].

Conformance rules : perform the "syntactic" checking of the R-Schema. We means by this term the syntax of the model and the specification language.

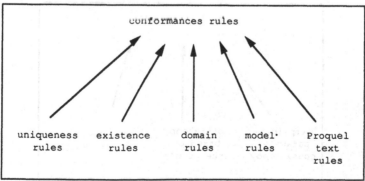

Figure 9 : Hierarchy of conformance rules

In this class, we can see five sub-classes shown by the previous figure.

Uniqueness rules : verify the uniqueness of a schema component. For instance, **"the event code must be unique in the set of event codes"** or **"the attribute name of an object must be unique in the set of object attribute names"**.

Existence rules : check that each R-Schema component is defined. For instance, **"the name of the object which is modified by the operation must be defined in the operation specification"**.

Domain rules : check the value of a schema component according to the domain definition. For instance, **"An event type is either 'internal event' or 'external event' or 'temporal event'"** and **"an operation type is either 'INS' or 'UPD' or 'DEL'"**.

model rules : correspond to cardinality rules between components of the R-Schema. For instance, **"an event must trigger at least one operation"** or **"an operation must modify at most one object"**.

Proquel text rules : express that for each component of the R-Schema expressing Proquel text, must be correct according to the syntax of the Proquel language. In other words that means these texts must be validate by the Proquel Interpreter. For instance, **"an event predicate must be correct according to the Proquel syntax"**.

Consistency rules : check that there is no contradiction in the specifications and that no contradiction can be deduced from the R-Schema.

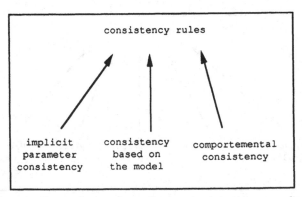

Figure 10 : Hierarchy of the consistency rules

We can decompose this class as the hierarchy illustrated by the following figure.

We present three examples of consistency rules.

The first is associated to the notion of "CONTEXT" in Proquel. We use the implicit parameter "CONTEXT" to refer to the object instance on which an event can be ascertained. The following control can be expressed : **"each field prefixed by "CONTEXT" and used in the operation text must correspond to an attribute of the object on which the event triggering operation is ascertained"**. This rule belongs to <u>"implicit parameter consistency"</u> sub-class.

The second example can be seen, for instance, when an object is accessed with modify statements in condition text, whereas **"a condition text should not modify an object's state"**. This control checks the consistency between the content of Proquel condition text and the condition definition in the model. It belongs to the sub-class <u>"consistency based on the model"</u>.

The last case is deduced from the specification when we can have contradictory behaviours of the application in the same specification. This defines the <u>"comportemental consistency"</u> sub-class. As an example of this sub-class, consider the following R-Schema illustrated in figure 11 : in the dynamic transition of the event, an unconditional operation OP1 sets an attribute of OB1 to 2, whereas another unconditional operation OP2 sets the same attribute to 5.

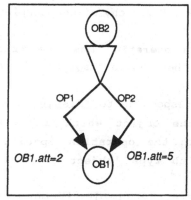

Figure 11 : graphical representation of dynamic transition

Rubis does not recognize execution order between operations belonging to the same dynamic transition. The execution of OP1 before that of OP2, or of OP2 before that of OP1, or their parallel execution must give the same result. It is evident, in this example, when EV1 is fired, the final value of "att" depends on the execution order of OP1 and OP2. The indeterminate result of the dynamic transition is a proof of specification inconsistency. The following rule detects this kind of inconsistency :

R31 : **"When an object instance is modified by more than one operation in the same dynamic transition, the triggering conditions must be mutually exclusive"**.

The detection of these types of inconsistencies can not be automated from the Proquel specification as they are data dependent. This is an interactive rule which can not be implemented using the Proquel language because we want to use a graphical way to explain the situation to the designer.

Completeness rules : verify that there is no isolated or missing component of the R-Schema. We propose the decomposition of this class as follows :

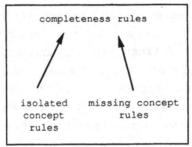

Figure 12 : Hierarchy of the completeness rules

For example, **"an operation must be triggered by at least one event"**. This rule belongs to <u>"isolated concept rule"</u> sub-class.

Another case corresponding to <u>"missing concept rule"</u> sub-class is, **"the name of the object which is modified by an operation and mentioned in the operation specification must be defined as an object with type 'object'"**.

Accuracy rules : detect probable inconsistencies in the R-Schema concerning the accuracy of the specifications as they relate to the application.

These rules point out some critical situations to the designer enabling them to be examined in more detail, thus determining whether or not these situations to the designer are in fact correct.

For example, the vivacity of a dynamic graph is a notion taken from the quasi-vivacity of Petri Net Theory [BRA.83], [BER.79]. This control is expressed by the rule R11 **"each operation that may be triggered by an event may be processed"**. We define a *dynamic transaction* as the dynamic transition of an external or temporal event, and with the dynamic transitions of subsequent internal events depending chronologically on the dynamic transition of the preceding event. The rule is checked by presenting each dynamic transaction to the designer and confirming the occurrence feasibility of each internal event and each operation belonging to this dynamic transaction.

Let us consider a second example, the analysis of the *dynamic circuits*. A dynamic circuit is defined by the following rule : **"when an event depends chronologically on itself, we detect a dynamic circuit. It is 'infinite', if the sequence of related events is infinite. This happens when all the operations belonging to this circuit are unconditional and when event predicates are always true after the operation execution. The infinite circuit is not necessarily incorrect but it is forbidden in the Rubis system because it can not be prototyped"**. This rule is checked by presenting each dynamic circuit to the designer and its correctness being confirmed.

III.3 Implementation of these rules

We have tried to limit the programming work with the definition of the generic type according to the hierarchy as presented previously. For example, consider the hierarchy of the completeness rules illustrated by figure 12. In our case, the "is-a" hierarchy expresses more the genericity notion issued from abstract data typed languages like ADA [BAR.88] [BOO.88] than inheritance notion coming from object-oriented languages as Smalltalk [PIN.88] [MEY.88].

So, the "Missing Concept" rule and "Isolated Concept" rule are two generic types of rule on which we associate a program model representing the rule. Then, we adapt this program model to the particular situation of R26, for example, by instantiation of input parameters defined in this program model described below.

The program model is a Proquel function as shown in figure 13.

```
FUNCTION missing_concept_rule ($type_mc : STRING,
                              $relation_mc : RELATION_NAME,
                              $attribute_mc : ATTRIBUTE_NAME,
                              $type_wmc : STRING,
                              $relation_wmc : RELATION_NAME,
                              $attribute_wmc : ATTRIBUTE_NAME,
                              $attribute_id_wmc : ATTRIBUTE_NAME)
VAR $result : BOOLEAN;
VAR $x : TUPLE;
BEGIN
FOR EACH $x IN (SELECT [$attribute_wcm], [$attribute_id_wcm]
                FROM [$relation_wcm])
  DO BEGIN
      IF (NOT EXISTS [$relation_mc]
              WHERE [$attribute_mc]=[$x.attribute_wmc])
        THEN BEGIN
              $result:=FALSE;
                affichage_erreur($type_mc,$x.attribute_wmc,
                                 $type_wmc,$x.attribute_id_wmc);
              END;
        ELSE $result:=TRUE;
    END;
  RETURN ($result);
END;
```

[$y] : corresponds to the value of the variable $y

Figure 13 : Proquel Function of the "Missing Concept" rules

The following defines the meaning of the input parameters of the program model in figure 13 :

- **$type_mc** represents the type of the 'missing concept',
- **$relation_mc** represents the Meta-base relation (or table) where the 'missing concept' ($type_mc) is stored,
- **$attribute_mc** represents the identifier attribute of the previous relation ($relation_mc),
- **$type_wmc** represents the type of the 'concept' which refers the 'missing concept' ($type_mc),
- **$relation_wmc** represents the Meta-base relation where the previous concept ($type_wmc) is stored,
- **$attribute_wmc** represents the attribute which refers the 'missing concept' ($type_mc) in the previous relation ($relation_wmc),
- **$attribute_id_wmc** represents the identifier attribute of the relation represented by $relation_wmc.

The program corresponding to the rule R26 consists to the following instantiation :

- $type_mc : **'operation'** is the missing concept,
- $relation_mc : **'ope'** is the Meta-base relation name where is stored all the operations,
- $attribute_mc : **'opn'** is the attribute name in the relation 'ope' which represents the operation code,
- $type_wmc : **'event'** is the concept where 'operation' is referred and misses,
- $relation_wmc : **'trigger'** is the Meta-base relation name where are stored the operations triggered by events,
- $attribute_wmc : **'opn'** is the attribute name in the relation 'trigger' which refers the operation triggered by a given event,
- $attribute_id_wmc : **'evtn'** is the attribute name in the relation 'trigger' which represents the event code.

We apply this principle for all rules which are automated and we use the Proquel language to implement these rules.

III.4 Control Levels

In this section, we present the definition of three control levels according to three successive development stages of the R-Schema. Then, we describe how we trigger these different levels.

The basic principle which must be respected by the Validation Module is to accept the incomplete specifications because the design process is incremental. Nevertheless, a satisfying level is insured at certain development stages of the R-Schema. We have determined the three following levels :

Level 0 is the imposed level on all the specification interfaces. We have chosen to trigger only a sub-set of conformance rules for keeping the flexibility of each interface given to the designer. For instance, if we define an operation which modifies the object OB2 and OB3, the rule which says that **"an operation modifies only one object"**, is not respected. In this case, the zeroth level of control is not verified.

169

Level 1 corresponds to the development of the complete conceptual schema where all the executable texts of condition, operation, factor and event predicate are not necessary defined. We check here :
  -the conformance rules which do not belong to the previous level and
   do not concern executable texts,
  -the completeness rules which do not concern executable texts,
  -the consistency rules which do not need executable texts.
For instance, consider the R-Schema where an operation modifies the object OB1, is defined and this operation is not triggered by any event. This incorrect feature is detected by the rule R26 which expresses that **"an operation must be triggered at least by one event"**. This incompleteness is recognized at this level.

Level 2 corresponds to the development of the executable complete conceptual schema. At this level, all the checking rules based on executable Proquel texts are run, in addition to the rules of the preceding levels. For instance, consider the R-Schema where the object OB1 used in the text of the condition C2, is not defined. This error is detected at this level by the rule R30 which expresses that **"each object used in the text of condition must be defined"**.
Each higher level subsumes the lower levels. The triggering of the different level controls is either automatic or when the designer wants to check the R-Schema.

Level 0 checking is automatically performed when an specification is entered with any design interface. The level 2 checking is either automatically performed when the designer activates the prototyping tools or when the designer wants to check the specification. Level 1 checking is performed when the designer wants to check the R-Schema. Levels 1 & 2 can check the entire R-Schema or just a part of it. The set of controls can be decomposed to the controls on the static or dynamic schemas.

IV Correcting Aid Module

We limit this section to the presentation of the basic principles of the correcting help provided to the designer in the Rubis system and to the brief presentation of the organization of the suggested corrections.

The aim is to assist the designer to correct the errors of the R-Schema highlighted by the checking module.

In general, it is possible to identify two causes of errors, a misunderstanding of the theory underlying and a bad implementation of this theory. The Correcting Aid Module integrates two kinds of help corresponding to two errors classes :

-if <u>a misunderstanding of the Rubis model concepts or Proquel language constructions</u> is the cause of errors, we help the designer by giving the concept definition corresponding to the detected error and providing a set of examples and a set of exercises for correcting the situation. This solution is taken from the "tutoring software" in which the learning strategy is composed of three items: **definitions, examples and exercises** [LEF.84]. We provide this help for each checking rule. For the errors detected by the conformance rules, this help allows to the the designer to correct the R-Schema. This is provided when the designer requests it because of a failure to understand the reasons for the highlighted error.

-<u>if a bad design or bad usage of model concepts</u>, is the cause of errors, we help the designer by the answer to the following question:
What are the changes to be made to correct this situation ?
For each detected error, we suggest to the designer **a set of possible corrections**. The designer can choose one of them or refuse the proposed suggestions. This help is provided when the designer requests it because of the failure to understand how to correct the situation.

For implementing the suggested corrections, we apply the same approach used to implement the checking rules. We use the hierarchy of rules described previously (cf section III.2) and we define for each generic type of rules a set of possible corrections which is implemented by a model program. This model program will adapt to the particular mistakes detected by the checking rules by the different values taken by the input parameters.
We illustrate this approach by the example of the completeness mistakes. The hierarchy of the completeness mistakes is the same as that of completeness rules : "missing component" mistakes and "isolated component" mistakes.
When we have a mistake detected by the "missing component" rule, we can suggest two possibles corrections :
    -if the missing component is useful, we define it,

-if the component may cause a referential error by erroneously referring to a non existent component, so we correct the reference.

We can adapt this general situation with the different values of the following input parameters to the mistake detected by a checking rule :
- *tm* : type of the missing component,
- *itm* : instance of the type defined by *tm*,
- *tom* : type of component where tm is referred,
- *itom* : instance of the type defined by *tom*,
- *trel* : type of the relationship between the types *tm* and *tom*.

Let us consider the sub-set of the R-Schema where is defined :

-the objects OB1 and OB3,
-the internal event EV1 occurring on the state change of OB1 and triggering the operation OP1 shown in following figure 14,
-the operation OP1 modifying the object OB2.

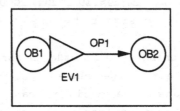

Figure 14 : Dynamic graph of the R-Schema

A mistake is detected by the rule R2 because the object OB2 modified by the operation OP1 is not defined. Each mistake detected by the rule R2 is adapted from the general situation by the following instantiation :
-the type of the missing component (tm) = 'object',
-the type of the component where 'tm' is referred (tom) = 'operation',
-the type of relationship between 'tm' and 'tom' (trel) = 'modified by'.
In our particular mistake, we adapt the help associated to the rule R2 with the following values of the input parameters :
-the instance of the missing object (itm) = 'OB2',
-the instance of the operation where the object is referred (itom) = 'OP1'.
So, we apply this approach for all mistakes detected by the Validation Module.

V Conclusion

In this paper, we have presented the Rubis system which provides :
   -a model and a specification language to aid in the development of
   the specification of the R-Schema,
   -a module to determine the correctness of the R-Schema,
   -a module to assist in the correction of any mistake detected by the
   previous module,
   -a prototyping mechanism to allow the execution of the specification
   on test cases,
   -various interfaces to input the specification in the Rubis system.

We have discussed in more detail the checking rule architecture and the
checking rules taxonomy. Then we have presented the principles of the
Correcting Aid Module.
These two modules are integrated in the Rubis system implemented in the
SUN 3/60 workstation.
The perspective of this work is, on the practical way, to achieve the
implementation of these two modules and, on the theorical way to improve
the Correcting Aid Module to the architecture of "intelligent tutoring
software" [NIC.88] where the module adapt the help to the designer which
uses it. Our goal is also to integrate more checking rules in the
Validation Module like the quality heuristics for R-Schema improvements
or checking rules based on the knowledge of the application domain
described in [WOH.88].

ACKNOWLEDGEMENTS : We wish to thank Bob Jansen for reading and
commenting this paper.

REFERENCES :

   [BAR.88] BARNES J. : "Programmer en ADA" , InterEditions (ed), 1988.

   [BER.79] BERTHOMIEU B. " Analyse structurelle des réseaux de PETRI :
            méthodes et outils ", Thèse de Docteur Ingénieur, Toulouse,
            1979.

   [BOO.88] BOOCH G. : "Ingéniérie du logiciel avec ADA, InterEditions
            (ed), 1988.

   [BOU.86] BOUFARES F.,ELKABBAT J., JOMIER G.,OUNALLY H. : " Le
            système de Bases de Données Relationnelles PEPIN3", Rapport
            de Recherche ISEM N°34, Univ. PARIS SUD, Mai 1986.

   [BRA.83] BRAHMS : " Théorie et pratique des réseaux de PETRI",
            Masson (ed) 1983.

[BRO.82] BRODIE M.L., SILVA E. : "Active and Passive Component Modelling : ACM/PCM", in [CRI.82].

[BRO.83] BRODIE M.L. : "On the development of Data Models", in On Conceptual Modelling, Perspectives from Artificial Intelligence, Databases, and Programming Languages, Edited by Brodie M.L., Mylopoulos J., Smidt J.W., Springer-verlag,1983.

[CAU.88] CAUVET C. : " Un modèle et un outil d'aide à la conception des systèmes d'information ", Thèse de doctorat de l'université Paris VI, 1988.

[CRI.82] " Information Systems Design Methodologies : a comparative Review", Olle T.W., Sol H.G., Verrijn-Stuart A.A. (eds), North-Holland (pub), 1982.

[LEF.84] LEFEVRE J.M. : " Guide pratique de l'E.A.O.", Cedric Nathan, 1984.

[LIN.88a] LINGAT J-Y., COLIGNON P., ROLLAND C. : "Rapid Prototyping : the PROQUEL Language", Proc. of the 14 th VLDB Conference, Los Angeles, 1988.

[LIN.88b] LINGAT J-Y : " RUBIS : un système pour la spécification et le prototypage d'applications Bases de Données ", Thèse de doctorat de l'université Paris VI, 1988.

[MEY.88] MEYER : " Objected-Oriented Software Construction ", Interactive Software Engineering, 1988.

[NIC.88] NICAUD J.F., VIVET M. : "Les tuteurs intelligents : réalisation et tendances de recherche", TSI Vol 7, 1988.

[NOB.88] NOBECOURT P., ROLLAND C., LINGAT J-Y. : " Temporal Management in an Extended Relational system ", BNCOD6. Conference, England, July 1988.

[ROLL.82] ROLLAND C., RICHARD C. : " The REMORA Methodology for Informatiion systems Design and Management " in [CRI.82].

[ROLL.87] ROLLAND C., FOUCAUT O., BENCI G. : " Conception des systèmes d'information : la méthode REMORA ", Eyrolles (ed), 1987.

[ROLL.88] ROLLAND C., CAUVET C., NOBECOURT P., PROIX C., COLIGNON P.,LINGAT J-Y., SOUVEYET C. : " The RUBIS system ", CRIS88, Computerized Assistance during the Information System Life Transition, September 1988.

[SMI.77a] SMITH J.M., SMITH D.C.P. : " Database Abstractions : Aggregation", Comm. of ACM, Vol 10, n°6, 1977.

[SMI.77b] SMITH J.M., SMITH D.C.P. : " Database Abstractions : Aggregation and generalization", ACM Trans. on Database Systems, Vol 2, n°2, 1977.

[WOH.88] WOHED R. : "Diagnosis of conceptual schemas", IFIP WG2.6/WG8.1 Working Conference on "the role of Artificial Intelligence in Databases and Information Systems", Canton, July 1988.

A Natural Language Interpreter for the Construction of Conceptual Schemas

Leone Dunn and Maria Orlowska

Key Centre for Software Technology
Department of Computer Science
The University of Queensland
St. Lucia, Q.4067 Australia

ABSTRACT

The problem of designing a relational database for an information system is a complex one; it involves the analysis of an informal, and often incomplete, statement about some enterprise and then formal application of the established theories.

This paper describes the first phase of the design of a natural language interpreter for constructing NIAM (Nijssen's Information Analysis Method) conceptual schemas. The entire system is intended as a tool for modelling relational databases. The analyst interacts with the system about a particular Universe of Discourse (UoD) using example sentences in natural language. From the example input, the system constructs the conceptual schema of a particular UoD. During the process, the analyst may subsequently retrieve and alter the information until the conceptual schema design phase is complete. The model is used to construct the relational database. The first phase of the system described in this paper constructs a 'first pass' at elementary fact types, the basic units of knowledge representation in NIAM. This involves the following:

- allocating entity type names and role names on the basis of sentence instances supplied by the analyst;

- automatic support for splittability decision, the key factor in determining elementary fact types.

1. Introduction

The problem of designing a relational database is a complex one. Not for nothing is the Universe of Discourse (UoD) represented as a cloud. Not for nothing have information systems researchers spent the past fifteen years or so developing conceptual theories to formalize this cloud. For example, the E-R model[1] and NIAM[2].

If we take NIAM for instance, there are also a number of precisely defined steps that guide the analyst through the conceptual schema design phase of the paper model. Even then, the analyst has problems in going from the unstructured definition of a UoD to the identification of the basic units of information in NIAM namely, the identification of elementary fact types and their component parts - entity types and roles. (It is assumed the reader is familiar with NIAM. Otherwise they are referred to [2]).

For example, the following sentences describe a very limited UoD:

(1)   Wirth wrote Pascal in 1975.

(2)   Smith migrated to Australia in 1925.

Allocating the surface objects *Pascal, Australia, 1975/1925* to entity types (semantic classes) e.g. **language, country, date,** is problematic. The decision as to whether *Wirth* and *Smith* are common entity types is more difficult. Whether these objects should be allocated to a common semantic class, such as *person*, or whether they should be allocated to separate classes, such as *creator* and *migrator*, depends on the context of a particular UoD.

Assuming that type allocation has been successful, another problem is determining whether the fact types, *person wrote language in date* and *person migrated to country in date*, are elementary, or whether they are splittable into smaller semantic units. Neither syntactic nor semantic criteria alone can determine splittability. The same fact types could be splittable in one UoD but not in another. The decision as to whether a fact type is splittable depends on other factors, namely whether a referent is unique and specific in a particular UoD.

The major issue in designing the interpreter was to provide a simple, easy-to-use facility that assists the expert through these initial difficult stages of conceptual schema design as automatically as possible, though some user interaction is necessary. Other major factors influencing the design were:

*   The system is intended as a tool for designing real life (and often very large) databases. It is not intended as an experimental toy;

*   The system is domain-independent. It is intended that the system can be used for designing conceptual schemas for any UoD;

*   Natural language is the means of interaction with the system. Natural language was chosen because it frees the applications expert from having to learn the complexities of

every new CASE tool that becomes available.

The research area focussing on database design tools is currently very active[3]. One tool designed specifically for constructing NIAM conceptual schemas is the Semantic Data Dictionary (SDD). The SDD assumes as a starting point the existence of the elementary fact type. The major part of this research is aimed at assisting the analyst in the identification of elementary fact types and therefore does not overlap.

2. System Architecture

The main function of the interpreter is to assist the expert in designing a relational database for an information system by means of the NIAM conceptual schema. It allows the user to define the UoD using (a subset of) natural language. It provides automatic support for the determination of uniqueness constraints and for the splittability decision, the key factors in determining elementary fact types. It assists the user in solving the problem of naming conventions (common entity types and roles), another key factor in determining elementary fact types. It also provides automatic support for selecting the derived fact types from the set of elementary fact types. Once the elementary and derived fact types have been established, the relational tables can be automatically created. Therefore, the system is conceptually divided into the following modules. The Type Allocation Module, the Elementary Fact Type Construction Module, the Naming Convention Module, The Derived Fact Type Construction Module, and the Relational Database Construction Module. Figure 2-1 shows the overall structure of the system.

The Type Allocation Module and the Elementary Fact Type Construction Module are described in this paper.

3. The Natural Language Interpreter

The core of the Type Allocation Module is the natural language interpreter. Like most natural language processing systems, the interpreter was designed for a specific task, namely, the construction of NIAM conceptual schemas. Because of the nature of the task, ie the fact that the the system is domain-independent, requiring the interpreter to engage in knowledge acquisition where the input is almost always unknown, existing theories and methodologies commonly used in natural language processing systems could not be used in the present system.

3.1. Background Issues

Natural language processing (NLP) is one of the oldest areas of artificial intelligence (AI) research. In recent years, a lot of research has been undertaken on context-based disambiguation. That is, the use of context to disambiguate sentence and text meaning for language interpretation[4][5] and utterance-planning [6][7].

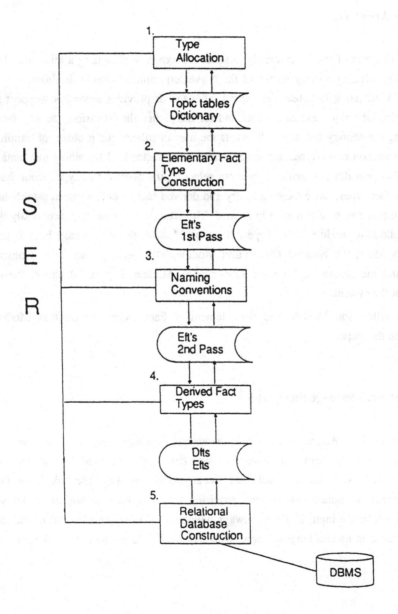

Figure 2.1 System Architecture

Most systems developed so far assume large bodies of prestored knowledge,making use of the now widely-accepted knowledge representation formalisms, such as [8][9][10][11][12] and the like. Learning systems, though concentrating on much smaller UoDs[13] also make use of these 'predictive' discourse structures. When unknown words or phrases are encountered in the input, the stereotyped encoded situations provide a predictive context for disambiguating meaning. The present NLP system, which is to be used as a database design tool, has to be more flexible. It would be inefficient to prestore knowledge in a system of this type. The knowledge required would have to be at such a high level of abstraction requiring complex inferencing mechanisms to disambiguate the meaning of the input. Also, due to the potential size of the system - a UoD description may contain thousands of fact types, it was not feasible to engage heavily in knowledge acquisition dialogue, as is the case with some of the more experimental systems designed for knowledge acquisition [14]. Rather than prestore knowledge, an interactive parser has been developed[16], which has some commonalities with one developed for a Japanese machine translation project[15].

The ambiguities dealt with at this stage by the interpreter are schema ambiguities, ie. ambiguities of (fact) types and (fact) instances[16]. The 'common entity type' problem , which had to be taken into account in the initial design stages, is a problem for all conceptual models and not considered to be a weakness of the present system. For large databases, a dictionary of synonym classes has to be set up prior to beginning the UoD description. The system then helps the analyst by collecting types and querying synonym classes[17].

4. The Type Allocation Module

Type refers to the entity types, or semantic classes of objects in the UoD. The major function of type allocation is to translate the natural language input sentences into their underlying semantic forms. Each instance of a natural language sentence represents one role-type pattern in the UoD. The semantic pattern of each input sentence is identical to the topic table, described below in 4.3.

4.1. Input to Type Allocation

The input to the type allocation module is a subset of natural language summarized by the following grammar.

1. Sentence -> NP Vgp Obj* (Reduced_S)*
2. NP -> (det) instance|(det) type|(det) type "," instance

3. Obj -> (Prep) NP

4. Reduced_S -> AND Vgp Obj*

5. Vgp -> (Aux) Verb

6. det -> the,this,that,those,a,an,all,each,....

7. instance -> any nominal string

8. type -> any nominal string

9. verb -> any verb string

4.1.1. Examples

(a) NP (Noun Phrase) strings.CS112(instance),the student,Adams(det type "," instance), the 3rd of January,1989(det instance), person(type), all students(det type).

(b) Vgp (Verb Group) strings. studies(verb), is enrolled(aux verb).

(c) Obj (Object) strings. on the 3rd January,1989(prep NP),CS112(NP).

(d) Reduced_S strings. and studies CS112(AND Vgp Obj), and is held in CS 718 and is taught by Halpin(Reduced_s Reduced_S).

(e) Sentence strings. The following sentences are interpreted by the grammar.
CS112 is held on Mondays at 3pm during semester 1 and is taught by Halpin.
The 3rd of January is a date.
Jones is enrolled in a BSc and studied CS112 and scored 7.
All students have id-codes.

4.2. Grammatical Restrictions

The subset of natural language was chosen for the initial version of the interpreter because of its suitability for database description. While it is not expected that the user enter only functional dependencies, at the same time the system is not in tended as an experiment in natural language processing. Future versions of the system will extend the natural language processing capability without change to the existing theory or methodology. At present, the following restrictions apply.

(a) The only form of the sentence that is recognized is the declarative. Questions and commands are not processed at this stage.

(b) Complex sentences joined by and are parsed only if they have a common subject NP. No other ellipsis is dealt with.

(c) Sentence modification is adverbial by means of prepositional phrases only. Adjectival modifiers, such as relative clauses and other adjectival phrases are not dealt with in the present system.

(d) Only complete information about types may be entered. Other sentence connectives, such as *or* will not be parsed.

(e) Quantification is syntactic only. If a noun phrase begins with a quantifier, such as *all,each,every* etc., the input sentence is treated in the same way as any other input sentence. The semantics of quantification is also intended for future versions.

4.2.1. Type Allocation Input/Output

(a) The Instance - Type Dictionary. The form of the Instance - Type Dictionary table is:

```
---------------------------------
Word    Category    Type
---------------------------------
```

where Word refers to the lexical item itself, Category refers to the syntactic category of the lexical item, and Type refers to the entity type, or semantic class of the word (where relevant). The structure of the dictionary is uniform for both language specific and world knowledge. (b) Topic Tables. The topic table has the following form TT = [S,<R1,O1>,<R2,O2>,...<Rn,On>], as shown below:

Subject	Role	Objects
Syntactic Type:	Role1	Syntactic Type:
Semantic Type:		Semantic Type:
Instance:		Instance:
Unique:		
	.	.
	.	.
	Rolen	Syntactic Type:
		Semantic Type:
		Instance:
		Unique:

It conforms to the linguistic theory convention of representing (complex) sentences as a sequence of grammatical relations. Grammatical relations in this grammar consist of both syntactic and semantic features. That is, working from left to right, a sentence consists of a subject and a number of role-object pairs, which make up the predicate. Objects are classified in this grammar as either direct or indirect. Direct objects are the noun phrases or prepositional phrases immediately following the verb(s) in the sentence. Prepositional objects are all other noun or prepositional phrases in the sentence. This is necessary for the construction of NIAM elementary fact types.

Subjects and objects have four features which are used by various modules in the system:

SyntacticType - refers to subject or object type,

SemanticType - refers to the entity type of a subject or object,

Instance - refers to the actual surface word or phrase,

Unique - refers to an integer value used for numbering uniqueness
     constraints.

Roles are expressed by the main verb and any prepositional case roles present. The case roles used by this system are shown in 4.5.

For every sentence entered by the user a topic table is constructed. The topic is the subject or focus of the sentence. It is the entity type about which attributes, or relationships to other entity types are classified. So that in a UoD which talks about students and their enrolments, the topic or subject of the sentence is the student. The subject must appear in first place. On the other hand,if the UoD were about degrees, for example, the topic would be degree and must be expressed with degree in the first position. It is possible to represent any sentence using this approach.

Example. The topic table constructed for the first example input sentence given in 4.1. is (including only SemanticType features for subject and object): TT=[subject,<is-held-on,day>,<at-loc,time>,<during-loc,semester>- ,<is-taught-by,lecturer>], as in:

Subject	Role(s)	Object Type(s)
SyntacticType:Subject	is_held_on	SyntacticType:Direct
SemanticType:Subject		SemanticType:Day
Instance:CS112		Instance:Monday
Unique:		Unique:
	at_location	SyntacticType:Prep
		SemanticType:Time
		Instance:3pm
		Unique:
	during_location	SyntacticType:Prep
		SemanticType:semester
		Instance:semester 1

182

                            Unique:
    is_taught_by   SyntacticType:Direct
                            SemanticType:Lecturer
                            Instance:Halpin
                            Unique:

4.3. Output of the Type Allocation Module

(a) Type Tables. For each topic table constructed during type allocation , a corresponding type table is presented to the analyst on the completion of this stage. A type table T has the form T = [S,O1,O2,O3,...On] eg.

Object-Type	Object-Type1	Object-Type2	....	Object-Typen
Subject-instance	Object-instance1	Object-instance2	....	Object-instancen

That is, the columns are ordered corresponding to the underlying form of the declarative sentence, where S stands for the subject entity type and O stands for object types. The semantic types are used as column headings. The example instance from the topic table is presented as a row value. The type table corresponding to the above topic table is T = [subject,day,time,lecturer].

subject	day	time	lecturer
CS112	Mon	3pm	Halpin

The analyst is requested at the completion of type allocation to populate these tables with a small but significant set of examples relevant to a particular UoD. Rather than have the user key in a natural language sentence for each instance, this method reduces the amount of dialogue interaction and has less potential for conflicting or redundant information.

4.4. Prestored Knowledge

The only prestored knowledge in the system, along with the parser, is a table of entries for closed word classes used by the parser. These are:

Word	Category	Type
in,on,under,..	preposition	location
from,out of,off	preposition	source
to,into,onto	preposition	goal
with,by	preposition	instrument
via,per,over	preposition	path
for	preposition	purpose
the,this,that,..	determiner	nil
a,an	determiner	nil
each,all,every	determiner	nil
some	determiner	nil
is,are,was,were	aux,verb	nil
has,have,had	aux,verb	nil

4.5. Function of Type Allocation

The Type Allocation module is responsible for the following:

- interpretation of the natural language sentences ;

- maintenance of the Instance-Type Dictionary;

- allocation of types and roles;

- rejection of more than one instance of the same instance-type / role-type pattern;

- querying the possibility of the same input sentence having been represented in a different form;

- querying any type inconsistencies or incomplete information;

- interacting with the analyst concerning any additional or updated information relating to type specification;

- providing the user with empty type tables in preparation for elementary fact type construction.

4.6. Algorithm PROCESS_SENTENCE

The high-level algorithm for processing input sentences.

Input: a subset N of natural language sentences S.

Output: a set of Topic Tables TT representing the underlying semantic form of sentence(s). The updated Instance_Type dictionary ITD.

PROCESS_SENTENCE(N)

begin

while N do begin
parse S and interactively determine fact types and instances; If instance then check dictionary
else if type then check topic information
else reject sentence; If information correct then store
 else send message to user querying inconsistencies
     revise accordingly
 end;
return(TT,ITD)
end.

The worst case time complexity of this algorithm is O(n2).

Conceptually, the construction of the dictionary and the construction of the topic tables are two separate stages. When the parser encounters an input sentence of the form <instance> IS A <instance/type>, the dictionary construction module is invoked. The high-level algorithm for dictionary construction is as follows:

4.7. Algorithm DICTIONARY_CONSTRUCTION

Input: A subset N of natural language sentences of type IS_A.

Output: A set of updated Instance-Type Dictionary tables ITD.

DICTIONARY_CONSTRUCTION(N)

begin while N do begin
 parse IS_A;
 check dictionary for instance;
 If instance exists and corresponding type matches input type
    send message to user and reject pattern
 else if instance exists with different type
    send message to user to confirm type pattern(s);
 check type in dictionary;
 if type exists and corresponding instance matches input instance
    send message to user and reject pattern
 else if type exist with different instance
    send message to user to confirm patterns;
 update instance-type knowledge in dictionary
end;

return(ITD)
end.

Discussion

If the analyst had entered the sentence *Adams is a student*, and had repeated at some stage the example, the system would reject the pattern. If, on the other hand, the analyst had entered *Adams is a manager*, the system queries the seemingly conflicting information to determine whether the fact that Adams is a student has to be deleted, or the fact that Adams is a manager has to be added. This option is relevant when instances may be of more than one type in the UoD eg Adams is both a student and a manager. Similarly, if the analyst had entered Jones is a student, ie where more than one instance of the same type were entered. The system checks first with the user to confirm whether two in stances of the same type pattern are necessary, before rejecting the pattern.

Example Dialogue. (User is in lowercase, system is in upper case).

> What do you know?
> system lists types and instances.
> Adams is a student
> I ALREADY KNOW THAT
> Jones is a student.
> I HAVE ADAMS IS A STUDENT. DO YOU WANT MORE THAN ONE PATTERN?
> yes (pattern stored).
> no (pattern rejected).
> Adams is a manager
> I HAVE ADAMS IS A STUDENT
> DO YOU WISH TO CHANGE ANYTHING?
> delete Adams is a student. or,
> add Adams is a manager.

The instance-type dictionary and the topic tables are constantly being accessed and updated during type allocation. If the parser encounters input sentences other than the IS_A sentence type, it assumes that a fact and thus a topic table has to be checked. The high-level algorithm for type allocation is as follows.

4.8. Algorithm TYPE_ALLOCATION

Input: A subset N of natural language facts F. Output: A set of updated topic tables TT.

TYPE_ALLOCATION(N)

begin while N do begin

```
parse F;
allocate types and roles;
check types and roles with information in topic tables(s);
If collection of types and roles exists in same syntactic form
    reject pattern
else if collection of types and roles exists in different
    syntactic form then
        verify with user whether same or different topic; store types and roles in relevant topic
table
end;
return(TT)
end.
```

Discussion

Assuming that the following sentence is the first sentence entered for a particular UoD, and ignoring the type/instance queries which were discussed above. (11) Adams is enrolled in a BSc and studied CS112 and scored 7. The parser works from left to right checking each word in the input string and matching these words with the entries in the dictionary and user - supplied in formation. Assuming that all word strings are matched and the parse is successful, the following role-entity type pattern is created: (a) person is enrolled in degree and studied subject and scored rating. If another sentence is entered, such as (12) Jones is enrolled in a BA and studied PD102 and scored 6. This sentence would be rejected by the system , as the role-entity type pattern created (b) person is enrolled in degree and studied subject and scored rating, is identical to the pattern created previously for sentence (11). Similarly, if the analyst had entered a sentence such as (13) Wirth wrote Pascal in 1973, giving the role- entity type pattern (a) person wrote language in location date. The following sentence translating to the same role- entity type pattern as (13)(a), though presented in a different syntactic form, (14) Pascal was written by Wirth in 1973, would be queried by the sytem,allowing the user the option of introducing a new topic, leading to the construction of additional tables, or being simply reminded that the pattern already exists.

If the interpreter encounters an unknown string during parsing, a message is sent to the user requesting further information. For example, if sentence (12) above were entered by the user and Jones had not been entered during stage 1 (instance-type specification),the system would not find a match for Jones in the dictionary. The user then has the option of specifying the sentence in the form described in 4.1 above, namely(18) The student, Jones is enrolled .....etc. This method of knowledge acquisition is not feasible for large UoD's for obvious reasons.

On completion of type allocation, the system presents the role entity type patterns to the user in the forms shown (14)(a)(b) above. If additional information were to be added , for example the fact that student got position 3, the sentence may be entered here. eg (19) Adams got position,3. At this stage the information would be appended to the table under discussion, rather than a new table being created.

Similarly, if a role - entity type pair were to be deleted, the user may delete at this stage. On completion of type allocation, a type table is presented to the user, corresponding to the topic tables.

Example Dialogue

> Adams is enrolled in a BSc and studied CS112 and scored 7.
> OK, or, if string Adams does not exist
> WHO OR WHAT IS ADAMS?
> The student , Adams is enrolled in a BSc....etc
> Jones is enrolled in a BA and studied PD102 and scored 6.
> I ALREADY HAVE THAT PATTERN.
> Adams got position,3.
> OK
> Wirth wrote Pascal in 1973.
> OK
> Pascal was written in 1973 by Wirth.
> IS THIS THE SAME AS PERSON WROTE LANGUAGE IN DATE?
> yes.
> OK, or
> no,
> OK, I'M CONSTRUCTING A NEW TOPIC TABLE.
> YOUR TYPE PATTERNS ARE
  STUDENT IS-ENROLLED-IN DEGREE STUDIED SUBJECT SCORED RATING GOT
POSITION.
> DO YOU WISH TO CHANGE ANYTHING?
> no, or
> delete got position.
> OK

5. Elementary Fact Type Construction

Elementary fact types are important for the construction of the relational database tables. Incorrect elementary fact type structures can lead to redundancies or information loss in the database. Elementary Fact Type Construction involves two interdependent stages:
 (a) determination of uniqueness constraints;
 (b) construction of the elementary fact types. Uniqueness constraints in this system differ from the NIAM method, in that they are determined on the basis of the output report, rather than on the conceptual schema. Stages (a) and (b) are almost fully automatic.

5.1. Input to the Elementary Fact Type Construction Module

Type tables corresponding to the topic tables (described above in 4.1) and illustrated again below.

5.2. Output from the Elementary Fact Type Construction Module

Candidates for elementary fact types in the following form:

Bft = Type1,Type2

.
.

Nft = Type1,Type2,..Typen

This system differs from NIAM in that it takes as a starting point binary fact types. That is, potential unary fact types are converted to binary fact types. Most of the fact types expected will be nary. The analyst may change the elementary fact types constructed by the system on completion of this stage. The naming conventions for NIAM elementary fact types are at this stage incomplete. That is, they are not in the form of entity - type role pairs (described in [2]). The system has not yet checked for common entity types (also described in [2]). Derived fact types also have to be determined before the efts are complete for ralational tables to be constructed.

5.3. Function of Elementary Fact Type Construction

The Elementary Fact Type Construction module performs the following tasks:

- automatically determines uniqueness constraints;
- validates these uniqueness constraints (unique columns) by offering the user a counter example;
- constructs a 'first pass' at elementary fact types, based on previously acquired linguistic knowledge (4.2) and the uniqueness constraints;
- validates the elementary fact types with the user and allows any alterations to be made.

Discussion

The analyst is presented with type table(s) corresponding to topic tables constructed in stage 2 of type allocation,for example:

Student   Degree   Subject   Rating

Adams   BSc   CS112   7

and requested to populate these tables with a small but significant poulation, an example of which would be:

Example 1.

Student	Degree	Subject	Rating
Adams	BSc	CS112	7
Adams	BSc	CS100	6
Adams	BSc	PD102	5
Brown	BA	CS112	7
Brown	BA	PD102	6
Collins	BSc	CS100	5

Based on the data supplied, the system then automatically determines the unique (composite) columns by searching each individual column, pairs of columns, triples of columns in all possible combinations till the number of columns in the table has been covered. In the above example, only student-subject are unique. When a unique (composite) column is encountered, a counter example is offered to enable the user to validate the correctness of this. Counter examples are constructed by taking the value from the first row of the suspected unique column(s) and joining with a non equal value from a neighbouring column. For example, in the above table, the student-subject column is unique. The system constructs the string <Adams BA CS112>, and asks the user to verify whether such a row is possible. In other words, can the student-subject values be repeated. If the response is no, then the column type is marked with an integer value (1..number of columns in the table), in the unique field of the topic table. The integer values help to determine the elementary fact types. Although the size of the type table(s) to be searched is not large (they are only a subset of a universal relation), corresponding to a complex English sentence (we can expect possibly ten type columns) , the complexity of the search is reduced by the following assumptions.

1. The columns of the table are ordered with subject as first argument, direct object(s) as second and third arguments, and modifying prepositional objects in this case as subsequent arguments working from left to right.

2. The table is such that the subject is the topic of the sentence. All subsequent types are attributes of the subject, or stand in some semantic relationship to the subject. Otherwise a different sentence pattern would have been chosen in 2.1.. Based on these assumptions we state the following.

Observation 1. If a table T = [S,O1,O2,O3,....On] and the uniqueness constraint covers the subject column only, then the table consists of binary fact types of the form Eft = [<S,O1>,<S,O2>,<S,O3>,....<S,On>].

Proof. Project on the unique column in the above combinations. As the column projected on is unique, the cardinality of the tables created is the same as the original table. Because the object columns are functionally dependent on the unique subject, no new rows (ie no new information) are created after joining.

Observation 2. If a table T = [S,O1,O2,O3,...On] and a direct object is covered by a unique-ness constraint (in the absence of a unique grammatical subject),then elementary fact types are binary and are constructed by combining the first unique direct object column with each other column giving Eft = [<UniqueColumn,S>,<UniqueColumn,O2>,..<UniqueColumn,On>].

Note. Types marked as prepositional objects in the topic tables are ignored as potential uniqueness constraints, as these are semantically only adjunct arguments, not belonging to the semantic core of the sentence.

Proof. Project on the unique column in the above combinations. As the column projected on is unique, the cardinality of the tables created is the same as the original table. Because the subject and/or object columns are functionally dependent on the unique object , no new rows are created after joining.

In the case where no single subject or direct object column is found to be unique the second stage of the search is to pick up composite unique columns (where uniqueness constraint covers 2 to n-1 columns) and determine columns that are functionally dependent on the unique columns.

Observation 3. If a table T = [S,O1,O2,O3,..On] and the uniqueness constraint covers the subject (or the first direct object) column, then the elementary fact types are either the original unique columns + each other column that overlaps in uniqueness with the first column, or a reduced column + each remaining unmarked column.

Proof. Project on the unique columns, combined with other columns as stated above. By projecting on the unique columns,the cardinality of the split tables remains the same as the original. Each other column is a function of the (reduced) unique column. Therefore on joining no new rows are created.

Example 2.

Given the following user-populated type table:

Subject	Credit Points	Semester	Enrolment	Lecturer
CS100	8	1	500	PP
CS102	8	2	500	GR
CS112	8	1	300	TH
CS113	8	2	270	TH
CS380	16	1	50	PB
CS380	16	2	45	AL

Eft1 = Subject,Semester,Enrolment (original unique columns + FDs).
Eft2 = Subject,CreditPoints (reduced unique columns + FDs)
Eft3 = Subject,Lecturer   "   "

Note. The method illustrated above, does not take into account overlapping uniqueness constraints which leads to the problem with B.C.N.F.

In cases where the uniqueness constraint covers a whole row of the table,the following observation applies.

Observation 4. If a table T = [S,O1,O2,O3,...On] and the uniqueness constraint covers the whole row of the table, then the elementary fact types are either (a) binary, as in Eft = [<S,O1>,<S,O2>,..<S,On>]. In cases where for each unique subject column value, the product of the unique types in the remaining columns = the number of rows for each entry in the table; or, (b) nary. That is, Eft = [S,O1,O2,O3,...On].

Example 3.			Example 4.		
Person	Skill	Language	Person	Vehicle	Company
Smith	cook	English	Smith	car	GMH
Smith	cook	Greek	Smith	truck	GMH
Smith	cook	French	Smith	4WD	Toyota
Smith	type	English	Smith	car	Toyota
Smith	type	Greek	Jones	4WD	GMH
Smith	type	French	Jones	car	GMH
Jones	type	English			

In Example 3 above,

Eft1 = Person,Skill
Eft2 = Person,Language.

In Example 4 above,

Eft = Person,Vehicle, Company.

6. Conclusion

This concludes a description of the first stage in a relational database design tool. The method described is simple, easy to follow, and requires reasonable interaction with the user. The remaining steps in the process ie naming conventions and the determination of derived fact types will be presented in another paper. The theoretical aspects of the remaining modules have been developed. This phase of the system is currently under implementation.

References

[1] Chen,P.(1976)."The Entity Relationship Model: Towards a Unified View of Data",ACM TODS 1,No.1.

[2] Nijssen,G.M. and Halpin,T.J."Conceptual Schema and Relational Database Design: A fact oriented approach". Prentice Hall of Australia,Pty,Ltd.

[3] Maciaszek,L.A.(1987)."Conceptual Database Design Methodology and Tools".Technical Report,No.87/10,Dept. of Computing Science,University of Wollongong,NSW,Australia.

[4] Alshawi,H.(1987)."Memory and Context for Language Interpretation".Cambridge University Press,London.

[5] Hirst,G.(1988)."Semantic Interpretation and the Resolution of Ambiguity".Cambridge University Press,London.

[6] Wilensky,R.(1981)."PAM(Plan Applier Module)". In Inside Computer Understanding, Schank and Riesbeck,eds.

[7] Appelt,D.E.(1985)."Planning English Sentences".Cambridge University Press,Cambridge,New York.

[8] Simmons,R.F.(1973)."Semantic Networks:Their Computation and Use for Understanding English Sentences". In Computer Models of Thought and Language, Schank and Colby,eds.

[9] Charniak,E.(1981)."The Case-Slot Identity Theory".In Cognitive Science,No.7.

[10] Charniak,E. and Minsky,M.(1975)."A Framework for Frame-based Systems".

[11] Schank,R. and Abelson,R.(1977)."Scripts,Plans,Goals and Understanding". Lawrence Erlbaum Assoc.,Hillsdale,New Jersey.

[12] Schank,R.(1982)."Reminding and Memory Organization". In Strategies for Natural Language Processing. Lehnert and Ringle,eds.

[13] Rumelhart,D.E. and McClelland,J.L.(1985)."On Learning the Past Tenses of English Verbs".In Parallel Distributed Processing.Vol. 2. Rummelhart,ed.

[14] Haas,N. and Hendrix,G.(1983)."Learning By Being Told". In Machine Learning, Michalski et al eds.

[15] Tomita,M.(1985)."Efficient Parsing for Natural Language".Kluwer Academic Publishers.

[16] Dunn,L.(unpublished manuscript)."An Interactive Parser for Conceptual Schema Disambiguation".U.Qld.

[17] Dunn,L.(unpublished manuscript)."Designing Relational Databases with Natural Language".U.Qld.

How to Combine Tools and Methods in Practice — a field study

Kari Smolander, Veli-Pekka Tahvanainen, Kalle Lyytinen

Project Syti
University of Jyväskylä
Dept. of Computer Science
Seminaarinkatu 15
SF-40100 JYVÄSKYLÄ
FINLAND
email: syti@jytko.jyu.fi,
syti@finjyu.bitnet

Abstract

In spring 1989 we surveyed the experiences of some Finnish companies in methodology modelling (*metamodelling*) and adaptation of tools and methodologies to each other (*methodology adaptation*). The companies represented software production, banking, wood and metal industry, and wholesale trade. The study was carried out as a field study where we interviewed method developers, systems analysts and their supervisors. The goal of the survey was to find out whether there was need for metamodelling or methodology adaptation in general and how this need had been satisfied. The study shows that a little experience had been gained in adapting data dictionaries to methodologies but no such attempts had been made with CASE tools. One reason for this was that few methodological guidelines were extensively employed and supported in organisations. In general no systematic approach had been followed in the adaptation. We also explored possible causes for encountered difficulties and conditions for successful metamodelling and methodology adaptation. A crucial success factor was the adaptability and ease of use of the tool. In general the causes for the success are similar to those of information systems development in general. These include sufficient resources and management support, concrete benefits for those who do the actual work and friendly user interfaces.

1. Introduction

As the field of CASE matures more research is needed in focusing on problems in using CASE technologies. So far, this has been little researched area, though the literature on this topic is continually growing (see *e.g.* Le Quesne 1988, McDaniel 1989, I/S Analyzer 1989, Kemerer 1989, Orlikowski 1988)

Most of the studies have focused on general attitudes and opinions of CASE technology, productivity changes, or changes in systems analysts' skills and work patterns. So far there are no empirical studies on how matching of tools to methods (or vice versa) is done and what the outcomes of such attempts are. In the theoretical literature, there are, however, several solution strategies for the problem of matching CASE technology with the existing development practices and tools (*cf.* Bubenko 1988). What are the outcomes of and contingencies in the use of various strategies in practice is still largely unexplored.

The goal of this paper is to report the results of a field study where we examined how metamodelling and methodology adaptation had been tried out in some large Finnish IS departments. The major focus of the study was to gather the experiences of the organisations of methodology adaptation and metamodelling. We also attempted to shed light on how much activities are needed in the adaptation and how CASE technologies are changing this need.

The paper will proceed as follows. First we discuss the general setting of the study, explain the research methodology and define some key concepts applied in the field study. In sections 3 and 4 we describe how methodologies and software tools are being used and how they are valued. In section 5 we take a closer look at methodology adaptation, discuss reasons for it, and describe the methods used in the process and the process differences in studied organisations. Section 6 illuminates the necessary requirements for a successful adaptation based on our observations. Lastly, we briefly summarise the results of the field study and compare them with related research outcomes.

2. Research methodology

The impact of CASE technologies is little researched topic. In largely unexamined fields of study, it is usual to start with case-studies to gain understanding and to generate a valid research hypothesis (Benbasat *et al.* 1987). Therefore we saw it appropriate to begin our research with a qualitative field study. During this study we interviewed seventeen method specialists and IS managers in eight Finnish companies. In four organisations we interviewed one person, in three organisations three persons, and in one organisation four persons.

The companies were (in Finnish scale) large and they had highly developed and well-staffed IS departments. All companies were interested in CASE technologies and almost all had some experience of it. We divided the organisations into three major groups: "Software production" (two companies), "Banking" (three companies) and "Trade and industry" (three companies). In one software house we visited two fairly independent departments so there are actually nine *quasi*-organisations in the study.

The interviews took place in the late January and early February 1989. The interviews were carried out by two interviewers which helped to keep a relaxed and open atmosphere during the conversations as the other interviewer could concentrate on the conversation and the other on keeping track of the dialogue. No tape-recorder was used. The interviews were semistructured and they followed the interview format exhibited in the appendix. The results of the interviews were discussed with the representatives of the companies after the interviews so they fairly well reflect the opinions expressed during the interviews.

We also followed the following strategy when we interviewed more than one representative in one firm. The general questions about the organisation (see the appendix) were asked from the group of interviewees whereas the spesific questions about metamodelling and methodology adaptation were asked personally. This turned out to be a good practice, as we thereby received varied opinions and different examples from the interviewees.

The results of our study should not be generalised too strongly because of the relatively small number of organisations included. In this sense the research could be viewed as *hypothesis generation* research. However, as the organisations were usually relatively large and had well-developed IS departments, they probably were more mature to adopt new technologies such as CASE tools or data dictionaries. Therefore, the outcomes of our study may apply to organisations in general in the longer run.

With these caveats, we believe that the study uncovers some interesting factors that affect the success or failure of CASE tools, data dictionaries and methodology adaptation approaches.

3. Conceptual preliminaries

As the empirical study focussed on metamodelling and methodology adaptation it is necessary to define these terms (and a host of other terms) in the way they were employed throughout the study.

Methodologies are conceptually distinct from methods which are generally defined as:

Explicit prescriptions for achieving an activity or set of activities required by the life cycle model used to develop a software product. (Charette 1986 p. 64.)

Well-known examples of methods are Structured Analysis (De Marco 1978), ER-modelling (Chen 1976) and project management methods. A method embodies a conceptual structure which defines what the method is about. The conceptual structures of the most widely known methods include such concepts as *activity, entity, relationship* etc. The process of modelling the what aspect of methods deals with describing their conceptual structure in some notation. This involves using another conceptual structure (and method) to describe another method *i.e.* "going outside" the method domain proper (shifting to "metalevel").

A methodology, in turn, is defined in the context of this study as an ordered collection of methods as suggested by a framework *e.g.* a life cycle model[1].

By *metamodelling* we mean in this paper a process of describing (modelling) a methodology *i.e.*, its methods and their interdependencies in order to implement the methodology in a CASE tool, data dictionary or the like.

A *tool* is defined here as an instrument for the execution of some procedure. More specifically, a tool incorporates software with which a IS design task can be done. We are mainly concerned in the following with CASE tools as well as to some extent with data dictionaries.

Methodology adaptation can be defined as the adjustment of a given IS design methodology and an IS design tool (*e.g.* a data dictionary or a CASE tool) to each other. (See also Lyytinen, Smolander, Tahvanainen 1989.)

This happens in *de novo* situations where they have not been matched with each other before. In such a case some modification has to be made in order to get the most out of the methodology and the tool. A tool can be adapted *e.g.* by changing its inherent data model. A methodology can be "tuned" for example by changing the syntax and/or semantics of its description language.

4. Methodical practices in organisations

Many companies visited had no methodology at all (as defined above). Instead, many companies had a sort of development *framework*, dividing the IS development into logical

---

[1] In general there is very much confusion about the use of terms such as "method", "methodology" and "technique".

and/or temporal phases (a phasing structure). Usually these frameworks did not suggest any particular methods but left the phases vaguely defined and loosely adaptable. In this sense, all organisations had developed (or transferred) some systematic practices, denoted here as "methodical practices" how the systems work should proceed.

In general, the attitude towards methods varied largely. In some companies they were defined and documented, but their use was voluntary. In some others method use was in principle obligatory and to some extent controlled.

The only widely used method was a species from the conceptual modelling fauna which usually included a locally modified ER-notation. Conceptual modelling was mentioned in six of the nine organisations covered. This was mostly used in the database design.

Some formalised phase models had been developed in connection with the data dictionaries. The most common of them was some variation of a Finnish design methodology TISMA which is actually a loose framework.

No other method nor methodology was widely used. The following were mentioned once during interviews: MBI, JSP, SA/SD and (an adaptation of) ISAC. Thus, only few organisations applied methods to model processes (as opposed to modelling data structures).

Despite the small number of methods in use, the methods were nevertheless considered useful. The general attitude was that the prevailing practice of letting every analyst to do things in his/her own way was yet more harmful and should therefore be abolished. The interviewees expressed that all organisations were striving a strategy towards a broader coverage of methods in the development work. As most organisations aimed at the use of CASE tools, it was also widely accepted, that a wider understanding and use of methods was needed.

Tables 1a and 1b summarise opinions about the benefits and drawbacks of the methods. In table 1a one can see that methods were not considered to improve software quality. Rather, their value flows from better common understanding of design options and problems. A majority of the interviewees mentioned the standardisation to improve joint understanding. On the other hand, only four interviewees mentioned better quality as an outcome of the method use. Surprisingly, no interviewee mentioned increased productivity though better understanding could be expected to result in better productivity. Information systems that meet the requirements can be expected to be produced more effectively and with less errors.

The biggest mentioned drawbacks of the methods were their rigidity and complexity (table 1b). The most frequent drawback was the unflexibility of methods: they compell the

Benefits of methods use	
+ Enhanced standardisation of documents and systems work and therefore easier communication in working groups.	16
+ Methods make systems work easier and faster.	7
+ Better quality of produced applications.	4
+ Methods structure the systems work and make project management more easy.	4
+ Enhanced maintainability of applications.	4
+ Less dependency from key persons.	3
+ Large databases are easier to construct.	2
+ Testing is more easy.	1
+ Naming problems are easier.	1

Table 1a. Noted benefits of methods use

Drawbacks of methods use	
− A strict procedure is enforced, that is unsuitable for some purposes.	7
− Methods mean more work and more bureaucracy and slow down the actual development work.	6
− Methods are often complicated and difficult to learn. Training for them takes time and costs money.	5
− Work load in the first phases of systems work increases. The benefits are seen only later.	3
− The maintenance of the descriptions is tedious.	1
− Methods are not mature yet.	1

Table 1b. Mentioned drawbacks of methods use

analysts to follow a rigid design procedure that is not necessarily fit to all situations. The next common drawback is controversial: in table 1a we have seven people claiming that methods ease systems development. In table 1b we see six interviewees claiming just the opposite: methods mean more work and slow down the development. One explanation for this controversial situation is the following: whether methods are seen to ''fit'' to a design situation depends largely on the analysts' personal background, his/her education, attitudes, earlier experience etc. However, this variation was not explained during this study and is a research issue to be tackled in the future.

5. Tool support in organisations

In general the organisations hesitated to introduce CASE tools because the outcomes were still unknown and the investments considerable. Nowhere, however, the attitude towards CASE technologies was negative or the interviewees had no expectations at all. In addition, the interviewees expected that the use of CASE tools would grow rapidly in the next years. This was especially true in those organisations where a new methodology was being planned to be used side by side with the tool.

Every organisation had discussed the use of CASE tools and most had tried out some tool(s). In the majority of the organisations the use was still experimental. In no organisation was a CASE tool supporting the whole systems development life-cycle. In most cases the CASE tools applied were "front end" tools that supported analysis and design tasks. In one company the tool was also supporting information systems planning tasks.

In some companies a suitable methodology – tool combination had been found and a wider application was in the beginning. Only few companies had taken CASE tools in "production" yet, and even in those companies where the tool or tools had been put in the production line the experiences were preliminary.

In production, or just moving into introductory phase were the following tools: Excelerator®, IEF™, IEW®, Managerview and Teamwork. In addition at least Deft, CASE2000 and IDMS/Architect had been explored for use. The tool variation in organisations was considerable. Only IEW (three sites) and Excelerator (two sites) were used in more than one organisation. Oddly enough, the organisations seemed to have few methodological reasons for choosing these tools. Only in one place was IEW used in concordance with the Information Engineering methodology™ (Martin 1987).

Data dictionaries were less common. Only four organisations had a central repository. Worth noticing is that all the banks used a centralised data dictionary. The reason for this could be that banks have large centralised applications that can be managed with data dictionaries. The banks also had centralised IS departments in which the benefits of using data dictionaries are quite obvious. Data dictionaries in use were: Datamanager (2), IDD (1), and DDDS (1). Usually the data dictionaries covered a larger share of the system design tasks, but the emphasis with these tools was on technical design and programming tasks.

The usage pattern of data dictionaries seemed to evolve in two directions: first, they were to be introduced in new organisations (there were at least two sites that had plans for purchasing one). Second, new, more active tools were to be acquired in order to better support the maintenance of applications. Many interviewees considered very important that the data dictionaries should acquire their data automatically without requiring an extra task of feeding data into the tool. One opinion emphasised contingencies in using data dictionaries: *i.e.* there should exist an option of not using the data dictionary. In some situations data dictionaries make the work only more rigid and do not allow for "bending the rules".

Tables 2a and 2b summarise the recorded opinions about the benefits and drawbacks of the tools. In contrast to methods, tools were mostly seen to enhance quality. In addition, tools were expected to increase productivity, and ease maintainability. However, the major drawback of current tools was their low quality. Many respondents argued that tools only marginally support their primary functions and they are not yet a mature technology.

Benefits of tool use	
+ Better general manageability: less errors and enhanced quality.	11
+ Better productivity as descriptions come out easier.	8
+ Documents always up to date: easier maintenance and better changeability.	6
+ Naming easier.	4
+ Better quality documentation.	4
+ Documents and descriptions always in the same format.	2
+ Projects better managed.	2
+ The use of applications easier.	1

Table 2a. Tool use benefits mentioned

Drawbacks of tool use	
− Tool is of poor quality.	5
− Tool is costly, resource and time consuming.	4
− Tool requires much learning. May become too high a threshold for new users.	3
− Tool use means additional work.	3
− Maintenance of descriptions is tedious.	2
− Methods must be strictly followed. Great danger of making a mistake.	1
− Expectations often too high.	1

Table 2b. Tool use drawbacks mentioned

If we compare the benefits of methods and tools we can observe that increased quality was seen to flow almost exclusively from the use of tools. In principle, one could expect quality to increase through a disciplined use of a methodology which produces better results. This reveals an underlying belief in the interviewees' thinking: methods and methodologies are not used unless there are tools to support them. Another interesting *raison d'etre* is found in their thoughts of increased productivity: wider productivity issues (a working system for the right tasks in time) are not so much considered as limited efficiency *i.e.* the cost-efficient use of project resources. However, a disciplined use of methodologies could be expected to affect positively on the former whereas it might even work against the latter goal.

6. Methodology adaptation in the organisations

6.1. Reasons for methodology adaptation

Organisations usually face the adaptation problem when a new tool is purchased or when their methodology is changed. The new tool may not support the methods used, or the old methodology is found insufficient in some sense. An adaptation to prevailing methods had been attempted with all the the data dictionaries. On the other hand, no adaptation had been attempted with any CASE tool.

Table 3 tabulates the reported reasons for methodology adaptation. The most common reason for methodology adaptation is that a new tool is purchased. It is also common that the prevailing methodology is found insufficient or there are no widely used, standard methods in use. In some cases the tools may have technical shortcomings requiring adaptation *e.g.* when the interfaces are inappropriate.

Reasons for methodology adaptation	
• The new tool does not support the earlier methods or its description base schema is not fit for the descriptions.	8
• The previous methodology does not work well. A new methodology is needed.	6
• The interfaces or some other features of the tool do not fit.	3
• No previous coherent methodology.	3
• Both tools and methods are made in-house.	1
• The type of applications produced has changed.	1

Table 3. Reasons for methodology adaptation

6.2. Adaptation strategies

In the time of the interviews some methodology adaptation had been attempted in six companies. In some of them the work was still unfinished. In four cases out of the six the data dictionary had been adapted to the methods used, in the remaining two a methodology was modified to fit for CASE tools.

No formal metamodelling methods or strict procedures had been followed: the adaptation had been done more or less *ad hoc* using a trial and error procedure. In some cases there had been some attempts to describe the methods by themselves. This is quite natural for the conceptual modelling methods.

The most common strategy was to adopt the methods supported by the tool or pick up a tool that supported the methodology used. A special case was to construct a new methodology (mainly from existing parts) for the CASE tool. The organisations were reluctant to give up old methods if they were in widespread use. However, on many sites no standard methodologies were used, so adopting a new methodology was not a greater effort than introducing CASE tools and associated training.

From the interviews we can generalise five adaptation strategies[2].

(1) *No adaptation*: the tool is used "as is" and only those parts that fit the prevailing methods are applied. This is a common strategy with CASE tools and also followed with data dictionaries when nothing else succeeds. (4 cases, banking, software production.)

(2) *Purchase both the methodology and the tool and see that they fit for each other.* This was the most common way to adopt CASE tools. If the old methods are unsatisfactory or no methods are widely used, this may also be the most efficient strategy. (3 cases, trade and industry, software production.)

(3) *Adapt the purchased tool to own methods.* This had been attempted with all data dictionaries. No CASE tools had been adapted in this way. (4 cases, banking, software production.)

(4) *Standardise the ways in which to develop the descriptions according the prevailing methods with a CASE tool.* In other words, create translation rules for

---

[2]Several strategies had been used in some organisations with different tools or due to the failure of one strategy. Hence the counts do not seem to sum up correctly.

notations. This may be feasible if it is not possible to use one CASE tool in the organisation. Supposedly this strategy is appropriate for software houses that need to work with the customer's methods and tools. (One case, software production.)

(5) *Build a tool, a methodology or both in-house.* The building of an own tool requires a large organisation for development and is feasible only in environments where standard tools are unsuitable. An own methodology may be developed more easily to support a CASE tool if its own built-in methodology is found inadequate. (2 cases, trade and industry, software production)[3]

It is to some extent arguable, how much "true" methodology adaptation had been done in all cases. Some borderline situations are the development of a methodology for CASE tools (strategy 5 above) and the adaptation of an existing methodology to the organisation (e.g. some local adaptations of a life-cycle model and observed local variations of ER-modelling). None of these examples fits very well for the concept of *methodology adaptation.*

Surprisingly, no organisation had adapted an existing methodology to a tool. Some steps in this direction had been made in some organisations: in one organisation more exact descriptions had had to be developed with the method due to the introduction of a tool. In one organisation a project was being started at the time the survey was done that aimed partially at this end.

6.3. Success of adaptation strategies

The interviewees had great difficulties in evaluating the success of the strategies they had followed at the time of the study. Strategy 1 seemed to work quite well in most cases, as it relies largely on the existing methodological base. However, it is problematic if the company does not have any sound methodological base or if it wants to renew and extend it.

At the time wider experience of adaptation was available only of the second and third strategy. With the third strategy the adaptation had either been unsuccessful or succeeded

---

[3]Bubenko (Bubenko 1988) has developed a similar type of classification for the introduction of CASE tools into the organisation. He does not focus on the methodology adaptation proper, and therefore there are obvious differences from our classification. In his classification two of the basic strategies are purchasing the tool and the methodology or making an own tool. These correspond to our strategies 2 and 5 above. Two other basic strategies mentioned in his article are the integration of several tools and the purchase of a customised CASE tool from some outside vendor. These could also be applied to the situation we were interested in. We did not, however, observe these strategies in our field study.

only partially. Though less experience was available of the second strategy the opinions were more positive as the interviewees reported of no larger disappointments. Strategies four and five were both in the preliminary phase and therefore their evaluation was not possible.

6.4. Differences in the adaptation strategies due to the industry sector

We further analysed whether the industry sector had any impact on the preferred adaptation strategy. We could not find any significant differences between banking and software production. Trade and industry differed greatly from the other two because they had not attempted to do any adaptation proper. On the other hand they had usually followed strategies 2 and 5.

This observation was somewhat surprising because we expected the software production group to do adaptation more readily than the two other groups, because of the primary role of systems development productivity in their competitiveness and their better skills in using tools. However, this hypothesis was not confirmed. It seems that the client and product oriented work to some extent **inhibits** the software houses to try adaptation. The software production companies seemed, however, to be better in adopting new methods than companies in other industry sectors.

These differences between banking and software houses and the trade and industry sectors can be explained by two factors. First, in banking and software production the IS departments are usually large (the average number of personnel in the studied companies was over 500 people) and the pressure to standardise development practices therefore greater *i.e.* these companies usually had developed and tried out some methodological principles. Second, these companies had usually specialised method development departments and therefore they had obtained more skills and knowledge to attempt methodology adaptation.

In banks and in software production we observed nearly all five strategies having been adopted. However, the industry sector did not seem to affect the success. For example in banks every organisation had done adaptation in one form or another. But the solutions and outcomes differed from one bank to another: one complete failure, one partial success and a project under way when the study was made.

6.5. How the tools and methods in use affect the methodology adaptation

We also explored how the methodology and tool used in the adaptation process affected the type and success of the strategy followed.

First, the failed adaptations (strategy 3) all concerned data dictionaries. According to the interviewees these failures were mostly caused by the shortcomings of the respective tools. The available data dictionaries were too inflexible to be adapted in any real sense. With CASE tools similar arguments could not be observed, because they had not been adapted but instead used "as is".

Second, our study does not suggest any particular requirements for the methodologies to be adapted, since there was no data available of cases in which an existing methodology would have been adapted to some tool. In one project this was being tried out with a data dictionary at the time the interviews were made. Another borderline situation of method is the strategy 4 above, where the CASE tool use is standardised even though the tool is not used according to its native methods. These cases were still in the planning stage so there was no data available on their success.

Third, the available hardware platform has a crucial effect on the adaptation strategy. There is a dearth of data dictionaries for mainframes other than IBM and compatibles. Therefore, organisations had had to live up with programs that were not flexible enough for successful adaptation or even for normal use. The CASE tools used were excessively PC-based. One organisation had rejected a tool partially because it required more exotic (MacIntosh) hardware.

7. Requirements for successful methodology adaptation

As noticed above the success of the adaptation attempts varied considerably. Major difficulties and problems in methodology adaptation are depicted in table 4.

Difficulties and problems in methodology adaptation	
• The functions of the tool (user interface, reports) or its descriptive power lacking or too limited.	9
• The benefits for application builders negligible, the use of the tool is seen as an unnecessary burden.	3
• Technical difficulties, tool malfunctions.	3
• The adaptation project took too long.	1
• The adapted methodology inexact, not fitting for the tool.	1
• No support from the tool vendor.	1

Table 4. Difficulties and problems in the adaptation

From table 4 we can see, that the most common difficulties were shortcomings in or plain malfunctions of the tool. The next significant problem group was the lack of immediate benefits for the users. Many interviewees pointed out that there must be some benefit for every user — the adopted tool is not used unless it gives some concrete advantage.

A significant factor not explicitly mentioned in all cases is the lack of management support. A difficult task of methodology adaptation often involves major changes in how systems development is carried out. This can not be accomplished if sufficient resources are not available[4]. Often, however, the resources were insufficient which makes the analysts feel that their work is not seen as important. In these cases it is also easy for the analyst to blaim the tool as the main culprit, even if the shortcomings could have been removed if more resources were given to the project. The lack of management support was also explicitly mentioned as a reason for unsuccessful adaptation. Also awkward and rigid user interfaces caused the adaptation to fail. Not surprisingly, all these reasons are widely known in the general literature concerning failures of information systems (Lyytinen & Hirschheim 1987).

We also asked about the requirements for the successful adaptation. The results of this question are summarised in table 5. The two most frequent requirements were: management support and training and user support (20 observations in together). Other necessary requirements are the ease of use of the tool and tangible benefits gained from its use (7 and 5 observations). Somewhat surprising is, how little importance is given to the functionality of the tools in comparison to table 4, where the shortcomings of the tool were seen as the major factor for failed adaptations. An explanation is, that the interviewees thought of CASE tools when they were asked for criteria for successful adaptation. All experiences of adaptation, in turn, they had about data dictionaries.

Requirements for methods were quite common (12 observations): they must be known both in theory and in practice and they must be both flexible and precisely defined.

8. Summary

The widespread use of tools was just beginning in large IS departments — especially in the case of CASE tools. A reason for this lies partially in the available tools and partially in the inertia of the organisations and in their reluctance to invest on large scale in the (still) costly CASE technology. More powerful and flexible CASE tools and CASE shells with better integration to other tools (repositories, document generators and 4GLs) will

---

[4] For similar arguments regarding the use and usefulness of CASE see (Wilson 1989), where some crucial preconditions for the use of CASE are outlined.

Requirements for a successful adaptation	
• Management support is necessary: enough resources must be provided, company policies must support the adaptation.	10
• User support: enough training for new working practices, support must be there when needed, because it is difficult to estimate correctly the required work in projects that use new tools and methods, there should be some help for the task.	10
• The tools need to be easy to use and function as automatically as possible. There must be interfaces to development and documentation tools.	7
• Thorough knowledge of the methods and systems work is necessary.	6
• Methods must be flexible, but precise.	6
• The users have to accept the tools. Their use must give real benefits for everyone involved. Feedback from users must be taken into account.	5
• The tool has to be customisable.	4
• The tool has to be well understood.	2
• The aims must not be set too high.	1
• Methods discipline must be taken care of.	1

Table 5. Requirements for the success of the adaptation

heal some of these problems. Also when the price/performance ratio improves organisations will be more willing to large scale investments.

Our study shows that organisations express a rich array of ways to adopt CASE technologies and the adaptation process is often painful. Several failures were reported, but many organisations also had carried out the adaptation successfully.

However, there seems to be no general strategy that is good in all situations. Several factors, such as the size and the type of IS department, application portfolio, evolution of methodological practices and skills in the organisation, management commitment and support, expectations of CASE technology, available hardware platforms, and evolution of the CASE market itself affect the shaping and choosing of the strategy.

Organisations did not generally choose the strategy based on careful analysis and consideration. Instead, the strategies seemed to be more or less invented on the fly. Therefore organisations were quite flexible in changing their strategies if major obstacles should occur. We did not encounter any systematic methodological procedures followed in metamodelling and adaptation.

We could generalise five generic strategy options that organisations are likely to follow in introducing the CASE tools. Some of them were more common with data dictionaries which were also included into the study.

The study reveals that the success of the methodology adaptation is crucially dependent on the amount of resources available. If the work is seen as important and is given enough time and work, it is more likely to succeed. The introduction of CASE and the accompanying method discipline is a major change in the IS development which needs to be taken into account through proper training, cultural change and the like. The quality of the tools is also an important success factor: their reporting capabilities (graphic pictures as well as textual reports) and user interface must be advanced and customisable. The use of the tools must give some direct benefits to everyone involved, they should contain many automated functions and have a functional interface to programming tools, code generators and the like.

Most of the success factors we encountered are fairly well known from implementation studies of "ordinary" IS applications. This suggests that methodology adaptation and the introduction of design tools needs to be considered as a species of software development. Its success or failure depends to a large extent on the same factors as developing a "conventional" information system.

References

. , "Building more flexible systems," *I/S Analyzer* **27**(10) pp. 1-12 (October 1989).

. Benbasat, Izak, Goldstein, David K., and Mead, Melissa, "The Case Research Strategy in Studies of Information Systems," *MIS Quarterly* **11**(3) pp. 369-386 (September 1987).

. Bubenko, jr., Janis A., *Selecting a strategy for computer-aided software engineering (CASE)*, SYSLAB University of Stockholm, Stockholm (June 1988).

. Charette, Robert N., *Software Engineering Environments: Concepts and Technology*, Intertext/McGraw-Hill, New York (1986).

. Chen, Peter Pin-Shan, "The entity-relationship model - toward a unified view of data," *ACM Transactions on Database Systems* **1**(1) pp. 9-36 (March 1976).

. De Marco, Tom, *Structured Analysis and System Specification,* Yourdon Press, New York (1978).

. Kemerer, C.F., "An Agenda for Research in the Managerial Evaluation of Computer-Aided Software Engineering (CASE) Tool Impacts," in *Procs. of the 22nd Hawaii International Conference on System Sciences,* (January 1989).

. LeQuesne, P. N., "Individual and Organisational Factors and the Design of IPSEs," *The Computer Journal* **31**(5) pp. 391-397 (1988).

. Lyytinen, Kalle, Smolander, Kari, and Tahvanainen, Veli-Pekka, "Modelling CASE environments in Systems Development," in *Procs. of CASE89 The first Nordic Conference on Advanced Systems Engineering,* , Stockholm (1989).

. Lyytinen, K. and Hirschheim, R. A., "Information System Failures: A Survey and Classification of Empirical Literature," *Oxford Surveys in Information Technology* **4** pp. 257-309 (1987).

. Martin, James, *Information Engineering,* Savant Technical Report 1987.

. McDaniel, Paul D., "Using PSL/PSA to Model Information System Planning for The United States Department of the Army Headquarters," in *Procs. of CASE89 The first Nordic Conference on Advanced Systems Engineering,* , Stockholm (1989).

. Orlikowski, W. J., "CASE Tools and the IS Workplace: Some Findings from Empirical Research," in *Procs. of the 1988 ACM SIGCPR Conference on the Management of Information Systems Personnel,* (April 7-8, 1988).

. Wilson, D. N., "CASE: guidelines for success," *Information and Software technology* **31**(7) pp. 346-350 (September 1989).

APPENDIX:Interview format

1. Background

These questions inquire the relationships between methodology adaptation and the size of the organisation, the industry sector, the educational background of its personnel etc.

It is possible to answer to these questions in advance. If some printed material is available, it will be very useful. We recommend that you collect the necessary information in advance.

1.1. The company

What is the industry sector the company is operating in?

The most important types of customers/most important customers?

1.2. The systems work in the company

By systems work we mean here the production of applications as a whole (at least from systems design to maintenance), not just system design or programming. By methods we mean predefined ways of producing, classifying, and describing design information, not merely drawing techniques or phase models.

The hardware and systems software in use?

The volume of IS work (number of personnel, percentage of company turnover?)

The education of the IS personnel?

The organisation of the IS work?

*   As part of the company

*   Internal organisation (units, their working areas)

*   How is methods development organised?

The design methods in use? In-house changes in them?

How widely are methods used (percentage of personnel and projects)?

Is methods use mandatory? How is it supervised?

The benefits/drawbacks of methods use/not using methods?

The ratio of development/maintenance work?

How many projects are currently running?

Are there any CASE tools or data dictionaries in use/proposed for use? Which?

How are these linked to code generation?

If a data dictionary is used, how many objects/object types are currently defined in it? Number of inherent types/added synonyms/aliases?

What benefits/drawbacks have the tools had? Why?

Is coding made in-house or by some subcontractor?

How are the design documents passed over to programmers?

Some examples of current applications? How are applications managed?

How large are the applications (manyears/lines of source code)? (<1, 1 to 5, 5 to 10, >10 manyears; <10000, 10 000 to 50 000, 50 000 to 100 000, >100 000 lines)

What types of applications are in use? (Batch oriented, real time, interactive, other)

Does the type of application make difference in the methods used in design? How?

Are IS architectures made?

- By whom?

- With which methods?

1.3. The interviewee

The position in the organisation (title, work area)?

Educational background?

Experience in work?

Phone/email for checkings?

2. Methodology adaptation

Here we try to describe methodology adaptation in the company or the need for it. We are especially interested in the benefits and drawbacks of the situation and their causes.

By methodology adaptation we mean the matching of a IS design method and a tool (CASE tool, data dictionary). Methodology description means here that the method to be adapted is descibed with some (possibly some other) method and description technique.

2.1. The need for adaptation

Has the company experienced need for methodology adaptation?

When and why?

Has some adaptation been done?

If not and there would have been need to, why not? How else is the problem solved?

What other (if any) solutions were considered for the problem?

2.2. The making of the adaptation

What tool(s) and which method(s) was (were) involved?

Who did the work, who was responsible for it?

How was the adaptation done (tool, method, ad hoc...)?

How was the method described (E-R model, other)?

Did the adaptation succeed (not at all/badly/moderately/well/perfectly)?

How much resources did the work take?

Difficulties encounterd?

Were changes in the method or in the tool needed? In which? What kinds of changes?

2.3. Benefits and drawbacks

What benefits and drawbacks followed from the adaptation/abandoning the adaptation? (In comparison to the other possibility)?

In which situations do the benefits/drawbacks occur?

What are the benefits/drawbacks due to (method, adaptation, compability of methods, tools, changes made, personnel, other)?

The conditions for a successful adaptation (training, prevailing knowledge, tools, methods, management support)

2.4. Other remarks

Other remarks on the topic?

Comments on the interview?

Application of Relational Normalforms in CASE-tools

Béla Halassy

Computing Application and Service Co. (SZAMALK)
Szakasits A. u. 68., 1502 Budapest, Hungary

Abstract

A new interpretation of relational normalforms is discussed. The goal is
to present such a normalization algorithm that aids process-design, too.
Practical experiences of applying normalform synthesis and decomposition
are highlighted. NF problems are recited and reinterpreted. Normalforms
are revised for completeness. The notion of semantical normalization is
explained. The concept of 'thread' versus 'cover' is suggested. The use
of threads in a coupled data- and process-design is recommended.

1. Background

Based on a long (1976-1987) theoretical and practical experimentation,
our research group has prepared a CASE-tool, named SYDES. This acronym
stands for SYstems DEsigner System. The name covers an information
systems design method, a software supporting the method and a systems
theory, which is the frame of both.

SYDES is a Ianus-faced product. It is a CASE-shell, by the aid of which
arbitrary categories (object-types) can be defined. Analysts may specify
design attributes of categories, conventional values of attributes and
informal descriptions of the enlisted factors. Categories may belong to
the data, event/process or environment aspect of the system. They are
classified according to conceptual, logical and physical levels. In
short: analysts are able to design their own designer system by SYDES.

On the other hand, some categories, properties and conventional values
are predefined in SYDES. E.g. entity, attribute, relationship, process
and event are prespecified SYDES-categories. This means that analysts
do not have to prepare their own designer system, if design-factors
provided by SYDES were sufficient.

Design-quality control is the most valuable function of SYDES. Many
design criteria are built into the system. These are validated at entry
of design information and by separately run analysis programs. We apply

mathematical and semantical evaluation methods. Normalform analysis is one of these. It is employed in a much revised form. The objective of this paper is to present our normalization process, which is closely coupled to the tasks of process-design.

We had a good reason to revise normalforms and normalization. Our first design-aid, SZIAM generated 3NF relations from attribute functional dependencies (FDs). We have used a normalform-synthesis method. (SZIAM has been licensed by IBM). The tool was applied for several large data-modelling tasks (including over 2000 attributes). We had some acceptable results. However, the method of synthesis proved to be very inefficient at such scales. We also had to conclude that data-design is an half-eyed giant, a Cyclops without a parallel process-modelling. The latter is required to capture more semantic meaning of data.

For the above reasons, the synthesis line was dropped. We have prepared a new product, ADAM & EVA. ADAM stands for analytic data modelling. This part of the tool supported normalform-decomposition (4NF). The other subsystem, EVA helped designers to define event-activity networks. The two functions were closely coupled. The product was double-sided in the sense that both a specially extended relational model and a similarly extended entity-relationship model could be prepared by its aid. (For some of virtues, the product has been licensed by BMW AG., FRG.)

We applied a particular decomposition method, which preserved some of the virtues of data-synthesis. Theory was again followed by practice. ADAM & EVA was used in several large applications. The conventional NF-decomposition have failed in many cases. It produced imcomplete, i.e. not connective data-designs. This fact was mostly due to incorrect semantic interpretation of data. We had to realize that data-modelling is rather a semantical than a mathematical endeavour. The next section shows, how our thoughts of normalforms/normalization had been changed.

2. The Nature of Normalforms and Normalization

Information system design-aids may help us to draw nice pictures, like entity-relationship diagrams. They can support management of design-information by 'meta-databases' or 'information resource dictionaries.' Nice tools guide the analysts through the complex design-process. All these tasks are inherent to a design-aid. Nevertheless, we intend to think that quality-assurance must be the most important function of CASE-tools.

Design-products must represent reality correctly. They have to be non-redundant, complete and unambigouos. CASE-tools should include quality-control processes as to ensure specification of optimum designs. We have found that normalforms were powerful means for design quality checking. An appropriate normalization process leads to a proper data-design. At the same time, it may improve the efficiency of process-design as well.

The nature of normalforms and that of normalization should be revised, before these concepts are used for quality-assurance of design-products. A very simple, but tricky example highlights the present problems of normalization.

In 1984, we had to face a design-tool applying the user-view integration approach. This data-design method assumes that the 'global' structure of a database can be deduced from 'private' data requirements of end-users. We have presented two simple views to that tool. (Please, observe our notation. Entity-types or relations, are shown in capital. Primary keys of data units are underlined. Parts of composite keys are connected by '+'. Attributes of entities are enlisted in paranthesis.)

(2.1) a/ ORDER (<u>Order-no</u>, Product-no, Quantity-ordered)
      b/ ORDER (<u>Order-no+Product-no</u>, Quantity-ordered)

Five analysts have worked on this simple case, envoluing not more than four presented concepts, for two hours - without success. The design-aid has failed. Why?

Two basic approaches are applied for normalization: decomposition and synthesis. Let us see, how far we get with any of those.

Both views are in correct normalforms (they are, as we shall see), so they cannot be normalized by decomposition. One may want to unite these two relations into one. The effort is useless: the keys are different. So, let us rename ORDER of b/ to ORDER-1! That would not help, either. The design of (2.1) suggests, that its relations are connectable by Order-no as a foreign-key (cp. 'referential integrity'). They are not.

Normalform synthesis leads to an even greater disgrace. It is based on mechanical normalform-rules. Quantity-ordered is defined by Order-no (View a/). It depends on Order-no+Product-no (View b/), as well. These two statements suggest the partial dependency of Quantity-ordered. Thus View a/ will be the only relation resulted from synthesis.

Let us have a different look at the case of (2.1). We ask the end-user about the meaning of those four concepts. In other words, a semantical

analysis is executed. After a few simple questions, we shall understand
that there are two kinds of orders: customer- and purchase-orders. The
concepts in View a/ and View b/ are homonyms. Customer-orders (View a/)
are always related to a single product, while purchase-orders (View b/)
may have several items.

Conclusion: in terms of normalforms both views are perfect. None of them
has to be or can be normalized. However, homonyms must be eliminated. An
unambigouos capturing of the two views would result in the next design:

(2.2) CUSTOMER-ORDER (C-Order-no, Product-no, Quantity-ordered)
      PURCHASE-ORDER (P-Order-no+Product-no, Quantity-ordered)

Nicely-cut examples are presented in publications. Life is more complex.
Design-tasks may envolve hundreds or even thousands of concepts. An army
of designers and a great bunch of end-users are working at the design.
Communications falter. End-users do not immediately capture the meaning
of 'dependencies', and they may make erroneous statements. Analysts are
working in separate groups, so synonyms and homonyms are hard to avoid
in the overall design. Contradictions, misunderstandings and even lies
are parts of the game...

Design-tools have to help analysts in discovering all discrepancies. It
took only a few seconds with our ADAM & EVA tool to solve the problem of
(2.2). Please, observe, that this was not a fancy-case. We have faced
this very situation at the information modelling of a suit-factory.

Having applied data-modelling techniques at several dozens of companies
and institutions, we came to the following conclusions:

. Normalization and normalforms are mathematical notions; quantitative
  measures to improve a data-design. They are of no use, if the basis
  of normalization was not free of homonym and synonym concepts. The use
  of normalform decomposition or synthesis must be preceeded by a very
  careful semantical analysis, i.e. clarification of concepts.

. Normalform analysis may show, that preliminary statements of concepts
  were of bad quality. Like in case of (2.1). We have executed a special
  normalization. We came to the conclusion that nothing is wrong with
  normalforms; the concepts themselves had been badly formulated. A
  problem of quantitative nature has called our attention to the real
  qualitative trouble.

. Data-design is an iterative process, which follows the 'se-ma-for'
  principle. Semantics first, mathematics next, and the former again.

Our previous findings may be of no great news to some experts. However, we have met many designers, who had applied normalization principles mechanically. We have read many 'classics' of normalization, too. They seem to neglect the aspect of semantics completely, as we shall prove in the next section.

3. Incompleteness of Normalforms

Normalforms are said to be complete in the sense, that 5NF covers the most important kinds of dependencies. 5NF is the ultimate normalform. That we do not doubt. However, we have discovered that the series of NFs had been incompletely defined internally (!). This statement is easily proved by the following decision-table. Before its interpretation, we hasten to declare that we do not intend to implement new NFs into the present cavalcade of dependencies. We just have some semantical remarks.

(3.1)

	1	2	3	4	5	6	7	8
A --> B	P	P	P	P	D	D	D	D
B --> C	P	P	D	D	P	P	D	D
A --> C	P	D	P	D	P	D	P	D

Three functional dependencies (-->) of three attributes (ABC) are shown. 'P' stands for a trivial dependency. In this case a primary-key defines its own part. Like A=(X+Y) --> B=(X). 'D' shows a normal dependency. The key defines a descriptive, non-key attribute.

It is easy to see, that Rule 8 stands for transitive dependency (3NF). Rule 4 explains partial definition (2NF), and Rule 7 covers key-breaking (BCNF). Rule 2 is impossible: if C is part of B, which is contained in A than C must be a key-part of A. But how should the other rules be interpreted? We have found no reasonable treatment of them in the available literature. (Note: This table was composed back in 1980.)

There are two cases. If it is not important, whether a defined attribute is part of the key (P) or not (D), than there is no sense to make any distinction among 2NF, 3NF and BCNF. In all these rules dependency A --> C is transitive (it is not partial or key-breaking). However, if this distinction makes sense, than the series of normalforms is, indeed, internally incomplete. It does not cover four rules of Table (3.1). We believe that these remaining rules must be treated separately, if a correct semantic interpretation (semafor-principle) is to be applied.

Examination of the remaining dependency-structures (rules) follow.

Rule 1 is a set of trivial dependencies. It would be a mistake to handle this case as transitivity, partial-dependency or key-breaking. (This particular rule implies all of these three normalform-problems. A --> C is transitive. A=(X+Y+Z) --> B=(X+Y) --> C=(X) is partial. The last part of this series is key-breaking.) An example:

(3.2) CITY (<u>Country-code+District-code+City-code</u>)
        City-id=Country-code+District-code+City-code

Rule 6 may be considered as a 'group-dependency'. A key defines a group of attributes, which defines its parts. A --> B=(X+Y) --> C=(X). There is no way to resolve this set of dependencies. However, one may ask the question: is C=(X) semantically identical to the part of B=(X+Y)?

(3.3) ACCIDENTS (<u>Accident-no</u>, Date, Month)
        Date=Year+Month+Day

Note: A relation is supposed to contain elementary attributes only. This 'law' is often neglected in data-designs. Thus the question: 'Is Month identical to the part of Date?' is a crucial one.

We have named Rule 5 as 'intersection', since two keys have a common part and one defines the other. A=(X+Y) --> B=(X+Z) --> C=(X). An incorrect normalization would ban A --> B. (Note, that A --> C is not transitive, it is trivial. B --> C cannot be eliminated, either.)

(3.4) DISPO-ITEM (<u>Dispo-item-id</u>, Order-item-id, Quantity)
        Dispo-item-id=Dispo-id+Product-id
        Order-item-id=Order-id+Product-id

The relational model does not recognize attribute-groups. This causes a lot of troubles. Order-item-id should be a foreing-key (cp. referential integrity), but in the 'orthodox' approach there is no way to define it. Thus the question arises: How to connect dispo-items to order-items? Rule 3 is called by us as 'hierarchical key', because one part of the key defines another part. A=(X+Y) --> B(X) --> C(Y). This is neither the 'normal' key-breaking dependency, nor a partial one. There is one only way to resolve this problem: to change the key. Normalization cannot help. A semantical solution is required.

Observe that this last case is the same as the one provided in (2.1). Our design-aid was able to call our attention to a semantical problem, because it had examined hierarchical keys and it have noticed a trouble of mathematical nature. Our tool handles the rules of (3.3) and (3.4) in a similar, semantically based fashion.

In summary: One may face situations, in which normalization-routines cannot help. However, they may call the attention to deeper troubles of semantical roots. Having eliminated homonyms, synonyms, incorrect keys, one may redo normalization according to the 'semafor' principle. This idea is explained in the next section.

4. Semantical Normalization

One may read several publications about 'linear-time' normalization processes, trying to overcome 'quadratic' or 'exponentional' routines. This is very nice: it is good to have optimal normalization algorithms. Unfortunately, they are not up to the issue.

Some analysts pretend to believe, that one has a nicely defined set of relations and attributes, so let us apply a good normalization algorithm and then we shall have the appropriate data-design. Some design-tools follow this principle. They remove incorrect dependencies automatically (decomposition-based tools) or they do not allow speecification of a bad dependency (aids of synthesis). Again, they are not up to the issue.

The two key-points of normalization are interpretation and design time-frame. In nice, small, academic examples one has a predefined set of concepts. In reality, data-design may take several months, and one part of the system must work, before another part is designed. There is nothing like a 'universal relation' or 'minimum cover'. The analyst must apply a 'co-normalization', trying to add new fractions to an already existing database in the best possible fashion. This was stated for the time dimension. Now let us examine the interpretation aspect.

If an A --> B --> C dependency occurs and the A --> C dependency is entered/discovered, than most of the normalization tools would remove the latter definition automatically. Our first design-tools have worked according to this logic, too. Then we have found, that well over 60% of normalform problems resolved by the design-aid were due to semantical misinterpretations. In other words: in terms of mathematics the third (A --> C) dependency was incorrect, though actually - in semantical terms - either A --> B, or B --> C had been falsely specified. (This is plain algebra. There are three dependencies. The chances that the third one is incorrect, are at 33%.)

Data-designs grow because of the time-frame. New attributes and new relations are added to a working environment. We do not endeavour here

221

to explain, how and why does the sequence of such additions influence
the mathematical result of normalization. It is enough to state that
the present mathematical basis of data-design is incapable to cope with
this problem of growth.

In summary: Conventional normalization algorithms are not acceptable.
They are not based on a semantically sound set of concepts, or at least
they do not seem to care about them. Normalization is a bunch of very
mechanical routines, with no back-loops for semantical corrections.

In SYDES, a different method is practiced. Designers may define their
entities (relations), data-items (domains) and their connections
(attributes of relations) 'by heart'. Having defined the basic items,
the analyst may run analysis-routines of SYDES. These will inform her or
him about possible normalform problems. Not just about the ones, known
from the literature. SYDES works on the basis of the (3.1) table. The
designer may follow three routes:

. Consider NF problems as quantitative troubles. When A --> B --> C,
  attribute C is to be removed from the relation identified by A. This
  is the 'orthodox' approach.

. Ignore NF problems. One should recognize that while a 2NF data-unit is
  worse than a 3NF relation in terms of joins, it may have many virtues
  in other design aspects. This is the practical approach.

. Consider NF problems as qualitative troubles. When A --> B --> C,
  any of the functional definitions (including A --> C) may be resulted
  from incorrect interpretations. This is the semantical approach.

This is the essence of SYDES-logic. Tools cannot examine the qualities
of concepts defined by human beings. Nevertheless, when constructed for
this purpose, they can call our attention to semantical problems by
evaluating quantities. This is the essence of semantical normalization.
The basis of such a normalization process is described below.

5. The Concept of 'Threads'

Conventional NF-decomposition methods cannot be used for database
design. The unit of normalization is a suggested relation, without
any structural reference to similar such units. The problem in (2.1)
cannot be solved by this procedure. The notion of referential integrity
will not help either. One question is, whether individual relations are

well-defined or not. A second matter of investigation is, if the whole
set of defined relations were optimally designed. A very simple example
highlights this problem:

(5.1) CUSTOMER (<u>Customer-id</u>, Customer-address)
     ORDER   (<u>Order-no</u>,   Customer-name)

Both relations of (5.1) are in 'perfect' normalform. However, the design
as a whole is a complete mess.

Having recognized the shortcomings of decomposition, new ideas arised,
like covers and universal-relations. They are not really useful. Let
us suppose, that one has 1000 attributes (only). Stating dependencies
among them would require about 500 thousand investigations, if one
wanted to find all possible dependencies. This work cannot be done.

The unit of decomposition (single relations) and that of synthesis
(universal relation, cover) are not acceptable. We seem to be stuck.

A foreign-key in a relation is an attribute of that relation, which
refers to the key of another relation. The key of the first relation
functionally defines all of the attributes of the second one. Like
Order-no defines all customer attributes through Customer-id in (5.2).

(5.2) CUSTOMER (<u>Customer-id</u>, Customer-name, Customer-address)
     ORDER   (<u>Order-no</u>,   Customer-id)

Please, observe, that a foreign-key gives rise to a hierarchy. The real-
world phenomena to be represented by information are referred to as
entities. They are classified to entity types. ORDER and CUSTOMER in
(5.2) are entity-types represented by relations. By nature, they are
in hierarchical connection: a customer may have many orders, but each
order belongs to a single customer. This fact is reflected in the design
by Customer-id of ORDER pointing to CUSTOMER.

(5.3)

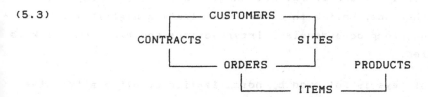

Two entity-types may be connected directly. They may have an indirect
hierarchical relationship, or they may be independent of one another.
In (5.3), ORDERS is directly related to CONTRACTS and indirectly to
CUSTOMERS, while it is independent from PRODUCTS. This means that ORDERS

has a direct reference to CONTRACTS (Contract-no); an indirect coupling to CUSTOMERS (CONTRACTS contains Customer-no) and no connection is made to PRODUCTS (none of the superordinates of ORDERS has Product-no).

In SYDES, we use the 'thread' term. A thread is a bottom-up directed line of entities leading from the lowest entity to the highest one. In case of (5.3), we have three threads. Items/orders/contracts/customers; items/orders/sites/customers and items/products. Threads are represented by keys of entities. They are nothing but chains of dependencies.

A thread is an intermediate unit. It is neither a single relation, as used in normalform-decomposition, nor a universal one, applied in the logic of normalform-synthesis. As we had seen, none of these methods can be used in a real practical data-design. The question is, what is the trade-off of implementing the thread-concept.

All kinds of incorrect (e.g. transitive, partial etc.) dependencies are easy to discover along the threads. Before such a normalization, cycles must be eliminated. The following set of dependencies is circular, so it is a cycle: A --> B --> C --> A. (Note, that some designers would see a cycle in (5.3), too. That example does not have a cycle.) The nature of entity-relationships are also entered to threads. Mandatory and optional connections (strong and weak FDs), partial and total as well as subtype relationships may be specified. This helps us to examine connectivity of the data-model. (Whether all entities are accessible from the others.)

Normalization of keys is the first task to be executed, because of possible cycles. Any of the dependencies may be incorrect in a cycle. Not necessarily the one, at which the cycle had been closed. Human reinterpretation is required. Dependencies must not be removed by a tool automatically. Having eliminated occasional cycles, transitive, partial and other problems are searched for. SYDES manages composite keys both as singular units ('A') and as collections ('A=X+..+Z'). A composite key may define another one, unlike in other normalization algorithms. Thus key-breaking and group dependencies, intersections and hierarchical-keys can be discovered.

Normalization of keys is followed by normalization of other attributes. Threads cannot be used directly to examine occasional FDs between items on parallel branches, such as ORDERS and PRODUCTS in (5.3). This may seem to be a major shortcoming. It is in theory, but not in practice. We have experimented with threads for quite a long time. We have found that at most 13% of 'hidden' dependencies had been undetectable by our process at very large data-models. These dependencies, and many more, could not have been detected by conventional normalization either.

One may argue, that such a normalization process is not linear. It is not. However, normalization is not a one-time effort. The time required for normalization is T * E. 'T' stands for the time of one execution of the analysis and 'E' shows the number of iterations. Normalform problems are mostly due to human failures, like semantic misinterpretations. If an incorrect dependency occurs, a semantical analysis is required. The really bad dependency must be removed, not the one suggested by a tool. Removal of a dependency or migration of an attribute from one relation to another has the consequence that normalization must be repeated.

Threads are very nice means to find the proper place of attributes in one only analysis run. Thus 'T' may be higher as in linear-processes, but 'E' is definitely lower. This is explained by an example:

(5.4)   A --> B --> C --> D --> e   and   A --> e

Key-attributes are shown in upper-case. We have a single descriptor attribute 'e'. When having 3000 attributes, a universal relation is out of question. When applying decomposition, 'e' would migrate from A to B, then from B to C, then from C to D. This is the point, at which its transitivity can be detected. Four iterations ('E'=4) were required. This transitivity is easy to discover at once when using threads.

Threads are redundant. They are overlapping. This is a storage problem only. It has nothing to do with time required for normalization. Common subthreads are analyzed by SYDES only once in one walk-through.

Conclusion: Threads may not be the most efficient means for a single execution of a normalization algorithm. Howewer, they are very useful for semantic normalization to reduce number of runs. In addition, our heuristic process increases the overall efficiency of the desig-effort and the overall optimality of the design-product. This idea is developed in the last section.

6. Threads in Process-Modelling

We cannot agree to the 'data-design first' principle. In nice, small applications that route may be followed. It is unusable in large projects. Data- and process-modelling are parallel efforts, which are coupled at a particular phase of the development.

One of the design subtasks of this coupling is definition of so called
navigation pathes. A navigation path is a set of entities managed by a
particular process-unit. The set is ordered in the sequence of accesses.
At a more detailed level of design, specification of such navigations
include access-mode, type of operation executed on the entities, set of
attributes taken from given entities and their usage-mode. Navigation
pathes can be supplemented with access- and hit-ratio information. These
information can give rise to automatic prototyping of programs. At the
same time, definition of pathes is a good control for data-modelling.

Let us see a simple example related to (5.3). The task of the process is
as follows:
"Find all those customers, who have ordered product 'x' for their sites
located at 'y'." A possible navigation path for this query is in (6.1):

(6.1)

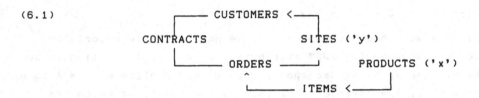

Such pathes are inherent parts of a process-design, so they have to be
stored in the design-dictionary. As to define them, one must have the
network of entities at hand. This is required for analysis reasons. One
must investigate the next questions:

   . Are entities managed by the process specified at all?
   . Are they internally connectable, or external control is required?
   . What is the reasonable sequence of entity management?
   . Are there any possible alternate routes?
   . What is the direction of access?

Navigation may be directed upwards and downwards. The entity, at which
this direction changes, is referred to as an inflexion point. In case of
(6.1) ITEMS is such.

How to manage the required entity-relationship 'diagram'? Storing all
possible pathes would be nonsense in case of several dozens or hundreds
of entities. However, such pathes are very easy to project from threads.

One can specify starting (PRODUCTS), inflection (ITEMS), intermediary
(ORDERS, SITES) and closing (CUSTOMERS) points of navigation pathes.

We have a Hungarian saying: "Two flies for one flap". Threads are very
useful in process-design. Covers and universal relations are not. Thus
data-normalization and 'process-normalization' can be coupled in SYDES.

Processes themselves can and must be 'normalized'. Process structures may also be ambigouos, incomplete or redundant. Some of the entity operations (addition, deletion, modification) may be missing. Some could have been defined duplicately. Parallelled by statements of operation-type, thread-manipulation may give us a convenient basis for analysis of entity life-cycles. When two processes are mapped to threads in the same way, i.e. they manage the same entity-types in the same sequence, the analyst may consider to design of one process instead of two.

Constraints are very important notions in modelling information systems. Normalforms themselves are particular kinds of them, but other types of constraints should also be implemented. Conditional process-branches, entity-association (not just referential) rules, subtyping of entities, appropriate usage of role-names are just a few of them to mention. These constraints pertain to a pair, a chain or a special subset of entities, and not just to one of them. These constraints are easy to define and validate by the aid of threads.

SYDES allows for definition of external input and output of a process as virtual relations. These are implicit starting and ending leaves of a navigation path. Data-flows can be represented in this way. Coupled to entities of threads, a most important constraint can be validated. A process must be able to provide its output from its input and the items of the navigation path. SYDES supports an HIPO-like process-analysis.

7. Conclusions

CASE-tools should envolve relational normalforms for analysis of data-structures. Conventional normalization algorithms are better to avoid. Completeness of NF-concepts must be revised and groups have to be used at least in the analysis and design phases. Normalization is to follow the 'semafor' principle. Threads are very powerful constructs to reduce the number of iterations during the design process. They lend themselves for an easy navigation definition as well as for stating constraints. They proved to raise the overall efficiency of the development effort.

The Conceptual Task Model: a Specification Technique between Requirements Engineering and Program Development (Extended abstract)

S. Brinkkemper*° and A.H.M. ter Hofstede*°

* Software Engineering Research Centre, P.O. Box 424,
3500 AK Utrecht, the Netherlands;
° Department of Information Systems, University of Nijmegen,
Toernooiveld, 6525 ED Nijmegen, the Netherlands

ABSTRACT

In current practice of information system development, as well as in its support tools, there exists a gap between the informal requirements engineering activities and the more formal program development stage. To overcome this, a specification technique, called the Conceptual Task Model (CTM), is introduced, that is related explicitly to the results of the global requirements specification, i.e. process models and data models, and that can be input to code generation. The CTM technique is based on and defined in terms of Predicate\transition nets. CTM integrates the specification of the data manipulation function with control structures and local and global data models. The possibilities for the automated support of CTM are discussed. Finally, the precise relation with the process model and some other theoretical issues are presented.

KEYWORDS:

Process model, data model, conceptual task model, predicate\transition nets, CASE-tool.

1.   INTRODUCTION

The requirements engineering phase and the program development phase, as they are commonly distinguished in the information system development life cycle, do not fit to each other properly with respect to the intermediate specification of the process view of the system. Output of requirements engineering should be a formal, complete, precisely defined problem specification, from which during program development code is derived manually or generated automatically.

The requirements engineering techniques used are unfortunately of an informal and global nature in order to capture the system in a concise and comprehensible way. Data flow diagrams and Entity-Relationship diagrams in some or other notation describe the process view and the data view of the system respectively. The data models are used to generate the data definition part (DDL) of the application software. Regarding the data manipulation part (DML), the processes at the bottom level of the data flow hierarchy, the so-called *tasks* [Brinkkemper 89a], are detailed by means of pseudo coding techniques, such as mini-specs [Yourdon 79] or action diagrams [Martin 85]. Since these contain informal statements, programmers usually need additional specifications and of course, pseudo code can never be input to code generation. In practice this leads to requirements engineering specifications only being helpful to define the scope and subject matter of the project, but a transformation of the process specification to programs is not made.

The crucial problem is therefore in the specification of the tasks, the processes at the bottom level of the process model. The tasks are processing data, that in its turn is specified in the data model. The tasks are refinements of the system processes and so their decomposition and contents will result in the modules and logic of the ultimate code.

We here want to introduce a new specification technique in which parts of the requirements engineering can be specified and that can be input to code generation. We impose on such a specification technique the following requirements:

1.   The technique should enable fluent transfer between the phases and steps. Cross-references between models should be explicit.

2. The technique should be complete with respect to control flow, i.e. triggers, decisions, dynamic constraints and iteration.

3. The technique should produce unambiguous models that can straightforwardly be input to code generation or programming.

4. The technique should have a sound formal theoretical basis to enable the verification of theoretical statements and the formulation of properties on models that underlie all sorts of validation analysis.

5. The technique should be diagrammatic in order to ensure fast comprehension of the models during all kinds of written and verbal communication.

6. The technique should be complete with respect to data manipulation: retrieval of (derived) data as well as updates of the data.

There are a lot of methods proposed for the specification of processes, although not especially intended to be used for task modelling. We mention here ACM/PCM [Brodie 82], REMORA [Rolland 82], IML [Richter 82], Structure Charts [Yourdon 79], Process algebra [Bergstra 86], JSD [Jackson 83], EXSPECT [van Hee 88] and Petri-nets [Reisig 85]. We have reviewed most of them on their applicability for task modelling by assessing the requirements above. Those existing techniques do to a large extent not satisfy all the requirements (see [Ter Hofstede 89]).

Task specification, as we propose it here using the Conceptual Task Model (CTM), continues with the results of the global process specification, for instance denoted in data flow diagrams, and the completed data models. The manipulation of the data is defined in terms of small parts of the data model, for which we use here NIAM [Nijssen 89] and RIDL [Meersman 82], but any combination of data modelling technique and data modelling language, such as for instance relational tables and SQL, could be used. The work here can be seen as an elaboration of ideas in of the work of Genrich [Genrich 87], Kung and Sölvberg [Kung 86] and Richter and Durchholz [Richter 82].

In the following chapter we will introduce the CTM formally, formulate some properties and give an example of a CTM-net. The implementation of a CTM support tool for its use in system development is discussed in chapter 3. Chapter 4 contains some theoretical issues, such as the formal correspondence of the task model with the process model. We conclude with some summarising remarks and options for further research. This work is an extended abstract of [Ter Hofstede 89], which in its turn is an extension of the research reported in [Brinkkemper 89a].

2. THE CONCEPTUAL TASK MODEL

In this section first the Conceptual Task Model (CTM) will be defined in terms of Predicate\transition nets and an example of a CTM-net will be presented. Then the CTM will be defined formally and the example will be related to the formal definition. Based on the formal definition we can formulate some properties a correct CTM-net must have.

2.1 PrT-net basis of the CTM

One way to introduce the CTM is to base it upon the formalism of Predicate/transition nets (PrT-nets). The advantage of this proceeding is that the semantics of the CTM is then (partly) defined through the semantics of PrT-nets.

PrT-nets are introduced by Genrich and others in a series of articles, starting with [Genrich 79], and at the moment concluded by [Genrich 87]. In short, PrT-nets are interpreted, inscribed high-level Petri nets, where inscriptions consist of variables for individuals (as opposed to the non-individual token of Petri nets) and truth-valued expressions, preferably in first-order predicate logic. For a detailed treatment of PrT-nets we refer to [Genrich 87].

A CTM-net is a PrT-net where

- Instead of the formalism of first-order logical formulas and their structures, the conceptual data modelling language NIAM in combination with the corresponding data manipulation language RIDL is used as supporting structure. Functions and expressions, which can be seen as special kinds of RIDL functions, are interpreted in this structure.

- A distinction is made between task places and information places. A conceptual schema in NIAM is related to both kinds of places. Each place of the PrT-net is either a task place or an information place. The conceptual schema of an information place determines the information structure of the tuples that can enter that place. The conceptual schema of a task place describes that part of the Universe of Discourse consisting of all the individuals of the tuples that can enter that place.

- An additional typing is related to each task place. When the arity of a task place P is n, a typing $<T1,T2,...,Tn>$ is associated with P such that for every tuple $<P1,P2,...,Pn>$ that can enter P we have that Pi is of type Ti (for all $1 \leq i \leq n$). The typing of a task place is a linear representation of the two-dimensional conceptual schema associated with that task place.

- Arrows may not be labeled with linear combinations of tuples, but only with single tuples.

We adopt three simplifying notational conventions. The first convention is that if we have n ($n > 1$) disjoint conditions (C1,C2,...,Cn), possibly combined with m ($m \geq 0$) other conditions (Q1,Q2,...,Qm), then instead of having n separate transitions for each condition, we introduce one combined transition containing all conditions, as shown in fig. 2.1. Output arrows coming from a transition containing condition Ci are now attached to the little box containing Ci inside the combined transition.

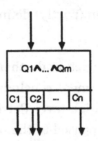

Figure 2.1 Combined transition for C1,C2,...,Cn

The second and third notational conventions are shown in fig. 2.2. These concern database I/O, which is bi-directional in the Predicate\transition formalism.

2.2 Example

In fig. 2.3, an example of a CTM-net is shown. This CTM-net calculates the rental proceeds of a film, which is defined as zero for new films and for rentable films as the number of tapes that contain that film times the rental price for that film.

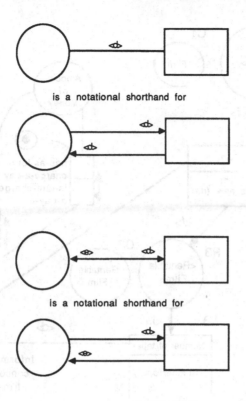

is a notational shorthand for

is a notational shorthand for

Figure 2.2 Double arrow convention for the CTM

In transition *T1* it is checked whether the film is new or not. Information of the information place *Information concerning films and tapes* is necessary to check this. If the film is new, a token consisting of that film is placed in the input place *P2* of transition *T2*. Transition *T2* then adds the current default value for new films (zero) to the tuple. If the film is not new, which is equivalent to the film being rentable, transition *T3* is enabled. Transition *T3* calculates the number of tapes that contain the processed film. Transition *T4* then searches for the rental price of the film and performs the multiplication of the number of tapes *n* and that rental price. Transition *T3* as well as transition *T4* need information from the information place *Information concerning films and tapes*. At the end of the calculation, task place *P5* will contain the film and its rental proceeds.

Near every place of the CTM-net, the corresponding conceptual schema is shown. These conceptual schemas contain information about the tuples that

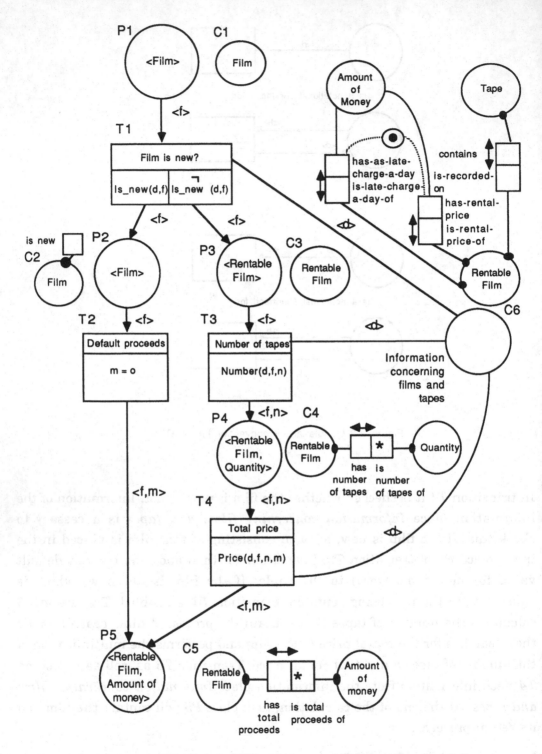

Figure 2.3 CTM-net for rental proceeds calculation

can enter the place to which the conceptual schema belongs. Conceptual schema *C2* for instance, asserts that every film that enters task place *P2* is new. The star in the conceptual schemas *C5* and *C6* denotes that the role, in which box the star is placed, is redundant.

The RIDL functions used in the transitions of fig. 2.3 are shown in fig. 2.4. In the function headings, we also showed the database on which these functions operate. In the function definitions we left this relation implicit.

```
PREDICATE Is_new (DATABASE d; FILM f);
BEGIN
        f IS NOT IN Rentable-film
END;

PREDICATE Number (DATABASE d; RENTABLE FILM f, QUANTITY n);
BEGIN
        n = NUMBER-OF Tape contains Rentable-film f
END;

PREDICATE Price (DATABASE d; RENTABLE FILM f, QUANTITY n, AMOUNT OF MONEY m);
BEGIN
        m = n * Amount-of-money is-rental-price-of Rentable-film f
END.
```

Figure 2.4. RIDL-queries belonging to CTM-net for rental proceeds calculation

Of course the CTM-net of fig. 2.3 is not the only possible solution to model the rental proceeds calculation. In fact it is a rather elaborate solution since it is possible to combine all the RIDL expressions in one transition. The disadvantage of that proceeding however is, that assertions about local information remain implicit. Another option is e.g. to have transition *T1* put a tuple *<f,0>* directly into task place *P5* if the film *f* is new. This obscures however the meaning of the zero. Guide-lines for modelling a task as a CTM-net will be reported soon.

2.3 Formal definition

After this introduction the definition of the Conceptual Task Model can be given in a formal way.

Definition 2.1 A CTM-net is a 12-tuple $(\Pi, T, P, \Sigma, \Psi, Z, I, \Phi, \Lambda, \Theta, X, \Omega)$, where

Π is a non-empty finite set of places,

T is a non-empty finite set of transitions (not combined transitions in the sense of fig. 2.1),

P is a finite set of parameterised RIDL expressions,

Σ is a non-empty finite set of conceptual schemas,

Ψ is a finite set of linear typings (a linear typing is a tuple of arbitrary length consisting of entity types),

Z is a non-empty finite set of variables,

$I \subseteq \Pi$ is a set of information places; $\Gamma = \Pi/I$ (by definition) is the set of task places,

$\Phi \subseteq \Pi \times T \cup T \times \Pi$ is a non-empty set of arrows, denoting that a place is input for or output of a transition,

$\Lambda \in \wp \wp(Z)^{\Phi}$ is a function from the set of arrows Φ to the set $\wp \wp(Z)$ of tuples of arbitrary length of variables chosen from Z, denoting the labeling of the arrows with a tuple of variables,

$\Theta \in P^{T}$ is a function from the set of transitions T to the set of parameterised RIDL expressions P, denoting which RIDL query belongs to which transition,

$X \in \Sigma^{\Pi}$ is a function from the set of places Π to the set of conceptual schemas Σ, denoting which conceptual schema belongs to which place,

$\Omega \in \Psi^{\Gamma}$ is a function from the set of task places Γ to the set of linear typings Ψ, denoting which typing belongs to which task place.

Now we relate the CTM-net of fig. 2.3 to this definition of a CTM-net. We will give examples of elements of each of the constituents of the 12-tuple:

P1,P2,..,P5 are elements of Π;

T1a, T1b and *T2* are elements of T (*T1a* and *T1b* are transitions that would become visible if we would unfold transition *T1* according to the notational shorthand of figure 2.1);

Number(d,f,n) is in P;

C1,C2,...,C6 are the elements of Σ;

<Rentable Film, Quantity> is in Ψ;

f, m and *n* are elements of Z;

Information concerning films and tapes is the only element of I, *P1* is an element of Γ;

(P1,T1) is an element of Φ, denoting the arrow going from task place *P1* to transition *T1*;

((T3,P4),<f,n>) is an element of Λ, denoting the labeling of the arrow going from transition *T3* to task place *P4* with the tuple *<f,n>*;

(T4,Price(d,f,n,m)) is contained in Θ;

(P5,C5) is an element of X;

(P5,<Rentable Film, Amount of Money>) is an element of Ω.

2.4 Properties

To formulate the properties a CTM-net must have, we introduce some auxiliary functions and predicates in an informal way. Most of these functions and predicates cannot be given here in a formal way, since we do not have a formal definition of RIDL and NIAM at hand.

The function *entity* operates on a conceptual schema and yields the set of entity types occurring in that conceptual schema,

Type_in_expression (r, v, e) is true if and only if the formal parameter *v* is supposed to be of type *e* in expression *r*,

The function *merge* operates on a set of conceptual schemas and yields the integration of these schemas,

The predicate *part_of* defines a binary relation between conceptual schemas and is true if and only if the first conceptual schema is part of the second conceptual schema,

The function *domain* operates on a RIDL expression and yields the domain (this is a conceptual schema) of that expression.

Among others, the following properties must hold for the 12-tuple:

Property 2.1

$$\forall p \in I \; \forall t \in T \; [\; (p,t) \in \Phi \Leftrightarrow (t,p) \in \Phi \;]$$

This property states that an information place is never only input for nor only output of a transition.

Property 2.2

$$\forall p \in \Pi \; \exists t \in T \; [\; (p,t) \in \Phi \vee (t,p) \in \Phi \;]$$

Every place is input for or output of a transition. From this property and the first property one can derive that every information place is input for at least one transition and also that every information place is output of at least one transition. It must not be forgotten however, that the set of information places may be empty.

Property 2.3

$$\forall p \in \Pi/I \ [\ \cup \ \Omega(p) = \text{entity} \ (X(p)) \ ]$$

This property states that the set (not multi-set!) of entity types occurring in the typing of a task place equals the set of entity types occurring in the conceptual schema of that task place.

Property 2.4

$$\forall t \in T \ \forall v \in Z \ \forall e \ [\ \text{type\_in\_expression} \ (\Theta \ (t), v, e) \Rightarrow$$
$$\forall p \in \Pi/I \ \forall i \ [\ (((p,t) \in \Phi \wedge (\Lambda(p,t))_i = v) \Rightarrow (\Omega(p))_i = e \ ) \wedge$$
$$(((t,p) \in \Phi \wedge (\Lambda(t,p))_i = v \ ) \Rightarrow (\Omega(p))_i = e \ )] \ ]$$

This complex looking property simply states that the type of a formal parameter as can be derived from the typing of the task place to which it belongs should agree with the way this formal parameter is used (i.e. of which type it is supposed to be) in the expression of the transition to which it is a local variable.

Property 2.5

$$\forall t \in T \ [\text{part\_of}(\text{domain}(\Theta(t)), \text{merge}(\{c \mid c \in \Sigma \mid \exists \ p \in I$$
$$[(p,t) \in \Phi \wedge X(p) = c]\}))]$$

A RIDL expression in a transition should operate on the conceptual schemas of the information places connected to that transition, i.e. the domain of the RIDL expression $\Theta(t)$ of the transition t is part of the union of the conceptual schemas c of the information places p connected to t. This is a simple formulation of the type checking of queries and is derived from the more important rule that queries are formulated in terms of the data model. Of course more than property 2.5 can be stated about the relation of the query and the data model, but that is beyond the scope of this work. We only formulate the following simple corollary.

Corollary 2.6. The entity types in a RIDL expression are a subset of the entity types of the information places:

$\forall t \in T [\text{entity}(\text{domain}(\Theta(t))) \subseteq \text{entity}(\text{merge}(\{c \in \Sigma \mid \exists\, p \in I [(p,t) \in \Phi \land$
$X(p) = c]\})))]$

Take the RIDL expression *Price* in fig. 2.4 as an example. This query has the types *Rentable Film* and *Amount of money* as entity types, which occur both in the conceptual schemas *C6* of fig. 2.3.

There are more properties a correct CTM-net must have. We will defer discussion of one of those properties to section 4. For a discussion of other properties of correct CTM-nets, we refer to [Ter Hofstede 89]. Worth stating here is that a CTM-net should contain the complete specification of a task. This requirement however, is not verifiable, since the completeness of a specification depends on the completeness of the informants' specification.

3.   CASE TOOL IMPLEMENTATION

The CTM technique is hardly applicable in a manual way for the modelling of tasks of a realistic sized IS, due to the complexity of the resulting diagrams. Automated support of the technique in a tool, possibly combined with modelling techniques for activities, data and user interaction, is required. Properties are formulated, on which all sorts of analysis of application models can be based.

In fig. 3.1 we show a proposal for a screen layout of a tool supporting the modelling of tasks using the CTM. The data models of the places and the RIDL-queries of the transition are shown in separate pop-up windows. When these windows are left out, a plain PrT-net remains.

The tool may provide additional support for a modelling procedure in the sense as described in [Brinkkemper 88]. To be distinguished are the preliminary task modelling, identification of individual transitions, modelling of data at the places, formulation of the RIDL-queries and the checks on the components. When the transitions in a task are known, they can be put in a preliminary schema, with some intermediate task places connecting them. Those transitions can be modelled and analysed separately. After that they can be integrated for global analysis of consistency, connectivity or for other purposes.

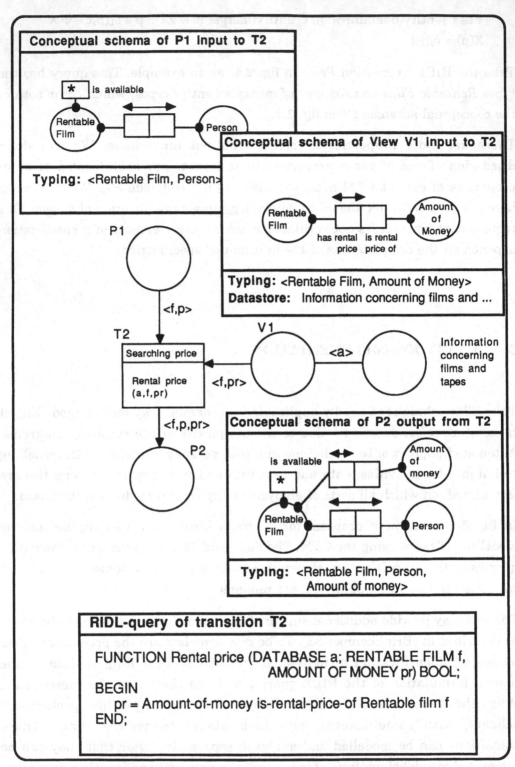

Conceptual schema of P1 Input to T2

* is available

Rentable Film — Person

Typing: <Rentable Film, Person>

Conceptual schema of View V1 Input to T2

Rentable Film — Amount of Money

has rental price   is rental price of

Typing: <Rentable Film, Amount of Money>
Datastore: Information concerning films and ...

P1

<f,p>

T2

Searching price

Rental price (a,f,pr)

V1   <a>   Information concerning films and tapes

<f,pr>

<f,p,pr>

P2

Conceptual schema of P2 output from T2

is available   Amount of money

* Rentable Film — Person

Typing: <Rentable Film, Person, Amount of money>

RIDL-query of transition T2

FUNCTION Rental price (DATABASE a; RENTABLE FILM f, AMOUNT OF MONEY pr) BOOL;
BEGIN
    pr = Amount-of-money is-rental-price-of Rentable film f
END;

Fig. 3.1 Screen layout of CTM tool

However, we propose in this section a practical diagramming convention, that deviates in two ways from the theoretical technique. This is necessary to improve the practical applicability. The discrepancies between the practical and the theoretical technique can be overcome by standard transformations, that can be derived from the descriptions below. The adaptations are the following.

First, we use data base views instead of database tuples. Since tasks need only a certain part of the data present in the data base, we define a view that models this part. This view is positioned on the arrow from the information place to the transition. An information place gets surrounded by such views. The conceptual schema of a view is a derivable part of the conceptual schema of the information place. Recall that the information places correspond with the data for which retrieval queries or update queries are formulated, whereas the data model at the task places stand for the parameters of the transition. Syntactical and semantical cross-checks of queries and parameters versus data models can be performed automatically.

All inputs and outputs of a transition are now specified by small conceptual schemas. An example of a view is shown in fig. 3.1 for the information place *Information concerning films and tapes*. The conceptual schema of view V1 is part of the conceptual schema C6 in fig. 2.3. In the PrT formalism such views are not prohibited, but the strong relation of the data in the data store with that in the data view must be described completely. This is not practical, since database management systems implement views very effectively.

Secondly, we propose for the tool implementation to support the decomposition of tasks. This decomposition obeys analogous rules as those for the decomposition of activities in data flow diagrams. The conceptual schemas at the places may also be decomposed, but the decomposition must always satisfy the requirement that tasks process data elements (see the definitions in [Brinkkemper 89a]).
In PrT-nets this is again not possible due to the unclear firing semantics of the decomposition, when data elements corresponding to more than one input or output place are optional.

Next to this and next to the discussions in the previous sections, we suggest three additional functionalities in a CTM-tool.

1. Support of modelling transparency. Because of the dependencies between the task models and the models of other types, like activity models and global conceptual schemas, developers working with the tool wish to be able to transfer directly from one type of model to the other via a dependency between the models. For example the transfer from a task model to the activity it belongs to. See [Brinkkemper 89b] for a discussion of the modelling transparency functionality of workbenches and the various degrees of it.

2. Syntactic and semantic analysis of data models and queries. As already suggested above, the presence and the type of the data that are processed or created in a transition can be analysed and compared with the queries specified. Furthermore, the violation of the constraints can be pointed out.

3. Support of re-use. A support tool can compare the patterns of the data models or of the transitions with existing models and suggest to make use of them.

For a discussion of system generation, reverse engineering and simulation in the CTM, we refer to [Ter Hofstede 89].

4. THEORETICAL ISSUES

In this section we will address some theoretical issues concerning the CTM. First the relation between the CTM and data flow diagrams is investigated. Then the computational power of the CTM is considered briefly. Finally some remarks about correctness of conceptual schemas at task places are made.

4.1 The relation between activities and tasks

Data flow diagrams generally consist of activators and flows. Flows represent information in motion, activators can be considered as functions on these flows. A well-known representative of data flow diagrams are the ISAC activity graphs or A-graphs [Lundeberg 80]. We will use an adapted version of these activity graphs here.

Definition 4.1 A data flow diagram is a 9-tuple $(S, A, D, F, R, Q, U, G, H)$, where

S is a non-empty finite set of states,

A is a non-empty finite set of activities,

$D \subseteq S$ is a set of data stores; $E = S \backslash D$ (by definition) is a set of flows,

$F \subseteq S \times A \cup A \times S$ is a non-empty set of arrows,

$R \subseteq E \times E$ is the subflow relation,

$Q \subseteq A \times A$ is the subactivity relation,

$U \subseteq S \times A$ is the substate-activity relation,

G is a non-empty finite set of conceptual schemas,

$H \in G^S$ is a function from the set of states to the set of conceptual schemas.

In [Falkenberg 89] some of the rules are stated this 9-tuple must fulfil. An example of such a rule would be that every state has a source, which could formally be expressed as:

$$\forall s \in S \, \exists a \in A \, [\, (a,s) \in F \,]$$

Definition 4.2 The set of tasks Y_d of a data flow diagram $\mathcal{D} = (S_d, A_d, D_d, F_d, R_d, Q_d, U_d, G_d, H_d)$ is given by:

$$Y_d = \{\, t \mid t \in A_d \, \neg \exists \, v \in A_d [\, (v,t) \in Q_d \,] \,\}$$

Informally, a task is an activity at the bottom level of the decomposition hierarchy, i.e. an activity that is not decomposed into other activities.

Definition 4.3 Let a be a task of a diagram $\mathcal{D}$, $a \in Y_d$, then

$$W_d(a) = \{\, s \mid s \in S_d \mid ((a,s) \in F_d \vee (s,a) \in F_d) \wedge (s \in E_d \Rightarrow \neg \exists \, t \in E_d [\, (t,s) \in R_d \,]) \,\}$$

$W_d(a)$ is the set of states which are input for or output of the task a and do not have any subflows.

These definitions enable us to formulate the relations between data flow diagrams and CTM-nets formally.

Suppose a is a task of data flow diagram

$$\mathcal{D} = (S_d, A_d, D_d, F_d, R_d, Q_d, U_d, G_d, H_d)$$

So $a \in Y_d$. Let

$$C_a = (\Pi_a, T_a, P_a, \Sigma_a, \Psi_a, Z_a, I_a, \Phi_a, \Lambda_a, \Theta_a, X_a, \Omega_a)$$

represent the CTM-net for task a.

The relation between the data flow diagram $\mathcal{D}$ and the CTM-net C_a is then expressed via an <u>injective</u> function f_a from the set of input and output states of task a in the data flow diagram $W_d(a)$ and the set of places of task a in the CTM-net Π_a:

$$f_a: W_d(a) \to \Pi_a.$$

For this function f_a the following properties must hold:

Property 4.4 Bijective data store mapping

$f_a \mid D_d \to I_a$ is bijective

This property states that the restriction of f_a to D_d is a bijective mapping on I_a, i.e. every information place of the CTM-net C_a is the unique image of a data store in the data flow diagram $\mathcal{D}$ which is input or output of the task a.

Property 4.5 Consistent input property

$$\forall \, s \in W_d(a) \, [(s,a) \in F_d \Leftrightarrow \exists \, u \in T_a \, [\, (f_a(s),u) \in \Phi_a \wedge (f_a(s) \in I_a \Rightarrow \Lambda_a((f_a(s),u)) = \Lambda_a((u,f_a(s))))] \,]$$

If a flow s, which is not decomposed, is input for task a in the data flow diagram $\mathcal{D}$, then there exists a transition in the CTM-net C_a which has the corresponding place $f_a(s)$ as input. If a data store s is input for task a in the data flow diagram $\mathcal{D}$, then there exists a transition in the CTM-net C_a which is connected to the corresponding place $f_a(s)$ by two arrows, one input arrow and one output arrow, with the same labeling. Conversely, if a place that is the image of a flow s, is input for a transition of the CTM-net C_a, then flow s must be input for task a in the data flow diagram $\mathcal{D}$. If a place, that is the image of a data store s, is input as well as output of a certain transition of the CTM-net C_a with both arrows having the same labeling, then data store s must be input for task a in the data flow diagram $\mathcal{D}$.

Note that when in a CTM-net a place is input as well as output of a certain transition and the arrow going from that place to the transition has the same labeling as the arrow going from the transition to that place, this means that the contents of that place is only used, not changed, by the transition.

Property 4.6 Consistent output property

$$\forall\, s \in W_d(a)\ [(a,s) \in F_d \Leftrightarrow \exists\, u \in T_a\ [\ (u,f_a(s)) \in \Phi_a \wedge (f_a(s) \in I_a \Rightarrow \Lambda_a((f_a(s),u)) \neq \Lambda_a((u,f_a(s))))]\ ]$$

The explanation of this property is analogous to the explanation of the previous property.

Property 4.7 Identical conceptual schemas property

$$\forall\, s \in W_d(a)\ [\ H_d(s) = X_a(f_a(s))\ ]$$

A state s in the data flow diagram of task a must be associated to the same conceptual schema as its corresponding place $f_a(s)$ in the CTM-net.

Normally activities, flows, places and transitions can be named. In this case s and $f_a(s)$ should also have the same name.

Based on the properties of the CTM and the ones specified above, some theorems can be formulated of which we present one.

Theorem 4.8 The domain of all queries of a task is specified in the conceptual schemas related to the data stores of the task.

Proof: Let a be an arbitrary task and let T_a be the set of all transitions of a.
Define $Q = \{q \in P_a \mid \exists t \in T_a\ [q = \Theta(t)]\}$. Q is then the set of all queries of the task a.
According to property 2.5 the domain of an arbitrary query $q \in Q$ is specified in conceptual schemas corresponding to information places p, that are input for the transition t: $(p,t) \in \Phi_a$.
From property 4.4 we deduce that this p is the image of a data store s: $p = f_a(s)$, and according to property 4.7 the conceptual schema $H_d(s)$ of s is the same as the conceptual schema $X_a(p)$ of p. QED

In the same style it can be proven that all data stores of the data flow diagram are used by queries in the tasks and that the images of any two states related to the task a in the data flow diagram are connected via a path in the CTM-net.

4.2 Computational power of the CTM

There are various approaches to capture the idea of computation. The class of the Turing computable functions is an example of such an approach. The principle that Turing machines are formal versions of algorithms and that no computational procedure will be considered an algorithm unless it can be presented as a Turing machine is known as Church's Thesis or the Church-Turing Thesis [Lewis 81]. If we can prove that in the CTM one can simulate any arbitrary Turing machine, we prove in fact that the CTM can compute any computable function. In [Ter Hofstede 89] a CTM-net is presented that simulates an arbitrary Turing machine.

4.3 Correctness of conceptual schemas at task places

A conceptual schema of a task place describes that part of the Universe of Discourse of those individuals that can enter that particular task place. The conceptual schemas output of a certain transition must be derivable from the conceptual schemas at the places input for that transition and the RIDL expression belonging to that transition.

As an example consider fig. 4.1. In the simple CTM-net shown there, either the conceptual schema in task place $P2$ or the conceptual schema in task place $P1$ is incorrect. In the conceptual schema of $P1$ we see that a manager never is a coworker and vice versa, while in the conceptual schema of $P2$ we see that it is forbidden to be manager and coworker of the same project. Tuple $<e,m,p>$ comes in and goes out of transition T, so every tuple $<e,m,p>$ that enters $P2$ was previously contained in $P1$. Hence the population of $P2$ satisfies the constraints belonging to $P1$. The conclusion must be that one of the schemas is incorrect.

The example shown was extremely simple, in general the situation is much more complex. Places can be output of more transitions, transitions can have more input places and schemas can change due to the RIDL expressions in the transitions and the schemas in the information places. For a more detailed discussion on correctness aspects of conceptual schemas at task places we refer to [Ter Hofstede 89].

5.   CONCLUSIONS

In this paper the Conceptual Task Model was introduced, which was intended to fill the gap between informal requirements engineering and program development. CTM-nets were defined as special kinds of PrT-nets and the CTM was defined formally accompanied with some of the properties of a correct

CTM-net. A CASE tool implementation of the CTM was discussed briefly and the relation between activities and tasks investigated. Finally the issues of computational power of the CTM and correctness of conceptual schemas at task places, were addressed.

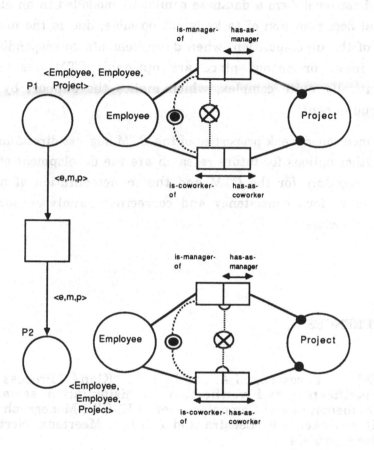

Figure 4.1 Incorrect CTM-net with respect to conceptual schemas

The CTM has several strong points. It was developed to fulfil the requirements on task modelling techniques as formulated in section 1. Fluent transfer between intermediate design results is supported due to the well-defined relation between activities and tasks and the incorporation of a data modelling technique. Tasks can be modelled on a conceptual level, thus enabling the analyst to abstract from particular machines and programming languages and their limitations. The CTM allows for code generation and the verification of all kinds of theoretical statements. Common constructs used in the processing of data elements as well as data manipulation and data retreival can be expressed easily. Finally, in principle every computable function can be specified in the CTM.

The CTM has however also some weak properties, inherited from its PrT basis. Update and retrieval form a database cannot be modelled in an elegant way. Hierarchical decomposition of tasks is not possible, due to the unclear firing semantics of the decomposition, when data elements corresponding to more than one input or output place are optional. CTM-nets tend to be diagrammatically quite complex, which makes the support by a tool an absolute requirement.

The above mentioned weak properties of the CTM suggest directions for future research. Other options for future research are the development of a detailed modelling procedure for the CTM and the implementation of a tool, that includes the various consistency and correctness analyses based on the formulated properties.

6. REFERENCES

[Bergstra 86]   Bergstra, J.A. and J.W. Klop, "Process Algebra: specification and verification in bisimulation semantics". In: Mathematics and Computer Science II, CWI Monograph 4, Eds. M. Hazewinkel, J.K. Lenstra and L.G.L.T. Meertens, North-Holland, 1986, pp.61-94.

[Brinkkemper 88] Brinkkemper, S. , N. Brand and J. Moormann, "Deterministic Modelling Procedures for Automated Analysis and Design Tools". In: Proceedings of the CRIS 88 conference on Computerized Assistance during the Information Systems Life Cycle, Eds. T.W. Olle, A.A. Verrijn Stuart and L. Bhabuta, Egham, England, September 1988, North-Holland, Amsterdam, pp. 117 - 160.

[Brinkkemper 89a]   Brinkkemper, S. and A.H.M. ter Hofstede, "The Modelling of Tasks at a Conceptual Level in Information Systems Development Methods". In: Workshop Proceedings for the CRIS review workshop, Eds. G.M. Nijssen and S. Twine, IFIP WG 8.1 meeting, Sesimbra, Portugal, June 1989.

[Brinkkemper 89b]   Brinkkemper, S., "The Essence and Support of Modelling Transparency", Position paper. In: Advance Working Papers, Third International Conference on Computer Aided

Software Engineering, Ed. J. Jenkins, Imperial College, London, UK, July 1989.

[Brodie 82] Brodie, M.L. and E. Silva, "Active and Passive Component Modelling: ACM/PCM". In: [Olle 82], pp.41-92.

[Falkenberg 89] Falkenberg, E.D., R. van der Pols and Th.P. van der Weide, "Understanding Process Structure Diagrams". In: Workshop Proceedings for the CRIS review workshop, Eds. G.M. Nijssen and S. Twine, IFIP WG 8.1 meeting, Sesimbra, Portugal, June 1989.

[Genrich 79] Genrich, H. and K. Lautenbach: "The Analysis of Distributed Systems by means of Predicate/Transition Nets", Semantics of Concurrent Computation. Evian 1979, Ed. G. Kahn, Lecture Notes in Computer Sciences, vol.70, Springer Verlag 1979, pp.123-146.

[Genrich 87] Genrich, H.: "Predicate/Transition Nets". In Petri Nets: Central models and their properties, Eds. W. Brauer, W. Reisig and G. Rozenberg, L.N.C.S. nr 254, Springer Verlag 1987, pp 207-247.

[van Hee 88] van Hee, K.M., G.J. Houben, L.J. Somers and M. Voorhoeve, "Executable Specifications for Information Systems", Computing Science Notes, nr. 88/05, Department of Computing Science, Eindhoven University of Technology, March 1988.

[Jackson 83] Jackson, M.A., "System Development", Prentice Hall, 1983.

[Kung 86] Kung, C.H. and A. Sölvberg, "Activity Modeling and Behavior Modeling". In: Information System Design Methodologies - Improving the Practice, Eds. Olle, T.W., H.G. Sol and A.A. Verrijn Stuart, Proceedings of the CRIS-86 conference, North Holland Publ. Co., 1986, pp. 145 - 171.

[Lewis 81] Lewis, H.R. and C.H. Papadimitriou, "Elements of the theory of Computation", Prentice Hall, 1981.

[Lundeberg 80] Lundeberg, M., G. Goldkuhl and A. Nilsson, "Information Systems Development - A Systematic Approach". Prentice Hall, Englewood Cliffs, 1980.

[Martin 85] Martin, J. and C. McClure, "Action Diagrams", Prentice Hall, Englewood Cliffs, N.J., 1985.

[Meersman 82] Meersman, R., "The RIDL Conceptual Language", Research Report ICIAS, Brussels, 1982.

[Nijssen 89] Nijssen, G.M. and T.A. Halpin, "Conceptual Schema and Relational Database Design: a Fact-Based Approach", Prentice Hall, 1989.

[Olle 82] Olle, T.W., H.G. Sol and A.A. Verrijn Stuart (Eds.), "Information System Design Methodologies - A Comparative Review". North Holland Publ. Co., 1982.

[Reisig 85] Reisig, W., "Petri Nets", EATCS Monographs on Theoretical Computer Science Springer Verlag, 1985.

[Richter 82]   Richter, G. and R. Durchholz, "IML-Inscribed High-Level Petri Nets". In: [Olle 82], pp.335-368.

[Rolland 82]   Rolland, C. and C. Richard, "The REMORA Methodology for Information System Design and Management". In: [Olle 82], pp. 369-426.

[Ter Hofstede 89] Ter Hofstede, A.H.M. and S. Brinkkemper, "Conceptual Task Modelling", Technical report nr. 89-14, Department of Information Systems, University of Nijmegen, September 1989.

[Yourdon 79]   Yourdon, E. and L. Constantine, "Structured Design", Yourdon Press, Englewood Cliffs, N.J., 1978.

Rule-Based Requirements Specification and Validation

A. Tsalgatidou

V. Karakostas P. Loucopoulos

EDP Department
Greek P.T.T
Megalou Vassiliou 6-8,
Rouf, Athens 118 54
Greece

Dept. of Computation,
UMIST, P.O. Box 88,
Manchester M60 1QD,
United Kingdom

Abstract

Requirements specification has only recently been acknowledged as one of the most important phases in the overall software life cycle. Since the statement of a complete and consistent set of requirements involves user participation, our approach investigates how user oriented formalisms and techniques could be employed for the specification and capturing of requirements. We propose the use of rules as a natural means for expressing the application domain knowledge, and introduce a number of techniques such as *semantic prototyping* and *animation* for the validation of the requirements.

Keywords: *requirements specification, executable specifications, rule bases, animation, Petri-nets, logic programming, conceptual modelling.*

Introduction

The expansion of the Information Technology sector in recent years has been responsible for increasing demands for bigger and more-complex computer applications. As, however, the computer systems' sophistication increases, the inadequacy of the traditional software development approaches becomes apparent. The major drawbacks of conventional software development methods are identified to be in the phase of requirements capturing/specification. While most of the approaches [deMarco 78] [Jackson 83] are good in describing the *artifact* (software system) through its various phases (i.e. as specifications, design and code) they fall short in their provision of adequate expressive power for describing the application domain. Even worse, many methods neglect to provide support for the analyst during the important phase of validating the captured requirements. Consequently, the state-of-the-art practice results in systems which do not meet user requirements, and which are expensive to maintain, since it is well known that the fixing of errors occurring due to misunderstanding of user requirements, is more expensive when the system has been implemented [Yeh et al 84].

We see the requirements specification phase as consisting of two major activities, namely requirements capturing, and requirements analysis [Dubois Hagelstein 86].

The objective of the requirements capturing phase is to depict the desired contribution of the software system in terms of application domain concepts and their interrelationships. The objective of the requirements analysis phase is to identify how the modelling assumptions are interrelated, and how they affect the future software system. As a consequence, the two phases pose different demands on the employed requirements formalism and technique. In order to model application domains of significant complexity we need an adequately rich formalism which provides a repertoire of concepts that is sufficiently rich for our ontological assumptions about the application domain and semantic accounts about every modelled aspect of the application domain [Mylopoulos 86]. In order to identify the consequences of our modelling assumptions we need a model with *deductive power* [Dubois et al 86].

Our approach is particularly suited for a class of applications known as *data intensive, transaction-oriented* information systems. These systems are characterised by large, often decentralized databases containing persistent application information, accounting for more than 80% of the investments in information systems in use today. We have observed that the requirements for such systems can be captured in terms of rules, conveying information about various aspects of the structure and behaviour of the domains. In this respect our line of research is similar to the one carried by approaches which advocate the rule-based specification of information systems [van Assche et all 88]. However, we pay particular attention to the validation aspect, and this is where this paper's discussion focuses on.

The structure of this paper is as follows. Section 1 introduces the modelling formalism used for capturing the static aspects of the application domain knowledge. In Section 2, the modelling techniques for the dynamic aspects of the application are modelled. A validation technique known as *semantic prototyping* is the subject matter of Section 3, whilst in the next section a *rule animation* technique, used for validating the system's dynamic aspects is discussed. We conclude with an overview and summary of our approach.

1   Static Modelling Constructs

The conceptual modelling formalism employed by our approach is an extension of entity-relationship based models [Chen 76] [Nijssen 89] enriched with the addition of constructs used for specifying domain knowledge which cannot be expressed by entities and relationships alone. In this respect, the formalism comes closer to contemporary conceptual modelling languages [Greenspan 84] and knowledge representation formalisms [Sowa 84].

The primary static modelling constructs are *entities*, *relationships* and *static rules*. Entities are the phenomena of interest within the application domain. Relationships are associations between the entities which are meaningful and useful from the information system's viewpoint. In contrast to the entity-relationship-attribute model and its variants, our approach does not make any distinctions between entities and attributes, as such distinctions are made usually on subjective criteria of the analyst. According to our viewpoint, attributes are equally important to entities, from an information system's perspective, and should be modelled as such. The purpose of a rule is to constrain the allowable set of entities and associations. The abstraction mechanisms employed by our approach in order to cope with the size and complexity of the application domains are *classification, generalization/specialization* and *aggregation* [Borgida et al 84]. Classification refers to the ability to model a set of similar concepts as a separate object, eg. the concept *product* is an abstraction over a set of products. Generalization/specialization refers to the ability to associate classes of concepts using superset/subset relations. A *high demand product* is a subclass of *product* in the sense that high demand products are also products.Similarly, *ordinary product* is another subclass of product. Finally, aggregation is the abstraction technique of viewing a concept as the sum of its parts (constituting components). A *product* can be considered as consisting of a *product code*, *product price* and *product description*.

Rules are pieces of knowledge used to further distinguish the application domain from similar ones. *Static rules* are an important modelling constructs in the sense that they increase our specification power beyond the definition of entities, relationships and cardinality constraints. A static rule is a linguistic expression which describes the state of affairs in the application domain at any time. A static rule for example may state that no *product* can be a *high demand product* and an *ordinary product* at the same time. This would be stated as follows.

static_rule1: high_demand_product <u>and</u> ordinary_product are <u>mutually disjoint</u>

Static rules can run to any size of complexity, relating for example, a number of different entity and relationship classes as in the following example: "High demand are those products which have associated with them a number of at least ten incoming orders of at least £100 each, over the last six months". This would be stated as follows.

static_rule2: product.X is high_demand_product if #(incoming_order.Y about product.X <u>and</u> incoming_order.Y of value > 100) < 10.

In summary, the static modelling constructs as applied to the modelling of a stock control system are shown in Figure 1.

2   Dynamic Modelling Constructs

The ability to model the dynamic aspects of an application domain is of paramount importance, therefore our approach provides a number of modelling constructs for this purpose. An application domain is perceived as changing due to a number of *events*. Events are the carriers of change within an application domain in the sense that they modify the structure of the domain by introducing, deleting or modifying instances of entities and relationships. Similarly to the modelling of static constructs we provide a number of abstraction mechanisms for modelling the dynamic constructs. Events are stated as *dynamic rules* which consist of three parts, namely

- a *when_part which* is a boolean expression over the state of affairs of the application domain, time conditions, and *signals* which are generated within the application domain (*internal signals*) or within its environment (*external signals*).

- a *precondition* which is a boolean expression over the application domain's state of affairs. A precondition describes the set of states in which an event can take place.

- an *action part* which is the set of actions introduced by the event in terms of

254

introducing/deleting new entities and establishing/destroying associations between them.

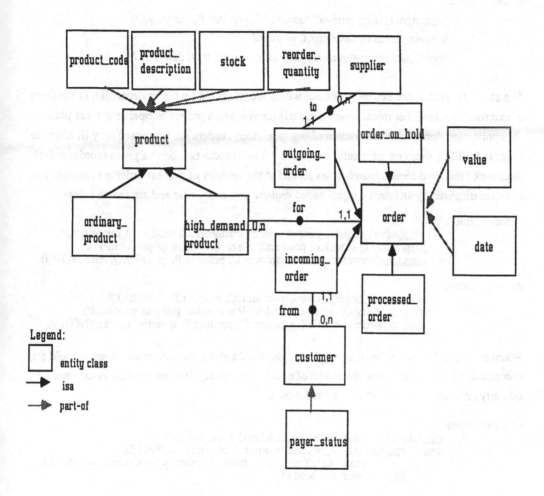

Figure 1: Conceptual model of a stock control system

In order to illustrate these concepts in more detail, consider the stock control system described in the last section.When a signal from the environment indicates that an order from a customer has arrived, then, if the status of the customer as a payer is bad, an instance of a backorder is created. If, however, the payer status of the customer is good then an instance of an order is created. This knowledge of the stock control system's dynamic behaviour is captured in two dynamic rules as follows.

dynamic_rule1:

        <u>when</u>signal_order_arrived(customer.C, product.P, quantity.Q)

        <u>if</u>payer_status of customer.C = 'bad'

thencreatebackorder(customer.C, product.P, quantity.Q, date(NOW)).

dynamic_rule2:

    whensignal_order_arrived(customer.C,product.P, quantity.Q)

    ifpayer_status of customer.C = 'good'

    thencreateorder(customer.C, product.P, quantity.Q, date(NOW)).

The above two rules, are examples of rules which are triggered by the environment, in the form of external signals. Other rules, however are triggered when a particular operation takes place in the application domain. In the domain of our case study, orders are processed only if, after the order is fulfilled, there remains sufficient stock for the products (above a given reorder point). Because of this, two more dynamic rules related to the activity of process order are entered. The rules are triggered by an internal signal called *request_process_order* and are shown below.

dynamic_rule3:

    whensignal_request_process_order(customer.C, product.P, quantity.Q)

    if(quantity.Q - stock of product.P > reorder_point of product.P)

    thencreateprocessed_order(customer.C, product.P, quantity.Q, date(NOW)).

dynamic_rule4:

    whensignal_order_arrived(customer.C, product.P, quantity.Q)

    ifnot quantity.Q - stock of product.P > reorder_point of product.P)

    thencreateorder_on_hold(customer.C, product.P, quantity.Q, date(NOW)).

When an internal signal called *process_order_on_hold* arrives, the orders which are on hold are processed. Also, a signal about the arrival of new stock will result in an increase in the product's quantity on stock. These are illustrated as follows.

dynamic_rule5:

    whensignal_process_order_on_hold(order_on_hold.O)

    then   createprocessed_order(customer.C of order_on_hold.O,

                    product.P of order_on_hold.O, quantity.Q of order_on_hold.O);

        destroyorder_on_hold.O.

dynamic_rule6:

    whensignal_new_stock_arrived(product.P, quantity.Q)

    thenincreasestock.S of product.P byquantity.Q.

The use of entity class hierarchies allows us to give inheritance semantics to the dynamic rules. A dynamic rule is said to apply also to a class' subclasses unless otherwise stated. An example of rule overriding is as follows. For high demand products, the orders are processed immediately, irrespectively of whether the stock may fall below the reorder point or not, if the customer who issues the order has a good payer status. Effectively, this means that dynamic rule 3 will be overwritten by dynamic rules 3.1 and 4.1, in the case of high demand products, as follows.

dynamic_rule3.1:

    whensignal_request_process_order(customer.C, high_demand_product.P,

                            quantity.Q)

    if   payer_status of customer.C = 'good'

    then createprocessed_order(customer.C, product.P, quantity.Q, date(NOW)).

dynamic_rule4.1:
        <u>when</u>signal_request_process_order(customer.C, high_demand_product.P,
                                        quantity.Q)
        <u>if</u>   payer_status of customer.C = 'bad'
        <u>then</u> <u>create</u>order_on_hold(customer.C, product.P, quantity.Q, date(NOW)).

The use of dynamic rule and entity hierarchies with inheritance overridance is illustrated in Figure 2.

3   Static Model Validation

Validation is an all-important phase, since its omission could result in misconceived and inappropriate models of the application domain, which will result in software systems that fail to realize their objectives. The validation phase is essentially an attempt to prove that the model is *internally consistent* and conforming to the users' conceptualization of the domain. Verifying the internal consistency of the model is a task that can be automated to a significant extent [Wohed 87]. This essentially requires that the model is expressed in a formalism with deductive power. We have opted for mapping the modelling constructs to an executable logic language, something that combines the advantages of a rigorous formalism with those of *rapid prototyping* [Budde et al 84]. Checking the internal consistency of the model involves the following activities.

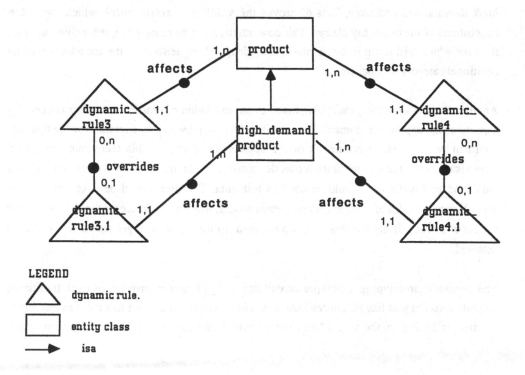

Figure 2. Entity and dynamic rule hierarchies

- Checking the well-formedness of the model, i.e. that it has been constructed according to the syntax rules of the modelling formalism. Checks in this category would include, for example, detecting cyclic *isa* hierarchies (i.e. two entity classes are mutually subclasses of each other), detecting inconsistencies in the use of aggregation relations (two concepts cannot be parts of each other at the same time), etc.

- Checking the consistency and completeness of the rules, i.e. detecting, self-contradicting or inconsistent rules.

Clearly, checking a model's consistency and completeness is not a task that can be fully automated, because of the difficulty to construct a complete logic theory to check the rules against. To overcome this problem we propose a technique known as *semantic prototyping* [Karakostas Loucopoulos 88] which advocates the active participation of the user in the validation phase. The technique draws results from the theory of logic [Tarski 56], by viewing the model as a logic theory which admits a number of interpretations. The technique proceeds by trying to *refute* the model's validity by trying to prove that it admits an interpretation (i.e. a set of instances of entities, relationships and rules) which is inconsistent. It also attempts to prove the model's agreement with the user's perception of the application domain by trying to find interpretations agreeable to the user. To make this approach clearer, consider the following example. Assume that the analyst manages to find a particular product which is classified both as *high demand* and *ordinary*. This disproves the validity of *static_rule1* which states the disjointness of the two entity classes. This contradiction can be resolved by reconciliations with the user which will result in *static rule1* being dropped, or perhaps in the introduction of an additional category of products.

Another facet of semantic prototyping involves the execution of *realistic scenarios* concerning aspects of the application domain. The user is guided step by step to explain how the test data conform with the static constructs of the application domain. This technique can reveal inconsistencies and omissions in the model definitions. For example, two real customer orders, a valid and an invalid one, could be used as test data. The user would be asked to explain, according to the rules of the application domain model, why he would accept the first, and reject the second order. If he was unable to do so, then a missing or wrongly stated rule could be detected.

The semantic prototyping technique constitutes a significant improvement over traditional validation techniques like *structured walkthroughs*. It can be automated to a large extent due to the use of Prolog as the target language on which the modelling constructs are mapped.

However, the technique requires an analyst with experience in the application domain, able to select the appropriate test cases, and to identify potential sources of inconsistencies within the model. The same applies to the validation of the dynamic aspects, discussed in the next section.

4 Dynamic Model Validation

The need to validate the dynamic aspects of the modelled domain has made necessary the invention of a number of techniques, similar to those used for static model validation described in the previous section. The techniques aim at proving the following things:

- the internal consistency of the model's behaviour
- its consistency with respect to the user's perception of the application domain
- the model's completeness.

Towards these ends, we have adopted a Petri Net representation of the dynamic rules, in order to give them formal semantic accounts and to define their interdependencies in a rigorous manner. The Petri-net formalism [Petri 62] and its variants (*augmented Petri Nets*) have received considerable attention in the area of information systems modelling [Zisman 76]. The graphical formalism introduced in this section uses *places* to represent signals (the WHEN part) and transitions are inscribed with the IF and THEN parts of the rules. Since every rule needs a signal to be triggered, all the transitions will have at least one input representing the triggering signal. In Figure 3 we give a Petri Net representation of the dynamic rules applying to class *product*, introduced in Section 2.

The major advantage of the net model is that its graphical representation coupled to its formal semantics leads to its validation using animation techniques. A prototype tool has been developed to edit and animate nets with places as signals and transitions inscribed by rules [Tsalgatidou 88]. Animation of the model can help in detecting redundant and conflicting situations by highlighting the rules inscribed to every transition every time a transition is enabled. Redundancy occurs when two or more rules can fire in the same situation giving the same results whereas conflict occurs when rules firing in the same situation produce contradictory results.

One of the model's feature's is that the number of tokens that each place can hold is countable. This feature enables the detection of circular rules by the assignment of output places to some transitions which would serve as counters of the number of times the transitions fire. A place assigned as output to a transition receives a token every time the transition fires. If this place is no input to any other transition, its tokens will not be consumed. Therefore the number of tokens that this output place will be holding will correspond to the number of times that the transition has fired. If such a place is continuously receiving tokens, this may be an indication of the existence of circular rules.

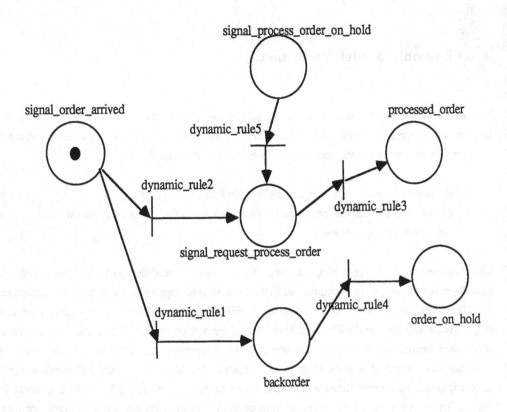

Figure 3: A Petri Net for dynamic rules affecting *product*

Missing rules can also be detected by animation. For example, if a signal, which is expected to trigger some actions, has been generated and nothing is happening, this may mean that some rules are missing. Another indication of missing rules is when there are some transitions which never become enabled. If the triggering part of the rule is internal to the system, this would mean that the necessary rule for the production of the signal is missing.

Conclusions

As the complexity of software applications continues to increase, it becomes more apparent that the traditional approaches focusing in specifying the artifact instead of its role within the application domain will become more unsuitable. For a large category of computer applications like embedded systems, office information systems and other knowledge based/expert applications the need to model the application domain in user-oriented terms becomes apparent [Borgida et al 85].

Our approach succeeds in providing the following.

- a rich formalism for expressing knowledge about complex domains in user-oriented terms, and

- techniques for validating the models' correspondence to the users perception of the application domain.

Compared to contemporary *knowledge-based* approaches to requirements modelling[Anderson Fickas 89] [Loucopoulos Champion 89] [Reubenstein Waters 89], we put more emphasis on the validation aspects, since it is them which become critical in large and complex applications. Currently, prototype validation tools, implemented in languages like Prolog and Pop-11, are running on Sun workstations. The plans for future enhancements of our approach include the automation of the semantic prototyping technique using *case-based* reasoning [Hammond 86], i.e. guiding the validation process using experience acquired from similar domains.

References

[Anderson Fickas 89]
Anderson, J. S., & Fickas, S. *A Proposed Perspective Shift: Viewing Specification Design as a Planning Problem.* Proc. Fifth Int. Workshop on Software Specification and Design, May 19-20, 1989, Pittsburgh, PA, USA.

[van Assche et al 88]
van Assche, F., Layzell, P. J., Loucopoulos, P., Speltincx, G. *Information Systems Development: A Rule-Based Approach.* Journal of Knowledge Based Systems, September 1988.

[Borgida et al 84]
Borgida, A., Mylopoulos, J., & Wong, H. K. Z. *Generalization/specialization as a basis for software specification.* In Brodie, M. et al (eds.)."On Conceptual Modelling: Perspectives from Artificial Intelligence, Databases and Programming Languages. Springer-Verlag, New York, 1984.

[Borgida et al 85]
Borgida, A., Greenspan, S., Mylopoulos, J. *Knowledge Representation as the Basis for Requirements Specification.* COMPUTER, April 1985.

[Budde 84]
Budde, R. (ed.) *Approaches to Prototyping.* Springer-Verlag, Berlin, 1984.

[Chen 76]
Chen, P. P. S. *The Entity-Relationship Model: Towards a Unified View of Data.* ACM TODS, Vol. 1, No. 1, March 1976.

[Dubois Hagelstein 86]
Dubois, E. & Hagelstein, J. *Reasoning on Formal Requirements: A Lift Control*

          System. Proc. Fourth Int. Workshop on Software Spec. and Design, April 3-4, 1987
          Monterey, CA.

[Dubois et al 86]
          Dubois, E., Hagelstein, J., Lahou, E., Ponsaert, F., Rifau, A., Williams, F. *Th*
          ERAE Model: A Case Study. In "Information System Design Methodologies: improving
          the practice", Olle, T., W., Sol, H., G., Verrijn-Stuart, A., A. (eds). North-Holland
          Publishing Company, IFIP 1986.

[Greenspan 84]
          Greenspan, S., J. *Requirements Modelling: A Knowledge Representation Approach t*
          Software Requirements Definition. Technical Report No. CSRG-155, University o
          Toronto, 1984.

[Hammond 86]
          Hammond, K. *"CHEF": A Model of Case-Based Planning*. In Proc. of the Fifth
          National Conf. on Artificial Intelligence, Philadelphia, PA, 1986.

[Jackson 83]
          Jackson, M. *System Development*. Prentice-Hall International, London, 1983.

[Karakostas Loucopoulos 88]
          Karakostas, V. & Loucopoulos, P. *Verification of Conceptual Schemata Based on*
          Hybrid Object Oriented and Logic Paradigm. Journal of Information and Softwar
          Technology, Vol. 30, No. 10, December 1988.

[Loucopoulos Champion 89]
          Loucopoulos, P. & Champion, R.E.M. *Knowledge-based Support for Requirement*
          Engineering. Journal of Information and Software Technology, Vol. 31, No. 3, Apr
          1989.

[deMarco 78]
          deMarco, T. *Structured Analysis and System Specification*. New York:Yourdon, 1978

[Mylopoulos 86]
          Mylopoulos, J. *The Role of Knowledge Representation in the Development*
          Specifications. In "Information Processing 86". Kugler, H. J. (ed.) Elsevier Scienc
          Publishers B. V., IFIP 1986.

[Nijssen 86]
          Nijssen, G. M. *On Experience with Large-scale Teaching and Use of Fact-base*
          Conceptual Schemas in Industry and University. In Proc. IFIP Conference on Dat
          Semantics (DS-1), Meersman, R. & Steel, T. B. Jr. (eds.), Elsevier North-Holland
          Amsterdam 1986.

[Petri 62]
          Petri, C. A. *Communication with Automata*. Suppl. to Tech. Rep. RAD C-TR-65-33`
          Vol. 1, Grifiss Air Force BAse, NY, 1966 (translated from "Kommunication m
          Automaton", University of Bohn, Germany, 1962.

[Reubenstein Waters 89]
          Reubenstein, H. B. & Waters, R. C. *The Requirements Apprentice: An Initial Scenaric*
          Proc. Fifth Int. Workshop on Software Specification and Design, May 19-20
          Pittsburgh, PA, 1989.

[Sowa 84]
          Sowa, J. F. *Conceptual Structures: Information Processing in Mind and Machin*
          Addison-Wesley Publishing Company, 1984.

[Tarski 56]
          Tarski, A. *Logic Semantics and Metamathematics*. Oxford Univ. Press, 1956.

[Tsalgatidou 88]

Tsalgatidou, A. *Dynamics of Information Systems: Modelling and Verification.* Ph.D. thesis, Dept. of Computation, University of Manchester Institute of Science and Technology, June 1988.

[Wohed 87]

Wohed, R. *Diagnosis of Conceptual schemas.* SYSLAB Report No. 56, Univ. of Stockholm, Sweden, 1987.

[Yeh et al 84]

Yeh, R. T., Zave, P.. Conn, A. P. & Cole, G. E. Jr. *Software Requirements: New Directions and Perspectives.* In "Handbook of Software Engineering", Vick, C. R. & Ramamoorthy, C/ V. (eds.), Van Nostrand Reinhold Company Inc., 1984.

[Zisman 76]

Zisman, M. D. *A Representation of Office Processes.* Dept. of Decision Sciences, Univ. of Pennsylvania, WP 76-1-03, 1976.

Requirements Specification in TEMPORA

C. Theodoulidis[1], B. Wangler[2] and P. Loucopoulos[1]

[1] Department of Computation,
UMIST,
P.O. Box 88,
Manchester M60 1QD,
UK

[2] SISU,
Swedish Institute for Systems Development,
Box 1250,
S-164 28 Kista,
Sweden

Abstract

The use of formal language is a way to introduce rigour in the specification of the requirements for information systems. This stage is traditionally considered as the most informal one of the life-cycle stages. Thus, the choice of a model best suited for this purpose is still an open issue.

In this paper we propose a data model called Enity-Relationship-Time (ERT), which is able to capture the structural components of such a specification. It is part of the TEMPORA conceptual model and it is an extension of the binary relationship model including a number of additional features such as the possibility to explicitly refer to past or future states of the system, to model complex objects, etc.

1.   Introduction

Recent years have witnessed a growing realisation that the development of large information systems is becoming increasingly more difficult as user requirements become broader and more sophisticated. Consequently, requirements analysis is becoming even more sensitive because the late discovery of misunderstandings of the users' needs is the source of the most expensive modifications to such systems [Greenspan, 1984; Balzer et al, 1983; van Assche et al, 1988]. By enforcing greater rigour during requirements analysis i.e., by introducing formal recording, would definitely help to avoid such misunderstandings, by removing ambiguities, redundancies and untimely choices [Mylopoulos, 1986].

Many recent approaches have suggested the use of a formal language for requirements analysis (see [CRIS-1], [CRIS-2], [CRIS-3], [Roman, 1985]). However, the features needed for a language suited for the formal expression of requirements are largely debated. Several existing languages inherit their basic concepts from other fields like data base modelling, knowledge representation or programming languages without paying enough attention to their appropriateness for expressing the customers' needs. This is the result of focusing mainly on languages and their foundations instead on understanding the process.

Much debate is currently under way as to the most appropriate set of requirements for conceptual modelling languages [Roman, 1985; Balzer et al, 1983]. An emerging consesus is the need for modelling

- Temporal Aspects. Such an extension would provide the often needed ability to reason about elements of the Universe of Discourse (UoD) which involve time. For example, historical data is required in hospital information systems in monitoring patient progress and relate current situation to previous ones. In other systems, planning is of equal importance. For example, in weather forecast systems one needs to be able to reason for the future based on current and previous data.

- Complex Objects. Such an extension would provide the ability needed for many applications for the abstraction of information that is going to be used as a single unit. For example, in CAD/CAM or CASE applications one needs to be able to deal with objects that consist of a number of components and to reason for them and at the same time to be able to deal with their components.

The process of requirements analysis is mainly an activity of modelling an application domain. This implies that certain things are needed for the natural description of various phenomena perceived in a Universe of Discourse (UoD)[Dubois, 1986; Dubois, 1987]. For example, we need:

- to classify phenomena perceived individually and associations among them,

- to classify phenomena perceived as complex structures,

- to express both static and dynamic constraints about the phenomena,

- to explicitly refer to a global time.

In section 2 of this paper we describe briefly the TEMPORA paradigm and its architecture together with the basic components of the specification environment. In section 3 we describe in detail the structural formalism of the TEMPORA conceptual model which possess the features described above. In particular, we discuss its basic concepts and externals together with the semantics of time and complex objects used.

2.   The TEMPORA paradigm

2.1   Introduction

The aim of the TEMPORA project is to improve the software development process through the exploitation of an approach which explicitly recognises the role of business policy within an information system and visibly maintains this policy throughout the software development process, from requirements specifications through to an executable implementation [van Assche et al, 1988; Loucopoulos, 1989]. This implies that the TEMPORA paradigm views the development of an information system as the task of developing or augmenting a knowledge base of business rules [TEMPORA, 1988]. In particular the need to explicitly represent business rules, to be kept distinct from the procedures and elementary data operations which implement them, has been recognised in a previous ESPRIT project [RUBRIC, 1989a; RUBRIC, 1989b] and this philosophy is continued in TEMPORA.

The TEMPORA project builds on the rule-oriented system development paradigm and extends this work in two directions. The first direction is concerned with the utilization of a commercial DBMS as the underlying data management mechanism. The second direction is concerned with enhancing the paradigm with the explicit modelling of temporal aspects at both specification and application levels.

2.2   Overview of the TEMPORA Conceptual Component

The TEMPORA paradigm is that development of an information system should be viewed as the task of developing or augmenting the policy knowledge base of an organisation, which is used throughout the software development process, from requirements specification through to the run-time environment of application programs. Within TEMPORA, this knowledge base is concerned with the definition of the principal facts and operations within the organisation together with the rules which guide these operations and ensure the integrity of these facts.

It has been seen from the outset of TEMPORA that realistic modelling of the application domain demands temporal modelling. This is because nowadays "time-less" models are considered to be with respect to information systems conceptual modelling requirements, like "programming in machine code instead of using high-level programming languages" [Falkenberg, 1988]. As a consequence, the TEMPORA model must be capable of dealing with historical information issues as well as being capable of modelling temporal business rules. An abstract view of the TEMPORA conceptual components and their interrelationships is shown in the diagram of figure 1. In this figure there are two levels namely the specification level and application level. At the specification level three models are defined, the ERT model, the Process model and the Rule model while at the application level we have a database schema and a language which describes and manipulates the information contained in it.

The structural component is expressed as an extended binary-relationship model called Entity-Relationship-Time (ERT) model. It is extended because it accommodates directly the representation of time as a distinguished entity and also, it caters for the representation of complex objects.

The process component deals with the definition of operations. A process is the smallest independent unit of business activity of meaning, initiated by a specific trigger and which, when complete, leaves the business in a consistent state. By analysing processes in terms of the ERT model we end up with a set of primitive actions suffered by an entity such as salary increase.

Control of the behaviour of a system is modelled in terms of rules. Two general classes of rules are recognised: static rules which are concerned with the integrity of the database and dynamic rules which are concerned with the control of transactions. More specifically, static rules are expressions that must hold in every valid state of the database. It can be said to hold (or not hold) simply on the basis of the extension of the database with respect to a single state. In other words, the static rules represent either integrity constraints on the ERT model or derivations on it. Dynamic rules are expressions that define valid state transitions in the database. It can be said to hold (or not hold) only by examining at least two states of the database. In effect, the dynamic rules specify the interaction of state components and/or event occurrences and they represent either dynamic integrity rules or control of operations.

3.   The Entity-Relationship-Time (ERT)   Model

3.1   The basic concepts

Besides the temporal dimension and the provision of complex objects, ERT differs from the original Entity Relationship model [Chen, 1976] in that it regards any association between objects in the unified form of a relationship thus avoiding the unnecessary distinction between attributeships and relationships [Kent, 1979; Nijssen, 1988].

The ERT model represents explicitly *entity types* and *value types*. For each relationship the ERT model recognises *sentence predicates* which are used to make statements (e.g. "a PRODUCT is sold at a PRICE") and *referent functions* which are used as a selection mechanism for entities or values (e.g. "a PRODUCT ... sold at a PRICE .."). In essence, these are two linguistic ways of expressing the same diagrammatic structure.

Time is introduced in the ERT model as a distinguished entity class. More specifically, we timestamp each time-varying entity class and each time-varying relationship class with a time period class. That is, we assign a time period for every time-varying piece of information that exists in a schema. For example, for each entity class we associate a time period which represents the period of time during which an entity is modelled (existence period of an entity). The same argument applies also to relationships i.e., with each time-varying relationship we associate a time period which represents the period during which the relationship is valid (validity period of a relationship).

The structural components of the TEMPORA model are based upon an extended binary entity relationship modelling formalism using the following concepts.

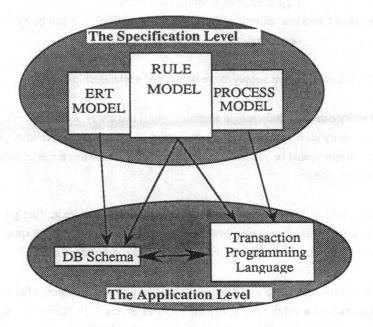

Figure 1: Overview of the TEMPORA Conceptual Component

Entity	is anything, concrete or abstract, uniquely identifiable and being of interest during a certain time period.
Entity Class	is the collection of all the entities to which a specific definition and common properties apply at a specific time period.
Relationship	is any permanent or temporary association between two entities or between an entity and a value.
Relationship Class is	the collection of all the relationships to which a specific definition applies at a specific time period.
Value	is a lexical object perceived individually, which is only of interest when it is associated with an entity. That is, values cannot exist in their own.
Value Class	is the proposition establishing a domain of values.
Time Period	is a pair of time points expressed at the same abstraction level.
Time Period Class is	a collection of time periods.

Complex Object is a complex value or a complex entity. A complex entity is an abstraction (aggregation or grouping) of entities, relationships and values (complex or simple). A complex value is an abstraction (aggregation or grouping) of values.

Complex Object Class is a collection of complex objects. That is, it can be a complex entity or a complex value class.

In addition, the following axioms apply to the concept of a relationship class.

1. An entity can only participate in a relationship if this entity is already in the population of the entity class specified in the relationship. Furthermore, the validity period of the relationship should be subperiod of the intersection of the existence periods of the two involved entities.

2. Each entity in a subclass population has also a reference (e.g., foreign key) in the population of its superclasses. In addition, the existence period of the specialised entity should be a subperiod of the existence period of the generalised entity.

3. If an entity belongs to a population of an entity class, it cannot also belong to the population of a value class at any time and vice-versa. Furthermore, any two entity classes which are not themselves subclasses of a third entity class and all have no common subclasses, must be disjoint at any time point. Note that this definition does not prevent entities from moving between entity classes during their lifetime.

In addition, an entity or relationship can be derived. This implies is that its value is not stored by default. Also, for each such derivable component, there is a corresponding derivation rule which gives the members of this class or the values of this relationship at any time.

We accommodate explicitly generalization/specialization hierarchies. This is done through the ISA relationships which have the usual set-theoretic semantics. More specifically, we assume that two subclasses of the same entity class and under the same specialization criterion are always disjoint.

3.2 External Representation of ERT

Figure 2 presents the current notation for the ERT externals. Note also that in the graphical model we cater for representation of some of the most common rules such as partial/total ISA relationships and cardinality constraints for relationships.

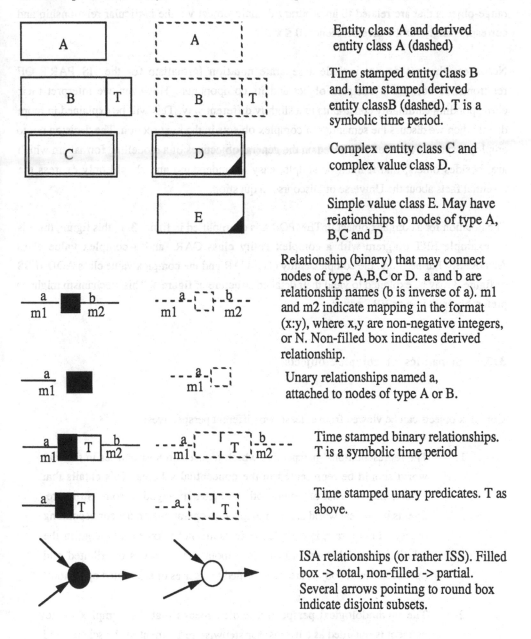

Entity class A and derived entity class A (dashed)

Time stamped entity class B and, time stamped derived entity classB (dashed). T is a symbolic time period.

Complex entity class C and complex value class D.

Simple value class E. May have relationships to nodes of type A, B,C and D

Relationship (binary) that may connect nodes of type A,B,C or D. a and b are relationship names (b is inverse of a). m1 and m2 indicate mapping in the format (x:y), where x,y are non-negative integers, or N. Non-filled box indicates derived relationship.

Unary relationships named a, attached to nodes of type A or B.

Time stamped binary relationships. T is a symbolic time period

Time stamped unary predicates. T as above.

ISA relationships (or rather ISS). Filled box -> total, non-filled -> partial. Several arrows pointing to round box indicate disjoint subsets.

Figure 2. Graphical notation for the ERT externals

Cardinality constraints may be given to all relationships (including the IS_PART_OF relationship) and also for their respective inverse relationships. These are expressed in the format (x-y), where x indicates the minimum cardinality and y the maximum cardinality for the set of range-objects that are related to an arbitrary domain-object via the particular relationship and correspondingly for the inverse. Hence, $0 \leq x \leq y$.

Note here that we do not include a separate notation formalism for the IS_PART_OF relationships between a complex object and its components. However, we interpret their corresponding cardinality constraints in a slightly different way. This will be explained in more detail when we discuss the semantics of complex objects in the next section. The decision not to employ a specific notation was based on the general objectives of a modelling formalism which are, besides others, that it must be simple, easy to understand and should only express the essential facts about the Universe of Discourse in question.

The notation for a complex object in TEMPORA is exemplified in figure 3. In this figure, there is an example ERT diagram with a complex entity class CAR and a complex value class ADDRESS. Furthermore, the complex entity class CAR and the complex value class ADDRESS of figure 3 may be exploited to yield their detailed structure of figure 4. This mechanism might be preferably built into an ERT editor.

3.3 Semantics of complex objects

Complex objects can be viewed from at least two different perspectives:

1. The representational perspective which focuses on how entities in the real world should be represented in the conceptual schema. This entails that objects may consist of several other objects arranged in some structure. Events in the real world are then mapped to operations on the corresponding objects. In contrast, if complex objects are not allowed, like e.g., in the relational model, then information about the object is distributed and operations on the object are transformed to a series of associated operations.

2. The methodological perspective which means that the complex object concept is regarded as a means for stepwise refinement of the schema and for hiding away details of the description. This in turn means that complex objects are merely treated as abbreviations that may expanded when needed.

The basic motivation for the inclusion of the complex entity/value class in the externals formalism, is to abstract away detail, which in a particular situation is not of interest, from the model. In addition, the semantics that we attach to complex objects are equivalent to *structural object orientation* as defined in [Dittrich, 1986].

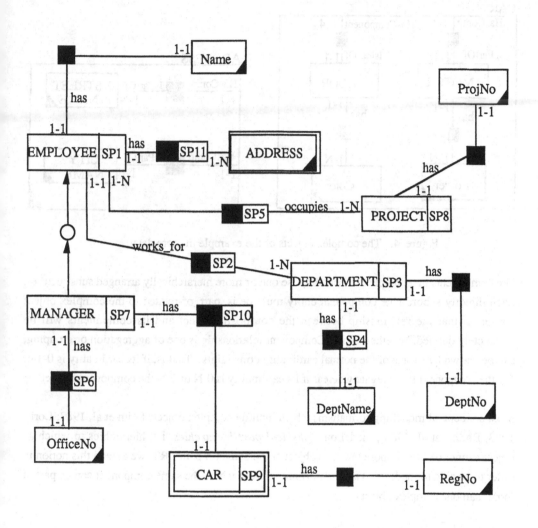

Figure 3. An example ERT schema

Many papers dealing with complex objects view a complex object as consisting of a conglomerate of objects and relationships. This means that they do not, distinguish between aggregation and grouping, but rather consider a general composition mechanism which also involves relationships/attributeships. This is the approach adopted in ERT. Graphically, composition is shown by surrounding the components with a rectangle representing the composite object type (see figure 4).

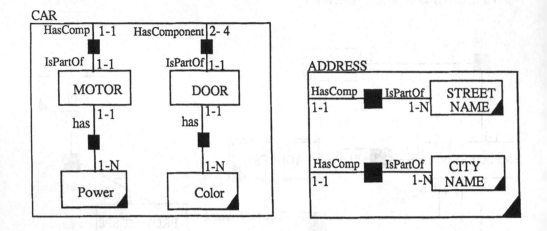

Figure 4. The complex objects of the example in more detail

The components of a complex object comprise one or more hierarchically arranged substructures. Each directly subordinate component entity must be is_part_of-related to the complex object border so that the relationship between the composite object and its components will be completely defined. Whether the HasComponent relationship is one of aggregation or grouping, can be shown by means of the normal cardinality constraints. That is, if its cardinality is 0-1 or 1-1 the component is aggregate whereas if its cardinality is 0-N or 1-N the component is a set.

Most conceptual modelling formalisms which include complex objects [Kim et al, 1987; Lorie, 1983; Rabitti et al, 1988], model only *physical part hierarchies* i.e, hierarchies in which an object cannot be part of more than one object at the same time. In ERT, we extend this notion in order to be able to model also *logical part hierarchies* where the same component can be part of more than one complex objects.

To achieve this we define four different kinds of IS_PART_OF relationships according to two constraints, namely the dependency and exclusiveness constraints. The dependency constraint states that when a complex object ceases to exist, all its components also cease to exist (dependent composite reference) and the exclusiveness constraint states that a component object can be part of at most one complex object (exclusive composite reference). That is, we accommodate the following kinds of IS_PART_OF variations [Kim, 1989] :

274

i) dependent exclusive composite reference

ii) independent exclusive composite reference

iii) dependent shared composite reference

iv) independent shared composite reference

Note that we do not accommodate specific notation for these constraints. Their interpretation comes from the cardinality constraints of the IS_PART_OF relationship [Wangler, 1989a]. That is, assume that the cardinality of the IS_PART_OF relationship is (α,β). Then, $\alpha=0$ implies non dependency, $\alpha\neq0$ implies dependency, $\beta=1$ implies exclusivity while $\beta\neq1$ implies shareness.

Finally, the following rules should be obeyed concerning complex objects:

- Complex values may only have other values as their components. In addition, the corresponding IS_PART_OF relationship will always have dependency semantics unless it takes part in another relationship.

- Complex entities may have both entities and values as their components. Every component entity must be IS_PART_OF-related to the complex entity.

- Components, whether entities or values, may in turn be complex, thereby yielding a composition/decomposition hierarchy.

In the next section, we discuss the complex objects under the time dimension. In particular, we elaborate on how complex object hierarchies evolve over time and the constraints that should always be valid during this process.

3.4   Semantics of time stamping

The time period representation approach has been chosen because it satisfies the following requirements [Loki-86; Villain, 1982; Villain, 1986]:

1. Period representation allows for imprecision and uncertainty of information. For example, modelling that the activity of eating precedes the activity of drinking coffee can be easily represented with the temporal relation *before* between the two validity periods [Allen, 1983]. If we try, however, to model this requirement by using the line of dates then we will have problems since we do not know the exact start and ending times of the two activities.
2. Period representation allows to vary the grain of reasoning. For example, we can at the same time reason about turtle movements and main memory access times.
3. Humans comprehend periods of time much more easily than time points.

The modelling of information using time periods takes place as follows. First, we assign to each time varying object in our model (entity or relationship), an instance of the built-in class *SymbolPeriod*. Instances of this class are system-generated identifiers of abstract time periods e.g., SP1, SP2, etc. Members of this class can relate to each other by one of the thirteen temporal relations between periods [Allen, 1983]. In addition, these members can be restricted by instances of the class *CalendarPeriod*. Instances of this class are all the conventional calendric periods e.g., 10/3/1989, 21/6/1963, etc. with absolute specified start and end points.

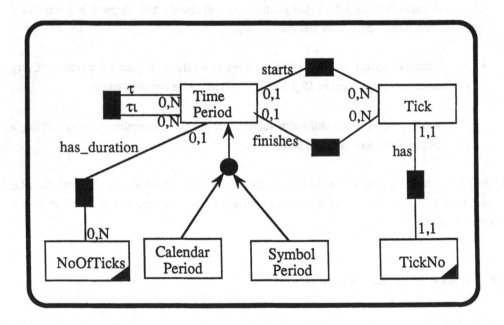

Figure 5. Time Period Metamodel

In figure 5, we show graphically the definition of these concepts. In this, the symbol τ represents a temporal relationship and the symbol τι its inverse. Also, in this figure we indicate the fact that the two classes *SymbolPeriod* and *CalendarPeriod* are disjoint. Note however, that the exact definition of the calendar period units is not included in this figure. The reason is because we want to keep it as simple as possible. For details the interested reader is referenced in [Wangler, 1989b]. The only think perhaps that we could add here is that for example, a date format like 21/6/1963 is just a shorthand notation of a calendar period.

According to the above discussion, we can time stamp the information in our conceptual model by using SymbolPeriod identifiers. However, we do not distinguish between time periods and time points. The fact that the abstraction level of a *SymbolPeriod* time stamp is say *day* can be inferred by its constraining temporal relations. For example, On the other hand, we can still represent explicitly in the conceptual schema the fact that an entity is time stamped only at the day abstraction level. This is done by distinguishing between different SymbolPeriod subclasses according to their abstraction level i.e., SP_D, SP_M,..etc. This last notation is not represented in the example of figure 3. We call this form of constraint a *resolution constraint* which when applied to a SymbolPeriod class restricts its members to calendar periods of the same resolution.

It is suggested that it would be convenient to represent directly in the conceptual schema some other notions of time such as duration and periodic time. The first consequence of this is that the expressive power of our external formalism is increased and also the readability of the schema. The definition of the duration class is shown in figure 6. Members of this class are simple durations expressed in any abstraction level. Each duration consists of an amount of calendar time units and it is uniquely identified by the combination of the real and calendar unit values. For example, the duration *"1,5 year"* is a valid duration according to our definition.

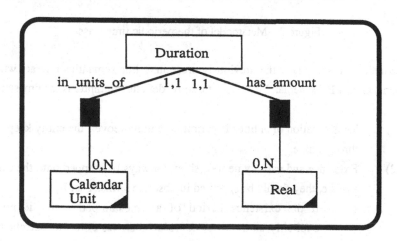

Figure 6. Metamodel of the duration class

The periodic time class is defined in figure 7. As shown in this figure, a periodic time has a base which is a calendar period, a duration and also it can be restricted by a symbol period. In other words, the interpretation of a periodic time can be expressed as "the base of every duration during symbol period". For example, the expression *"first week of each month during next year"* is a valid definition of a periodic time. In this case, the calendar period corresponds to "1-7 days", the duration corresponds to "1 month" and the restricting symbol period is the next year corresponding to [1/1/1991, 31/12/1991]. Finally, a periodic time is uniquely identified by the combination of its base and its duration.

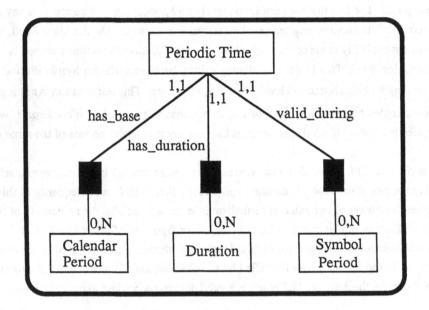

Figure 7. Metamodel of the periodic time class

In the sequel, we discuss how the previously presented time semantics interact with the other components of an ERT schema. First, we state some default assumptions for timestamping:

1) Reincarnation of entities is permitted and moreover, the entity keeps its identity through time.

2) Existence and validity periods should always be mapped onto the calendar time axis i.e, they should be specified in absolute terms. That is,

   - if the existence period of a timestamped entity is not specified explicitly as an absolute value then we take the current time as the starting point of its existence period.

   - if the validity period of a timestamped relationship is not specified explicitly as an absolute value then we take as its starting point the most recent starting point of the existence periods of the two involved entities.

3) Non timestamped entities and relationships are assumed always existing i.e., from system startup time until now.

In ERT, we do not timestamp value classes and the IS_PART_OF relationships in a complex value class should always be time invariant. This is because an aggregation or grouping of values is defined through the participating value components. These assumptions affect the way that we map ERT to the relational model.

As discussed already, the validity period of a relationship should be a subperiod of the intersection of the existence periods of the involved entities. This does not hold for the ISA relationships where from the current semantics employed, we conclude that the existence period of the specialized entity should be a subperiod of the existence period of its generalization and that the ISA relationship is always time invariant.

Timestamping, when applied to derived ERT components has slightly different semantics than usual. Since, the derived components are not stored by default, the interpretation of timestamps refers to their corresponding derivation formulas. That is, if a derived component is not timestamped then the derivation formula returns the value of it at all times i.e, for every valid state of the database. Alternatively, for the timestamped derived components, the derivation formula returns a value which is valid for the existence or validity period of this component. i.e., the derivation formula must somehow refer to this period.

Finally, timestamping in a time varying IS_PART_OF relationship is translated to the following constraints (see [Theodoulidis, 1989] for more details). The dependency constraint in a time varying IS_PART_OF relationship boils down to:

i) The existence periods of the complex object and the component object should finish at the same time with the validity period of the IS_PART_OF relationship.

Also, the exclusiveness constraint is translated to:

i) If an object A is part of the complex objects B and C , then the period during which A is part of B should have an empty intersection with the period during which A is part of C.

Concluding, the above presented time semantics permit us to keep historical information for the UoD, include a strong vocabulary for expressing temporal requirements [McBrien, 1989] and also, model the evolution of complex objects through time in a natural way.

4. Conclusions

The aim of this paper was to present a data model which provides the expressive freedom required for the purpose of requirements analysis, perceived mainly as a real world modelling activity.

The ERT model as discussed in this paper is used to describe the structural components of the TEMPORA conceptual model. It contains some features which bring it in the state of the art among the other models. More specifically, it accommodates directly the representation and manipulation of time and complex objects in a uniform way.

Currently, we are working on the Rule and Process models of our formalism. In particular, we head towards a natural-language based External Rule Language enhanced with some form of abstraction mechanism(s) and a Process model able to express business functions in a simple and uniform way. A number of extensions have been planned including the introducion of history of rules.

Acknowledgments

The work reported in this paper has been partly funded by the Commission of the European Communities under the ESPRIT R&D program. The TEMPORA project is a collaborative project and the partners who contribute to this are: BIM, Belgium; Hitec, Greece; Imperial College, UK; LPA, UK; SINTEF, Norway; SISU, Sweden; University of Liege, Belgium and UMIST, UK. More specifically, SISU is sponsored by the National Swedish Board for Technical Development (STU), ERICSSON and Swedish Telecomm.
The authors wish to thank everybody involved in the TEMPORA project for their helpful discussions and suggestions during the first year of the project.

References

[Allen, 1983]   Allen J.F. *Maintaining Knowledge about Temporal Intervals* CACM, 26(11) Nov.1983.

[Balzer et al, 1983]   Balzer, R., Cheatham, T.E, Green, C. *Software Technology in the 1990's: Using a New Paradigm*, Computer, November 1983, pp. 39-45.

[Chen, 1976]   Chen P.P-C. *The Entity-Relationship Model-Toward a Unified View of Data* ACM TODS vol.1 no.1, pp.9-36, March 1976.

[CRIS-1]   *Information Systems Design Methodologies*, T.W. Olle, H.G. Sol and A.A. Verrijn-Stuart(eds), North-Holland, 1982.

[CRIS-2]   *Information Systems Design Methodologies : Comparative View* T.W. Olle, H.G. Sol and A.A. Verrijn-Stuart(eds), North-Holland, 1983.

[CRIS-3]   *Information Systems Design Methodologies : Improving the Practice* T.W. Olle, H.G. Sol and A.A. Verrijn-Stuart(eds), North-Holland, 1986.

[Dittrich, 1986] Dittrich K.R. *Object-oriented Database Systems: The Notion and the Issues* (extended abstract), Proc. OODB, Pacific Grove, Ca, Sept.1986.

[Dubois, 1986] Dubois E., Hagelstein J., Lahou E. et al *The ERAE Model : A Case Study* in CRIS-3.

[Dubois, 1987]   Dubois E., Hagelstein J. *Reasoning on Formal Requirements: A Lift Control System*, Proceedings on S/W Specification and Design, 1987.

[Falkenberg, 1988] Falkenberg, E. *Knowledge-Based Information Analysis Support*, Proceedings IFIP TC2/TC8 Working Conference on 'The Role of AI in Databases and Information Systems', Canton, China, July, 1988, North Holland.

[Greenspan, 1984] Greenspan, S.J. *Requirements Modeling: A Knowledge Representation Approach to Software Requirements Definition*, Technical Report No. CSRG-155, University of Toronto, 1984.

[Kent, 1979]   Kent W. *Limitations of Record-Based Information Models*, TODS, 1979.

[Kim et al, 1987] Kim W., Banerjee J., Chou H.T., Garza J.F., Woelk D. *Composite Object Support in Object-Oriented Database Systems*, in Proc. 2nd Int. Conf. on Object-Oriented Programming Systems, Languages and Applications, Orlando, Florida, Oct. 1987.

[Kim, 1989] Kim W., Bertino E., Garza J.F. *Composite Objects Revisited*, SIGMOD RECORD 18(2), June 1989.

[Loki-86] ESPRIT P107- LOKI, *A Logic Oriented Approach to Knowledge and Databases Supporting Natural Language User Interfaces* Institute of Computer Science, Research Center of Crete, Greece, March 1986.

[Lorie, 1983]   Lorie R., Plouffe W. *Complex Objects and Their Use in Design Transactions*, in Proc. Databases for Engineering Applications, Database Week 1983 (ACM), San Jose, Calif., May 1983.

[Loucopoulos, 1989]   Loucopoulos, P. *The RUBRIC Project-Integrating E-R, Object and Rule-based Paradigms*, Workshop session on Design Paradigms, European Conference on Object Oriented Programming (ECOOP), 10-13 July 1989, Nottingham, U.K.

[McBrien, 1989] P.J. McBrien *TEMPORA: Language Definition and Library*, TEMPORA report, Imperial College, E2469/IC/T2.1/5.

[Mylopoulos, 1986]   Mylopoulos, J. *The Role of Knowledge Representation in the Development of Specifications*, In Information Processing 86, Kugler, H-J. (ed), Elsevier Science Publishers B.V. (c) IFIP 1986.

[Nijssen, 1988]   Nijssen G.M., Duke D.J., Twine S.M. *The Entity-Relationship Data Model Considered Harmful*, 6th Symposium on Empirical Foundations of Information and Software Sciences, Atlanta, Georgia (USA), October 1988.

[Rabitti et al, 1988]   Rabitti F., Woelk D., Kin W. *A Model of Authorization for Object-Oriented and Semantic Databases*, in Proc. Int. Conf. on Extending Database Technology, Venice, Italy, March 1988.

[Roman, 1985]   Roman G-C. *A Taxonomy of Current Issues in Requirements Engineering* IEEE Computer 18(1), 1985.
[RUBRIC, 1989a] RUBRIC, ESPRIT Project 928, *Concepts Manual*, Nov. 1989.
[RUBRIC, 1989b] RUBRIC, ESPRIT Project 928, *Implementation Manual*, Nov. 1989.
[TEMPORA, 1988] TEMPORA Technical Annex, Oct. 1988.
[Theodoulidis, 1989]   B.Theodoulidis *The IS_PART_OF Relationship Reconsidered (Working Note)*, TEMPORA report, E2469/UMIST/T1.1/15, Sept. 1989.
[Wangler, 1989a] Wangler B. *On the Semantics of Complex Objects in TEMPORA*, TEMPORA report, E2469/SISU/T1.1/13, October 1989.
[Wangler, 1989b] Wangler B. *On the Interpretation of timemarks in ERT schemas*, TEMPORA report, E2469/SISU/T1.1/14, October 1989.
[Van Assche et al, 1988] Van Assche, F., Layzell, P.J., Loucopoulos, P., Speltincx, G., *Information Systems Development: A Rule-Based Approach*, Journal of Knowledge Based Systems, September, 1988, pp. 227-234.
[Villain, 1982] Villain M.B. *A System for Reasoning about Time* Proceedings of AAAI-82, Pittsburgh, Pa., Aug.1982.
[Villain, 1986] Villain M.B., Kautz H. *Constraint Propagation Algorithms for Temporal Reasoning* Proc. of AAAI-86, 1986.

ESPRIT Today - An Overview

Janis Folkmanis
(Invited speaker)

Commission of the European Communities, DG XIII
Telecommunications, Information Industries and Innovation
200 Rue de la Loi, B-1049 Brussels, Belgium

Abstract

ESPRIT (European Strategic Programme for Research and Development in Information Technologies) is set in context of the European Communities' current Framework Programme for research (1987-1991) and ESPRIT's evolution since 1983 is briefly described.

The technical scope covered by ESPRIT is described and the market sectors affected are identified. An example of the effect ESPRIT projects are having on a particular technical area and related products is given.

Finally, the status of discussion on the new Community Framework Programme for research (1990-1994) gives a glance into the future of Community-wide IT research programmes.

Janis Folkmanis was born in 1954 in London, completing his studies (Engineering Science) in Exeter in 1977. Initially a development engineer with Ferranti Computer Systems Ltd., later consultant, for radar control systems, command and control systems, he was project leader for DBMS development at mbp GmbH (Dortmund) prior to joining the European Commission in 1988. He is currently project officer in directorate ESPRIT, with particular responsibility for projects advancing technology in the area of information management systems.

ESPRIT at the Age of Seven - its Industrial Impact Seen from a Participant's Viewpoint

Günter R. Koch
(Invited speaker)

2i Industrial Informatics
Haierweg 20, D-7800 Freiburg, FRG

Abstract

ESPRIT was launched in 1983 to increase the competitiveness of the European IT industry through cooperative R&D.

Starting with a historical view of the original motivations, the speaker will investigate the current status of ESPRIT, as well as give a report on advances and pitfalls of an SME (small or medium size enterprise) participating in the programme.

The talk will conclude with considering whether the programme has met its objectives, what the future in cooperative R&D will be, and which effects can already be noted with respect to the development of international markets.

Günter R. Koch, born 1947 in Freiburg, FRG, has a B.Sc. in Electrical Engineering and a M.Sc. in Computer Science from Karlsruhe University. He is founding chairman and technical director of 2i Industrial Informatics, and is responsible for the company's contributions within ESPRIT projects such as ToolUse, REX, and ATMOSPHERE.

He has been a member of a variety of committes and working groups within IFIP, Ada Europe and ESPRIT, and is Chief Executive Officer of the local Technology Center (TZF) in Freiburg. His current interests include software requirements engineering and transformations of specifications into design in the framework of industrial production automation.

From Software Engineering to Business Engineering: ESPRIT Projects in Information Systems Engineering

Pericles Loucopoulos
(Invited speaker)

Information Systems Group, Department of Computation
UMIST, P.O. Box 88
Manchester M60 1QD, UK

Abstract

During this talk it will be argued that approaches to the development and evolution of information systems need to progress from the traditional 'information viewpoint' to also encompass the 'enterprise viewpoint'. It will be argued that future development paradigms will need to provide advanced support to business system analysis in developing, maintaining and evolving high level, formal conceptual models for business applications. To this end, a number of research projects, in the context of ESPRIT, will be discussed and a number of future research directions will be outlined.

Pericles Loucopoulos is a professor of Information Systems in the Department of Computation, the University of Manchester Institute of Science and Technology (UMIST). He joined UMIST in 1984 after several years of commercial work in the systems department of a major firm of financial brokers. He holds a Ph.D. in Computing and is a Fellow of the British Computer Society. His research interests include system development methods, rule-based active database environments and requirements engineering. This work has been supported by awards funded by SERC under the Alvey initiative and by the Commission of the European Communities under the ESPRIT and AIM Research and Development programmes. He is the co-author of 3 textbooks and the author and co-author of over 50 papers.

Quality Auditing: The Necessary Step Towards the Required Quality Objectives

Donald Davies
(Invited speaker)

Compex, 19A High Street
Cobham, Surrey KT11 13DH, England

Abstract

In an era when many, some would say most, software projects fail to meet their objectives, by being late, over budget and causing extreme customer dissatisfaction, the quality audit of projects is a common occurrence. A common conclusion of quality audits is that a project has not followed up-to-date project management and quality methods. And a common recommendation is to set up a task force to make the imminent deliveries AND in parallel to introduce a Quality Project Management Method. What, then, characterises a good such method?

It involves setting up a dedicated team of qualified staff including specialists in QA, System Design, Acceptance Configuration Management, and providing an environment where effective work can be done; providing everyone with the space, equipment and information necessary and creating an atmosphere of determination to success, hard but not hurried work. Objectives, requirements and commitments are managed and status is regularly checked against the planned schedule, quality target and budget. Problems and risks are highlighted early and solved. Acceptance is managed. Staff is educated and motivated. The result of all this is to make deliveries on schedule and having them accepted and paid for. There is visibility of key activities, management awareness, no nasty surprises, successful projects, motivated staff and an all-round professional image.

Donald Davies has been a project manager since 1956. Starting with Stantec Zebra he managed a succession of projects for ITT, UNIVAC, ICL and Philips, including message switching projects and reservations projects for Canadian Army, SAS and Siljaline, banking projects for AMROBank and Swedish Post and several more. Apart from project work he has been system manager and also set up the support organisation for the ICL 2900 new range. He became a consultant in 1978 and for a time specialised in crisis management and undertook a series of recovery exercises in France, Holland and Sweden. Recently interested in teaching project management he has designed and run a series of workshops and introduced the idea of project competence centres. He is a director of Compex (Competence Centres) and Project Management Workshops Ltd.

Quality Engineering: Designing for Quality – the SW Engineering Challenge

Ulf Olsson
(Invited speaker)

Bofors Electronics
S-175 88 Järfälla, Sweden

Abstract

Hardware quality can be expressed as the probability that something will break and/or wear out. Software does not wear out, but it can break when exposed to overload (i.e., unexpected or unfortunate sets of inputs, resource failure, ...). A trustworthy system will behave in a controlled way under such circumstances: it will perform as well as possible, and will in general not compound the problem. Quality Assurance (QA) aims at removing the sources of untrustworthiness (bugs, errors, features) by forcing developers to prove to someone with project authority (but possibly with only superficial technical knowledge) that enough thought and work has gone into trying to reduce those risks.

This talk is an attempt to set QA in the perspective of the developers. The basic point of the argument is that QA is a *supportive* function. If not controlled, there is a risk that QA (and Configuration Management) procedures are formalized and expanded so far that they actually become counter-productive: less time is spent on the product as such; i.e., quality goes down. Obviously, there is a balance to be struck here. A few points will be made from our experiences, illustrating this and showing how we try to think at least as much about the properties of the *products* as about those of the *process*! Actually, the two go hand in hand: improving the process gives better products; improving the products provides helpful hints about where the process needs further enhancement.

Ulf Olsson graduated from Stockholm's Royal Institute of Technology in 1978, with a M.Sc. in Engineering Physics. Since then, he has been with Philips Elektronikindustrier (which became Bofors Electronics in 1989). He has been involved as a Software Engineer and Software Project Manager in a number of projects, including several Coastal Artillery systems, airborne as well as land-based radar extractors, and C3 systems. Since 1985, he has been involved in the SS2000 projects in various capacities, mainly concerning overall software design. In 1989, he was appointed Senior Specialist in the field of System Architecture.

Quality Control: A Cornerstone to Quality – Measurement and Motivation are Key Issues

Rikard Almgren
(Invited speaker)

RSA Software Quality Systems
Östergökssvängen 61
S-163 54 Spånga, Sweden

Abstract

The primary objective of quality control is to determine the extent to which a *product* exhibits required software qualities. Quality control may apply to static quality attributes, i.e., attributes of design, code and documents that one can measure without executing the product, as well as to dynamic quality attributes, which may be considerably more difficult to measure.

Objective and well defined quality requirements have to be developed and specified to serve as the yardstick by which quality controllers can measure quality. Quality requirements negotiated and agreed with the client constitute a well-defined contract regarding the criteria of high quality.

Quality control also measures the *process* quality to detect roadblocks in the development environment that interfere with achieving software product quality. High process quality is a prerequisite for producing high product quality. Appropriate set of development and configuration tools, continuous coaching of project members, clear project organisation and senior management commitment ensure high process quality and job satisfaction. Motivated personnel enforce success.

Rikard Almgren studied mathematics, computer science and economics at the University of Stockholm (B.Sc. 1974). He has five years of experience in developing real-time systems for air traffic control and defence systems, primarily in the areas of system software and methods & techniques. Experiences from the financial industries were gained over eight years at Philips where he specialised in methods & techniques, tools, and software quality engineering. He is a member of IEEE, ACM and the Swedish Quality Association (SFK).

Quality Management: The Business Asset and its Competitive Advantage

Alvaro de Portugal
(Invited speaker)

Deportic International Consultancy, Helmhof 16
2403 Vn Alphen aan den Rijn, The Netherlands

Abstract

Computer systems engineering is by definition the adoption of proven procedures for developing computer hardware and software. It is also the use of common methods for communicating design concepts within business application development. The acceptance of standards for managing quality in computer systems development is the mandatory first step towards managing and assuring Quality, and consequently, demands Senior Management commitment.

Introducing Quality Assurance Management implies a set-up of mutual commitments on Customer System Requirements, Information Resources Technology, Software Industry Standards, and Project Plan. Large projects require unambiguous Review and Reporting mechanisms such as Users Review, Technical Review, Senior Management Review, Change Control Boards and so forth. Success can be obtained by using an appropriate Project Management method, clear Review and Approval mechanisms, a tailored Quality Assurance approach, a collection of adequate development and configuration tools, and last but not least, by ensuring active customer involvement. The benefits are: quantified quality effort, monitored progress, accurate measurements and reports, enforced uniformity and improved communications. The final product is then of the required quality, up to the budget and to the estimated time-frame. Client satisfaction enriches business and competitive advantage.

Alvaro de Portugal, studied Electronics Engineering at the Universities of Porto and Coimbra (Portugal) and Brussels (Belgium); further on studied Economy at the University of Amsterdam (The Netherlands). He is a member of the Dutch Association of Informatici (VRI), Dutch Association of Management Consultants (OOA) and Dutch Association of Economical Advisors (NVOA). He has 20 years of international experience as a management consultant on Information Resources Technology Management, in particular, Project Management, Quality Assurance Management and Information Management in the following areas: wholesales, banking, insurance, government, industry, trade and general services. Author of several articles, work-papers and training courses and experienced lecturer.

Software Prototyping:
Implications for the People Involved in Systems Development

Pam Mayhew

School of Information Systems
University of East Anglia
Norwich, NR4 7TJ, England

Abstract

This paper explores the adoption of systems prototyping and, in particular, concentrates on the various ways in which this may affect those people associated with systems development.

One widely accepted prerequisite for successful prototyping is that it requires a fundamental change of attitudes for developers, users and managers alike. This all too frequently ignored requirement is discussed and illustrated.

Adopting a prototyping approach to systems development can have a significant effect on the roles played by both users and developers. These alterations in roles and responsibilities are examined. Particular attention is given to the role of the prototyper, as well as to the issues to be considered when choosing who should play this crucial part.

Examples are drawn from experience of both teaching prototyping within a University and its adoption in a commercial environment.

1. Introduction

During the 1980's systems prototyping has fast been transformed from a relatively unknown research topic to a widely discussed approach to developing computer based information systems. Consequently, there now exists a considerable amount of literature on the subject. The majority of these publications deal with one or more of the following areas:

- a general discussion of prototyping often concentrating on advantages and problem areas;

- a description of the execution of prototyping, often in an ad-hoc and retrospective fashion;

- a detailed presentation of a particular product, followed by an argument as to its suitability for use as a prototyping tool.

Unfortunately, a significant number of the available articles give the misleading impression that prototyping is a simple, even trivial process. This occurs in two main ways:

- the first implication is that with the currently available range of sophisticated development tools, prototyping is simply a matter of choosing and subsequently using an appropriate tool;

- the second misleading impression is founded in the notion of a "stereotype prototyping session" [Boar 1984]. This involves one user and one developer, sitting at one terminal making immediate changes to a simple problem system.

Some prototyping may be as straightforward as this, but the majority will not. A prototype must be developed just as any other piece of software. Its production will involve all the investigation, analysis, design, implementation and evaluation activities found in the more conventional approaches to software development. In addition to the construction and evaluation of useful prototypes, successful prototyping requires careful preparation, detailed organisation and effective control.

Despite the widely held debate on the use of prototyping, there are only a small number of documented cases of its actual adoption within commercial organisations. Furthermore, a disappointingly low percentage of these articles actually discuss and assess details of the manner in which the prototyping was organised and controlled.

In practice there are a wide range of issues to be taken into account when preparing to adopt a prototyping approach to development. These necessarily include many decisions that will affect the people who are to be involved in the prototyping, for instance: who is to participate?; how are participants to be selected?; what are their roles and responsibilities?; how are they to be prepared?; how is prototyping to be organised?

Careful attention to issues relating to the preparation and organisation of prototyping maximises the chances of it being successful. Since prototyping is critically dependant on those people who are participating, it is clear that decisions concerning people are central to the success of the entire prototyping process. This paper highlights some of these important issues.

Prototyping provides a hitherto unparalleled opportunity for the meaningful, active participation of users within the systems development process. Such a high level of participation must be expected to have implications for all the people involved. Hence this paper also explores the adoption of systems prototyping, with particular emphasis on the various ways in which this may affect those people associated with systems development.

2.   Towards Successful Prototyping

An understanding of what is meant by "successful prototyping" can be gained by considering a definition of systems prototyping. Prototyping is defined as:

"the process of constructing and evaluating working models of a system in order to LEARN about certain aspects of the required system and/or its potential solution."

The crucial component of this definition is the word "learn". If nothing has been learned from the prototyping process then it has been a waste of time and effort.

There are many issues which can be clarified by the use of system prototyping, such as establishing requirements; assessing alternative designs; and investigating the likely affect upon the organisation [Floyd 1984, Mayhew 1987a]. Assuming that the objectives of prototyping have been carefully planned and recorded in advance, one definition of successful prototyping is as follows:

"prototyping which enables LEARNING about those aspects of the required system that were identified as crucial at the outset."

Experience suggests that this might be a somewhat narrow definition, as prototyping often enables those involved to learn far more than just those aspects initially declared. In addition, such a high level of user participation inevitably affects the existing working environment, influencing such things as personal attitudes, expectations, relationships and responsibilities. It is important that the full implications of prototyping are taken into account during the early preparatory stages. In this way the chances of obtaining the maximum potential benefit from prototyping are enhanced, thus enabling "more successful" prototyping.

Three central factors have been identified as crucial prerequisites for successful prototyping [Law 1985], as follows:

- suitable tools;

- changes in attitudes;

- a methodology.

Appropriate tools must be available that enable both the speedy construction and the speedy modification of software prototypes. Almost every day sees the introduction of some new high-productivity system building tool onto the market. While few, if in fact any of these have been designed specifically as prototyping tools, many of them could be used in this way. Experiments have indicated that even the simplest tools enable much to be learned through prototyping [Mayhew 1987b]. For these reasons, it is unlikely that the adoption of prototyping is being hampered, to any large degree, by a lack of suitable tools.

A change in peoples' attitudes is given as the second requirement for successful prototyping. The use of a more experimental systems development method challenges many of the underlying principles of the now widely accepted structured approaches. Given the amount of effort which has often accompanied the introduction of these more formal development methods, it is hardly surprising that systems development managers are somewhat less than enthusiastic when they first encounter prototyping. A proposal to construct a system (or more) with the intention of disposing of it soon afterwards, seems the very anti-thesis of the prevailing doctrine which these same managers may have worked hard to establish. Since the management views on prototyping are highly likely to affect the decision of whether or not to pursue this approach to development, an adjustment in their attitudes is clearly necessary in order to enable successful prototyping.

Having decided to prototype part(s) of a required system, it must be appreciated that this will require both users and developers to work in a manner which is likely to be unfamiliar. Developers must be prepared not only to accept criticism but to elicit it effectively. Users must not expect perfection from early exploratory prototypes and must be encouraged to participate actively in the development of their system. Section 3, below, examines this "changes in attitude" prerequisite in further detail.

The third requirement is that of a methodology to support prototyping. Little has been published in this area, and there appears to be few guidelines as to how to put prototyping into practice [Riddle 1984]. In particular, questions such as: How do I introduce prototyping? How do I organise prototyping? and How do I control development that uses prototyping?, have largely remained unanswered [Harker 1988, Mayhew 1989, Vonk 1990, Mayhew 1990]. These methodological issues may be responsible for the reluctance of management to introduce prototyping into their organisations. The selection of prototyping participants, and the explanation of their roles and responsibilities, are two important topics to be taken into account when preparing to utilise a prototyping approach. These are discussed in detail below in Sections 4 and 5 respectively.

3.   Prevailing Attitudes and Misunderstandings

The introduction and subsequent use of prototyping to assist in systems development constitutes a change in working practices. Changing working practices is no simple affair, necessitating a re-examination of both attitudes and traditions [Andersen 1990]. Hence, an organisation adopting a prototyping approach for the first time may encounter problems, e.g. the users take one glance at the first prototype and immediately begin to broadcast the incompetency of the developers; an egotistic developer refuses to acknowledge criticisms that indicate the redundancy of a particularly ingenious and intricate piece of code.

The majority of potential problems are founded in a lack of understanding and appreciation on behalf of the people involved, including managers, developers and users. Each participant needs to be familiar with the concepts of prototyping, his/her role within the process and what can be expected of other participants. Sections 3.1, 3.2 and 3.3 below, discuss some of the misapprehensions among participants, their implications, and suggestions for avoidance.

3.1   Management Attitudes

It is the management's attitude to prototyping that affects the decision of whether or not to pursue a prototyping approach to development. They have to be able and willing to expect, encourage, and accept re-work and iteration as a natural consequence of prototyping.

Systems development managers need to be sympathetic and supportive of the application of alternative tools and techniques. It is advantageous to establish a development environment in which creativity is not stifled [Amabile 1989]. This appears to contradict various well-known and widely used structured development methods, which aim to divide development into a large number of well-defined tasks [Cutts 1987]. Being forced to carry out a predetermined sequence of these tasks is intended to leave little opportunity for individual creativity. Prototyping is unlikely to perform at its best within this type of rigid regime.

Individual project mangers need to be willing to search for and establish enhanced methods for project management. The main areas of concern include: the justification of adopting a prototyping approach; project estimation; and the actual management of prototyping.

User managers need to be aware of the differences between a traditional pre-specification type development approach and an experimental approach involving prototyping. In particular, it is imperative that user managers are aware of the users' central role in the actual prototyping process. It is important that the significant increase in user time for participation is recognised at the outset. The managers must be able to reassure participating users that this is going to be "time well spent" and that they will not be penalised for having completed less of their "real" work.

3.2 Developer Attitudes

Developers require a thorough appreciation of any new tools and/or techniques which they may be applying for the first time. They are also likely to be more successful if they approach pilot developments of this type in as open-minded a fashion as is possible. This is as true for the introduction of prototyping as it is for other unfamiliar methods.

In fact this problem may be exacerbated for the introduction of prototyping. The false image, as discussed above, of prototyping as the simple application of high-productivity tools, is doubtless partially responsible for this concern. Developers may view prototyping as completely different from the approaches with which they are familiar. Prototyping may be seen as a threat to their hard-earned position and status, by rendering their current knowledge and experience worthless. These worries spring from a lack of understanding of the concepts of prototyping. Developers must be made aware that prototyping is an additional approach at their disposal, not a replacement methodology.

The proposal that prototyping needs to be seen as a useful approach to combine with existing approaches, should not, however, disguise the fact that to perform prototyping can require profound changes in attitudes for some developers.

Since prototyping, if it is to enable learning, requires the development of working models prior to their being satisfactorily specified, developers are constantly in a position of demonstrating that their work is not yet "correct". Some developers may not take kindly to "making a fool of themselves" in this way. The tendency to want to show the parts of the development that are working properly, rather than to expose those parts with serious shortcomings is only human nature. However, this can seriously jeopardise the success of prototyping. Experience, as described below, indicates that this may be a difficult problem to overcome.

A group of some thirty, third year Computer Science undergraduate students, were given an assessed coursework exercise that involved prototyping. Each of these students had attended several courses dealing with the implementation of computer systems. They had also taken, in the previous year, a first course in systems analysis and design, which had exposed them to a wide range of tools and techniques, mainly from the Structured Analysis family of development methods. Prior to the coursework being distributed, the class had been taught the concepts and practices of prototyping, and had been warned of the possible need for the adoption of unfamiliar attitudes. In particular, the need for the prototyper to be prepared not only to accept criticism, but to actually elicit it effectively, was discussed.

Each student was provided with a reasonably detailed account of the operation of a small wholesaler of domestic electrical appliances. (S)he was then required to produce a prototype and utilise this during a session with a representative of the firm, who was in practice one of the two course tutors. The exact orientation of the prototype was to be decided by each student, although the scenario provided did give pointers towards those parts of the system which were important and/or poorly defined. Students were allowed approximately three weeks to prepare for their prototyping sessions, and were instructed to use dBASE III on an IBM PC AT. Given that this course represented only a sixth of each student's workload, it was clear that the prototypes could at best automate only part of the original system description.

Despite the fact that this set of student developers knew about prototyping and its potential pitfalls, the outcome of this exercise was disappointing. Apart from a small number of students, it appeared very difficult for them to operate in this unfamiliar manner. This manifested itself in several ways, including:

- the choice of functions to prototype was often based upon the ones which were described in most detail and hence offered the greatest opportunity for getting it right, rather than the greatest opportunity for learning;

- the emphasis during the actual prototyping sessions was on showing what had been developed rather than on learning;

- the firm's representative was frequently discouraged from being anything more than an observer;

- when the representative managed to ask a question about a certain function, (s)he was all too often faced with a response such as, "Oh, I haven't implemented that yet, but let me show you what this function does";

- the user representative was rarely made to feel that (s)he was a crucial component of the prototyping activity.

Many students were unable, because of the way in which they handled the sessions, to learn any more than what the user thought of the small part of the system that they had already managed to construct. The potential to learn via prototyping had been wasted as a direct consequence of the self-protective attitude displayed by the developers.

Clearly, development in a University student environment is different from that in a commercial organisation. Students were being assessed on this exercise. Their desire to show their development talents, unfortunately, took precedence over what they had been taught about prototyping. It appears that old habits do indeed die hard, even in a University environment. The worry is that there may well be a similar reluctance on behalf of commercial developers to expose themselves during prototyping. After all, the commercial developer, like the student, is rewarded by being seen to get things "right". It is extremely important that developers are prepared to admit that their knowledge is incomplete, and hence be in a position to learn via prototyping.

Prototyping often requires that prototypes are produced to short deadlines [McCracken 1981, Donovan 1977]. These deadlines are largely determined by the need to maintain user interest and enthusiasm. This can sometimes mean that models are not as complete as developers may have wished. This practice may be difficult for developers who have perfectionist tendencies to come to terms with. People with these attitudes, (which are highly commendable under different circumstances), must be reassured that even simple, incomplete prototypes enable much to be learned.

Developer participants in prototyping need to have a user-oriented attitude. They must be prepared to work in partnership with users. They must not just listen to the users' suggestions then automatically persuade them that the developer's approach is the only approach, but they must be willing to try these suggestions in practice. As above, this attitude may not be as easy to actually adopt as it is to appreciate in principle.

This problem was clearly illustrated during a prototyping session that was attended by the author. The session was progressing well until one user suggested some changes which challenged a part of the logical design. The designer responsible was also present at the session. Unfortunately, this particular part of the system was both one that had taken much effort to analyse, and one of which the designer was most proud. Despite the designer supposedly attending in a passive capacity, he was unable to contain himself. He quickly and forcibly did his utmost to quell the user's suggestions, and in so doing put at risk the entire prototyping process. This designer portrayed an attitude towards users that was potentially devastating to the prototyping situation.

A further examination of the selection of developer participants for prototyping can be found in Sections 4.1 and 4.2 below.

3.3 User Attitudes

The users who are to participate in prototyping need to be ready and willing to get meaningfully involved in the development of their systems. Hence, they must be prepared to dedicate the required amount of time to work in partnership with the developers. It is important that user participants are aware from the start of the significant amount of their time which will be needed for evaluation of the system prototypes. This also implies that users will play a greater role in development and consequently have an increased responsibility for its progress and eventual outcome.

The users must appreciate that the aim of prototyping is to enable the participants to learn about some aspect(s) of the required system. They must not expect prototypes, especially early exploratory ones, to be perfect operational systems. Conversely they must understand that what appears to be a highly suitable system, may in reality be a rather fragile, incomplete prototype under its professional exterior.

Most of these problems are unlikely to occur if the users are familiar with the theory and practice of prototyping. It is particularly important that users appreciate that their input is crucial to the process. Without their evaluation and feedback prototyping is a waste of time and effort.

3.4   Attitudes Summary

The attitudes of all people involved in prototyping, managers, developers and users alike, contribute to the success or otherwise of the prototyping process. Sympathetic attitudes can be encouraged through a carefully designed and executed education and training programme. It is important that the participants are happy to work in partnership for the benefit of the organisation rather than for their own personal kudos. Prototyping which takes place within such a supportive environment, where creativity is not stifled, has an improved opportunity to succeed.

4.   Selection of Participants

This involves selecting the number and make up of both developers and user representatives who are to participate in prototyping. Perhaps the most crucial decision to be made at this point is concerned with who is to play the role of the prototyper.

4.1   Selection of Prototyper

Those who have been involved in the early analysis and/or logical design are in a position of knowing a great deal about the system, as well as already having been involved with the users. An analyst/logical designer appears to be the obvious choice for the prototyper position. However, these people may have expended a great amount of time and effort in preparing the logical design and consequently they may have considerable "ego-involvement". It would be difficult for one of them to act as an impartial prototyper. There is a danger that the users could be persuaded that the logical design is as it should be.

Those developers who will be responsible for the physical design must also have a complete understanding of the system. However, it might be difficult for these people to act impartially as they may well be preoccupied with the implementation of the system. The danger here is that the users could be steered towards a particular conclusion because this was the simplest to implement.

Another possibility is to employ the person who is the most proficient with the chosen construction tool as the prototyper, in which case suggested alterations could be easily incorporated. The main concern in this case is that this person may be a programmer who might lack the valuable experience of dealing with the user population.

The personal qualities of the prototyper are also very important. Ideally, this person must possess the qualities traditionally required by a systems analyst, including patience, diplomacy, perception, acceptability and objectivity. Perhaps the most important attribute is that the prototyper must not be regarded as intimidating by the participating users. Should this be the case, they may be dissuaded from making suggestions and criticisms, thus adversely affecting the feedback so crucial for productive prototyping.

4.2   Selection of Additional Developers

It may also be advisable to involve additional developers in the prototyping sessions, in order to provide support for the prototyper. A logical designer could be made available to provide clarification at the request of either the prototyper or the users. A physical designer could be made available for consultation in order to advise the prototyper of the feasibility of proposed changes. However, care must be taken that these developers do not defend or propose solutions so enthusiastically that it is to the detriment of the prototyping process. In practice it appears to be extremely difficult to attend a prototyping session in a purely passive capacity.

A further developer may be required to attend the prototyping sessions. This person would be responsible for keeping a written account of the session for control purposes, in particular to record all incorporated changes and suggested alterations. This should allow the prototyper to give his/her full attention to the user participants. The person performing this secretarial role need not necessarily be the same for every prototyping session. The use of video could negate the need for this additional developer participant.

4.3   Selection of Users

One concern during the selection of user participants for prototyping involves choosing between the management, those people who will be responsible for the system under construction, or choosing the end users, those people who will operate it, or in fact choosing any intermediate level of employee. It is, of course, possible to choose participants from more than one group of employees. However if this is the case, and the intention is that they should all attend the same prototyping session, there is a possibility that this may lead to a loss of objectivity among those involved. Selecting individual user participants is usually the responsibility of user management and will depend upon such criteria as status, experience, attitudes and enthusiasm.

There are at least two alternative ideas concerning the selection of user participants based upon their attitudes and levels of enthusiasm. Selection of appropriate users who are already interested in the system and who are keen to participate is hardly likely to fail. However, the selection of an unsympathetic, potentially antagonistic user, while being a little more risky, offers an excellent opportunity for improving relationships within the organisation.

The author has witnessed this phenomena in action. A series of prototyping sessions were organised and the participating developers chosen. User management were responsible for the selection of the user participants. Two of the four users selected, openly declared that they had no wish to be present, but that they had been "directed" to attend by their senior management. The prototyping began in an unfriendly and suspicious atmosphere. However, the attitude of these users gradually softened as they began to appreciate that what they had to say really mattered. Suggestions they made were incorporated into the prototype system. Their support and responsibility for the task they had been assigned grew rapidly, and at the end of the second prototyping session, one was heard to make a comment concerning "personalising our own system". The speed at which this complete change of attitudes had occurred was staggering. Much later, the same two users willingly adopted the roles of local "champions" for the new system. They were also vocal with their opinion that they would insist upon being involved, via prototyping, in any future developments in their area.

This may, in fact, indicate a further complication in the selection of user participants. Despite some users being reluctant to take part in early prototyping ventures, the situation could quickly change with many people wanting to participate. If participation in prototyping begins to be linked with status, or perhaps rewards, this could pose further selection decisions.

An alternative method of selection could be founded on lines similar to those used for the consensus approach to participative development [Mumford 1979], in a more democratic manner.

The number of participating users must also be established. The usual assumption is that prototyping takes place with one developer and one user, however, this may have disadvantages, as follows:

- it does not enable user debate;

- it does not encourage general system ownership;

- it could be intimidating for the one user;

- it relies upon the knowledge and abilities of an individual.

Conversely, the more users that participate in the prototyping sessions, the greater the practical problems, e.g. many people attempting to view the same VDU. It has also been suggested that having multiple user participants slows down each of the prototyping activities, hence it is preferable to develop a prototype with one typical user, and then to use it as a pilot or initial prototype with all other users [Jenkins 1983].

Another consideration is whether the same user participants should attend all the prototyping sessions, or whether to involve different people. Having one set of user representatives throughout prototyping has the obvious advantage of continuity, thus reducing the familiarisation effort for each session, and enabling the users to become quite adept at their prototyping role. Introducing a number of different users has the advantage of involving more people with the project development and so providing a greater wealth of knowledge, experience and ideas. This also provides the opportunity for a wider understanding and appreciation of the system and consequently a wider sense of involvement, responsibility and ownership.

5. Roles Adopted

This section considers the roles that users and developers must play during systems development. It suggests that the users, in particular, are required to play a very different role when development incorporates prototyping.

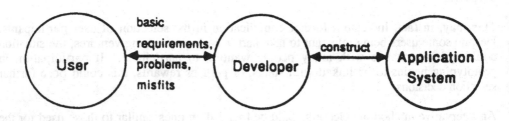

Figure 1 : Traditional Development Roles

Figure 1 shows a somewhat simplified view of the roles adopted during a traditional, prespecification approach to systems development. The provision of the application system is almost entirely the responsibility of the developers. Users are involved in a passive way, usually during the fact finding activities, and much later for acceptance testing. They participate when requested to do so by the developers. For the remainder of the time they can do little more than wait and pray. Meanwhile the developers are attempting to design, implement and test the system, to meet their own understanding of its requirements. More up-to-date structured methodologies have introduced numerous checkpoints at which the user is consulted. However, the participation remains at a relatively passive level, hence the user's role is little changed from that previously described.

The introduction of prototyping into systems development has a significant effect on the roles of both user and developer. The extent of the change depends upon the way in which the organisation adopts the approach. The roles shown in Figure 2 have been suggested as appropriate for prototyping [Naumann 1982]. The titles of both users and developers have been altered to more accurately reflect their new responsibilities. The user/designer is the active participant in this model having full responsibility for the design and evaluation of the prototype. The developer, who in this model has been reduced to a system builder, is now a relatively passive participant.

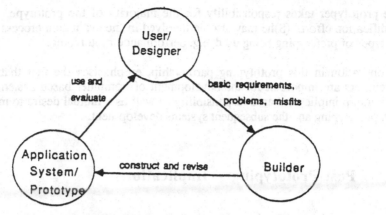

Figure 2 : Prototyping Rules - One Approach

The two previous models, although quite the opposite of each other, have an identical deficiency. They both fail to make full use of all those people involved. Figure 3 illustrates an approach to prototyping that draws upon the combined knowledge and experiences of both user and developer, here referred to as the prototyper. Users and developers form a partnership in order to develop prototypes, and hence learn about the required system. Users are required to play a far greater role in development. They are actively involved in the use and evaluation of prototypes. They may also build parts of them depending on the available tools and the type of prototypes being constructed, e.g. using report generators. In association with this greater role is an increased user responsibility, both for the progress of development and for the quality of the final product. Users are no longer merely the developers' customers.

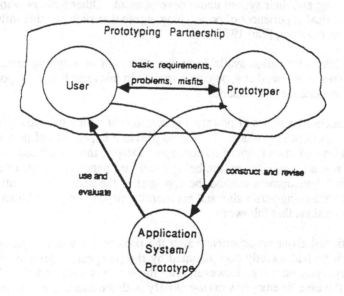

Figure 3 : Prototyping Roles - "Partnership Approach"

The prototyper takes responsibility for the majority of the prototype construction and modification effort. (S)he may also be involved in the evaluation process depending upon the types of prototyping being used, e.g. performance prototyping.

Co-operation in this prototyping partnership, emphasises the fact that both users and developers are important for the development of computer based systems. An effective partnership implies a shared responsibility as well as a mutual desire to make a success of both prototyping and the subsequent systems development.

6. Post-Prototyping - Implications

The intention of this section is not to reiterate discussions on the overall advantages and problems associated with prototyping, which have been covered in detail elsewhere, (see for example [Brittan 1980, Dearnley 1983]), but rather to highlight some of its implications for those people who have participated in the process.

As was mentioned previously, the majority of publications about prototyping are relatively theoretical. Those that do focus upon its practical application, generally concentrate on its affect on users, and comment less on the implications for managers and developers. The few empirical studies published in the area, also tend to concentrate on users' perceptions rather than to those of the other participants [Alavi 1984].

The experience related in Section 4 above, supports the widely held belief that prototyping appears to have a positive influence on the attitude of end-users towards both the development process and the information systems department. The example described two users who were initially unwilling to participate, yet who quickly became avid supporters of both prototyping and their system under development. Other authors who have published their own practical experiences of prototyping, agree that such positive influences really do occur, (see, for example, [Earl 1978]).

There is far less information available on the effects of prototyping upon developers and managers. There are few, if any, objective studies in this area, hence the points made below are based on experience and intuition.

The author attended a series of prototyping sessions at which the prototyper was a young, relatively inexperienced graduate. He had no previous experience of prototyping and at the outset had a limited knowledge of its concepts. Despite this, he agreed to take on the role. Since there was no possibility of him being overly influenced by years of experience using a more formal development method, he approached the task with a relatively open mind. Both his outward going personality and his friendly disposition proved invaluable during the prototyping sessions that followed.

When questioned about his experience after the prototyping was completed, the prototyper admitted that he had secretly been daunted by the prospect of demonstrating a system to multiple user representatives. However, once the sessions were underway he conceded that for most of the time he enjoyed working closely with the users. He had necessarily become far more involved with the detailed requirements of the system, than with any of his previous programming work. While he considered this increased level of involvement as more taxing, he readily admitted that a greater appreciation of the whole problem increased the enjoyment of his work. However, he also made the remark that he looked forward to getting back to some simple programming.

The main problem highlighted by this prototyper was that at times he felt rather vulnerable. He was referring to what he saw as a lack of a comprehensive support environment; there were few methodological guidelines to which he could turn for direction. The project manager, who like the prototyper had no previous experience of prototyping, also commented on the relative lack of guidelines to support his own role in the process. Perhaps this is an inevitable problem for an emerging approach, however, it is one that needs addressing in the near future.

Hence from the experience outlined above, it appears that the reactions of the developers, in particular those of the prototyper, are likely to be significantly influenced by the level and quality of available support for prototyping. Implications are likely to vary substantially depending on the personality of the prototyper.

Observations concerning the implications for management can also be taken from this same prototyping application. In the beginning, user management somewhat reluctantly agreed to the software developer's proposal to utilise prototyping during the early stages of development. However, when they began hearing the user participants enthusiastic reports of the prototyping, they became more interested in the process and made arrangements to attend the next session. They were delighted by the way in which their users were actively involved in the process, particularly as they had originally anticipated possible opposition to the new system. However, they were more guarded than their subordinates in their comments concerning the use of prototyping in the future.

If prototyping has been successful, (i.e. having developers working with users, in such a way as to enable their active, meaningful and satisfying participation, in the learning process), it encourages an improved organisation-wide attitude towards systems development. Future systems are likely to be designed and introduced with high levels of competence because the users are now better informed and educated concerning the application of technology within their organisation. At the same time the developers have improved their understanding of the activities of the user departments [Land 1983].

7. Summary

Prototyping involves far more than choosing, and subsequently using a tool to build working models of a system. Successful prototyping requires substantial preparation, as well as careful organisation and management. Many important decisions must be taken concerning the people who are to participate in the prototyping. The effectiveness of prototyping is largely dependent on the individuals involved, in particular the prototyper and the user representatives. Hence it is crucial that proper care and attention is given to those issues concerning the prototyping participants.

A large number of articles have examined the potential advantages of prototyping, e.g. reduced development effort, reduced testing time, more effective solutions, fewer maintenance requests, greater user satisfaction. There are additional benefits, however, which despite being difficult, if not impossible, to quantify, are nevertheless extremely important. These benefits stem from the positive effect that prototyping so often has on its participants. Working closely, with a single objective to learn more about the required system, both users and developers can expand their knowledge and improve their mutual understanding. This fosters an atmosphere of co-operation between the systems developers and the user community, which can only improve the chances of successful developments in the future.

It is essential that organisations are aware of the possible implications of prototyping on those people involved. Such an appreciation enables the organisation to plan for prototyping that will take full advantage of all the extremely important potential benefits described above.

8. References

[Alavi 1984]
  Alavi, M., "An Assessment of the Prototyping Approach to Information Systems Development", Comm. ACM, Vol.27, No.6, June 1984.
[Amabile 1989]
  Amabile, T., "Improving Creativity in Systems Design", Panel 15, ICIS 89, Boston, December 1989.
[Andersen 1990]
  Andersen, N,E. et.al., "Professional Systems Development: Experience, Ideas and Action", Prentice-Hall, 1990.
[Boar, 1984]
  Boar, B.H., "Application Prototyping: A Requirements Definition Strategy for the 80's", Wiley, 1984.
[Brittan 1980]
  Brittan, J.N.G., "Design for a Changing Environment", Computer Journal, Vol.23, No.1, 1980.
[Cutts 1987]
  Cutts, G., "Structured Systems Analysis and Design Methodology", Paradigm, 1987.
[Dearnley 1983]
  Dearnley, P.A. and Mayhew, P.J., "In Favour of System Prototypes and Their Integration into the System Development Cycle", Computer Journal, Vol.26, No.1, 1983.
[Donovan 1977]
  Donovan, J.J. and Madnick, S.E., "Institutional and Ad-Hoc DSS and Their Effective Use", Database, Vol.8, No.3, Winter 1977.
[Earl 1978]
  Earl, M.J., "Prototyping Systems for Accounting, Information and Control', in "Accounting, Organisations and Society", Vol.3, No.2, 1978.
[Floyd 1984]
  Floyd, C., "A Systematic Look at Prototyping", in "Approaches to Prototyping", Eds. R. Budde, K. Kuhlenkamp, L. Mathiassen, H. Zullighoven, Springer-Verlag, 1984.
[Harker 1988]
  Harker, S., "The Use of Prototyping and Simulation in the Development of Large-Scale Applications", The Computer Journal, Vol.31, No.5, 1988.

[Jenkins 1983]
   Jenkins, A.M., "Prototyping: A Methodology for the Design and Development of Application Systems", Indiana University, Graduate School of Business, Discussion Paper 277, 1983.
[Land, 1983]
   Land, F. and Hirschheim, R., "Participative Systems Design: Rationale, Tools and Techniques", in Journal of Applied Systems Analysis, No.10, 1983.
[Law 1985]
   Law, D., "Prototyping: A State of the Art Report", NCC, 1985.
[Mayhew 1987a]
   Mayhew, P.J. and Dearnley, P.A., "An Alternative Prototyping Classification", The Computer Journal, Vol.30, No.6, 1987.
[Mayhew 1987b]
   Mayhew, P.J., "An Investigation of Information Systems Prototyping", Ph.D. Thesis, UEA, Norwich, UK (1987).
[Mayhew 1989]
   Mayhew, P.J., Worsley, C.J. and Dearnley, P.A., "Control of Software Prototyping Process: Change Classification Approach", Information and Software Technology, Vol.31, No.2, March 1989.
[Mayhew 1990]
   Mayhew, P.J. and Dearnley, P.A., "The Organisation and Management of Systems Prototyping " to be published in Spring 1990, in "Information and Software Technology".
[McCracken 1981]
   McCracken, D.D., "A Maverick Approach to Systems Analysis and Design", in "Systems Analysis and Design: A Foundation for the 1980's", Elsevier-North Holland, 1981.
[Mumford 1979]
   Mumford, E., "Consensus Systems Design: An Evaluation of this Approach", in "Design and Implementation of Computer Based Information Systems", Sijthoff and Noordhoff, 1979.
[Naumann 1982]
   Naumann, J.D. and Jenkins, A.M., "Prototyping: The New Paradigm for Systems Development", MIS Quarterly, Vol.3, September 1982.
[Riddle 1984]
   Riddle, W.E., "Advancing the State of the Art in Software Systems Prototyping", in "Approaches to Prototyping", Eds. R. Budde, K. Kuhlenkamp, L. Mathiassen, H. Zullighoven, Springer-Verlag, 1984.
[Vonk 1990]
   Vonk, R., "Prototyping: The Effective Use of CASE Technology", Prentice-Hall, 1990.

Experiences from Prototyping

Peter F. Elzer
(Invited speaker)

Asea Brown Boveri Corporate Research Heidelberg
Eppelheimerstrasse 82, D-6900 Heidelberg 1, FRG

Abstract

Prototyping is one of the most useful complements to the traditional linear life cycle of software development, which greatly improves user participation in the specification and design of software. It gives the user an immediate concrete impression of the functionality and behaviour of the software under development. This is especially important for the development of interactive software and man-machine interfaces. However, the full potential of prototyping can only be exploited if the right tools are used. Particularly powerful and flexible tools have emerged in the area of expert system development.

The presentation therefore concentrates on the author's experience with a development environment for expert systems for the design of various components of a system for knowledge based support of operators of industrial processes: GRADIENT (=GRAphical DIalogue environmENT), a project funded by the Commission of the European Communities within the ESPRIT programme. It will be shown that the integration of sufficiently powerful graphic capabilities with the more strictly expert system oriented functionality of the tool set was the key factor for the success of such a tool set as a prototyping environment. It will also be discussed how prototyping helped to overcome the skepticism of the users towards "new and unproven techniques" and to achieve broad acceptance and support of an innovative design.

Peter F. Elzer, born 1942 in Nürnberg, has a M. Sc. in Experimental Physics and a Ph.D. in Computer Science from the University of Erlangen-Nürnberg, FRG. In 1969-1978, he led the research group that specified and implemented PEARL, a Process and Experiment Automation Real-time Language, at the University of Erlangen-Nürnberg. 1978-1979 he was on the management team for the development of Ada at DARPA (Defense Advanced Research Projects Agency) in Washington D.C., and 1979-1981 he was product manager for support software for aerospace applications at DORNIER Systems in Friedrichshafen, FRG. Since 1982 he has been with ASEA Brown Boveri in Germany, first as senior group leader for the development of power distribution control systems, then as research group leader for applications of knowledge based systems in power systems. Current research interests include knowledge-based systems, man-machine interfaces, reuse of software, and management of software projects. Dr. Elzer has authored over seventy publications on various aspects of software development.

IRIS – A Mapping Assistant for Generating Designs from Requirements [1]

Yannis Vassiliou, Manolis Marakakis, Panagiotis Katalagarianos
Lawrence Chung[2], Michalis Mertikas, and John Mylopoulos [2]

Institute of Computer Science
Foundation for Research and Technology - Hellas
Heraklion - Crete
Greece

Abstract

The problem of generating information system designs from requirements specifications is addressed, with the presentation of a framework for representing requirements and a mapping assistant, IRIS[3], that facilitates the design generation process. Requirements are viewed as knowledge bases and the knowledge representation formalism for the prototype, also the language for implementing IRIS, is Telos which provides facilities for describing entities and relationships and for representing and reasoning with temporal knowledge. The generation of a design is achieved with a mapping process from requirements which is: (i) Locally guided by dependency types determining allowable mappings of an element of a requirements model, (ii) globally guided by non-functional requirements, such as accuracy and security requirements on the intended system, represented as goals describing desirable properties of the intended system and used to guide local decisions.

The paper details a prototype implementation (IRIS) of the proposed mapping framework and illustrates its features through a sample session.

[1]This is a report on results from the DAIDA project, funded in part by the European Commission through the Esprit programme under contract no. 892 [Jarke86]; financial support for this research was also received from the Institute of Computer Science of the Foundation for Research and Technology - Hellas (FORTH), the National Science and Engineering Research Council of Canada and the University of Toronto.
[2]Department of Computer Science University of Toronto, Canada
[3]IRIS was a famous Greek goddess, considered to be the personal assistant of Zeus.

1 Introduction

A *requirements model* includes both *functional* and *non-functional* requirements [Roman85]. Functional requirements provide constraints on the functionality of the intended system and for the case of information systems may include (a) a description of the environment within which the intended information system will eventually function, hereafter the *environment model*, (b) a description of the functions carried out by the information system, hereafter the *system model* and (c) a description of the interactions between the intended system and its environment, hereafter the *interaction model* [Borgida89]. Since the subject matter of requirements modelling is some part of the world, it is reasonable to view requirements models as *knowledge bases* which capture knowledge about an environment, e.g., a corporation or an office, but also describe how the intended information system is to be embedded in and interact with that environment ([Zave81] [Jackson83] [Mylopoulos86] also adopt this point of view).

In addition to functional requirements, a requirements model also includes *non-functional requirements* which impose global constraints on the operation, performance, accuracy and security of any proposed solution to the functional requirements model. For example, considering a hypothetical expense report system for research projects, non-functional requirements may require that the intended system run on a PC, and that the expense information be accurate and secure in the sense that it is only available to key persons within each project.

An *information system design* describes the structure of the information managed by the intended system as well as the behavior of the processes manipulating that information. As such, it can be viewed as a formal specification of the system to be built in the spirit of formal specification work [Hayes87]. However, unlike formal specifications intended for other programming tasks, such as the development of an operating system, those of interest here include descriptions of highly complex data structures and generally simple algorithms. *Semantic Data Models* have been offered as extensions of conventional data models appropriate for the development of information system designs [Borgida85]. Such models attempt to capture a human's conceptualization of the structure and behavior of an information system while omitting implementation details.

The generation of a system design involves many refinements in mapping each of the various components of requirements models down to different constituents of system designs. Without adequate guidance on how to make refinements, the generation of a system design is an extremely difficult task. Some of the problems that need to be faced in generating system designs include:

1. *Coping with omissions in functional requirements*: In requirements models, details are omitted concerning entities, cause-effect chains, and requirements violations. Since system designs result from successive refinements of requirements models, we need to discover rules that assist the introduction of the omitted details for various components of requirements models.

2. *Supporting non-functional requirements*: Little work exists on how to use non-functional requirements in the generation of a system design.

3. *Exploiting representational commonalities*: The languages or formalisms chosen for

requirements modelling and system design hopefully may share knowledge representation features. Methods need to be developed for the exploitation of commonalities in order to simplify the mapping process.

4. *Correctness of mapping*: Each design should be consistent to the requirements specification from which it was generated. However, no formal framework is available to date that guards against invalid mappings. Thus, we need to devise ways for ensuring the correctness of mappings.

It should be noted that not all the parts of a requirements model are mapped down to designs. The components of the systems model are only mapped to designs. The rest of the requirements model prescribes the nature of interaction of the information system and its environemnt and the meaning of the information maintained by the system.

The paper presents IRIS, a mapping assistant prototype/demonstrator of a *dependency-based, goal-oriented* methodology to the mapping problem. The methodology is *dependency-based* in the sense that the mapping of parts of the requirements model into a design is guided by predefined allowable dependencies. Data entities in the design, for example, may only be derived from, and therefore depend on, entities in the functional requirements model, while activities may be mapped onto transactions or scripts.

At the same time, the methodology is *goal-oriented* in the sense that non-functional requirements are treated as possibly conflicting goals to be satisfied, to a greater or lesser extent, by the generated design. For each requirement goal, our proposed methodology offers a set of refinement methods to designers to help them guide the mapping process. Each refinement method allows the decomposition of a posted goal into sub-goals and is based on an explicit model for each class of non-functional requirements handled by the methodology (e.g., accuracy, security, operational, performance).

The work reported in this paper was carried out in part within the framework of the DAIDA project, whose goal is to build a software engineering environment for developing and maintaining information systems. Key features of the project are: (a) requirements models and designs are viewed as knowledge bases and representation languages are chosen accordingly, (b) a knowledge base management system which maintains a complete design record for an information system is developed, and (c) mapping methodologies from requirements models to designs to implementations are created.

Telos, TDL (Taxis Design Language) and DBPL[4] are the languages adopted for requirements modelling, design and implementation respectively. The Global Knowledge Base Management System, or GKBMS, manages general knowledge used to guide the users of the environment in the development of a requirements model and in the mapping of that model to a design and later on an implementation. The GKBMS also maintains a history record of decisions and dependencies among requirements, design and implementation components. A detailed description of the DAIDA architecture and the initial aspirations of the project are beyond the scope of this paper and are described in [Borgida89], while the GKBMS component is presented in [Jarke89].

---

[4]The former languages are introduced in the paper mainly with examples and small explanations. DBPL is a database programming language developed at the University of Frankfurt, which offers a Modula 2-like programming framework extended it with sophisticated relational database management facilities [Schmidt88].

The language for requirements modelling, used in this paper, is *Telos*[Koubarakis89].[5] Telos adopts a representational framework which includes structuring mechanisms analogous to those offered by semantic networks [Findler79] and semantic data models [Hull87]. In addition, Telos offers an assertional sublanguage which can be used to express both deductive rules and constraints with respect to a given knowledge base. Two novel aspects of Telos are its treatment of attributes, promoted to a first class citizenship status, and the provision of special representational and inferential facilities for temporal knowledge. Descriptions in a Telos knowledge base are partitioned into *tokens* and *classes*, depending on whether they represent particular entities, say the person John or the number 23, or abstract concepts, say those of Person or Number. Classes are themselves instances of other more generic classes, namely, *metaclasses* that are, in turn, organized along an instantiation hierarchy.

Apart from this representational framework, shared to a large extend by the adopted design language and many other semantic data models, Telos views a requirements model as an account of a history of events and activities, thus emphasizing the use of *time* in the description of a corporation or office within which the intended information system will function. The model of time adopted is based on time intervals [Allen81]. Every Telos proposition includes, along with other structural information, a temporal interval which specifies the lifetime of the represented entity or relationship. Time intervals are related to each other through temporal relations such as *before, during* and *overlaps* (thirteen possibilities in all) during the description of individuals or through assertions. Inferences with respect to temporal relations are handled by a special inference procedure rather than a general purpose inference mechanism, with obvious performance advantages. In addition, each Telos expression has a temporal component which acts as a filter on its possible values.

Design specifications, according to the DAIDA world view, present a conceptual view of the information system by structuring the data and transactions which constitute the system according to their intended meaning rather than their implementation. TDL (short for Taxis Design Language) facilitates the development of such specifications by offering a uniform semantic data model for describing data, transactions and long-term processes [Borgida89]. As with many other semantic data models, the one adopted here offers the notions of entity and relationship along with aggregation, generalization and classification intended as structuring mechanisms.

TDL offers a variety of *data classes* for modelling the entities that are relevant to the application domain and at the same time will eventually be stored in the database(s) of the information system. Data classes include as special cases conventional data types (Integer, String, enumerated and subrange types), but also labelled Cartesian products *aggregate classes*, whose instances have equality decided structurally, and *entity classes* which have their extensions (collections of instances) externally updated.

Each type of data class has associated *attribute categories* which indicate the kinds of attributes that are applicable to their members. It should come as no surprise that subclass hierarchies are supported and their use is encouraged throughout the design. Note that as a specification language, TDL makes no commitment on how such attributes are to be stored (arrays, records, relations), nor whether the information provided by the

---

[5]Telos has evolved from CML ([Stanley86]) which, in turn, is an enhanced version of RML, a requirements modelling language proposed in ([Greenspan84]).

attribute will be obtained by look-up or computed by a function. It is the prime goal of the design-to-implementation mapping process to make and justify these decisions.

Turning to its procedural sublanguage, TDL offers functions and two types of procedures that effect state changes: *transactions*, intended to define atomic database operations, and *scripts*, intended to model long term processes. Each transaction is supposed to specify a set of allowable state transitions through pre/postcondition constraints on the values of the state variables (attribute functions, parameters and class extensions).

TDL assumes frame axioms, i.e., state components that are not affected by a transaction, are assumed to remain unchanged. This is one of the fundamental differences between TDL and Telos.

As indicated earlier, to model activities with prolonged duration (e.g., running a project) as well as to describe the system's interaction with its users, TDL supports the notion of *scripts* [Barron82], [Chung84]. A script is built around a Petri-net skeleton of states connected by transition arcs which are augmented by condition-action rule pairs. The rules allow reference to the passage of time, and permit the exchange of messages following Hoare's CSP mechanism.

While it is beyond the scope of this paper to fully and formally introduce Telos and TDL, it unavoidably dwells into some notational details of the two languages while describing the mapping assistant. Effort is made to keep this to a minimum without losing scientific validity and content.

Section 2 describes the dependency-based, goal-oriented mapping framework adopted and analyses some of the technical problems that arise in mapping requirements to designs. Section 3 goes over an example session using IRIS to give a feel of the framework and the facilities that could be expected. A functional requirements model, concerning project expense accounts, which is used as running example throughout the paper is also presented. Major mapping issues such as the problem of representation are discussed in Section 4. Finally, Section 5 presents the status of the implementation and some concluding remarks.

2   IRIS: A Prototype Mapping Assistant

This paper emphasizes the dependency-based aspect of the mapping problem, while more details on the complete goal-oriented methodology and the use of non-functional requirements for the mapping process can be found in [Chung89].

The role of IRIS is to assist the designer who makes the final decisions. Dependency types define the options available to him/her, while dependencies relate design objects and the corresponding requirements objects. Automatic selection of dependencies is performed only in situations where there is a single applicable dependency and the system need only inform the designer of the selected dependency. The mapping assistant interface employs a graphical presentation of objects and dependencies at two different levels of detail.

2.1   System Architecture

The mapping activity transforms the system model component of a requirements specification into a conceptual design. A fundamental consideration throughout the mapping process is the interplay of requirements entities and activities with corresponding design data

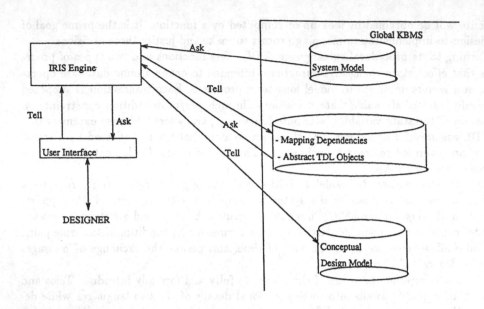

Figure 2.1 General Architecture of the Mapping Assistant

classes, transactions and scripts. The dependencies and dependency types used by the mapping assistant are represented in Telos, along with requirements and design objects. IRIS, the mapping assistant, assumes the following types of dependencies: classification (dealing with mappings of classes), attribute (dealing with the mapping of attributes), IsA (for IsA hierarchies), and instantiation (for instantiation hierarchies). Figure 2.1 depicts the general architecture of the mapping assistant, the knowledge relevant to the mapping task and the assistant's interaction with the user.

2.2 Representation of Design Objects in Telos

The features, syntax and semantics, of the conceptual design language TDL have been modeled as Telos metaclasses organized along isA hierarchies. These metaclasses have as instances classes which represent components of the conceptual design, i.e., TDL classes. All these individual and attribute metaclasses are instances to the omega_class, TDL_Object and will be referred to as *abstract TDL objects*. At the top of the metaclass isA hierarchy is TDL_MetaClass with specialized subclasses TDL_DataClass, TDL_Procedure and TDL_Script.

Generally, the Telos representation of TDL designs encompasses two layers, the first consisting of metaclasses modelling features of the design language (TDL) and is application-independent, while the second consists of simple classes representing the conceptual design model for a particylar application. The organization of abstract TDL objects is depicted in Figure 2.2.

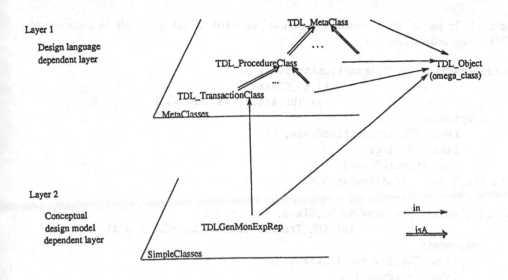

Figure 2.2 Two-layer representation of the design model in Telos

The discussion that follows focuses on the modelling of attribute categories of the design language. These have been defined as Telos attribute metaclasses organized along isA hierarchies. TDL_AttributeClass is treated here as the most general attribute metaclass with specializations: TDL_DataAttributeClass, TDL_TransactionAttributeClass and TDL_ScriptAttributeClass. These metaclasses are further specialized to lead to definitions of TDL attribute categories.

```
AttributeClass TDL_AttributeClass in M1_Class, TDL_Object with
     components
          from: TDL_MetaClass;
          label: String;
          to: TDL_MetaClass;
          when: AllTime;
end TDL_AttributeClass
```

The component attributes of this definition indicate the internal structure of the proposition TDL_AttributeClass [6] The Telos attribute class Produces shown below is the attribute metaclass modelling the TDL attribute category Produces. The from component of each attribute class specifies the valid objects where that attribute class can

---

[6]The internal structure of every Telos proposition includes four components, labelled respectively *from, label, to, when*. Since the *when* component of all definitions below is *AllTime*, it will be omitted from definitions that follow.

313

be used. In particular, Produces can be used as attribute category only in instances of TDL_TransactionClass.

```
AttributeClass TDL_TransactionAttributeClass
                          in M1_Class
                          isA TDL_AttributeClass with
    components
        from: TDL_TransactionClass;
        label: String;
        to: TDL_MetaClass;
end TDL_TransactionAttributeClass

AttributeClass Produces in M1_Class, TDL_Object
                      isA TDL_TransactionAttributeClass with
    components
        from: TDL_TransactionClass;
        label: produces;
        to: TDL_Object;
end Produces
```

The *not setOf* feature of TDL is represented in the model of abstract TDL objects by the built-in Telos attribute category single, an attribute which is not single is by default setOf.

Justification is another interesting attribute metaclass which relates each abstract TDL object with an instance of the selected mapping dependency, which effected the creation of that object.

For instance, using some the constructs discussed, the TDL transaction GenMonExpRep

```
TRANSACTION GenMonExpRep WITH
    IN
        exp: SETOF Expense;
    LOCALS
        pr : Project;
        m: Month;
        per: String;
    CONSUMES
        exp: SETOF Expense;
    PRODUCES
        expRep: MonthlyEmplExpenseReport;
    GOALS
        : (expRep.mo' = m) AND (expRep.amount' = SUM(exp))
          AND (expRep.proj' = pr)
    END
```

is represented in Telos by the class TDLGenMonExpRep as demonstrated by:

314

```
IndividualClass TDLGenMonExpRep
                in S_Class, TDL_TransactionClass, TDL_Object with
    justification
        : MonMbrExpRptToTDLGenMonExpRep_Dep
    tdl_in
        exp: TDLExpenses
    locals, single
        pers: TDL_String;
        m: TDLMon
    produces, single
        exr: TDLMonEmplExpRep
end TDLGenMonExpRep
```

2.3 Representation of Mapping Dependencies

Telos classes and metaclasses model the mapping dependencies between a requirements model and a corresponding conceptual design. The dependency metaclasses, modelling dependency types, define conditions under which there can be a dependency between a requirements and a design object. For the purposes of the prototype system, a dependency name, by convention, indicates the type of both the source requirements object and the target TDL object. For instance, the dependencies Activity_Transaction_Dep and NecessarySingle_Unchanging_Dep model the mapping of Telos activity classes into TDL transactions and the mapping of a Telos necessary and single attribute to a TDL unchanging attribute respectively. Every dependency metaclass has at least two necessary attributes named respectively telosObject and abstractTDLObject which indicate the corresponding requirements and design objects.

Dependency metaclasses for Telos activities and TDL transactions are shown below. The attribute telosObject in the dependency Activity_Transaction_Dep is inherited from Activity_Procedure_Dep. The integrity constraint in Activity_Procedure_Dep states that the life of the instances of Activity_Procedure_Dep co-end with the life of the transformed activity. The mapping of the attributes of an object from the requirements model are represented by the attribute attributeDep. All the dependency classes are instances of the omega_class Omega_Dep. The most generalized dependency metaclass is Telos_TDL_Dep. The attribute isaDep models the mapping of isA relationships.

```
IndividualClass Telos_TDL_Dep in M1_Class, Omega_Dep with
    necessary
        telosObject: SystemClass;
        abstractTdlObject: TDL_MetaClass
    attribute
        isaDep: ISA_Dep
end Telos_TDL_Dep


IndividualClass Activity_Procedure_Dep
```

```
                        in M1_Class, Omega_Dep,
                        isA Telos_TDL_Dep with
    necessary
        telosObject: ActivityClass;
        abstractTdlObject: TDL_ProcedureClass
    integrityConstraint
        : $(Forall x/Activity_Procedure_Dep)
            (coends(when(x), when(x.telosObject))$
end Activity_Procedure_Dep

IndividualClass Activity_Transaction_Dep
                        in M1_Class, Omega_Dep
                        isA Activity_Procedure_Dep with
    necessary
        abstractTdlObject: TDL_TransactionClass;
        attributeDep: TransactionAttribute_Dep
    attribute
        isaDep: Activity_Transaction_ISA_Dep
end Activity_Transaction_Dep
```

The dependency OutputSingle_Produces_Dep models the mapping of an output attribute from a Telos activity class to a produces attribute in a TDL transaction. The integrity constraint in OutputSingle_Produces_Dep, states that before mapping an attribute of a Telos object the type of that attribute, an attribute class, should have been mapped. Attribute_Dep is the most general dependency metaclass for attributes.

```
IndividualClass Attribute_Dep in M1_Class, Omega_Dep
    attribute
        telosAttribute: AttributeClass;
        abstractTdlAttribute: TDL_AttributeClass
end Attribute_Dep

IndividualClass  TransactionAttribute_Dep
                        in M1_Class, Omega_Dep
                        isA Attribute_Dep
end TransactionAttribute_Dep

IndividualClass ActivitySingle_Dep in M1_Class, Omega_Dep
                        isA TransactionAttribute_Dep
end ActivitySingle_Dep

IndividualClass ActivitySetOf_Dep in M1_Class, Omega_Dep
                        isA TransactionAttribute_Dep
end ActivitySetOf_Dep

IndividualClass OutputSingle_Produces_Dep
                        in M1_Class, Omega_Dep
```

```
                         isA ActivitySingle_Dep with
   necessary
       telosObject: Output;
       abstractTdlObject: Produces
   integrityConstraint
       :$ (Forall x/OutputSingle_Produces_Dep)
          (Exists existingDep/Activity_Transaction_Dep)
          (existingDep.telosObject=from(x.telosObject) and
          (existingDep.attributeDep = x))$
end OutputSingle_Produces_Dep
```

According to these definitions, the mapping of the activity class
&MonMbrExpRpt

```
IndividualClass &MonMbrExpRpt
                     in S_Class, ActivityClass, SystemClass
                     isA &GenExpenseReport with
   input
       exp: &Expense
   control
       pers: &Person;
       m: &Month
   output
       exrep: &MonEmplExpRpt
   activationCondition
       : (Exists t/Date)(now during t and
                         LastDayOfMonth(t, m))
end &MonMbrExpRpt
```

leads to the following dependencies:

```
IndividualClass MonMbrExpRptToTDLGenMonExpRep_Dep
                     in S_Class, Activity_Transaction_Dep
                     isA Dep_S_Class with
   telosObject
       : MonMbrExpRpt
   abstractTdlObject
       : TDLGenMonExpRep
   attributeDep
       : MonMbrExpRpt_exp_Dep;
       : MonMbrExpRpt_pers_Dep
       : MonMbrExpRpt_m_Dep;
       : MonMbrExpRpt_exrep_Dep
end MonMbrExpRptToTDLGenMonExpRep_Dep
```

```
IndividualClass MonMbrExpRpt_exrep_Dep
                        in S_Class, OutputSingle_Produces_Dep
                        isA Dep_S_Class with
    telosObject
        : &MonMbrExpRpt!exrep
    abstractTdlObject
        : TDLGenMonExpRep!exr
end MonMbrExpRpt_exrep_Dep
```

Note that dependency metaclasses, as defined here, are independent of the application domain and only depend on the nature of requirements and design specifications. Selecting a dependency type results in the creation of an instance to the corresponding dependency metaclass.

3 A Sample Session

The prototype implementation of the mapping assistant IRIS was developed with the following requirements in mind:

- Assistance to the designer with the decisions he needs to make during the mapping process.

- Maintenance of the history of the mapping process.

- Offering simple-to-use tools that aid the mapping process.

Figure 3.1 shows the interface of IRIS, consisting of three separate areas:

- The Telos area, which provides access to Telos objects. (More precisely, the SML area, where SML is an extension of Telos with built-in attribute categories, Telos and SML are used interchangeably)

- The TDL area, which provides access to TDL objects.

- The dependency types area, which provides information on available dependencies.

Early on in the implementation of the mapping assistant, and consistently with other components of the DAIDA project, it was decided to use graphical representation to help the designer have a better view of the contents of the requirements and design specifications as well as the mapping process. Moreover, node highlighting and dynamic pop-up menus were adopted as display methods to suggest to the designer possible choices. In addition, the mapping assistant is equipped with a powerful TDL editor which minimizes the amount of information to be provided by the designer during the mapping of a requirements object into a design one.

Consider the following example, for the purposes of demonstrating the mapping process. Suppose that the designer decides to map the following isA hierarchy which is part of the requirements model:

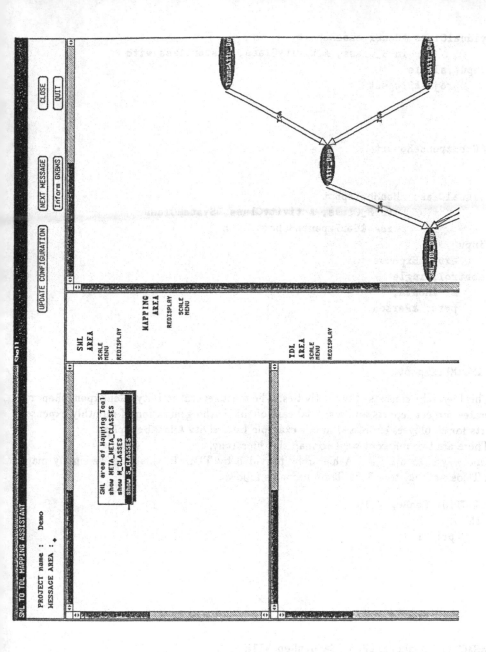

Figure 3.1 The Mapping Assistant Interface

```
IndividualClass &GenExpenseReport
                in S_Class, ActivityClass, SystemClass with
    input,single
        proj: &Project


        ...


end &GenExpenseReport


IndividualClass &MonMbrExpRpt
                in S_Class, ActivityClass, SystemClass
                isA &GenExpenseReport with
    input
        exp: &Expense
    control,single
        m: &Month;
        pers: &Person


        ...


end &MonMbrExpRpt
```

This hierarchy consists of two activities. The most general activity &GenExpenseReport generates project reports and a special case of this is the generation of monthly expense reports for employees expressed in our example by activity &MonMbrExpRpt.

There are two different ways to map this hierarchy.

One way is to use the isA hierarchy provided by TDL. In this case we simply map each Telos Activity to a TDL Transaction as follows:

```
TRANSACTION GenRep WITH
    IN
        pr: Proj;


        ...


END


TRANSACTION GenMonExpRep ISA GenRep WITH
    IN
        exp: SETOF Expense;
    LOCALS
        m: Mon;
        per: String;


        ...
```

END

An alternative way is to decide to eliminate this hierarchy from the design specification and to create instead the following transaction:

```
TRANSACTION GenMonExpRep WITH
    IN
        pr: Proj;
        exp: SETOF Expense;
    LOCALS
        m: Mon;
        per: String;


        ...


END
```

This alternative combines mapping of a requirements object with the projection of attributes to all specializations of a class and is referred to as *mapping with inheritance* in [Katalagarianos89]. For the example, &MonMbrExpRpt is mapped, with its own and inherited attributes, while &GenExpenseReport is not. The particular steps required for this mapping task are as follows:

1. *Selection of the level of the objects to be mapped.*

Each mapping task begins with the selection of a requirements object. Preliminary to this step, a pop up menu allows the designer to select the classification level of the object to be mapped by choosing

- Simple Classes.

- M1 Classes.

- Meta Meta Classes which consist from M2 classes up to Omega classes.

Action: Select Simple Classes item, figure 3.1.

Effect: All simple classes are presented graphically in the Telos area.

2. *Selection of the object to be mapped*

Next, a specific object is selected for mapping. To complete the mapping, the designer needs to first review its complete description. By clicking the right button of the mouse on a node which represents a particular class, a pop-up menu appears on the screen. Figure 3.2 shows the menu corresponding to class &MonMbrExpRpt. As &MonMbrExpRpt is a specialization of &GenExpenseReport, two different alternatives are offered to the designer for the mapping. Either he can choose the item *start mapping/show dep* which corresponds to the case of mapping the Telos isA hierarchy into a corresponding TDL one, or he can choose the item *mapping with inheritance/show dep*. Both items contain *show dep*, because if the selected class (or hierarchy) has already been mapped then the dependency graph corresponding to that previous mapping is going to be displayed.

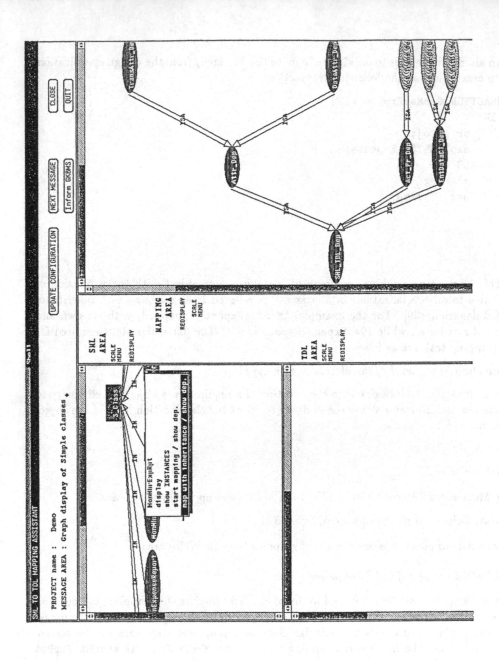

Figure 3.2 Telos Object Selection

Action: Select *mapping with inheritance*

Effect: Attribute displayer comes up (Figure 3.3). The inherited attributes are colored grey.

In order to map a class, the types of its attributes must have been mapped before. If this is not the case, the mapping assistant suspends the mapping process. The special sign "M" on some nodes on the attribute displayer shows that the classes represented by these nodes have been mapped.

3. *Start the mapping process for the object*

The next step is to decide how that object is going to be mapped without having in mind whether it has attributes or not for the time being. By clicking the right button of the mouse on the class node &MonMbrExpRpt on the attribute displayer figure 3.3, a pop-up menu comes up with the item *map*.

Action: Select *map*

Effect: Some nodes of the mapping rules area are turned into grey (highlighted), figure 3.4.

4. *Selection of the mapping rule to be used*

The designer has to decide which rule to chose from the grey ones figure 3.4. The system has highlighted the applicable ones for this mapping task. By clicking the appropriate highlighted node, a pop-up menu comes up.

Action: Select *Fire*

Effect: A TDL editor comes up with the frame of the TDL object to be created, figure 3.5.

5. *Start creating TDL Object*

The designer just fills up the slot with the name of the new TDL object.

Action: Click *create abstr* button of the TDL editor.

Effect: The dependency corresponding to the mapping performed is shown on the attribute displayer, figure 3.6.

6. *Continue with attribute mapping*

The next step is to proceed with the mapping of the attributes including the inherited ones.

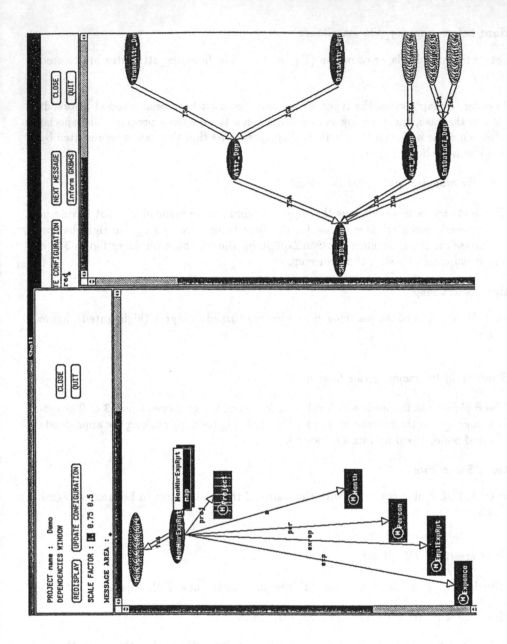

Figure 3.3 Attribute Displayer

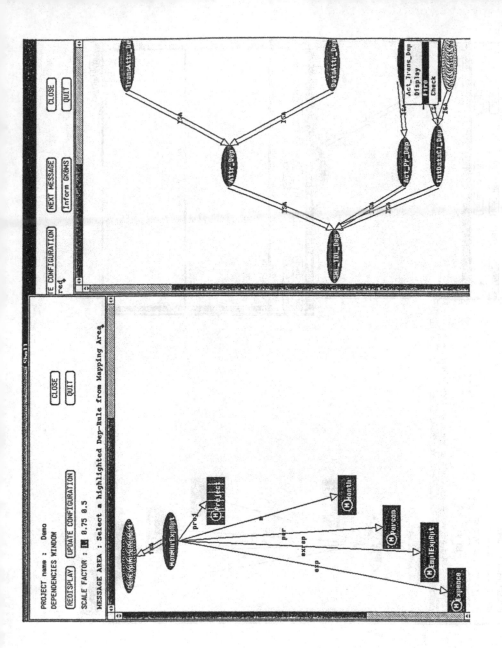

Figure 3.4 Dependency Hierarchies and Dependency Selection

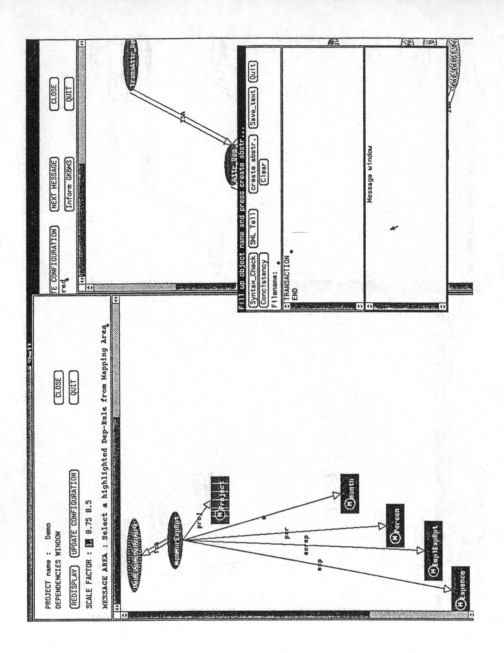

Figure 3.5 TDL Editor

326

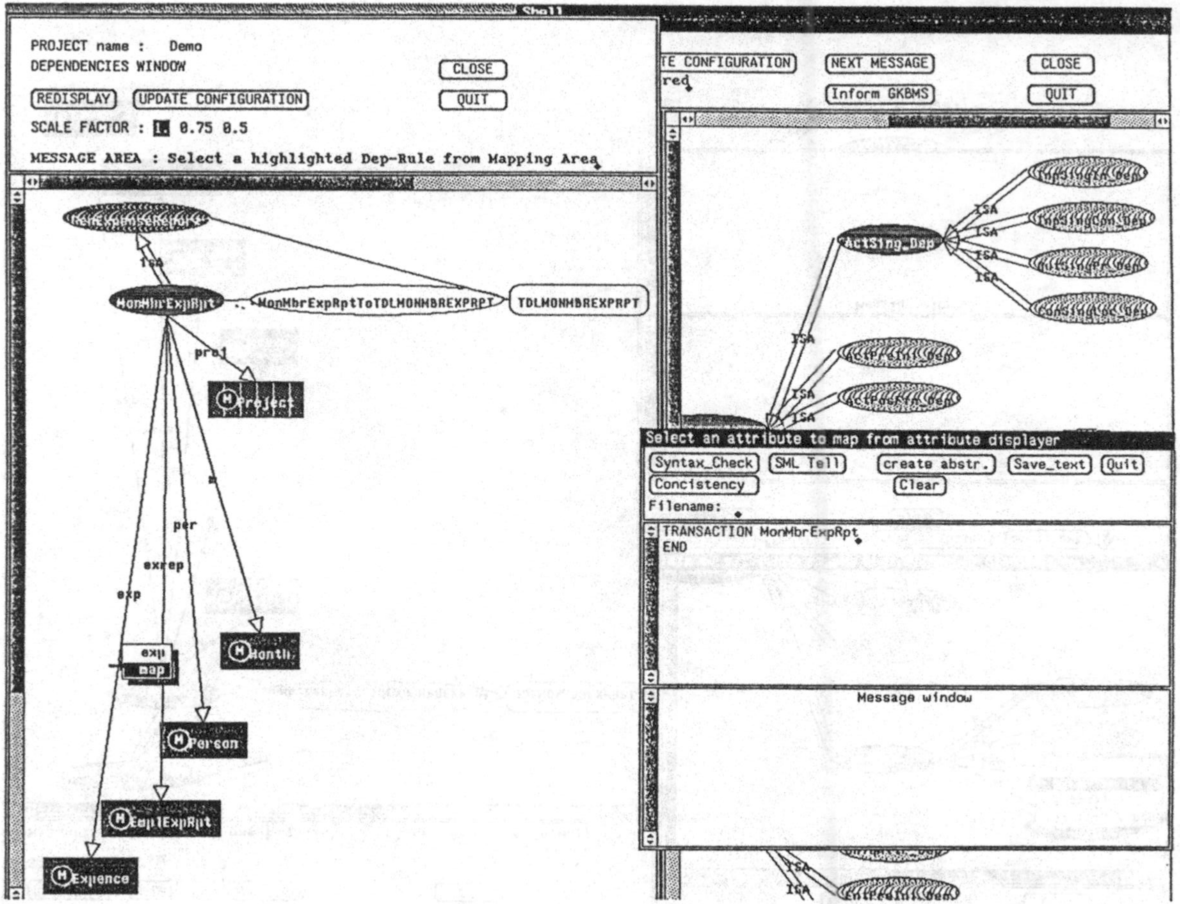

Figure 3.6 Dependency Graph

327

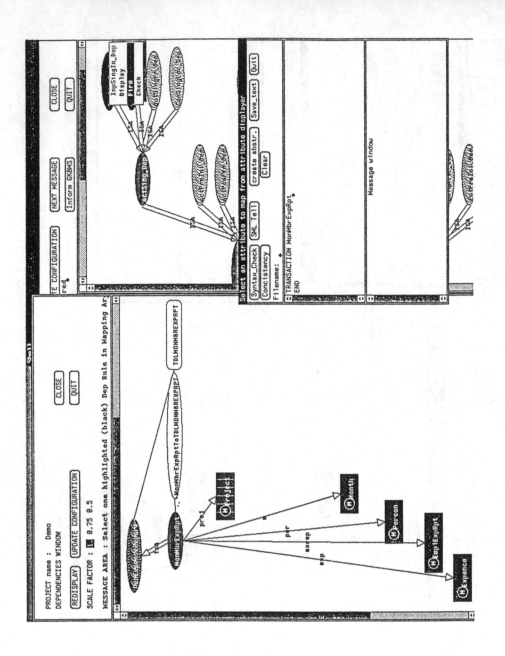

Figure 3.7 Dependencies for Attributes

328

Action: Click on an attribute link and select the only item *map* of the pop-up menu.

Effect: Some nodes in the mapping rule area are highlighted to grey, figure 3.7.

7. Selection of the mapping rule to be used for attribute mapping

Action: Select *Fire* by clicking the desirable highlighted node.

Effect: The form of the TDL attribute appears on the TDL editor.

The TDL attribute type is provided by the mapping assistant. The designer only gives the attribute name.

Action: Fill up the attribute name and press *create abstr.*

Effect: The dependency corresponding to the mapping of attribute is shown in the attribute displayer, figure 3.8.

Action: Repeat steps 6) and 7) until all the attributes have been mapped.

After all attributes are mapped the abstract TDL object and dependency instances corresponding to this mapping have been created.

Action: Press the button *SML Tell* of the TDL editor.

Effect: Abstract TDL object and dependency instances are being *Told* to TELOS KB.

Action: Press *Syntax Check* and then *Consistency* on the TDL editor.

Effect: TDL object is being *Told* to TDL KB. Class &MonMbrExpRpt is marked as mapped on the attribute displayer, and mappping is over. Figure 3.9 shows the corresponding dependency graph.

Special handling is offered by the mapping assistant when a requirements object that has already been mapped needs to be changed. In order to maintain consistency, all Telos objects influenced by this change have to be remapped. The designer does not have to follow the mapping steps described previously in order to remap these objects. Instead the mapping assistant finds the objects that have been affected by the change and asks the designer to take specific actions. For example, it may be recommended that the designer remove the changed objects and remap the new ones, or change specific objects created by the old mapping process without having to remap the changed object. The actions to be taken by the designer in such circumstances are intended to preserve consistency, of the requirements specification, the design specification or the mapping process.

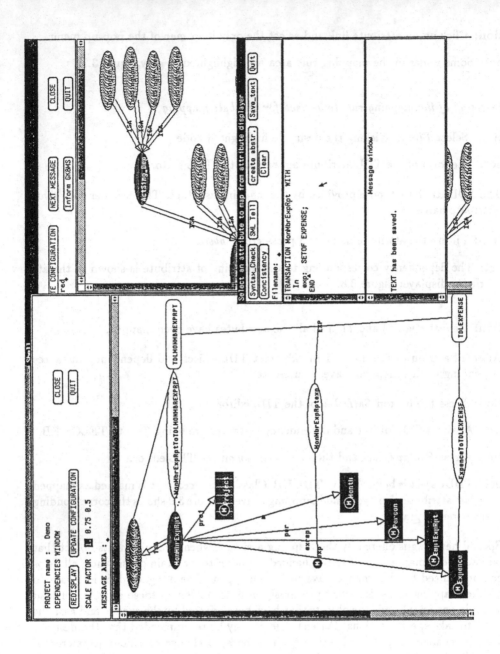

Figure 3.8 Dependency Graph Including Mapped Attributes

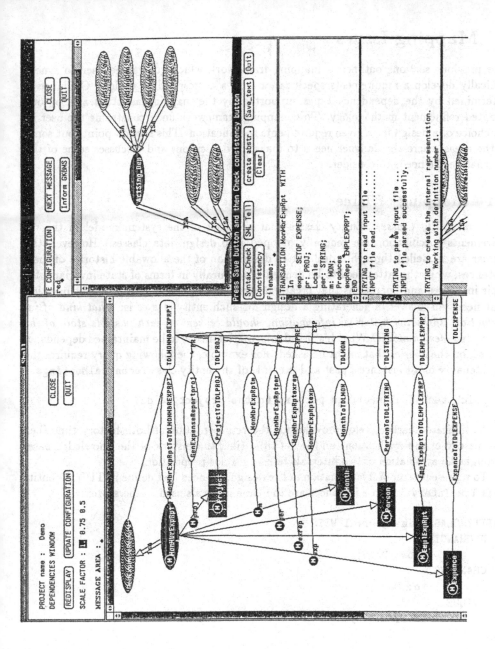

Figure 3.9 Dependency Graph from the Mapping of &GenExpenseReport

331

4 Mapping Issues

The previous sections outlined a mapping framework which guides the user to synergistically develop a requirements specification and a corresponding design. Guidance is determined by the dependency types supported by the mapping assistant and by our adopted refinement methodology. This mapping framework underconstrains the user in his choice of a design for a given requirements specification. This section points out some of the areas where the designer needs to make hard decisions and discusses some of the alternatives he needs to consider.

4.1 Mapping of Time

Time in Entity Classes: Entity classes that are part of the system model in the requirements specification are generally mapped into design data classes. However, the former are modelled through a declarative description of the allowable histories of their instances, while the latter need to be defined procedurally in terms of state invariants for their instances and operations that create, destroy and update them. The first question that needs an answer in generating a design for such entity classes is: *what kind of information, including historical information, should be kept in each possible state of the conceptual design model?* What historical information needs to be maintained depends, of course, on the queries that might be asked. For example, the following query requires the maintenance of all instances, past and present, of the entity class `TechnicalMeetings`.

```
Which technical meetings pertain to the project daida?
```

As indicated earlier, Telos provides for the representation of both history time (i.e., the history of the application) and belief time (i.e., the history of the knowledge base) through the association of two intervals to every Telos proposition.

To represent temporal information in the design, we need first define in TDL the entity class `TimeInterval` whose instances are the time intervals used in the system:

```
ENTITY CLASS TimeInterval WITH
    UNCHANGING
            from: Date;
    CHANGING
            to: Date;
    UNIQUE
            id(from, to)
END
```

Two useful concepts for conceptual design of databases with temporal information can be adopted from temporal databases [Snodgrass86], [Snodgrass87]: *validity time or existence period* which represents the time when the stored information was true (history time, in our terminology) and *transaction time* which represents the time the information was inserted in the database (belief time). Accordingly, every (design) data class may have two new temporal attributes, `validityTime` and `transactionTime`:

```
ENTITY CLASS Employee ISA Person WITH
   UNCHANGING
      eName: String;
   CHANGING
      eAddress: Address;
      worksOn: SET OF Project;
      salary: Amount;
      validityTime: TimeInterval;
      transactionTime: TimeInterval;
   UNIQUE
      id: (eName);
END
```

For requirements entity classes with invariant extensions, the value of `validityTime` is `AllTime`. Moreover, this attribute needs to be classified as unchanging. Likewise, `transactionTime` might be declared as unchanging and its value might be set to ∞ or to the time system operation was launched.

```
AGGREGATE CLASS Month WITH
   UNCHANGING
      month: 1..12;
      validityTime: [AllTime];
      transactionTime: [SystemLaunchTime];
   INVARIANT
      : (ALL x IN Month)(SOME y IN Date)
        (x.transactionTime = [y..31/12/2000]);
        {* System must be launched between y and
                                  31/12/2000 *}
END
```

Some objects represented in an information system will be inactive in the sense that their validity time has passed (consider, for example, a project that has terminated). Such objects may still be needed, depending on expected usage of the information handled by the system under development. *Relevance period* is another useful concept, intended to provide precisely this information. If the relevance period of an object is greater than its validity time, then past information must be maintained for that object as long as it is its relevance period. One way to structure inactive objects is through "conceptual archives": inactive objects are classified according to the day, week, month or year of their validity time, in addition to their other classifications. Alternatively, inactive objects might be classified according to their relation to the present. For instance, inactive instances of the class `Meeting` may be partitioned into one year collections through classes `LastYearMeetings`, `TwoYearAgoMeetings`, etc. Obviously, this scheme requires update operations. Note that in the DAIDA framework these issues are only dealt with at the design level and will lead to design objects, including data, transaction and script classes, which don't have requirements specification counterparts.

Time in Activity Classes: The declarative representation of temporal constraints in activities needs to be transformed usually into a more fine-grained state-transition view in the conceptual design. Since TDL treats transactions as atomic database operations, the transcations can only be used as design objects for activities with uninterruptible subactivities. Interruptible subactivities include communication, either between activities or between the system and end users. As with inactive entities, information about activities may have to be maintained after their termination.

Since scripts are long-term events, one may want to store in the information system not only an inactive script's validity time, but also the history of state and transition activations/de-activations. Transitions can be treated as generalized transactions for which the system maintains the input which triggered the transition, the goals (output) performed by the transition and the transition time interval.

As in the case of data classes the notion of relevance period must be applied here to prevent the rapid growth of the amount of past information.

4.2 Mapping of Assertions

In general, a temporal assertion in the requirements specification will have to be analysed and possibly reconfigured in order to be integrated in the system design. Here are some basic alternatives:

From Telos Assertions to TDL Assertions: One of the many difficulties here is that each entity in the constraints of the system model has a time interval associated with it, whereas each data class in the assertions of the conceptual design model is associated with a *validity time* interval which is defined in terms of two time points. For instance, the following constraint of the system model requires that *all expenses of an employee should occur during a meeting of a project in which he is involved:*

```
(Forall x/&Expense)(Exists mt/&Meeting)
        (x.meet = mt) and (x during mt) and
        (mt.proj subsetOf x.participant.proj)
```

This constraint might be mapped into

```
(ALL x IN Expense)(SOME mt IN Meeting)
    (x.meet = mt) AND
    AFTER(x.validityTime.from, mt.validityTime.from) AND
    BEFORE(x.validityTime.to, mt.validityTime.to) AND
    (mt.proj SUBSETOF x.participant.proj)
```

in TDL. Note that the resulting formula is considerably more opaque, due to the mapping of intervals into time points.

From Telos Assertions to Satisfaction by Design: Rather than transforming a constraint in the system model into assertions in the design, the developer may choose to enforce the constraints through system operations and interactions with its environment. Consider, for example,

```
(Forall x/&GenExpenseReport)
    (x  meets this.beginTime + 6mo)  or
    (Exists y/GenExpenseReport) (x  meets y + 6mo)
```

which requires, roughly speaking, that expense reports be generated every six months. Naively, this constraint might be enforced by a script transition that fires every six months and generates a report. However, having the system generate a report is only useful when the system has full information on the subject matter. Accordingly, a more pragmatic enforcement of the constraint may involve a cooperative scheme between the system and users where the system reminds them about an impending deadline, gets the information it needs[7] and proceeds to generate the report. Moreover, the designer may want to add constraints at the requirements or design level to facilitate this information-gathering process for the system. For instance, he may add the constraint that *no expense receipt should be submitted more than a month after the expense actually occurred* (requirements level) or *no expense summary can be inserted in the system more than a month after the relevant meeting took place* (design level). Alternatively, the system may be designed to send out periodic reminders, keep track of meetings – past, present and forthcoming – and send out specific reminders or use some other scheme.

Note that in all of the above scenarios, requirements constraints are enforced by the structure of transactions or scripts and even by the (helpful) behaviour of the environment.

4.3   Mapping of Generalization and Classification Hierarchies

Modelling the world is generally considered a more difficult task than designing a system. Telos recognizes this by offering levels of metaclasses intended to help the user define the concepts that are most appropriate for the modelling task at hand. TDL, on the other hand, is built around a *fixed* set of concepts for conceptual system design and has no use for metaclasses. To deal with this difference, all information associated with a requirements specification beyond the simple class level needs to be collapsed down to simple classes. This collapsing process can be complicated by the presence of generalization hierarchies at metaclass levels.

When dealing with a generalization hierarchy at the metaclass or higher levels, we have to suppress the hierarchy into some metaclass definitions and then have to map the resulting classification hierarchy. In the first step, a class B inherits all attributes from a class A (at a higher level in the generalization hierarchy) and becomes class B'. We may keep class A as is, or we may remove it if we know that it will never be instantiated. In the second step, corresponding classes at a lower level inherit attributes from B', thus eliminating the generalization. We eventually have only classification hierarchies that need to be mapped to TDL.

Elimination of classification hierarchies implies the loss of the ability to talk about sets of classes. Therefore, we have to explicitly associate semantics with them. The methodology employed allows to suppress classification hierarchies by explicitly defining all the knowledge, included in the description of a metaclass, in the instances of the particular metaclass.

---

[7]Obviously, this is still an idealization of what happens within an organization

335

5   Current Status and Conclusions

This paper proposes a novel framework for the generation of information system designs from given requirements specifications. The framework is based on a number of premises. Firstly, it adopts the DAIDA architecture which relegates different classes of decisions to different stages of the software development process. Secondly, it assigns a particular role to the mapping assistant in the software development process which involves primarily constraint enforcement and suggestion of basic alternatives. Thirdly, it employs a knowledge engineering approach for the mapping assistant, whereby the relevant knowledge sources are identified and their role in the performance of the mapping task is formally characterized and embedded in the framework's control regime. Finally, a single knowledge representation language is used as an appropriate linguistic vehicle for capturing all types of knowledge relevant to the mapping task.

The implementation of IRIS described in this paper is part of an effort to develop a prototype of the DAIDA environment. This prototype has already been demonstrated and is currently being extended and refined. It runs on SUN workstations and is implemented on top of BIM-Prolog, where the windows and graphics interface have been implemented in SunView and Pixrect.

The prototype implementation of the mapping assistant only employs approximately 30 dependency types at this point. We estimate that a reasonably complete implementation will require 50 -100 such types, in addition to analogous sets of decomposition, satisficing and refinement methods.

Some of the limitations of the implementation are due to the status of the Telos and TDL implementations. In particular, in the current implementation of Telos, performance degrades quite rapidly with the size of the knowledge base. The implementation of TDL supports the insertion, retrieval and update for data and transaction classes. Moreover, most of the assertion language has been implemented, while scripts and functions have only been partly implemented. The Telos and TDL implementations consist of 3 and 1.5Mb of Prolog code respectively and require more than 35Mb of virtual space to run efficiently.

Future plans for the implementation of IRIS include adding more dependency types and decomposition, satisficing and refinement methods. Also, extending and improving the implementations of Telos and TDL. Finally, refining the control structure which utilizes these knowledge sources to guide the generation and the justification of a design.

Bibliography

[Allen81] James F. Allen, *A General Model of Action and Time*, Proceedings 7th IJCAI, Vancouver, BC, Canada, 1981.

[Barron82] John Barron, *Dialogue and Process Design for Interactive Information Systems Using Taxis,* In Proceedings SIGOA Conference on Office Information Systems, Philadelphia, PA, SIGOA Newsletter, Vol. 3, Nos 1 and 2, pp. 12-20, 21-23 June 1982.

[Borgida85] A. Borgida, *Features of Languages for the Development of Information Systems at the Conceptual Level*, IEEE Software, Vol. 2, No. 1, Jan. 1985, pp. 63-72.

[Borgida87] Alex Borgida, John Mylopoulos, Joachim W. Schmidt and Eric Meirlæn, *Final Version of TDL Design*, Esprit Project DAIDA (892), deliverable DES1.2, Sept. 1987.

[Borgida89] Alex Borgida, Matthias Jarke, John Mylopoulos, Joachim W. Schmidt and Yannis Vassiliou, *The Software Development Environment as a Knowledge Base Management System.* in J. W. Schmidt and C. Thanos (Editors), Foundations of Knowledge Base Management. Springer-Verlag, 1989.

[Chung84] Lawrence Chung, *An Extended Taxis Compiler*, M.Sc. thesis, Dept. of Computer Science, University of Toronto, Jan. 1984. Also CSRG Technical Note 37, 1984.

[Chung89] Lawrence Chung, Panagiotis Katalagarianos, Manolis Marakakis, Michalis Mertikas, John Mylopoulos and Yannis Vassiliou, *From Information System Requirements to Designs: A Mapping Framework*, Technical Report FORTH/CSI/TR/1989/020. Institute of Computer Science - FORTH, Heraklion, November 1989.

[Findler79] Findler, N. (editor), *Associative Networks*, Academic Press, 1979.

[Greenspan84] S. Greenspan, *Requirements Modelling: The Use of Knowledge Representation Techniques for Requirements Specification*, Ph. D. thesis, Dept. of Computer Science, University of Toronto, 1984.

[Hayes87] I. Hayes (editor), *Specification Case Studies*, Prentice Hall International, Englewood Cliffs NJ, 1987.

[Hull87] R. Hull and R. King, *Semantic Database Modelling: Survey, Applications and Research Issues*, ACM Computing Reviews 19, No. 3, Sept. 1987.

[Jackson83] Michael Jackson, *System Development*, Prentice-Hall, 1983.

[Jarke86] M. Jarke (ed), *Development of Advanced Interactive Data-Intensive Applications (DAIDA), Global Design Report*, Esprit-Project 892, Sept. 1986.

[Jarke89] Matthias Jarke, Manfred Jeusfeld, Tomas Rose, *A Software Process Data Model for Knowledge Engineering in Information Systems.* Information Systems, Vol.14, No.3, Fall 1989.

[Katalagarianos89] Panos Katalagarianos, Manolis Marakakis, Michalis Mertikas, Yannis Vassiliou, *CML/Telos - TDL Mapping Assistant: Architecture and Development*, Esprit Project 892 (DAIDA), del. DES2.3, Institute of Computer Science, Foundation for Research and Technology, Heraklion, Crete, Greece, Febr. 1989.

[Koubarakis89] M. Koubarakis, J. Mylopoulos, M. Stanley and A. Borgida, *Telos: Features and Formalization*, Technical Report KRR-TR-89-4, Dept. of Computer Science, Univ. of Toronto, 1989.

[Mylopoulos86] *The Role of Knowledge Representation in the Development of Specifications,* In H. J. Kugler (ed.): Information Processing, Elsevier Science Publishers B. V., North-Holland, 1986.

[Roman85] Gruia-Catalin Roman, *A Taxonomy of Current Issues in Requirements Engineering,* In IEEE Computer, pp. 14-21, Apr., 1985.

[Schmidt88] J. Schmidt, H. Eckhardt, and F. Matthes, *DBPL Report.* DBPL-Memo 111-88, Fachbereich Informatik, johann Wolfgang Goethe-Universitat, Frankfurt, West Germany, 1988.

[Snodgrass86] Richard Snodgrass, *Temporal Databases,* Computer, September 1986, pp. 35-42.

[Snodgrass87] Richard Snodgrass, *The Temporal Query Language TQuel,* In ACM Transactions on Database Systems, 1987.

[Stanley86] M. Stanley, *A Formal Semantics for CML,* M. Sc. thesis, Dept. of Computer Science, University of Toronto, 1986.

[Zave81] Pamela Zave and Raymond T. Yeh, *Executable Requirements for Embedded Systems,* In Proceedings fifth International Conf. on Software Engineering, pp. 295-304, 1981.

RECAST:
A TOOL FOR REUSING REQUIREMENTS

M.G. Fugini §†, *B. Pernici* †

§Università di Brescia
†Politecnico di Milano,
piazza Leonardo da Vinci 32, Milano, Italy

Abstract

Reuse of development documents regarding application requirements makes the application development process more efficient and reliable. The REquirements Collection And Specification Tool (RECAST) being developed in the framework of the ESPRIT ITHACA project aimed at reusability under an object-oriented approach for Information System applications is presented in the paper.
Two types of application developers interact with RECAST: the Application Engineer, who maintains the knowledge about reusable components, and the Application Developer, who develops specific applications; their interaction with RECAST is presented. RECAST guides these developers using design knowledge stored in a Software Information Base (SIB).

1 Introduction

This paper describes RECAST (REquirement Collection And Specification Tool), a tool for reusing application requirements in development of Information Systems applications. RECAST is being developed as part of the ITHACA Project /Pro 89/, an ESPRIT II software environment research program encompassing European industrial and university organizations. The objective of ITHACA is to develop an advanced software development environment based on the object-orientation paradigm /Ara 88, Fis 87, Tsi 88, Tsi 89/ and on reusability. In particular, the *ITHACA Application Development Environment* (ADE) facilitates the reuse by the developers of various components of previously developed applications: application requirements, application designs, implemented objects, execution results, documentations /Gib 89b/. Consequently, the set of tools in the ITHACA Application Development Environment comprises requirement collection and specification tools, application configuration tools, object design tools.

The ITHACA Application development Environment is centered around the *Software Information Base* (SIB), a knowledge base storing information about available reusable components /Cos 89/. The SIB is accessed by the ITHACA tools in order to inspect available application components /Gib 89b/ in the context of the development of a new application to evaluate which existing components can possibly be reused totally or through refinement and modification.

Two types of designers are addressed by ITHACA tools: the *Application Engineer* (AE), and the *Application Developer* (AD) /ITH 89, Gib 89a/. The Application Engineer is responsible for development of application skeletons, that is, sets of generic application components (application requirements, specifications, design objects, executables, design documents, etc.) meaningful to certain application domains and therefore candidates for reusability in applications pertaining to those domains. For example, in the "accounting system" application domain, reusable components are specifications and designs of "journal", "client", "account" objects, and operations on them like "update", "post", "withdrawal". These reusable components can then be expanded by the AD in different ways in order to develop specific applications. The Application Developer develops specific applications. Using the ITHACA tools, the AD's development paradigm consists of the definition of the application requirements, selecting reusable components from generic applications, and progressively *refining* and *modifying* these components to meet the requirements of the specific application being developed. The AD uses the tools of the ITHACA environment, maintained by the AE, to search for reusable components in the SIB, for configuring the current application reusing as many components as possible, and for implementing new objects. The product of a specific application development can be further evaluated by the AE for identifying new components that are candidates to reusability; these may become part of the available reusable software of ITHACA and therefore be described in the SIB.

In the ITHACA Application Development Environment, *reusability* of software and of development information is the major goal. This goal regards all the development phases, thus, in particular, the application *requirement collection and specification* phase. Such phase is conducted under a reusability approach that allows the AD to reuse existing *requirement specifications* and to identify reusable *design objects* that meet the requirements.

The purpose of this paper is to describe how the RECAST tool addresses these issues by supporting the AD in requirement collection and specification under an object-oriented paradigm, by automatically *completing* the requirements when existing specifications are discovered by the tool for reuse, and by giving *suggestions* about existing design objects that can be possibly reused.

The next section of the paper describes the rationale of the approach to reusability of application development documents in the first phases of the software development life-cycle. Subsequent sections present RECAST architecture (Section 3), the requirement collection phase (Section 4), the requirement specification phase (Section 5), and a scenario of use of RECAST (Section 6).

2 Reusability of development documents

The focus of research on reusability has mainly been on reusing code /Bur 87, Fre 87/. However, reusing the results of previous software projects is important in all development phases in the software development life-cycle. The importance of reusing results from the early development phases has particularly been emphasized: Freeman /Fre 87/ suggests the reuse not only of code, but also of specifications, and Feather

/Fea 87/ suggests to reuse specifications, modifying specifications rather than their implementations when change is needed. Reuse of algebraic specifications, built and structured in a modular manner to facilitate reuse, is presented in /Wir 89/.

RECAST may be regarded as a *system generator*, based on knowledge of given application domains and on models for requirement definition, with reusability of development documents as a primary goal. RECAST is based on domain knowledge specialized for development of Information Systems in different application domains. The support of information bases, specification bases, and knowledge bases for different phases of the development of software systems has been proposed in the literature /Tsi 89, Jar 89, Per 89b, Pun 87, Pun 88/.

The relevance for reusability of intermediate stable forms of development documents has been emphasized /Weg 87/. We assume an Information Systems development life-cycle based on the following phases /ITH 89/:

- requirement collection
- functional specification
- configuration of designs (implementations)

Each of these phases produces **development documents** based on the domain knowledge and on a model for that particular development phase. The requirement collection phase produces a Requirement Collection Document, the specification phase a Requirement Specification Document, and the third phase an implementation of the system in the target O-O language.

RECAST produces and reuses documents in the first two phases above. The structure and the contents of these documents is discussed in the following sections.

The definition of requirements in RECAST is oriented to building a system rather than to describing the relationship of the system with the external world. Therefore, the requirements define the system model, rather than the world model, the goal being that of describing the aspects that characterize a specific application in a given application domain. The specification documents define the functionalities of the components of the system. These components are defined by RECAST on the basis of available knowledge on a given domain and on the requirements described by the AD for the specific application.

We assume that the SIB contains both reusable building blocks and information about the development process. RECAST reuses elements in the SIB in three ways:

- *requirements are collected following a predefined domain model.* The domain dependent model allows the designer to define the characteristics of the application, using a domain dependent vocabulary, mainly on the basis of examples. Requirements may define not only functional characteristics of a specific application, but also non-functional characteristics such as distribution of users and data on different sites, volumes of data and processing frequency. The use of domain languages has been proposed in the literature for this purpose (e.g., in the Draco system

Figure 1: Relationship among Requirements Collection, Requirements Specification and Application Design through the Requirements Model

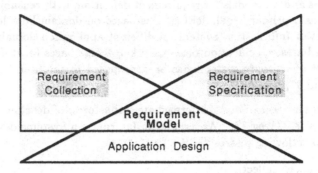

/Nei 87/); in RECAST, the domain model is inserted as knowledge in the SIB, for more flexibility (see Sect. 3).

- *functional specifications* are written *combining specification elements*. These elements can specify default functionalities for a given domain, or be selected and composed (automatically or semi-automatically) from the SIB, according to the requirements defined by the AD. In addition, the AD may refine existing modules and create new elements, which may be made available for reuse in future projects, both as reusable elements and together with their development information. As suggested in /Fea 87/, refinement in RECAST is mainly based on adding to, and combining features of, existing elements, rather than changing predefined features.

- *design objects* (corresponding to implementations) may be *associated to specification elements*, and provide the basis for implementation of the O-O target application.

These three reuse categories of RECAST are strictly related to each other by a Requirement Model (Fig. 1). The *Requirement Model* (RM) contains relationships between requirement, specification and design components, information about their structure, and about tools that can be used to define these components. Additional information describing the components and their relationships is also contained in the SIB with the purpose of facilitating their reuse.

In general, reusable components, although constructed by developers under a reusability approach, are maintained and inserted in the RM by the AE in order to control and guarantee the quality of the model.

The AD is guided through RECAST in the definition of the requirements of the specific

Figure 2: Architecture of RECAST

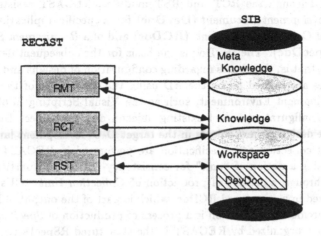

application using information contained in the RM. A set of tools is provided within RECAST (or called by RECAST) to help the AD in producing the requirement and specification documents for a specific application, as described in the following sections.

In RECAST, the domain model and language used for requirement collection may vary for different applications and different domains, while the specification language is an internal language of the tool, domain independent, and defined according to an extended object-oriented paradigm /Per 90/. The O-O paradigm in specifications facilitates the definition of standardized parts in the specifications and of interfaces between them. In fact, the description of object interfaces has been used for system specifications by many authors /Mey 89, Cox 87/. Moreover, in the Ithaca development environment, the goal is that of developing O-O applications. Therefore, while we keep the requirement collection phase open to any other approach, we suggest that the specification phase is chosen as the borderline between models used by developers during the requirements collection phase, based on domain dependent concepts, and the O-O world.

3   Architecture of RECAST

The architecture of RECAST is shown in Fig. 2; the tool is composed of the *Requirement Modeling Tool* (**RMT**), the *Requirement Collection Tool* (**RCT**), and the *Requirement Specification Tool* (**RST**). The three tools are centered around the knowledge provided by the *Requirements Model* (RM), which groups knowledge about the application domains and about the phases of requirement definition, together with a link to possible implementations, as shown in Fig. 1 and 2.

RECAST, with the RMT, assists the AE in filling in and modifying the RM, stored in the SIB. Through the RCT and RST modules, RECAST assists the AD in producing a *Development Document* (**DevDoc**) for a specific application, composed of a *Requirement Collection Document* (**RCDoc**) and of a *Requirement Specification Document* (**RSpecDoc**). The DevDoc is the basis for the subsequent development phases of ITHACA, that is, the phases regarding configuration of designs and implementations. These phases are carried on by the AD using the other tools of the ITHACA Application Development Environment, such as the Visual Scripting Tool, which supports application configuration out of existing objects, and the Object Design Tool, which supports the design of new objects in the target O-O development language /ITH 89/. Requirement collection and specification are performed in RECAST through a set of steps and using a notion of "unit" for consistency reasons. In particular, collection is performed through a process of production of *Collection Units* (CUs); these units are then organized in a structured RCDoc, which is part of the output of RECAST. Analogously, requirement specification is a process of production of *Specification Units* (SUs) which are then organized by RECAST in the structured RSpecDoc.

The RM is stored as a semantic network in the ITHACA SIB knowledge base. This network contains:

- knowledge about the requirement models, about application domains, and about the process of defining in RECAST new application domains and reusable components with the related development assistance rules ("meta-knowledge").
- knowledge about the requirement collection and specification process used in ITHACA ("knowledge").

The interaction of RECAST with the developers is obtained through *navigation* in the knowledge base using the RM (see Fig. 3) for:

- guiding the interaction with the developers ("dialogues") and interpreting the user choices ("answers");
- allowing the developer to use available *external tools* necessary to perform some of the activities related to requirement production. These can be general-purpose tools, such as editors, text formatters, graphical packages or interface managers, or special-purpose tools, for example application document generators and managers. These tools are linked to the RECAST environment and can be called by the user to perform some functions. Such links provide flexibility to RECAST because tools can be easily integrated in the requirement definition environment by the AE by simply adding to the knowledge of RECAST a link to the tool. In current work on RECAST, specialized tools that scan a document and derive its conceptual structure /Per 89a/ are being linked to RECAST;
- producing the RCDoc and the RSpecDoc;
- inspecting the set of available design objects to identify reusable objects, i.e., objects that meet the current requirements; acknowledgment about the existence

Figure 3: Role of the RM in RECAST

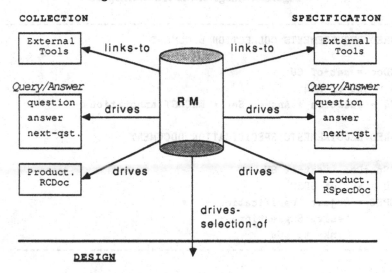

of such objects is inserted by RECAST into the DevDoc in the form of design suggestions.

In this paper, we focus on the description of the contents of the SIB for use by RECAST (Sect. 3.1. describes the designer working area, Sect. 3.2. and 3.3. the meta-knowledge and knowledge) and on the RCT and RST modules.

3.1 The developer workspace

The AD is provided by RECAST with a workspace where:

- information is moved from the SIB to be examined;
- external tools operate when invoked through RECAST;
- requirements are inserted as part of the current application requirements in two ways:

  a) upon creation by the AD
  b) automatically by RECAST, when reusable requirements are found in the SIB.

The requirements are transferred, created, deleted from the workspace according to CUs and SUs which are the atomic entities of consistency of RECAST and of the workspace.

A sample image of the workspace for the AD is shown in Fig. 4.: the structured RCDoc

Figure 4: Image of the AD workspace

```
------------------------------------------------------------------
STRUCTURED REQUIREMENTS COLLECTION DOCUMENT

      RCDoc = set-of CU
      CU = set-of REQ
      REQ = Question + Answer Set + RECAST annotations

STRUCTURED REQUIREMENTS SPECIFICATION DOCUMENT

      RSpecDoc = set-of SU
      SU = set-of SPEC
      SPEC = Object Specification +
             Design Suggestions +
             links to CUs
------------------------------------------------------------------
```

is progressively built as a set of CUs; analogously, the RSpecDoc is built as a set of SUs. A CU is a set of requirements (REQ in Fig. 5) derived by posing questions to the AD and by interpreting the user answer within an answer set. Additionally, REQ contains annotations given by RECAST about requirement collection, that is, about missing requirements that are automatically added by the tool reusing available CUs. In the specification phase, SUs are built as sets of specifications. A specification (SPEC in Fig. 4.) is derived by RECAST as a set of specification objects and as a set of design suggestions. Design suggestions are links to reusable design objects. In each SPEC, RECAST introduces a link to the requirements that lead to the generation of the SPEC.

3.2 Semantic network for requirements modeling

Requirements modeling in RECAST is based on a semantic network containing both meta-knowledge (generic knowledge for model construction) and knowledge (knowledge for modeling applications in a given application domain).

The semantic network that is used mainly by the AE for management of the RECAST environment is shown in Appendix 1. The meta-knowledge represented in this semantic network regards the task of the AE of defining a given RM. The definition of a RM consists of the definition of the **model characteristics**, such as the application domains where the model can be applied, whether the model data-oriented (e.g., an ER model) or process-oriented (e.g., Petri nets), and whether external tools exist for model processing (e.g., a graphical editor for entering the model entities).

The next component of the RM definition process is the definition of the **model entities**

(**ENTITY** node in the semantic network). An entity, identified by its name, has a representation (e.g., graphical), and some attributes.

The definition of an RM then encompasses the definition of the model links, i.e., of the relationships among entities (**LINK** node). A link, identified by its name, has some **CHARACTERISTICS**: origin and destination entities (this also defines the link direction), and a type. The type can be standard, such as "is-a" or "part-of" link, or can be defined by the AE. In the network, the "is-a" links are used as a classification mechanism and the "part-of" links are used for defining the components of a node. No inheritance mechanism holds in the network. External tools mentioned earlier in this section are connected to LINK nodes; this mechanism allows the AD or AE to be aware of the availability of external tools while traversing links.

Navigation of the AE through this meta-knowledge occurs according to the modalities that will be illustrated in the next section. The purpose of navigation for the AE is to be guided in the maintenance of the environment; besides the introduction of new models, the AE navigates for exploring the base of reusable requirement elements, for creating connections among requirements, specifications, and designs, for defining application domain knowledge and organizing it in structured hierarchical subdomains. The AE is also responsible for linking external tools to the environment and for defining the questions and answers associated to links.

In Appendix 2, a sample semantic network of RECAST knowledge is depicted. This network describes the knowledge used by RECAST to guide the requirements collection and specification by developers in specific applications and it is constructed according to RECAST meta-knowledge, in terms of ENTITY nodes, LINK nodes, and their characteristics. The network shows, as an example, the Requirement Definition Process in the "Public Administration" application domain. It is assumed that an AD is collecting the requirements of an application in this domain and that a definition process based on a model (PADM model in App. 2 a) exists especially oriented to developing applications in the Public Administration Domain. A method for application development in the Public Administration domain is being used in ITHACA as a common ground for evaluating the functionalities of the various ITHACA tools /Kap 89a, Kap 89b/. The application being developed is a system for a City Council; this system automates the procedure of releasing authorizations to private organizations to hold public events (concerts, exhibitions, etc.). App. 2 b) shows the information needed for requirements collection and App. 2 c) the information needed for requirements specification. The use of the knowledge illustrated in App. 2 is described in detail in Sect. 4 and Sect. 5., and an example of RECAST use based on this knowledge is shown in Sect. 6.

3.3 RECAST interaction with the developers: links and navigation on the semantic networks

RECAST guides the Application Developer and the Application Engineer in navigating along nodes and links of the semantic networks that constitute its base of knowledge, performing actions and calling available external tools associated to network links. *Link traversal* is the basic mechanism for generating queries to the developers and for calling external tools during specific tasks of the requirement definition process.

Default queries can be automatically associated to standard links ("is-a" and "part-of"). The default query:

```
YOU CAN SELECT ONE OF THE FOLLOWING DEFINITIONS:
   list of choices
```

is associated to "is-a" links; the developer is requested to select among possible choices listed by the tool. The choices are derived by RECAST from the semantic network, which describes "is-a" relationships between elements of the model.

The following default query:

```
WHICH PART DO YOU WANT TO SELECT?
   list of choices
```

is associated to "part-of links"; the developer is requested to select among possible components linked with a "part-of" link in the semantic network.

Optionally, links may have associated **questions** for interaction with the developer during requirements collection and specification according to the models defined by the Application Engineer. To each link type, an **answer set** is associated, which contains information to elaborate the user answers. An **inverse question** may be associated to links for their traversal in inverse mode. Questions attached to links may refer to tools (EXTERNAL TOOL node in App. 1.) which can thus be called and used from within RECAST.

Links have a **state**. The state can assume the following values:

- *potential*: the link is not visible to the AD because it does not belong to the currently selected path, (e.g., because the AD is working within a given application domain and therefore a sub-network has been selected);

- *active*: the link is visible to the AD because it belongs to a currently selected path; potential and active links provide the Application Developer with a view mechanism on the semantic network;

- *selected*: links can be selected by the AD when they are relevant to the current application and moved to the AD's workspace; with this mechanism a view on the semantic network is defined for a specific application (designer workspace for the specific application).

All the links in the semantic networks are potential, that is, can be traversed. Some of them become active, that is, can be traversed, depending on answers to previous queries; for example, if the AD decides to use the Entity-Relationship model for defining data schemas in the "accounting systems" application domain, the links necessary to create CUs and SUs according to the E-R model and according to available reusable requirements in that domain become active.

The semantic network can be traversed in two modes:

- retrieval mode
- update mode

In the first mode, the AE or the AD explore the RECAST knowledge or the AD's workspace in order to find concepts useful in the development or to examine the current contents of the workspace. The update mode occurs when concepts are selected from the network and information is copied from the SIB into the workspace. In retrieval mode, traversal of active links prompts the corresponding queries; no actions are undertaken on the SIB, but each link traversal operation activates other links. In update mode, the selection of a link determines insertion operations on the workspace.

4   Requirements collection tool

The Requirements Collection Tool is realized in RECAST using the navigation mechanism and knowledge in the semantic network concerning requirements collection. Requirements collection is carried out by progressively creating Collection Units (see App. 2a and 2b) composed of *functional* and *non functional* requirements. Functional requirements regard the application entities and procedures, that is the functionalities of the application; non functional requirements regard the application interface, the hardware and software characteristics of the application, the organization, and a variety of quantitative parameters and constraints (such as, expected response times, data volumes, computer loads). Some examples of non functional requirements are shown in App. 2b.

The output of requirements collection is the structured RCDoc. This document is composed of a set of CUs which are organized by RECAST in the RCDoc through some *Structuring Rules*. Such rules determine where collected information has to be placed in the RCDoc and how this document can be accessed in order to find "related" information. CUs are produced by RECAST according to the Q/A paradigm for requirements collection illustrated in the previous section.

The remainder of this section describes navigation of RECAST through the semantic network of App. 2. for: setting the AD requirements definition environment for the City Council application (Sect. 4.1.); navigating in the network along specific knowledge referring to the preparation of CUs according to the selected method (Sect. 4.2.).

4.1   Setting RECAST environment for the AD

RECAST drives the AD in setting a collection and specification environment, that is, in selecting the adequate knowledge for the application at hand. Setting the environment is achieved with RECAST navigating along the knowledge and selecting a model and the application domain for a given specific application to be developed. In the network of App. 2 a), three types of models are shown: Structured Analysis, PADM model /Kap 89a/, and SADT & ER models /Som 89/. Application domains have an associated size and a description that brings to three subdomains: the Public Administration domain, the domain of Chemical Applications, and the domain of Financial Applications. In our case, the AD selects the Public Administration domain, which is composed of a set of phases: each phase produces a set of CUs; CUs are in turn possibly made of CUs.

4.2   An example of requirements collection knowledge

In the network of App. 2 b), the knowledge associated to the production of CUs within the Public Administration domain with the PADM method /Kap 89a/ is illustrated (only active links are shown). The network shows the representation of the requirements model developed for the PADM method. A CU is made of entities (functional requirements) and of non functional requirements. The basic entity of this model describes procedures and is called *case type* /Kap 89a/; a case type is composed of a schema (flowchart) of *steps*. Steps of a case type have associated *documents*; we suppose that the reusable base of documents contains three document types: the OFFICIAL DOCUMENT, the REQUEST document, and the APPROVAL document. Each type of document has a default form which is shown to the AD: the AD decides whether such form is suitable to his purposes and can be reused. This is shown in App. 2b for the REQUEST only. The REQUEST document has a default definition; alternatively, an example of REQUEST can be entered by the AD and one of RECAST external tools can be called (e.g., the INTRES tool which understands document structures by examples /Per 89a/) or entering an example. Depending on which link is traversed in the network, the proper external tool is called by RECAST into the AD workspace. A case type also comprises the definition of *agents* who represent business roles involved in the use of the application. Here, an agent can be an EXTERNAL OFFICE (of the organization who requires the authorization to the public event) or an OFFICE of the City Council.

A tool which facilitates the reuse of existing elements in the description of case types has been defined /San 90/; the tool allows the definition of case types by example, based on available case components; defined examples are generalized and aggregated by the tool in order to define case types.

5   Requirements specification tool

The goal of requirements collection and specification in ITHACA is to enable the developer to reuse as many existing specification components as possible. We have seen how RECAST guides the developer in requirements collection, helping him to identify and to choose from, or to define, predefined reusable components. In a similar way, functional specifications are constructed from predefined specification elements stored in the SIB.

In the following section, we discuss how specification elements are retrieved from the SIB, composed in specification units and linked to design objects (implementations) by the RST module of RECAST.

5.1   Requirements specification units

The Requirements Specification Document (RSpecDoc) describes the functional specifications of a specific application. The requirements specification document is composed of a set of specification units (SUs). Specification units describe specification components or composition of specification components. The requirements specification tool (RST) uses the navigation mechanism provided by RECAST, as in the case of the RCT. Contrary to the case of the requirements collection phase in RECAST, the model used for requirements specification is an internal model known to RECAST, common to all application domains. This choice is justified by the necessity of developing a homogeneous specification components base, providing components which are reusable across application domains. The internal specification model is based on an extended O-O paradigm: the Objects with Roles Model (ORM) /Per 90/. An object-oriented paradigm has been chosen for requirements specification in ITHACA for two main reasons: the object-oriented paradigm provides abstraction and encapsulation constructs that make definition of specifications and their composition easier; the target development environment in ITHACA is object-oriented, therefore specifications at all levels and designs are performed according to this paradigm. The ORM model provides a high level representation model for objects: object properties and methods are partitioned using the concept of role. An object interface may be different according to the different roles that the object may perform, and the internal state of the object. Within a role precedences of application for methods and constraints may be defined with transition and constraint rules (the reader interested in a detailed description of ORM is referred to /Per 90/).

Specification components are stored in the SIB in form of ORM pre-defined objects and their components (roles, messages, properties, states and rules). Information associated to the semantic network instructs the tool to support the mapping from requirements collected according to domain specific models to specifications units defined according to the RECAST internal specification model.

In the following section, we discuss how specification elements are retrieved from the

SIB and composed in specification units.

5.2 Derivation of functional specifications

The Application Developer is assisted by RECAST in deriving requirements in three ways:

- providing *default objects.*

  For deriving object descriptions, we may assume that a number of requirements is implicit in a given application domain; in these cases, there is no need to ask the Application Developer to collect these requirements, and the tool for requirements specification is able to complete the collected requirements with application domain dependent default assumptions. For instance, in the Public Administration domain it is obvious that some document preparation functions must be provided. Therefore, there is no need to ask the AD if these functionalities are needed, rather it is necessary instead to collect requirements about the quality of the documents to be produced, the volume, the characteristics of the secretarial personnel, the security and access constraints, and so on. Basic functionalities, such as editing, formatting, printing documents are not to be explicitly stated and are inserted in the specification document by default.

- *(semi-) automatically deriving ORM objects.*

  We assume that collection units and specification units can be either in interpreted or non-interpreted form /Gib 89a/. Interpreted units refer to sentences in a language whose syntax is known by RECAST, non-interpreted units store development results, independently of the model used to develop them (e.g., free text, or non-interpreted diagrams and charts). The mapping rules are used to support the developer in mapping from collected requirements to specifications; an automatic (or semi-automatic) mapping can only be performed for units in interpreted form. A mapping has the following results:

  - new specification units are created

    - active links are created from collection units to specification units; each of these links has attributes defining its query/answer interface, tool invocation, as described for the next-phase links.

A mapping may be performed using a number of techniques, with the goal of combining collection units and selecting from the specification base in the SIB the appropriate specification units. Fig. 5.a shows the structure of mapping rules, which define, corresponding to a CU, which are the possible corresponding SU. Mapping rules are useful when the previous collection phase has been performed mainly in a guided way, thus yielding interpreted requirements. Mapping rules are associated to links in the semantic schema, which are activated when the "next-phase" link is traversed from a PHASE entity (see App. 2a) to the next one.

a) Mapping rule from requirements to specifications

```
REQUIREMENT UNIT -----> ORM OBJECT, ROLE, OPERATION
```

b) Mapping rule from requirement specifications to designs

```
{ORM OBJECT set}, {ROLE set}, {OPERATION set} ----->
DESIGN OBJECT, DESIGN ANNOTATIONS
```

- *refinement by the developer.*
  The developer must complete the definition of specification units, until all collection units are mapped into specification units. In particular, non-interpreted requirements have all to be mapped into specifications manually. In some cases, also interpreted requirements may require manual refinement.

The mapping from requirements to specifications according to the ORM model is represented in the RM following the schema of App. 2 c). Entities and links of the semantic network of the RM are handled as in the requirements collection part of RECAST, that is:

- some links and entities are predefined for a given application domain by the Application Engineer. In particular, some transformation tools are associated to some of the links; the mapping tool is associated to the "next-phase" link.
- specialization of basic components may be created by the Application Developer in two ways:

  1. some entities and links are automatically created or activated by the mapping tools.
  2. some entities and links may be created by the Application Designer as a refinement of pre-existing entities.

ORM design tools can be called traversing appropriate links in the semantic network.

5.3 Design suggestions

Design suggestions for pre-defined specification units are automatically provided through the Requirements Model. As with the mapping rules presented in the previous section, these associations may be performed dynamically, through domain-dependent rules contained in the RM, taking into consideration several aspects of the requirements, the domain knowledge, and existing specifications (Fig. 5.b).

Design suggestions are basically of two types:

- object class names
- annotations about suggested implementation strategies (for instance, references to previous implementations, similar implementations, possible basic components for the implementation).

Some examples of mapping from requirements to specifications, including some design suggestions, are presented in the following section, describing a scenario of use of RE-CAST.

6 Scenario of use of RECAST

In this section, we describe a scenario of use of RECAST, calling also some external tools for requirements specification.

The scenario is described illustrating an example dialog with an AD interacting with RECAST. The example is taken from the Public Administration application domain /Kap 89a/.

Collection phase

First, the developer sets up the appropriate environment answering questions about the general characteristics of the application at hand. We assume that the developer will have to answer these questions only the first time a session is started. We do not show here the dialog for setting up the environment, but we focus on the collection of requirements about functionalities in a specific application. As presented in Sect. 3., queries are formulated according to the semantic network of App. 2. We assume that the developer is using the method for the Public Administration domain (PADM in App. 2a). This example of interaction shows how queries are composed automatically by RECAST, directly from the structure of the semantic network, and from information associated to links. Referring to App. 2b, an example of dialogue session is reported in Fig. 6., where a star (*) marks selected options.

The dialogue shown in Fig. 6. shows how a collection unit is composed. An entity is defined, in particular a case type. A case type is being defined. The name "approval" is assigned to the case type. A case type has a schema of steps, and the step "preparation" is being defined. Since the STEP is a reusable component, RECAST allows the AD to see available steps (TYPICAL DEFINITION in App. 2b): additionally, a tool is available to define steps by examples (associated to the "is-a" link from the EXAMPLE OF STEP entity to the ENTER EXAMPLE entity in App. 2b) /San 90/.

We suppose that the AD has selected the DOCUMENT entity associated to the STEP, selecting the "has-part" link from STEP to DOCUMENT. The option of defining a specialization of an entity in the semantic schema is always present. In the example,

```
PUBLIC ADMINISTRATION HAS COLLECTION UNITS

COLLECTION UNIT
WHICH PART DO YOU WANT TO SELECT?
*   ENTITY
    NON-FUNCTIONAL

ENTITY
YOU CAN SELECT ONE OF THE FOLLOWING ENTITIES:
*   CASE TYPE

CASE TYPE
CASE NAME:
    approval
WHICH PART DO YOU WANT TO SELECT?
*   SCHEMA OF STEPS
    DOCUMENT

SCHEMA OF STEPS
WHICH PART DO YOU WANT TO SELECT?
*   STEP
YOU CAN SELECT ONE OF THE FOLLOWING ENTITIES:
    STEP DEFINITION

STEP
STEP NAME:
    preparation
WHICH PART DO YOU WANT TO SELECT?
    FOLLOWS
    AGENT
    STATE
    ACTION
    SELECTION CONDITION
*   DOCUMENT


DOCUMENT
YOU CAN SELECT ONE OF THE FOLLOWING DOCUMENTS:
*   REQUEST
    APPROVAL
    OFFICIAL

REQUEST
WHICH PART DO YOU WANT TO SELECT?
    DEFINITION
*   DEFINE SPECIALIZATION

REQUEST SPECIALIZATION
NAME:
    police-doc
ATTRIBUTES:
    none

POLICE-DOCUMENT
*   DEFINITION

DEFINITION
YOU CAN SELECT ONE OF THE FOLLOWING DEFINITIONS:
*   EXAMPLE
    FREE TEXT

EXAMPLE
YOU CAN SELECT ONE OF THE FOLLOWING EXAMPLES:
    TYPICAL DEFINITION
*   ENTER EXAMPLE

PLEASE ENTER THE EXAMPLE
    .........
```

Figure 6: Example of dialogue driven by RECAST

the AD is defining a new document type "police-doc". After definition of the new document type, control of the dialogue returns to the pre-defined semantic network; the new defined document type is entered and considered as a regular entity in the semantic schema (see dashed box in App. 2b). An example of REQUEST document may be entered (a tool for entering document definitions, such as an editor or a scanner, is called by RECAST at this point).

Specification phase

With the same mechanism shown for the requirements collection, it is possible to change phase ('next-phase' link), and prepare the specification units corresponding to the collection units built with the illustrated dialogue. In the specification phase, mapping is performed directly by the AD and is assisted by mapping rules.

Figg. 7. and 8. provide a simplified version of the City Council application using RECAST for specification of requirements.

Fig. 7a illustrates the existing predefined ORM specification objects. An ORM object has a name, a set of roles, and, for each role, a set of applicable operations (shown in curly brackets). Only the principal characteristics of each object are shown. Fig. 7b depicts the default ORM objects provided by the AE in the Public Administration domain; some of these objects are usually taken globally, such as the "document" and "official-document" objects, while other objects may be selected considering only the roles relevant in the specific application.

Fig. 8. shows some mappings from requirements to specifications in the Public Administration domain. In Fig. 8a, some general mapping rules are shown. In Fig. 8b, the actual mapping from application requirements in the City Council example to specifications is shown. Note that some of the derived roles appearing in Fig. 8b are derived automatically from default objects and/or from mapping rules; other roles have been selected from the SIB and added to the specifications by the developer, or deleted from suggested specifications.

7 Concluding remarks and future work

Reusability of requirements is one of the goals of the ITHACA Esprit II Project; in this paper we have illustrated the basic features of the RECAST tool that is being implemented in the ITHACA framework for reusing development documents related to requirements.

The approach to reusability of requirements on which RECAST is based is a guided collection of the requirements of a specific application, together with a from these requirements to specifications reusing as many available specification elements as possible. In guiding the collection of requirements and in supporting the selection of suitable specifications, RECAST uses knowledge about requirement models and about application

Figure 7: Predefined components

a) PREDEFINED ORM OBJECTS

person/office
    roles: request-handler
           reminder/informer
           document-preparer
           asker-for-approval
           approver

document
    roles: been-prepared
               role-messages: {input, visualize/retrieve}
           been-delivered
               role-messages: {print, archive, send}

official-document
    roles: been-prepared
               role-messages: {sign}

external-office
    roles: approver
           been-informed

b. PUBLIC ADMINISTRATION DEFAULT SPECIFICATION OBJECTS

document

official-document

external-office
    roles: been-informed

person/office
    roles: document-preparer,reminder/informer, asker-for approval

357

Figure 8: Mappings

a. MAPPING RULES

```
----------------------------------------------------
Collected               Specification components
Requirement             to be selected:
                        ORM object          role
----------------------------------------------------


office                  person/office
office-director         person/office      approver
request                 official-document  all roles
----------------------------------------------------
```

b. MAPPING OF EXAMPLE REQUIREMENTS

```
-----------------------------------------------------------------
Requirements               Specifications
                           ORM object        role
-----------------------------------------------------------------


office                     person/office     document-preparer,
                                             reminder/informer,
                                             asker-for-approval,
                                             request-handler
office-director            person/office     approver,
                                             reminder/informer
                           document          been-prepared,
been-delivered
                           official-document been-prepared,been-delivered

                           external-office   been-informed
-----------------------------------------------------------------
```

domains stored in a knowledge base (Software Information Base).

Connections of RECAST with the other tools of the ITHACA Application Development Environment are being studied. Experiments on sample applications are currently being performed, based on a ground of implemented objects in a given application domain (the Public Administration application domain). Ideas on reuse of requirements are being validated on these objects using the ORM specification model; work on refinement of this model is also being done.

Acknowledgments

We acknowledge the contributions of the ITHACA partners in the Tools Group through discussions and comments.

This work was partially supported by a research contract between Datamont and Politecnico di Milano within the ESPRIT II project Ithaca (Project N. 2121) of the Commission of European Communities. We also acknowledge the contribution of the participants to Project "Informatica e Calcolo Parallelo - Obiettivo Infokit" of the Italian National Research Council through discussions on the topics presented in this paper.

References

/Ara 88/ G. Arango, R. Cazalens, and J.-C. Mamou, "Design of a software reusability system in a object-oriented environment", *Rapport Technique Altair 25-88*, Nov. 30, 1988.

/Bur 87/ B.A. Burton, R.A. Wienk, S.A. Bailey, et al., "The reusable software library", *IEEE Software*, July 1987.

/Cos 89/ P. Costantopoulos, M. Jarke, J. Mylopoulos, B. Pernici, E. Petra, M. Theodoridou, and Y. Vassiliou, "The ITHACA Software Information Base: Requirements, Functions, and Structuring Concepts", in /ITH 89/.

/Cox 87/ B. Cox, *Object-oriented programming*, Addison-Wesley, 1987.

/Fea 87/ M.S. Feater, "Reuse in the context of transformation based methodology", in /Fre 87/.

/Fis 87/ G. Fisher, "Cognitive view of reuse and redesign", *IEEE Software*, July 1987.

/Fre 87/ P. Freeman, *Tutorial: Software Reusability*, IEEE Computer Society, 1987.

/Gib 89a/ S. Gibbs, V. Prevelakis, D. Tsichritzis, "Software Information Systems: A Software Community Perspective", in /Tsi 89/.

/Gib 89b/ S. Gibbs, G. Kappel, "The ITHACA Application Development Environment - Process Models and Tools Scenario", in /ITH 89/.

/ITH 89/ ITHACA Tools Group, "Tools Group Interim Report", July 1989.

/Jar 89/ M. Jarke, DAIDA Team, "DAIDA: Conceptual Modeling and Knowledge-based Support" (draft version), Sept. 1989.

/Kap 89a/ G. Kappel, "Proposed reference example for the TWG in ITHACA", ITHACA.CUI.89 (Revised Version), Sept. 1989.

/Kap 89b/ G. Kappel, "Reusable software components for application of the Public Administration domain", ITHACA.CUI.89.E.#12, Sept. 1989

/Kou 89/ M. Koubarakis, J. Mylopoulos, M. Stanley, M. Jarke, "Telos: A knowledge representation language for requirements modelling", Int. Rep. KRR-TR-89-1, Univ. of Toronto, Jan. 1989.

/Mey 89/ B. Meyer, *Object-Oriented Software Construction*, Prentice-Hall Intl. Series in Comp. Sc., 1989.

/Nei 87/ J.M. Neighbors, "The Draco approach to constructing software from reusable components", in /Fre 87/.

/Per 89a/ B. Pernici, G. Vaccari, R. Villa, "INTRES: INTelligent REquirements Specification", Proc. IJCAI Workshop on Automating Software Engineering, Detroit, Aug. 1989.

/Per 89b/ B. Pernici, F. Barbic, M.G. Fugini, R. Maiocchi, J.R. Rames, C. Rolland, "C-TODOS: An automatic tool for office systems conceptual modelling", ACM Trans. on Information Systems, Oct. 1989.

/Per 90/ B. Pernici, "Objects with Roles", ACM/IEEE Conf. on Office Information Systems, Boston, MA, April 1990.

/Pro 89/ A.K. Proefrock, D. Tsichritzis, G. Mueller, M. Ader, "ITHACA: An integrated toolkit for Highly Advanced Computer Applications", in /Tsi 89/ and in Office and Business Systems Results and Progress of ESPRIT Projects in 1989, DG XIII, CEC, 1989.

/Pun 87/ P.P. Puncello, F. Pietri, P. Torrigiani, "ASPIS: a project on a knowledge-based environment for software development", CASE 87, 1987.

/Pun 88/ P.P. Puncello, P. Torrigiani, F. Pietri, R. Burlon, B. Cardile, M. Conti, "ASPIS: a knowledge based CASE environment", IEEE Software, March 1988.

/Pun 89/ W.W.Y. Pun, R.L. Winder, "A design method for object-oriented programming", in Proc. ECOOP'89, S. Cook ed., Cambridge University Press, 1989.

/San 90/ A. Sanfilippo, Dynamic INTRES, Graduation Thesis, Politecnico di Milano, 1990.

/Som 89/ I. Sommerville, Software Engineering, 3rd ed., Addison-Wesley, 1989.

/Tsi 88/ D. Tsichritzis (Ed.), *Active Object Environments*, Centre Universitaire d'Informatique, University of Geneva, June 1988.

/Tsi 89/ D. Tsichritzis (Ed.), *Object-Oriented Development*, Centre Universitaire d'Informatique, University of Geneva, July 1989.

/Weg 87/ P. Wegner, "Varieties of reusability", in /Fre 87/.

/Wir 89/ M. Wirsing, R. Hennicker, R. Stabl, "MENU - An example for the systematic reuse of specifications", University of Passau *Technical Report MIP - 8930*, 1989.

Appendix 1 - Semantic network of RECAST meta-knowledge

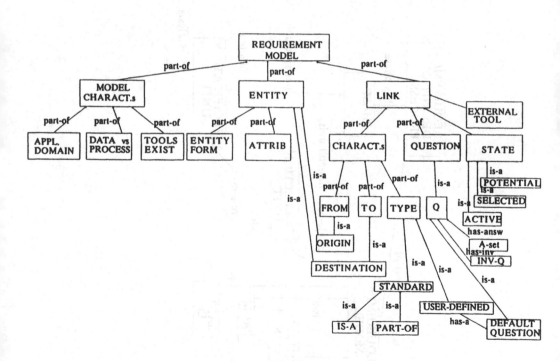

Appendix 2 - Semantic network of RECAST knowledge

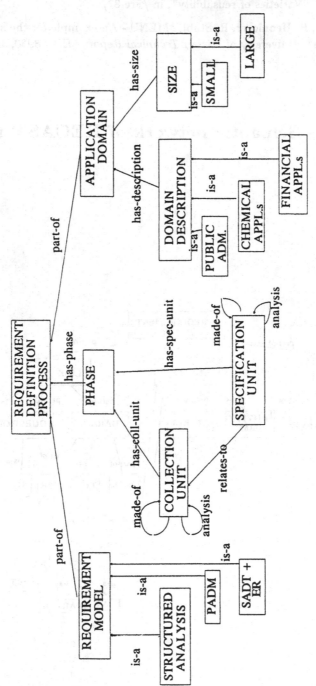

App. 2a

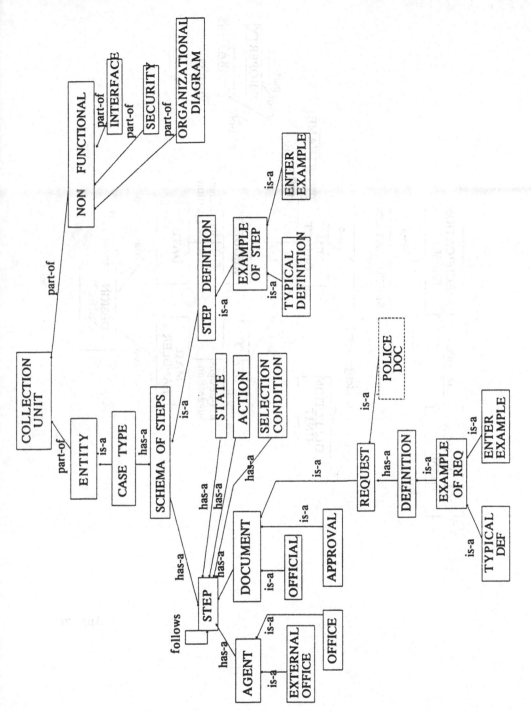

App. 2b

363

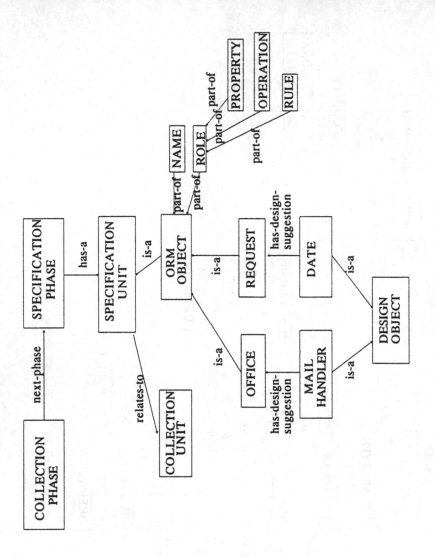

App. 2c

364

A Design Tool for Object Oriented Databases

Mokrane Bouzeghoub, Elisabeth Métais

Laboratoire MASI, Université P. et M. CurieCentre de Versailles,
45 avenue des Etats-Unis78000 Versailles

Farid Hazi, Laurent Leborgne

Infosys, 15, Rue Anatole France 92800 Puteaux La Défense

Abstract:

This paper describes a design methodology for an object oriented database, based on a semantic network. This approach is based on the assumption that semantic data models are more powerful and more easy to use than current proposed object oriented data models. They are especially more poweful in representing integrity constraints and various relationships. Object oriented data models are generally based only on class hierarchies and inheritance, plus their ability to represent the behaviour of objects. But this latter capability is generally provided through an algorithmic language which cannot be considered as a conceptual language. In this paper, we combine the two categories of data models and give a procedure on how to translate the conceptual model to the logical model.

1. Introduction

Like relational databases, the design of an object oriented database is a complex art which needs many expertise in the domain. The simultaneous modeling of the structural aspect and the behavioural aspect of objects increases the complexity of the design. The current object oriented data models are mainly defined by a few basic constructors (like the tuple constructor and the set constructor) and a taxonomy of objects (i.e. hierarchy of classes and inheritance). The power of object oriented data models is highlighted by their ability to describe the dynamic behaviour of the objects (methods). However, as generally proposed in the object oriented database systems, this dynamic description is made in a procedural language; this fact makes the specification of the methods too difficult at the conceptual level. Another weakness of current object oriented data models is that, except through methods, they do not easily permit to specify integrity constraints on the objects.

This work was partly supported by GIP/ALTAIR, PRC/BD3 and INFOSYS

Except for the dynamic aspect, the expressive power of semantic data models is stronger than that of object-oriented data models. Various relationships and integrity constraints can easily be specified. Class hierarchies and inheritance are generally defined in the same way. The dynamic aspect can be fulfilled by introducing the concept of behaviour in the semantic data models. In some sense, this was already done in the AI domain by the concept of script which has been developped to enhance the expressive power of semantic networks and frames. We follow the same approach and describe the behaviour of a semantic data model by means of production rules. This kind of a declarative language permits to avoid the complexity of procedural languages which are generally used in object oriented data models. The behaviour of each object in the semantic data model will be described by one or several rules expressing either integrity constraints or any management rules concerning objects.

A large number of database design tools are based on semantic models. Secsi is one among others [BOUZ 85][BOUZ 86]. Many experience we got from this previous project Secsi (e.g. interactive acquisition of knowledge, completeness of specifications, consistency checking) is reused in the new domain of object orientation.

This paper highlights on one hand the object-oriented database design methodology we have developped, and on the other hand the design tool which supports this methodology. This methodology is based on two design levels: a semantic object oriented level and an operational object oriented level. The process of interactive acquisition, completeness and consistency checkings of the behavioural rules is particularly emphasized in the first level. At the second level, we use as an operational object oriented model the O_2 model, which was developed by Altaïr project [BANC 87]. Then a mapping process between the two models is proposed. Besides the data structure mappings, the transformation of a semantic object oriented schema into an operational object oriented schema consists, among others, in the generation of procedural methods (C written) from a declarative language specification (production rules). A design tool prototype based on this approach has been developed and demonstrated [BOUZ 89].

Secsi is a database design assistant which is based on two models: a semantic data model, called Morse, and the relational data model. The semantic data model is built upon the usual concepts of aggregation and generalization which were refined in more basic constructors: aggregation of atomic objects, aggregation of molecular objects, classification of objects and generalization of classes. To enhance the semantic power of this model, several constraints are defined: domains, keys, cardinalities, dependencies, intersections and disjunctions.

2. The Semantic Data Model

A semantic netwok is an oriented diagram where the nodes represent real world objects and the arcs represent semantic relationships between these objects. In addition, constraints can be defined over these nodes and arcs [BOUZ 84]. In the following, such a semantic network data model is designated by the name Morse. The following subsections detail the different concepts used in Morse.

2.1. The objects of the model

An object is a generic term to designate the different real world individuals refered to in Morse schemas. We distinguish four categories of objects: in one hand *instances of atomic objects* (IA) and *instances of molécular objects* (IM), in the other hand *classes of atomic objects* (NA) and *classes of molecular objects* (NM). Then, in the following, we use the term object in a generic way, and whenever necessary, we use the more specific term.

The distinction between atomic objects and molecular objects permits to highlight their structural links for a better specification of the corresponding constraints. In traditional databases, classes of atomic objects are practically never used; files containing only one field (or one column relation) is generally considered as irrelevant to the application. Database operations (retrieve, insert, delete) are generally defined over classes of molecular objects (file, relation). Then, in the classical data models, atomic objects exist only as properties or values to characterize molecular objects. In semantic data models and in object oriented data models, atomic objects can exist (and then be identified) independently of the molecular objects to which they are related.

Atomic objects have values taken from basic domain such as: integer, real, boolean and string. The set of all atomic values in all domains are refered to by the name VA. Molecular objects have molecular values which are composed from the corresponding atomic objects which constitute the molecular object.

2.2. The semantic links

Semantic links are basic binary relationships between the different categories of objects mentioned above. These binary relationships formalize the well-known concepts of *aggregation* and *generalization* [SMIT 77]. Specific refinement of these concepts are introduced to take into account the distinction between atomic objects and molecular objects. The aggregation concept is refined as *atomic aggregation* and *molecular aggregation*. Generalization is refined as *instance generalisation* and *class generalization*.

a) The atomic aggregation (or aggregation of atomic objects) permits the construction of a new molecular object X by juxtaposition of a sequence of atomic objects $A_1...A_n$ which are generally, but not necessarily, of different domains. The molecular object is related to each of its atomic components by a couple of binary arcs **a(A_i,X)** and **p(X,A_i)** which represent the reverse directions of the same binary relationship relating a molecular object to its atomic component.

```
a(Number, VEHICLE),                    p(VEHICLE,Number),
a(Type, VEHICLE),          or          p(VEHICLE,Type),
a(Power, VEHICLE),                     p(VEHICLE,Power),
a(Color, VEHICLE).                     p(VEHICLE,Color).
```

b) The molecular aggregation (or aggregation of molecular objects) permits the construction of a new molecular object Y by juxtaposition of a sequence of other molecular objects $X_1...X_n$. Each semantic relationship is represented by a couple of binary arcs **r(X_i,Y)** and **o(Y,X_i)** which represent the reverse directions of the same binary relationship which relates two molecular objects.

```
r(VEHICLE,ORDER),          or          o(ORDER,VEHICLE),
r(CLIENT,ORDER).                       o(ORDER,CLIENT).
```

c) The instance generalization (or generalization of instances) is often called **classification**. It permits to build a new class of object instances X by union of other object instances $O_1...O_n$. It's a way to define a class by extension. As the amount of objects in a given class could be very high, this abstraction is not often used in database schemas; then all schema objects are considered as classes defined intensionaly by their basic domains or their aggregations. This kind of abstraction is represented in the semantic network by the pair of arcs **c(O_i,X)** and **i(X,O_i)** (for classification/instanciation) which represent the reverse directions of the same binary relationship.

```
c(C1,Color)                    i(Color,C1)
c(C2,Color)        or          i(Color,C2)
c(C3,Color)                    i(Color,C3)

c(v1, VEHICLE)                        i(VEHICLE, v1)
.........                      or      .........
c(vn, VEHICLE)                        i(VEHICLE, vn)
```

d) The class generalization (or generalization of classes) permits to build a new class of objects X as a union of other classes $X_1...X_n$ by concentrating only on their common properties (components). This kind of abstraction is represented by a pair of arcs **g(X_i,X)** and **s(X,X_i)** (generalization/specialization) which represent the reverse directions of the same binary relationship. These arcs allow to build hierarchies of classes.

```
g(CLIENT, PERSON),                    s(PERSON,CLIENT),
g(AGENT,CLIENT),                      s(CLIENT,AGENT),
g(PRIVATE_PERS,CLIENT),               s(CLIENT,PRIVATE_PERS).
```

The inheritance is one of the interesting properties of generalization hierarchies; each atomic or molecular component of an object X can be transfered by inheritance to objects X1...Xn, if these latters are sub-classes of X. Inversely, each instance of a sub-class is an instance of its super-classes. We say that components of objects propagate toward the leaves of the hierarchy whereas the instances propagate toward the root(s) of the hierarchy.

As for all abstractions there are two equivalent representations (equivalent reversed arcs), we use only one specification which subsumes the other (for example p, o, c and g) except if constraint specification is needed for the implicit arc.

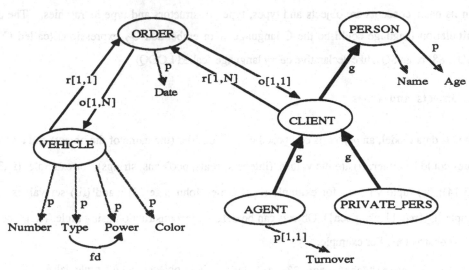

Fig.1: An example of a semantic network

2.3. Integrity constraints

Different integrity constraints can be specified in a Morse semantic network to enhance its capability to capture more meaning from the real world. Among these constraints, we can mention domains, cardinalities, functional dependencies, keys, intersection and disjunction of classes, etc. In the semantic network, some of these constraints are defined over nodes, others are defined over arcs. The constraints are specified either as a complementary information of binary arcs or as new predicates. For example, cardinality constraints are expressed as complementary information over a/p arcs and r/o arcs, while other constraints like functional dependencies are represented by a new **fd** arc:

```
        a(Number,VEHICLE,[1,1]),              p(VEHICLE,Number,[1,1]),
        a(Type,VEHICLE,[1,N]),                p(VEHICLE,Type,[1,1]),
        a(Power,VEHICLE,[0,N]),      and      p(VEHICLE,Power,[1,1]),
        a(Color,VEHICLE,[0,N]).               p(VEHICLE,Color,[1,3]).

        r(VEHICLE,ORDER,[0,1]),      and      o(ORDER,VEHICLE,[1,10]),
        r(CLIENT,ORDER,[1,N]).                o(ORDER,CLIENT,[1,1]).

        fd(VEHICLE,lhs(Type),rhs(Power))
```

Graphically, a given semantic network can be represented as portrayed in figure 1.

3. The Object Oriented Data Model

The O_2 data model belongs to the category of the so-called object oriented data models [LECL 87]. Then its basic concepts are objects and types, type constructors and type hierarchies. The data manipulation language could be the C language with embedded O_2 expressions (called CO_2) [HAUX 88] or an SQL like declarative query language (called LOOQ).

3.1. Objects and types

In the O_2 data model, an *object* is composed of an identifier (the name of the object) and a value. Values could be either: (i) atomic values (integers, reals, booleans, strings), for example: $(i_1,22)$, $(i_2,3.14)$; (ii) tuple values, for example $(i_3, [name:"John",age:22])$; and (iii) set values, for example $(i_4,\{red, black, green\})$. Objects can be defined by construction using tuple ([...]) and set ({...}) constructors. For example:

```
        (i5, [name:"John", age:22, v:i6])    is an object having a tuple value,
        (i6, {v1,v2,v3})                     is an object having a set value.
```

Objects can mutually reference each other. For example,

```
        (i7, [name:"John", wife:i8]),
        (i8, [name:"Mary", husband:i7]).
```

Intuitively a *class* is a mean for representing a set of objects with their behaviour. A class is composed of two parts: (i) a type which contains the structure that characterises all the instances of the class, (ii) methods which contain operations which will be applied to these instances. A class may have a basic type (integer, real, boolean, string) representing atomic objects, a tuple type representing objects with tuple values or a set type representing objects having set values. The following expressions are examples of classes :

```
Person = [name : string, age : integer]
Employees = {p : Person}
```

The *tuple* and *set* constructors could be composed to create more elaborated types (e.g. sets of tuples or tuples of sets). For example:

```
Person =[name:string,age:integer,vehicles:{[number:integer,color:string]}]
```

The O_2 data model makes a clear distinction between identified objects and non identified objects. The formers can be stored and manipulated independently, while the latters exist only as property values of other objects. For example, in the following specification , persons and vehicles could be manipulated independently:

```
Person = [name:string, age:integer, vehicle:Vehicle]
Vehicle = [number:integer, color:string]
```

But in the following example, the object vehicle exists only as a composite attribute value of person:

```
Person=[name:string,age:integer, vehicle:[number:integer,color:string]]
```

The object identity makes possible the sharing of objects. For example:

```
Person = [name:string, age:integer, vehicles:Vehicles]
Vehicles = {[number:integer, color:string]}
Garage = [code:string, address:string, vehicles:Vehicles]
```

where Person and Garage may share same objets of the class Vehicles. A partial order between types defines a hierarchy of types within which the inheritance concept permits to transfer components from one type toward its subtypes [LECL 88].

A method is a procedure which is associated to a type in order to describe the behaviour of the instances of this type. Methods introduce the notion of **encapsulation** which permits the manipulation of objects without any knowledge about their structure, nor about the internal code of the procedures corresponding to these methods.

3.2. Programming in CO_2

The CO_2 language is an embedded database language (CO_2) into a procedural host language (C) [HAUX 88]. Besides the usual programming of algorithms, it permits to specify and access database objects. Objects are manipulated through methods. A method is characterized by its signature (its name, its type and the type of its parameters) and its body (procedure). The following example shows the declaration of types and the programming of methods in CO_2:

```
add class   Person with extension          /* type declaration */
  type tuple(name:string,age:integer,address:string,children:set(Person))

add class Agent inherits Person             /* hierarchy of classes */
  type tuple (code:string, salary:integer)

  method category: string is public        /* method declaration */

  body category:string   in class Agent CO2  /* method procedure */
  {       if (self->salary > 50)
          return("VIP");
  }
```

The keyword **inherits** defines a hierarchy of types. The keyword **with extension** creates a named value which contains the instances of the class and then permits set operations on this class. The keywords **type** and **method** respectively define the object data structure and its associated method signature. Its following keyword **is public** makes the object-integrity method visible from anywhere. The keyword **body** introduces the procedure which implements the method. Its following keyword **in class CO2** defines the class for which this body is defined; this is useful to solve ambiguities of names, as method bodies can be specified independently of the class description. The brackets {} delimit the C source statements of the procedure.

The definition of a database schema in CO_2 needs the knowledge of the objects structure, the status of objects, i.e. identified object or non identified object (value), and the sharing of the objects.

4. Mapping from the Semantic Level to the Operational Level

The CO_2 model describes both static aspect (data structures) and dynamic aspect (methods). Relationships between objects or object classes are not represented by a specific concept; but they are represented by a uniform way based on objects composition and objects sharing. As in the relational model, references are the unique way to represent relationships between objects. Integrity constraints are not considered as specific concepts of the model; they are defined in a uniform way as any procedure describing the behaviour of an object. The object identity allows to make a clear distinction between objects having their own existence, and values which are only relevant when characterizing other objects. The object identity is represented in CO_2 by different syntactic forms.

The semantic data model Morse concerns only the static aspect. The different categories of aggregation arcs allow to specify different types of relationships between objects. Integrity constraints are represented as declarative assertions on the data structure. Objects identity is explicitly handled only for molecular objects. Indeed, in the traditional databases, we make a strict dichotomy between molecular objects which are generally identified with an associative manner using attributes, and the atomic objects which exist only as attribute values for molecular objects.

In the following we are only interested on the mapping from Morse to CO_2 and not for the reverse mapping. First we consider the structural mappings between the two models, then we study the representation of constraints with methods, and finally the general mapping process. This plan is made only for the soundness of the paper; in fact structural mapping rules often depend on the integrity constraints [BOUZ 88].

4.1. The mapping between objects

An atomic object defined in Morse is equivalent in O_2 to either an identified atomic object or to an atomic value (non identified object) inside an other object. A molecular object defined in Morse is equivalent to either an identified tuple structured object or to a tuple value in O_2. A class of objects defined in Morse is partly equivalent to a class of objects defined in O_2. Indeed, and as stated before, Morse classes describe only the static aspect of the objects, while O_2 classes describe their behaviour too, thanks to methods. Figure 2 summerizes the correspondance between the Morse objects and the O_2 objects.

MORSE CONCEPTS	O2 CONCEPTS
Atomic object	Atomic object / atomic value
Molecular object	Structured object / tuple value
Class	Class
Subclass	Subclass
Instance	Object
Object identifier	Object identifier

Fig. 2: Correspondance between the Morse objects and the O2 objects

4.2. The mapping between constructors

Both atomic and molecular aggregation defined in Morse are equivalent to the tuple constructor of the O_2 model. More precisely, we have to include what is considered as domain constraints in Morse to obtain what is considered as attribute basic type in O_2. For example, the following Morse specification:

```
p(PERSON, Name)                    dom(Name,string)
p(PERSON, Age)                     dom(Age,integer)
o(PERSON, Address)
p(Address, Number)                 dom(Number,integer)
p(Address, Street)                 dom(Street,string)
p(Address, Postcod)                dom(Postcode,integer)
```

will be mapped into O_2 as:

```
Person=[Name:string,Age:integer,Addr:Address]
Address=[Number:integer,Street:string,Postcod:integer]
```

which can be described in CO_2 by the following statements:

```
add class Person
    type tuple (Name:string,Age:integer,Addr:Address)

add class Address
    type tuple(Number:integer,Street:string,Postcod:integer))
```

if we consider that all of Name and Age are values of the Person (thus they are not identified), but the Address is an object by itself (thus it is identified). Addr is called a reference; it is considered as an attribute of Person which references an other object, i.e. Address.

The classification/instanciation defined in Morse is partly equivalent to an O2 class defined **with extension**. In fact the Morse abstraction can define a class only by extension, without necessarily describing its structure. The generalization/specialization is equivalent to the inheritance hierarchy in O_2. In Morse, a given class can be defined by generalization from other classes even the structures of these latters are unknown. Inversely, a Morse subclasse can be defined as a restriction of a superclass, but without any refinement on its structure. This makes the generalization/specialization more general than a partial order of types which is defined in O_2.

MORSE CONCEPTS	O2 CONCEPTS
Atomic aggregation	Tuple constructor
Molecular aggregation	Tuple constructor
Classification / Instanciation	Class defined by extension
Generalization / Specialization	Inheritance hierarchy

Fig. 3: Mapping between the Morse and the O_2 constructors

374

The inheritance is defined in Morse as a logical property which propagates components and constraints of generic classes to their subclasses. In the O_2 model, there is a uniform formalisation of hierarchies of types and inheritance (partial order of types). Figure 3 summarizes the different mappings between the Morse constructors and the O_2 constructors.

4.3. The mapping of the constraints

Semantic integrity constraints are useful for many reasons: (i) to check the consistency of the object structure and values, (ii) and possibly to assist in the decision process which determines whether a Morse object coincides or not with an O_2 object. Except for the usual domains which are represented by basic types in O_2 (integer, real, boolean, string), all the other Morse integrity constraints are represented by methods in the O_2 model. In the following, we illustrate this latter case with cardinalities and functional dependencies. Methods which implement integrity constraints are particular in the sense they are not directly invoked by the users but by other methods which guarantee the encapsulation of the concerned object. Figure 4 summarizes the different mappings between the Morse constraints and the O_2 concepts.

MORSE CONCEPTS	O2 CONCEPTS
Domain	basic type / method
Cardinality	set constructor + method
functional dependency	method
key	method
intersection / disjonction	method

Fig. 4: Mappings between the Morse constraints and the O2 concepts

a) Methods implementing cardinality constraints:

Formally, cardinalities characterize binary relationships (a/p and r/o arcs) by specifiing the frequence of object participation in a given binary relationship. More precisely, a cardinality is a couple of values [m,n] which respectively specify the minimum and the maximum number of a given relationship instances to which the same object could participate. Cardinalities where n=1 are called monovalued cardinalities and those where n>1 are called multivalued cardinalities. In the following, we study the methods by which we will implement these constraints. As we have several situations, we will only focus on three examples.

Case 1: p(X,Y,[1,1]) : which specifies that for a given instance of X, there is only one instance of Y. For example:

```
p(PERSON, Name,[1,1])          Dom(Name, string)
p(PERSON, Age,[1,1])           Dom(Age, integer)
```

will be implemented into O_2 as:

```
add class PERSON
      type tuple (Name:string,Age:integer)
      method  Nulle_value:boolean

      body Nulle_value:boolean in class PERSON CO2
      {      if(                ( ! (self->Name == (o2 string) NULL))
                   &&           ( ! (self->Age == (o2 integer) NULL)) )
             {return (true);} else return (false);
      }
```

Case 2: o(X,Y,[1,N]): which specifies that for a given instance of X, there is N instances of Y. For example:

```
o(PERSON, Address,[1,N])
p(Address, Number,[1,1])       Dom(Number, integer)
p(Address, Street,[1,1])       Dom(Street, string)
p(Address, Postcod,[1,1])      Dom(Postcod, string)
p(Address, Town,[1,1])         Dom(Town,string)
```

will be mapped into O_2 as:

```
add class PERSON
   type tuple(Addr:setof(Address))
   method  Bounded_set(min:integer, max:integer):boolean

add class Address
   type tuple(Number:integer,Street:string,Postcod:string,Town:string))

body Bounded_set(min:integer, max:integer):boolean
      in class PERSON CO2
      {      O2 set(Address) x;
             x = (self->Addr);
             if ((min =< count(x)) && (count(x) =< max))
             {return (true);}  else return (false);
      }
```

Case 3: Unique value (key): If we specify cardinalities for the reverse arcs of the semantic network, we obtain other kind of constraints like unique values or keys:

```
a(Name, PERSONNE,[1,1]).
```

This constraint can be represented into CO_2 as follows:

```
    add class PERSON      with extension
        type tuple (Name:integer)
        method  Unique_value:boolean

    body Unique_value:boolean in class PERSON CO2
        {       O2 PERSON p;
                integer RES;
                RES = 1;
                for (p in  PERSON  when p->Name == self->Name)
                {RES = 0};
                if (RES == 1) {return (true);} else return (false);
        }
```

b) Methods implementing functional dependencies

In the relational data model, functional dependencies are used to represent elementary facts between attributes, and then serve as a basis for the normalisation process. In the Morse semantic data model, functional dependencies are just considered as constraints between atomic objects within a molecular object. In an object oriented data model, these constraints can be implemented as methods checking the consistency of the object values.   For example,

```
        p(VEHICLE,Number)              df(VEHICLE,lhs(Type),rhs(Power))
        p(VEHICLE,Type)
        p(VEHICLE,Power)
```

can be implemented as following in O_2:

```
    add  class VEHICLE   with extension
                type tuple(Number:integer,Type:string,Power:integer)
                method Funct_dependency : boolean
                body Funct_dependency: boolean in class   VEHICLE CO2
                  {O2 VEHICLE v;
                   integer RES;
                   RES = 1;
                   for (v in VEHICLE when (strcmp (self->Type, v->Type))
                                            && !(self->Power == v->Power))
                        {RES = 0});
                   if (res == 1) {return (true);} else return (false);
                   }
```

We shall see later that they can be used in the similar way of the relational model to what can be considered as object definition.

4.4. The object identity and the object sharing

In the Morse semantic data model, everything is considered as an object. Each object has a unique representation, then objects can be shared between different other related objects. In the O_2 object oriented data model, there are objects and values; objects are sharable while values are not. So, when mapping a Morse schema into an O_2 schema, we have to decide whether a Morse object can be considered as an O_2 object or as an O_2 value. This decision mainly depends on the user's desire in the way to implement his database. He can arbitrarily decide whether a given Morse object is an O_2 object or value. For example, for the mapping of the following Morse schema (figure 5), he can envision many solutions:

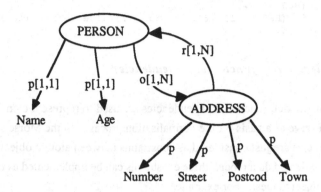

Fig.5: Morse objects

Solution 1: one O2 object PERSON describing the whole Morse structure:

```
PERSON=[Name:string, Age:integer,
        Address:{[Number:integer,Street:string,Postcod:integer,Town:string]}]
```
All other components are considered as values characterizing a person.

Solution 2: Two O2 objects corresponding to the two Morse molecular objects:

```
PERSON=[Name:string, Age:integer, Addr:ADDRESSES]
ADDRESSES={[Name:integer, Street:string, Postcod:integer, Town:string]}
```
In this case each person's addr is a reference to a set of addresses.

Solution 3: Three O2 objects whose one is an identified set:

```
PERSONNE=[Name:string, Age:integer, addr:ADDRESSES]
ADDRESSES: {ADDRESS}
ADDRESS=[Name:integer, Street:string, Postcod:integer, Town:string]
```
There are two kinds of objects describing addresses: the first one (ADDRESSES) describes sets of addresses, the second one (ADDRESS) describes tuples whose each corresponds to a given address.

Solution 4: One O2 object ADDRESS corresponding to the whole Morse structure:

```
ADDRESS:[Number:integer,Street:string, Postcod:integer, Town:string,
```

```
Person:{[Name:string, Age:integer]}]
```
In this case, persons do not have any existence, they are just characterizing addresses.

There are many other solutions where we can consider that towns or telephones are independant objects. To decide between all these solutions, a computer design tool can help in the decision process by taking into account several heuristics derived from the following parameters:

- *Cardinality constraints* defined over arcs a/p and r/o of the semantic network: if the minimal cardinality of one of these arcs is equal 0, then the origine object of the arc can exist independently of the related one.

- *Functional dependencies* defined between atomic objects of the semantic network: as in the relational model, a set of functional dependencies can determine a group of Morse atomic objects which may correspond to an O_2 object. In this case, we can just highlight these groups but the final decision remains to the human designer.

- *Keys* defined for molecular objects: generally keys are used to provide an associative access to objects. It is generally considered as an external way of identifiing objects.

- *Users'operations* and general constraints defined on the Morse objects: basic operations like insert, delete and update, can be considered as the main means to identify objects. We shall see in the next section how these operations are defined in the Morse semantic data model.

4.5. The generator of the CO_2 code

The generator of CO_2 code is composed of a set of mapping rules which transform objects, relationships and constraints of Morse toward objects and methods of O_2. As each Morse object may satisfy one or several integrity constraints, each corresponding O_2 object or value may satisfy one or several methods called "constraint-methods". These latter methods are particular in the sense they are activated by other methods which realize the encapsulation of the object. Then each update operation on a given object should activate by message passing the set of constraint-methods associated to this object. This set of constraints is called the "object-integrity". It can be itself considered as a general constraint-method associated to an object. Thus each update operation has to know only one general constraint-method instead of knowing the set of all specific constraint-methods.

The CO_2 code generator is composed of two parts: (i) one part generates the definition of the object data structure and the constraint-methods signatures, (ii) the other part generates the body of the object-integrity method and the bodies of the corresponding specific constraints-methods. The two parts consist of dynamicaly filling a predefined frame which is organized into slots containing keywords of the CO_2 language (figure 6).

add class	class_name_1 [**inherits** class_2] **with extension**	
type	(component_1 : type_1, component_2 : type_2, ... component_n : type_n)	
method	method_signature_1 ... . method_signature_n	
	body	signature_method_1 **in class** class_name_1 CO2 method_body_1
	body	signature_method_n **in class** class_name_1 CO2 method_body_n

Fig.6: The code generator frame

An example of code generation could be the following:

```
add class PERSON
    type tuple(Name:string,Age:integer,Addr:setof(ADDRESS))
            with extension
    method  Integrity:set(string) is public
            Nulle_value:boolean
            Unique_value:boolean
            Bounded_set(min:integer, max:integer) : boolean

    body Integrity:set(string) in class PERSON CO2
        {  o2 set(string) ENS;
           SetRes = set();
           if (!( [self  Nulle_value] )) {SET += set("Nulle_value");};
           if (!([self Unique_value] )) {SET += set("Unique_value");};
           if (!( [self  Bounded_set] )) {SET += set("Bounded_set");};
           return (SetRes);
        }
```

Each object-integrity method (i.e. the method Integrity of the class Person in the previous example) returns a set type value. This set (e.g. SetRes in the previous example) contains the names of the constraint-methods which were not satisfied during the update operation. Depending on wether this set is empty or not, the programmer can commit or not the update operation. For example, we define a new insertion method which creates an object and assigns a value to each of its attributes. In the definition of this method, we must activate the corresponding integrity constraint

380

to be sure that the update is allowed with respect to the integrity constraints.

```
add method insert:boolean in class CO2 PERSON
  body insert:boolean in class CO2 PERSON
        {       o2 set(string) ENS
                SetRes = [self Integrity];
                if (SetRes == (o2 set(string)) set())
                    {PERSON += set(self)}; return (true);}
                else { printf ("Integrity constraints not respected: ");
                    display (SetRes);
                    return (false);}
        }
```

In the previous code generation, the cost of the integrity checking process is not considered. Constraint-methods are specified in such a way they semantically correspond to the declarative assertions of the semantic network. The experience in traditional databases has shown that integrity checking is a very expansive process. If we want to avoid the multiple scanning of the same class, we have to merge in the same procedure the different constraint-methods which have been defined for this class. This problem is not addressed in this paper.

5. Extending the Semantic Data Model to Represent General Constraints

This section intends to extend the Morse semantic network to represent more generalized integrity constraints. These general integrity constraints should be any first order logic formula whose variables refer to the content of the semantic database. Before presenting this extension, let us give a formal representation of a semantic database as well as for its conceptual schema and for its extension. This representation is not intended to represent real databases but just to give a formal abstract representation in order to correctly specify integrity constraints.

5.1. The representation of a semantic database

A Morse database schema is composed of:
- the list of names of all classes of atomic objects (i.e. instances of NA),
- the list of names of all classes of molecular objects (i.e. instances of NM),
- for each atomic object, its domain values (basic type),
- for each molecular object, its data structure (i.e. the set of all its p/a and o/r arcs),
- for each binary relationship (i.e. p/a and o/r arcs), its cardinalities,
- for each multiple reference to the same component, the different roles played by the component in the abstraction.

For Example:

```
i(NA,P_name,string)              p(PERSON,Name,[1,1][1,N])
i(NA,Age,integer)                p(PERSON,Age,[1,1][1,N])
i(NA,number,integer)             p(VEHICLE,Power,[1,1][0,N])
i(NA,Power,integer)              p(CONTRACT,Premium,[1,1][1,1])

i(NM,PERSON)                     o(CONTRACT,PERSON,[1,1][1,N])
i(NM,VEHICLE)                    o(CONTRACT,VEHICLE,[1,1][1,1])
i(NM,CONTRACT)                   g(CLIENT, PERSON)
```

As previously stated, everything in Morse is an object. Then each atomic or molecular object is formally identified. The relationship between an atomic object identifier and its corresponding value is represented by a specific predicate v. The relationship between a molecular object identifier and its corresponding structured value is represented by a sequence of v predicates. This systematic identification of all objects implies a systematic sharing of objects. Then values of objects are represented only once. This identification permits also an independent manipulation of all object classes. The generalization arcs (i.e. g/s) are not directly represented in a database extension. They are captured by the inclusion of sets of identifiers with respect to the generalization hierarchy. In the following is an example of extension of the previous database schema:

```
i(PERSON,P1)      i(Name,N1),     v(N1,dupond)    i(Age,A1)    v(A1,33)
i(PERSON,P2)      i(Name,N2),     v(N2,durand)    i(Age,A2)    v(A2,44)
i(PERSON,P3)

i(VEHICLE,V1)     i(Number,I1)    v(I1,123)       i(Power,W1)  v(W1,5)
i(VEHICLE,V2)     i(Number,I2)    v(I2,345)       i(Power,W2)  v(W2,7)
i(VEHICLE,V3)     i(Number,I2)    v(I2,345)

i(CONTRACT,C1)    i(Premium,M1)   v(M1,5500)
i(CONTRACT,C2)    i(Premium,M2)   v(M2,6000)

p(P1,N1)                          p(V1,I1)                     o(C1,P1)
p(P1,A1)                          p(V1,W1)                     o(C1,V1)
                                                               p(C1,M1)
p(P2,N2)                          p(V2,I2)                     o(C2,P1)
p(P2,A2)                          p(V2,W1)                     o(C2,V2)
                                                               p(C2,M2)
p(P3,N2)                          p(V3,I3)
p(P3,A2)                          p(V3,W2)
```

Obviously this representation is not defined for implementing real databases, but just as a formal representation for a formal reasoning. It can be considered as an abstract representation of the content of a given database. This representation permits a better understanding of the constraint specifications, and provides a convenient framework for a CASE tool.

5.2. The representation of general integrity constraints

A general integrity constraint is a first order closed formula, restricted to only conjunction connectors and at most only one implication symbole. The following expressions are allowed constraints: P(X), P(X) & Q(Y), P(X) —> Q(Y), P(X) & Q(Y) —> R(X,Y). Variables can be quantified existencially or universally. The universe of discourse in which these formulas are interpreted is constituted as follows:

- a set of constants: composed of (i) the union of atomic objects domains (VA), (ii) the union of atomic objects identifiers (IA) and molecular objects identifiers (IM) and of (iii) the union of class names of atomic objects (NA) and class names of molecular objects (NM),
- a set of variables taking their values in the previous defined universe of discourse,
- a set of predicates: composed of (i) all atomic and molecular aggregation relationships (i.e. p/a and o/r arcs), (ii) instance generalization and class generalization relationships (i.e. c/i et g/s arcs), and (iii) usual mathematic predicates: $<, >, \leq, \geq, =, \neq$.

For example, over the previous database schema, we can define a general integrity constraint which states that if the vehicle power is greater than 10 and the person's age is less than 20, then the contract premium is at least equal to 5000:

IC1: $\forall P \ \forall C \ \forall V \ \forall G \ \forall S \ \forall M \ \exists VG \ \exists VS \ \exists VM$
      [i(PERSON,P) $\land$ i(VEHICLE,V) $\land$ i(CONTRACT,C)
      $\land$ i(Age,G) $\land$ i(Power,S) $\land$ i(Premium,M)
      $\land$ o(C,P) $\land$ o(C,V)
      $\land$ p(P,G) $\land$ v(G,VG) $\land$ VG<20
      $\land$ p(V,S) $\land$ v(S,VS) $\land$ VS>10]
      —>[p(C,M) $\land$ v(M,VM) $\land$ VM$\geq$5000].

We can also state that the age of every person is greater than 17.

IC2: $\forall P \ \exists G \ \exists VG$ i(Person,P) $\land$ i(Age,G) $\land$ p(P,G) $\land$ v(G,VG) $\land$ VG>17

As these constraints are specified using the same semantic arcs as for describing the static data structure, they can be represented by a semantic network in which each variable or constant is represented by a node. Variable nodes are considered as instances of object classes. The quantifier corresponding to each variable is represented as a complementary information of the arc i relating a variable to its class. For example, i(Person,x,$\forall$) describes a variable x universally quantified over the class Person. As the order of the quantifiers is meaningful in a given formula, an indice is associated with the quantifier. For example, i(Person,x,$\forall$,1). Finally, new binary arcs (inf, sup, equ, einf, esup, diff) are added to the semantic network to represent the predicates: $<, >, =, \leq, \geq$. To give more meaning to this representation, we must complete each predicate to specify whether it belongs to the left hand side or to the right hand side of the rule representing the integrity constraint.

IC1:
    i(PERSON,P,",1,left,IC1)   i(VEHICLE,V,",2,left,IC1)
    i(CONTRACT,C,",4,leftright,IC1)   i(Age,G,",5,left,IC1)
    i(Power,S,",6,left,IC1)   i(Premium,M,",7,right,IC1)

    o(C,P,left,IC1)   o(C,V,left,IC1)

```
p(P,G,left,IC1)        v(G,VG,left,IC1)       inf(VG,20,left,IC1)
p(V,S,left,IC1)        v(S,VS,left,IC1)       sup(VS,10,left,IC1)
p(C,M,right,IC1)       v(M,VM,right,IC1)      sup(VM,5000,right,IC1)
```

The following schema illustrates the representation of the constraint **IC1**. The lower part represents the static data schema, the upper part represents the behavioral schema. In this latter one, we have separated the rule left hand side part and right hand side part; although some nodes appear in the both parts.

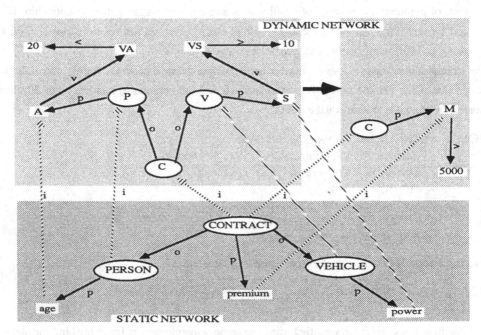

Fig.7: An exemple of rule representation

As for the database extension, this representation is an abstract representation for a better understanding and consistency checking of integrity constraints.

5.3. The semantic object oriented language

The Morse language is a formal language to represent the detailed description of a conceptual schema. This language is not intended to be used by end-users nor to implement real databases. Consequently, we need two things: a friendly user interface to specify data structures and constraints, and a real database managment system to implement the database schema. This subsection describes the former requirement, the latter one is supported by the O_2 system after mapping Morse specifications into O_2 specifications.

a) Specification of data structures

(1) Each set of p or o predicates which defines the structure of a molecular object class is replaced by the following statement, if the structure is composed of atomic objects:

```
X(A₁:dom₁,…,Aₙ:domₙ)
<=> i(NA,A₁,dom₁), …,i(NA,Aₙ,domₙ), i(NM,X)
    p(X,A₁), …, p(X,Aₙ)
```

or by the following if the structure is composed by molecular objects:

```
X(Y₁,…,Yₙ)
<=> o(X,Y₁),…, o(X,Yₙ), i(NM,X)
```

or by the following statement if the structure is either composed of atomic objects and molecula objects.

```
X(A₁:dom₁,…,Aₙ:domₙ,Y₁,…,Yₘ)
<=> i(NA,A₁,dom₁), …,i(NA,Aₙ,domₙ), i(NM,X)
    p(X,A₁), …, p(X,Aₙ)
    o(X,Y₁),…, o(X,Yₙ)
```

If the cardinality constraints are specified, we shall have the following description:

```
X({A₁:dom₁}[am₁,an₁],
            …,
            Aₙ:domₙ,[amₙ,anₙ],
            {Y₁},[rm₁,rn₁],
            …,
            Yₘ,[rmₙ,rnₙ])
<=> i(NA,A₁,dom₁), …,i(NA,Aₙ,domₙ), i(NM,X)
    p(X,A₁,[1,N][am₁,an₁]),
    …,
    p(X,Aₙ,[1,N][amₙ,anₙ]),
    o(X,Y₁,[1,1][rm₁,rn₁]),
    …,
    o(X,Yₘ,[1,1][rmₙ,rnₙ])
```

(2) Each set of generalization arcs can be declared as follows:

```
g(X,Y)                    <=>      X:Y
g(X,Y1),…,g(X,Yn)         <=>      X:Y1,…,Yn
g(X1,Y),…,g(Xn,Y)         <=>      X1,…,Xn:Y
```

b) Specification of general constraints

The external interface to specify general constraints must allow the user to specify easily his integrity constraints defined over the external description of the data structures (i.e. previous data language). Each integrity constraint is specified as a fist order assertion or a production rule. This specification must be made at any place in the application description. The external language must have the same expressive power as the Morse formal language, but must be more concise and more easy to learn and to use. The external constraint language is built from the Morse formal language as follows:

(1) The alphabet of the external language is roughly the same as that of the internal language; except that "∧" and "—>" symbols are respectively replaced by "and" and the two keywords "if" - "then" to distinguish between the left part and the right part of a given rule. The quantified variables ∀x et ∃x are respectively replaced by {x} and [x] to alleviate the absence of the mathematical symbols in common keyboards.

(2) The domain of interpretation of the external language is the same of that of Morse language: we distinguish names of atomic object classes (NA) and molecular object classes (NM), atomic and molecular object identifiers (respectively IA and IM) and the values of atomic objects (VA).

(3) The following restriction is made for variables: the scope of each defined variable is the set of instances of a specific class. We use the notation x/class_name to represent this declaration.

(4) The value of an atomic object is delivered by the function "." defined as a composition of two elementary functions f1 and f2 defined as follows: let I_X be the set of instances of X, P_X the set of atomic components of X, IA the set of all atomic identifiers and VA the set of all atomic values, and let x, at, a_i, va_i be respectively elements of the previous categories:

f1: I_X x P_X —> IA

$\quad$ (x,at) ——> x.at = a_i / i(at, a_i) ∧ p(x,a_i)

$\qquad\qquad\qquad\qquad\qquad$ ➡ $\quad$ x.at = f2(f1(x,at))

f2: IA —> VA

$\quad$ a_i ——> va_i / v(a_i,va_i)

(5) The access to a a molecular object through another molecular object is made by the function "->" which delivers only the molecular object identifier. This function is defined as following: let I_X be the set of instances of X, O_X the set of molecular components of X, and IM the set of all molecular object identifiers, and let x, mol, m_i be respectively elements of these categories.

I_X x O_X —> IM

$$(x,mol) \longrightarrow x\text{->}mol = m_i / i(mol, m_i) \land o(x,m_i)$$

(6) The only allowed terms are constant terms, variable terms and functional terms obtained by "." et "->" function symbols.

(7) The only allowed predicates are: $<, >, \leq, \geq, =, \neq$.

(8) The well-formed formulas are those of the first order predicate calculus, elaborated with the conjunction (and) and the implication (If...Then).

<u>Example 1</u> : The salary of any employee is les than that of all managers.

      IC1:   `{m/Manager} {e/Employee} e.salary < m.salary.`

<u>Example 2</u> : Each student's mark is between 0 and 20.

      IC2:   `{s/Student} {m/mark} s.m≥0 and s.m≤20.`

<u>Example 3</u> : If a student has at least one mark less than 16, then his honors is not a first class.

      IC3:   `{s/Student} [m/mark] If s.m<16 Then s.honors ≠ "first class".`

<u>Example 4</u> :For each contract relating a person and a vehicle, if the age of the person is less than 20 and the power of the vehicle greater than 10, then the premium of the contract is at least equal to 5000.

```
IC4: {p/Person} {v/Véhicle} {c/Contract}
     If c->Person=p and c->Vehicle=v and p.age<20 et v.power>10
     Then c.premium≥5000.
```

To facilitate the rule expression, we can introduce the following composition of functions:

```
     If x->y->z    Then ......
```

which is equivalent to:

```
     If x->Y = y and y->Z = z    Then ......
```

In the same way, the following:

```
     If x->y.Z = 'v'    Then ......
```

composition is equivalent to:

```
     If x->Y = y and y.Z = 'v'    Then ......
```

With these compositions, the example 4 can be writen more simply as follows:

```
IC4: {p/Person} {v/Véhicle} {c/Contract}
     If c->p.age<20 and c->v.power>10    Then c.premium≥5000.
```

5.4. Code generation from general integrity constraints

This subsection deals with O_2 code generation from logical formulas describing integrity constraints. In the process described in this section, we have not considered the case where several different logical formulas may generate a unique constraint-method. We just focus on the case where a formula may generate one or several methods. Before this generation process, a semantic controle of each formula is done. Then we discuss the method definition and attachment.

a) Consistency checking of integrity constraints

The consistency checking of the constraints aims to verify in one hand the semantics of the constraints and in other hand their compatibility with the static database schema. It is composed of the following steps:
- Each constraint variable must be defined over an existing class of the static database schema,
- For each function symbol there must correspond an aggregation arc in the static semantic network,
- Arguments of the same predicates have compatible types,
- No predicate is subsumed by another predicate,
- Check wether different predicates of the same formula are contradictory or not,
- As we have not considered the exception handling, no constraint has to be contradictory with another one.

b) Methods definition and attachment

An integrity constraint is a first order formula specified on a semantic network. To give an interpretation to this formula (by assigning one of the logical values: true or false) with respect the application universe of discourse represented in a database, we must generate one or several enforcement procedures depending on different kinds of updates envisioned for the database (insert, delete, modify). For example, from the following constraint expression which asserts a classical referential constraint,

```
RC: {p/PERSON} [a/AGENCY]
    If p.Agency_name = "n"   Then  a.name = "n".
```
we may generate two enforcement procedures:
- one procedure M1 triggered by the insertion of a person (or the modification of his agency_name), which checks whether the referenced agency exists in the AGENCY class or not,
- one procedure M2 triggered by the deletion of an agency (or the modification of its name), which checks whether referencing persons exist or not.

Then, we notice that from one constraint specification, we may generate different controle procedures, attached to different objects. We call each of these procedures a constraint-method. As the example shows, each constraint-method is attached to a specific class. A given constraint-method attachment is characterized by the following tuple: (`Const_Name, Class_name, Set_of_updates`) where set of updates can be {insert, delete, modify,...}. Then an integrity constraint specification may be characterized by a set of attachments of this form. For example, the set of attachments characterizing the constraint RC is the following:

```
RC_A:           { (M1, PERSON, {Insert, Modify}),
                  (M2, AGENCY, {Delete, Modify}) }
```

The code generation of constraint-methods from a logical constraint specification needs the knowledge of:

1) object classes involved in the constraint specification (known through variable declaration),
2) for each involved class, update operations which trigger this constraint (given by the end user or generated from buiseness rules).

Having this knowledge, the process of generating a CO_2 procedure from a logical formula is quiet simple. The same recipient frame described in the previous section is instanciated to generate CO_2 methods.

6. Concluding Remarks and Current Extensions

In this paper, we have described a general framework for a CASE tool devoted to the design of object oriented databases. The design approach is based on two levels: the semantic object oriented level and the operational object oriented level. The first level is based on a semantic data model which was extended to represent more information about the behaviour ob objects (general integrity constraints and deduction rules). The second level is more operational, and is based on an existing object oriented DBMS called O2. The design methodology described in this paper is implemented in the Secsi Expert system environment which already provides a design environment for relational databases.

This design tool is interfaced with O_2 object oriented database system. It automatically generates a CO_2 database schema and gives a very convenient way to populate the database and to check its consistency with respect to the constraint-methods generated. A syntactic analysis of specifications, an interactive acquisition aid of constraints and a set of consistency checking rules are also provided too. This design environment can be considered as a powerfull mean for validating user requirements against an image of the projected database application.

The new development mainly concerns the semantic checking of general integrity rules, a decision procedure for object identification, and a more efficient code generation procedure. The current work extends the system to aid in the acquisition and represention of buiseness rules from which it may generate the complete behaviour of a given database. Buiseness rules are expressed as a generalization of integrity rules, and then represented by production rules having in their right hand side database operations.

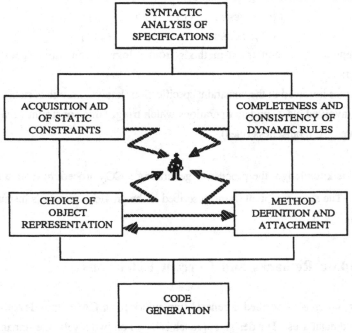

Fig.8: The architecture of the design tool

REFERENCES

[BANC 85] BANCILHON F., KIM W. & KORTH H.F., "A Model of CAD Transactions" 11th VLDB Conf., Stockholm 1985.

[BANC 87] BANCILHON F. "Les objectifs scientifiques du GIP Altaïr" , Rapport Altaïr 8/1987.

[BERN 82] BERNSTEIN P. & BLAUSTEIN B. "Fast Method for Testing Quantified Relational Calculus Assertions" ACM-SIGMOD Conf., Colorado, June 1982.

[BERT 84] BERTINO E. & APUZZO D. "Integrity aspects in Database Management Systems" Proceed. of Internat. Conf. on Trends and Applications of Databases" IEEE-NBS, Gaithersburg, USA 1984.

[BORG 85a] BORGIDA A. "A Language Features for Flexible Handling of Exceptions in Information Systems" ACM TODS Vol10, N°4, Dec. 1985.

[BORG 85b] BORGIDA A. "Accomodating Exceptions in Databases, and Refining the Schema by Learning from Them" 11th VLDB Conf., Stockholm, Sweeden 1985.

[BOUZ 84] BOUZEGHOUB M. "MORSE: a Functional Query Language and its Semantic Data Model" Proceed. of Internat. Conf. on Trends and Applications of Databases" IEEE-NBS, Gaithersburg, USA 1984.

[BOUZ 85] BOUZEGHOUB M., GARDARIN G. & METAIS E. "SECSI: An Expert System for Database Design" 11th VLDB Conf., Stockholm Sweeden 1985.

[BOUZ 86] BOUZEGHOUB M. "SECSI: un système expert en conception de systèmes d'information", Thèse de doctorat de l'université P. et M. Curie, mars 1986.

[BOUZ 88] BOUZEGHOUB M., METAIS E , MARAUX F., HAZI F., " Transformation du modèle MORSE en modèle O_2", Rapport de spécification, tâche 2 phase 1, Infosys-Masi-Altaïr, décembre 1988.

[BOUZ 89] BOUZEGHOUB M., METAIS E, MARAUX F., HAZI F., "Conception d'une base de données orientée objets à l'aide d'un modèle sémantique" Journées Bases de données avancées, PRC/BD3, Genève septembre 1989., Rapport MASI N°307, Univ. Paris VI Nov 1989.

[BOUZ 89] BOUZEGHOUB M., METAIS E, F., HAZI F., LEBORGNE L. "Aide à la spécification de l'intégrité sémantique dans les bases de données orientées objets" Rapport de spécification, tâche 1 phase 2, Infosys-Masi-Altaïr, septembre 1989.

[BROD 81] BRODIE M. "On Modelling Behavioural Semantics of Databases" 7th VLDB Conf., Cannes, France 1981.

[BROD 84] BRODIE M., MYLOPOULOS J., SCHMIDT Y. "On Conceptual Modelling: Perspectives from Artificial Intelligence, Data Bases and Programming languages" Springer-Verlag, NY 1984.

[BROD 86] BRODIE M. & MYLOPOULOS J. "On Knowledge Base Management Systems" (editors) Springer Verlag, 1986.

[BUCH 86] BUCHMANN A.P., CARRERA R.S. & VASQUEZ-GALINDO M.A. "A Generalized Contraint and Exception Handler for an Object Oriented CAD-DBMS", in [OODB 86]

[CREM 83] CREMERS & DOMANNG, "An Integrity Monitor for the Database System Ingres", 9th VLDB Conf., Florence 1983.

[GUST 83] GUSTAFSSON M.R., BUBENKO J.A. & KARLSSON T. "A declarative Approach to conceptual information modelling" in OLLE,SOL,VERRIJN-STUART (eds): Information System Methodology: a comparative approach, North Holland Publ. Co 1983.

[HAGE 88] HAGELSTEIN T. " A declarative Approach to information system requirements" J. Knowledge Based Systems, 1(4) 1988.

[HAMM 75] HAMMER M.M. & McLEOD D.J., "Semantic Integrity in Relational Database Systems" 1st VLDB Conf., Framingham, USA Sept. 1975.

[HAMM 81] HAMMER M.M. & McLEOD D.J., "Database Description with SDM: A Semantic Data Model" ACM TODS Vol6,N°3, Sept 1981.

[HAUX 88] HAUX L. , C. LECLUSE, P.RICHARD. "The CO2 V0.4 Language and Some Extensions, Release 3.1" Rapport interne Altaïr 4-88, octobre 1988.

[LECL 87] LECLUSE C., Ph. RICHARD & F VELEZ, V "An Object Oriented Data Model" C. Rapport Altaïr 10/ 1987.

[LECL 88] LECLUSE C, Ph. RICHARD & F VELEZ, V "Modeling Inheritance and Genericity in Object Oriented Databases, Version 1" C. LECLUSE & Ph. RICHARD, Rapport Altaïr 18/ 1988.

[LOUC 89] LOUCOPOULOS O. & KARAKOSTAS V. "Modelling and validating office information systems: an object and logic oriented approach" Software Engineering Journal, March 1989.

[MYLO 80] MYLOPOULOS J., BERNSTEIN P.A. & WONG H.K.T. "A Language Facility for Designing Database Intensive Applications" ACM TODS Vol-15, N°2, 1980.

[NICO 82] NICOLAS J.M. " Logic for Improving Integrity Checking in Relational Databases" Acta Informatica, July 1982.

[OODB 86] Object-Oriented Databases, Proceed. of the 1st Internat. Workshop, IEEE Computer Society Press 1986.

[SIMO 84] SIMON E. & VALDURIEZ P. "Efficient Alorithm for Integrity Control in Database Machines" Proceed. of Internat. Conf. on Trends and Applications of Databases" IEEE-NBS, Gaithersburg, USA 1984.

[SMIT 77] SMITH J.M. & SMITH D.C.P., "Database Abstractions: Aggregation and Generalization" ACM TODS June 1977.

[STONE 75] STONEBRAKER M. "Implementation of Integrity Constraints and Views by Query Modification" ACM-SIGMOD Conf., 1975.

[TSIC 82] TSICHRITZIS D. & LOCHOVSKY F. " Data Models" Prentice Hall 1982.

[TUCH 83] TUCHERMAN L., FURTADO A. & Casanova M.A. "A Pragmatic Approach to Structured Database Design" 9th VLDB Conf., Florence, Italy, 1983.

[TUCH 85] TUCHERMAN L., FURTADO A. & Casanova M.A. "A Tool for Modular Database Design" 11th VLDB Conf, Stockholm , Sweeden 1985.

[VALL 88] VAN ASSCHE F., LAYZELL P.J., LOUCOPOULOS P. & SPELTINCK G. "Information System Development: a rule based approach", J. Knowledge Based Systems, 1(4) 1988.

Vol. 379: A. Kreczmar, G. Mirkowska (Eds.), Mathematical Foundations of Computer Science 1989. Proceedings, 1989. VIII, 605 pages. 1989.

Vol. 380: J. Csirik, J. Demetrovics, F. Gécseg (Eds.), Fundamentals of Computation Theory. Proceedings, 1989. XI, 493 pages. 1989.

Vol. 381: J. Dassow, J. Kelemen (Eds.), Machines, Languages, and Complexity. Proceedings, 1988. VI, 244 pages. 1989.

Vol. 382: F. Dehne, J.-R. Sack, N. Santoro (Eds.), Algorithms and Data Structures. WADS '89. Proceedings, 1989. IX, 592 pages. 1989.

Vol. 383: K. Furukawa, H. Tanaka, T. Fujisaki (Eds.), Logic Programming '88. Proceedings, 1988. VII, 251 pages. 1989 (Subseries LNAI).

Vol. 384: G. A. van Zee, J. G. G. van de Vorst (Eds.), Parallel Computing 1988. Proceedings, 1988. V, 135 pages. 1989.

Vol. 385: E. Börger, H. Kleine Büning, M. M. Richter (Eds.), CSL '88. Proceedings, 1988. VI, 399 pages. 1989.

Vol. 386: J.E. Pin (Ed.), Formal Properties of Finite Automata and Applications. Proceedings, 1988. VIII, 260 pages. 1989.

Vol. 387: C. Ghezzi, J. A. McDermid (Eds.), ESEC '89. 2nd European Software Engineering Conference. Proceedings, 1989. VI, 496 pages. 1989.

Vol. 388: G. Cohen, J. Wolfmann (Eds.), Coding Theory and Applications. Proceedings, 1988. IX, 329 pages. 1989.

Vol. 389: D. H. Pitt, D. E. Rydeheard, P. Dybjer, A. M. Pitts, A. Poigné (Eds.), Category Theory and Computer Science. Proceedings, 1989. VI, 365 pages. 1989.

Vol. 390: J.P. Martins, E.M. Morgado (Eds.), EPIA 89. Proceedings, 1989. XII, 400 pages. 1989 (Subseries LNAI).

Vol. 391: J.-D. Boissonnat, J.-P. Laumond (Eds.), Geometry and Robotics. Proceedings, 1988. VI, 413 pages. 1989.

Vol. 392: J.-C. Bermond, M. Raynal (Eds.), Distributed Algorithms. Proceedings, 1989. VI, 315 pages. 1989.

Vol. 393: H. Ehrig, H. Herrlich, H.-J. Kreowski, G. Preuß (Eds.), Categorical Methods in Computer Science. VI, 350 pages. 1989.

Vol. 394: M. Wirsing, J.A. Bergstra (Eds.), Algebraic Methods: Theory, Tools and Applications. VI, 558 pages. 1989.

Vol. 395: M. Schmidt-Schauß, Computational Aspects of an Order-Sorted Logic with Term Declarations. VIII, 171 pages. 1989. (Subseries LNAI).

Vol. 396: T. A. Berson, T. Beth (Eds.), Local Area Network Security. Proceedings, 1989. IX, 152 pages. 1989.

Vol. 397: K. P. Jantke (Ed.), Analogical and Inductive Inference. Proceedings, 1989. IX, 338 pages. 1989. (Subseries LNAI).

Vol. 398: B. Banieqbal, H. Barringer, A. Pnueli (Eds.), Temporal Logic in Specification. Proceedings, 1987. VI, 448 pages. 1989.

Vol. 399: V. Cantoni, R. Creutzburg, S. Levialdi, G. Wolf (Eds.), Recent Issues in Pattern Analysis and Recognition. VII, 400 pages. 1989.

Vol. 400: R. Klein, Concrete and Abstract Voronoi Diagrams. IV, 167 pages. 1989.

Vol. 401: H. Djidjev (Ed.), Optimal Algorithms. Proceedings, 1989. VI, 308 pages. 1989.

Vol. 402: T.P. Bagchi, V.K. Chaudhri, Interactive Relational Database Design. XI, 186 pages. 1989.

Vol. 403: S. Goldwasser (Ed.), Advances in Cryptology – CRYPTO '88. Proceedings, 1988. XI, 591 pages. 1990.

Vol. 404: J. Beer, Concepts, Design, and Performance Analysis of a Parallel Prolog Machine. VI, 128 pages. 1989.

Vol. 405: C. E. Veni Madhavan (Ed.), Foundations of Software Technology and Theoretical Computer Science. Proceedings, 1989. VIII, 339 pages. 1989.

Vol. 407: J. Sifakis (Ed.), Automatic Verification Methods for Finite State Systems. Proceedings, 1989. VII, 382 pages. 1990.

Vol. 408: M. Leeser, G. Brown (Eds.),Hardware Specification, Verification and Synthesis: Mathematical Aspects. Proceedings, 1989. VI, 402 pages. 1990.

Vol. 409: A. Buchmann, O. Günther, T. R. Smith, Y.-F. Wang (Eds.), Design and Implementation of Large Spatial Databases. Proceedings, 1989. IX, 364 pages. 1990.

Vol. 410: F. Pichler, R. Moreno-Diaz (Eds.), Computer Aided Systems Theory – EUROCAST '89. Proceedings, 1989. VII, 427 pages. 1990.

Vol. 411: M. Nagl (Ed.), Graph-Theoretic Concepts in Computer Science. Proceedings, 1989. VII, 374 pages. 1990.

Vol. 412: L. B. Almeida, C. J. Wellekens (Eds.), Neural Networks. Proceedings, 1990. IX, 276 pages. 1990.

Vol. 413: R. Lenz, Group Theoretical Methods in Image Processing. VIII, 139 pages. 1990.

Vol. 414: A.Kreczmar, A. Salwicki, M. Warpechowski, LOGLAN '88 – Report on the Programming Language. X, 133 pages. 1990.

Vol. 415: C. Choffrut, T. Lengauer (Eds.), STACS 90. Proceedings, 1990. VI, 312 pages. 1990.

Vol. 416: F. Bancilhon, C. Thanos, D. Tsichritzis (Eds.), Advances in Database Technology – EDBT '90. Proceedings, 1990. IX, 452 pages. 1990.

Vol. 417: P. Martin-Löf, G. Mints (Eds.), COLOG-88. International Conference on Computer Logic. Proceedings, 1988. VI, 338 pages. 1990.

Vol. 419: K. Weichselberger, S. Pöhlmann, A Methodology for Uncertainty in Knowledge-Based Systems. VIII, 136 pages. 1990. (Subseries LNAI).

Vol. 420: Z. Michalewicz (Ed.), Statistical and Scientific Database Management, V SSDBM. Proceedings, 1990. V, 256 pages. 1990.

Vol. 421: T. Onodera, S. Kawai, A Formal Model of Visualization in Computer Graphics Systems. X, 100 pages. 1990.

Vol. 423: L. E. Deimel (Ed.), Software Engineering Education. Proceedings, 1990. VI, 164 pages. 1990.

Vol. 424: G. Rozenberg (Ed.), Advances in Petri Nets 1989. VI, 524 pages. 1990.

Vol. 425: C. H. Bergman, R. D. Maddux, D. L. Pigozzi (Eds.), Algebraic Logic and Universal Algebra in Computer Science. Proceedings, 1988. XI, 292 pages. 1990.

Vol. 426: N. Houbak, SIL – a Simulation Language. VII, 192 pages. 1990.

Vol. 427: O. Faugeras (Ed.), Computer Vision – ECCV 90. Proceedings, 1990. XII, 619 pages. 1990.

Vol. 428: D. Bjørner, C. A. R. Hoare, H. Langmaack (Eds.), VDM '90, VDM and Z – Formal Methods in Software Development. Proceedings, 1990. XVII, 580 pages. 1990.

Vol. 429: A. Miola (Ed.), Design and Implementation of Symbolic Computation Systems. Proceedings, 1990. XII, 284 pages. 1990.

Vol. 430: J. W. de Bakker, W.-P. de Roever, G. Rozenberg (Eds:), Stepwise Refinement of Distributed Systems. Models, Formalisms, Correctness. Proceedings, 1989. X, 808 pages. 1990.

Vol. 431: A. Arnold (Ed.), CAAP '90. Proceedings, 1990. VI, 285 pages. 1990.

Vol. 432: N. Jones (Ed.), ESOP '90. Proceedings, 1990. IX, 436 pages. 1990.

Vol. 433: W. Schröder-Preikschat, W. Zimmer (Eds.), Progress in Distributed Operating Systems and Distributed Systems Management. Proceedings 1989. V, 206 pages. 1990.

Vol. 436: B. Steinholtz, A. Sølvberg, L. Bergman (Eds.), Advanced Information Systems Engineering. Proceedings, 1990. X, 392 pages. 1990.

Manuscripts

Manuscripts should be no less than 100 and preferably no more than 500 pages in length.
They are reproduced by a photographic process and therefore must be typed with extreme care. Symbols not on the typewriter should be inserted by hand in indelible black ink. Corrections to the typescript should be made by pasting in the new text or painting out errors with white correction fluid. Authors receive 75 free copies and are free to use the material in other publications. The typescript is reduced slightly in size during reproduction; best results will not be obtained unless the text on any one page is kept within the overall limit of 18 x 26.5 cm (7 x 10½ inches). On request, the publisher will supply special paper with the typing area outlined.
Manuscripts should be sent to Prof. G. Goos, GMD Forschungsstelle an der Universität Karlsruhe, Haid- und Neu-Str. 7, 7500 Karlsruhe 1, Germany, Prof. J. Hartmanis, Cornell University, Dept. of Computer Science, Ithaca, NY/USA 14853, or directly to Springer-Verlag Heidelberg.

Springer-Verlag, Heidelberger Platz 3, D-1000 Berlin 33
Springer-Verlag, Tiergartenstraße 17, D-6900 Heidelberg 1
Springer-Verlag, 175 Fifth Avenue, New York, NY 10010/USA
Springer-Verlag, 37-3, Hongo 3-chome, Bunkyo-ku, Tokyo 113, Japan

ISBN 3-540-52625-0
ISBN 0-387-52625-0